Visual Basic .NET at Work:
Building 10 Enterprise Projects

Tony Martin
Dominic Selly

Wiley Computer Publishing

John Wiley & Sons, Inc.

Publisher: Robert Ipsen
Editor: Theresa Hudson
Managing Editor: Angela Smith
New Media Editor: Brian Snapp
Text Design & Composition: John Wiley Composition Services

Designations used by companies to distinguish their products are often claimed as trademarks. In all instances where John Wiley & Sons, Inc., is aware of a claim, the product names appear in initial capital or ALL CAPITAL LETTERS. Readers, however, should contact the appropriate companies for more complete information regarding trademarks and registration.

This book is printed on acid-free paper. ∞

This publication is designed to provide accurate and authoritative information in regard to the subject matter covered. It is sold with the understanding that the publisher is not engaged in professional services. If professional advice or other expert assistance is required, the services of a competent professional person should be sought.

Library of Congress Cataloging-in-Publication Data:

ISBN: 0-471-38631-6

Printed in the United States of America.

10 9 8 7 6 5 4 3 2 1

To my friends

Contents

Acknowledgments

Thanks go out to many people on a project like this book. I hardly know where to begin. I'll start with Dominic. I want to tell Dominic that he saved my at least 42 percent of my sanity by writing Project 6. Without his work and diligence, we wouldn't have made it on time. Besides, he's an ASP.NET genius, wrote an ASP.NET training course that he now teaches around the country, and is one of the most immediately likable people on the planet. Thanks, pal. Give me a call when it's time for that star party.

A mathematically incomprehensible amount of thanks, appreciations, and owed favors go to Kathryn Malm. She is the editor of this book. She is smart, funny, encouraging, and the primary reason you have this book in your hands now. Without her efforts, I would have been committed by now. Instead, I became committed to finishing the book. She's like that. With an email or a short phone call she revitalized my zeal and energy for this endeavor, and I enjoyed it a great deal because of her. Many warm thanks to you. She writes ~~good~~ well too!

Huge thanks to Yasser Shohoud at DevXpert (www.devxpert.com). Without the use of his expertise, this book would have taken much longer. He's one of the smartest programmers I know, and I encourage anyone interested in XML, Web services, or .NET to check out his company and the training he offers. Thanks very much, buddy.

A big thank you to everyone, friends and family, who always asked how the book was doing while it was being written. Whether you were genuinely interested or just being polite, it doesn't matter. That you thought to ask meant a lot to me. The most generous part of what you did was that you asked how the book was going, knowing full well that I was actually going to tell you. That's the mark of true friendship. Particular thanks to Shilpa Kumbhar, who took an interest in doing some XML research. I am thankful for your help. Sorry about all those OS reinstalls.

Thanks a bunch to everyone at Best Software, Inc. who put up with me during the writing of this book. They offered encouragement and asked about progress. Special thanks to Michael Ottomanelli for his sense of humor and flexibility that allowed me to finish on time.

Special thanks to my family: Mom, Lise, Wayne, Nico, Alex, Hannah, Poppop. All of you helped me get through this in one way or another, either by encouragement, talking with me about it, or just listening to me ramble. I love you all.

I would like to send out a special thank you to Mike, Betsy, Maggie, Moxie, and Sassy. This crew gave me the much-needed breaks during the writing of this book that helped keep me from going stir crazy. You are two of the nicest people and three of the nicest dogs anyone would ever want to know.

Warren, David, Susan, and Cheryl. You are the best friends anyone could ask for. You have been the cause of more high points in my life than I can count, and you were there for the low points. We could easily make a television show about our friendship, except that we are the only ones who would laugh at the jokes.

Thanks go out to Graham Chapman, John Cleese, Terry Gilliam, Eric Idle, Terry Jones, and Michael Palin. You helped get me through this book. Thanks also for the years of side-splitting laughter you've inflicted upon me and for making me walk around all day quoting lines from your skits, films, songs, and books, which I'll probably be doing for the rest of my life, being laughed at, ostracized, and generally beaten up. I'll get you for it.

Finally, I'd like to thank my Dad. Many times during the writing of this book, I would sit back and think about how you would handle one issue or another or just imagine that you were there to help me talk things out, and this helped a great deal. Thanks, and I hope you're having a blast.

About the Authors

Tony Martin has been a programmer for about 20 years now. He started in 1981 with such tools as CP/M and DOS. He has been involved in many aspects of software development and has a special interest in software development process and user interface design and construction. However, like many programmers, he will do about anything in which he can write code. He works regularly with Visual Basic, C++, and Visual Basic .NET and has the terribly unrealistic goal of someday understanding all 6,500 classes in the .NET framework. By the time this happens, the framework will have irreversibly changed and he'll have to start over.

There is more to Tony than just programming, and understanding his personality is an important part of understanding his programming books. Programming Tony shares a brain with Artist Tony. He draws, paints, writes fiction, but is mostly a photographer. He has a best friend who is a Border Terrier named Tirith that is laying upside down, feet in the air, and snoring as this is being written. Friends, family, and dog are all extremely important parts of Tony's life. He sees possessions as a delusion, but as far as delusions go, he likes his camera equipment and his DVD collection.

On a day when Tony is not programming, you are likely to find him romping through the woods, hanging out with friends, reading a book, visiting family, or creating some new work of art.

Dominic Selly is a Senior Software Engineer at Capella University (www.capella.edu), where courses are delivered entirely online. Visit Capella and use the 2-Minute Advisor to see some of the earliest ASP.Net code to go into production. Prior to Capella, Dominic was a Senior Software Engineer at Best Software where he led the data services tier working on their next generation Web-based accounting application.

Dominic is also a trainer of developers. He currently teaches the ASP.Net Bootcamp, which he developed (www.ASPDotNetBootCamp.com). Dominic also co-developed the Web Application Development certificate program at George Washington University, where he was an instructor. He has been a speaker at the SD and Connections conferences, and has been conducting trainings across the country for many years.

When he's not coding or training, Dominic spends his time trying to master the perfect determinism of the game of billiards.

Getting Started

There's no denying it. Microsoft has turned the Windows software development community on its ear with the .NET initiative. There have been debates and arguments among those who have firm opinions about whether .NET is a good thing or a bad thing. The bad guys say that the changes are too big, too sweeping to be accepted. They contend that the changes required are too great to adopt quickly and that they prevent people from migrating their existing applications to the new technology. They also complain about the changes made to the Visual Basic language for the same reasons.

These apprehensive people make good points. It will be difficult if not impossible to migrate large applications without redesigning and rewriting them. However, redesign will be required anyway to take advantage of the new features and benefits of the framework and the language. It will take significant amounts of time for engineers to become proficient with the new language and framework. The language changes are fundamental and the .NET framework, with over 6,500 classes, is huge. The effort will be worth it, though. The language is much more powerful and even safer to use. It is still fairly easy; just *different*. The new capabilities are amazing and will start making you think of new things to build. Even the Visual Studio environment is vastly improved. It's as if they built everything they heard programmers complaining about for the last three years.

I can use myself as a good example of why .NET and the changes to Visual Basic are good things. I was a little worried about .NET at first. I had been comfortable for years with VB, COM, DCOM, MTS, ASP, ADO, and all the other acrotechnologies (technologies named with acronyms). Why bother changing to this radical new way of building software? The promises were nice, but were they worth the work to get there? During the course of learning and using .NET and the new Visual Basic (VB), I realized that I was creating software that had advanced capabilities easily and swiftly. Once I got used to the language changes and the new way each technology worked, I realized how much programming power was at my disposal. And I hadn't even begun to scratch the surface of those 6,500 classes. Programmers like myself who will be using

.NET will turn out applications that nobody has even thought of before, and the world will be astounded.

But the most compelling reason that I think of to recommend .NET and Visual Basic .NET to other programmers is that after 20 years of programming, I thought I had seen about everything. Programming was still rewarding, but it was like doing anything for 20 years. It's hard to keep the subject lively and interesting. After using .NET for about a month, I caught myself *having fun again*. I was actually excited about the programs I was writing and actually called friends to tell them about them. It made me want to be a teacher of .NET and all it could do. Mostly, I wanted to build more software, because ideas came flooding into my head. I will be busy for months with some of them.

Obviously, you'll have to make your own judgments about .NET and its future. The industry certainly has a lot to say. For now, I'm having a blast and hope that this book will help you get to that place as well.

What This Book Is About

We have all read books about new technology that go on for pages and pages about something or other, slipping you little code fragments as they go. You're always waiting for that big example, the payoff for having waded through explanations and theory. And suddenly you come to the end of the chapter, having seen only a few trivial examples of the technology's use.

These books give you something to think about, but more work to do before you can really get started using what you have learned. Seeing the technology in action is critical to understanding how it works and is meant to be used. You need substantial examples to make this happen, examples that relate to the real world and tackle real problems.

The purpose of this book is to teach through example, using complete solutions to real problems that you as enterprise programmers need to deal with. You'll be taken on a tour of the major .NET technologies, seeing how each works and then working through a complete program using that technology. The chapters are really projects, complete programs that you can put to use in your own work or other programming. We're covering a lot of material, but the project-oriented approach lets you tackle one issue at a time.

Organization

The projects in the book are all organized the same way. Each starts with a statement of the problem that will be solved by the project, as well as a description of the solution. It will detail the supplies you need to build the project and the technologies that will be used. Usually an informative section follows the introduction and teaches what you need to know about the technology used in the project, explaining key concepts and some of the important details. The rest of the chapter is all about the project. You'll learn more about the technology by doing. At the end of each project is a list of suggestions for enhancing the project. The enhancements could be simple upgrades or completely new features, and they will give you something else to build on your own.

Throughout the book will be assorted tips that will help you out with something specific. If there is anything important you should know about, it will be given in a Sidebar for your reference.

Each chapter in this book is a project that focuses on a specific technology. There are 10 projects all told. Some build on previous projects, whereas others are completely standalone. I'll let you know which is which. They generally follow an order that assumes you know the technologies in the previous projects, but not in the following projects. Take a look at what each project is about:

Project 1: A WinForms Library.   Take a tour of the new forms technology and see how Microsoft has changed the way you will build standard Windows applications. You'll learn some advanced VB language features in the process, including inheritance, inherited forms, overloaded and overridden methods, and creating your own constructors. When you're done, you'll have a class library of standard forms on which you can base your own applications.

Project 2: Bug Tracking with ADO.NET.   We'll build a small bug-tracking application using ADO.NET as our database interface. You'll see what the new ADO.NET objects are like and how to use them. I'll show you how to use SQL statements along with ADO.NET to perform all the primary database operations. You will also see some ADO.NET data binding in action. This project makes use of Project 1.

Project 3: Bug Reporting with Web Services.   This project builds on Project 2. We will create a Web service that sits out on your Internet site and allows the users of your programs to report bugs that they find in your software. We'll create a client component that you can build into your own applications that provides the interface your users can use to enter bug data. It will then ship the bug off to the Web service for storage. The Web service does more as well, but we'll save that for the project. The client portion of this project makes use of Project 1.

Project 4: Application Performance Testing with .NET Remoting.   Remoting is essentially Microsoft's more flexible replacement for DCOM. I'll show you how to create your own remote components, configure them to work over an HTTP line, process requests, and ship results back. We'll build a component that logs performance data from your own applications as they execute. We'll also create a class for your own applications that will make it painless to instrument them for performance testing. You even get a fancy client program that will get performance data from the remote component and analyze it for you.

Project 5: Deployment Packages.   Visual Studio .NET has replaced the aging and inadequate Package and Deployment Wizard with new deployment tools that allow you to create truly professional installations. We'll create three different types of deployments using these tools, resulting in deployment packages for Projects 2 and 3. You may find yourself using these tools more often than your complex third-party installation software.

Project 6: A Web Portal with ASP.NET.   This project will show you how to use ASP.NET and its new capabilities to construct a complete company Web portal. You'll find that ASP.NET is really a completely new way of building Web sites that are more capable, faster, and easier to construct. This is a big project, so make some time for it.

Project 7: Schema Generator with XML.   You can't get through a day without hearing about XML. This project will show you how to make use of XML and XSD schemas to exchange data between disparate systems or even completely different companies. The project is a pair of programs, one for the provider of data and another for the consumer of the data. The provider program generates XML and XSD schemas from a database to pass to the consumer. The consumer program reads XML and XSD schemas, validating the data against the schema.

Project 8: User Authentication Login Screen.   It is always difficult to approach the topic of security. It is complex, sometimes tedious, and often arcane. Complete information about the topic seems to be difficult to locate. This project focuses on ASP.NET Web security, and we'll be creating a standard login screen you can use on your Web applications. We focus on forms security, but Windows security is even easier.

Project 9: Employee Information System Using the Mobile Toolkit.   This project explores the Microsoft Mobile Internet Toolkit. This is an extension to ASP.NET and Visual Studio .NET that allows you to use VB to create Web sites and applications for mobile devices, including Web-enabled cell phones. We will actually build a small company intranet site that allows employees to access company information through their cell phones. They will have access to information such as company announcements, weather alerts, the next paid holiday, and a complete company phone list (which you can dial directly from your cell phone without punching in any numbers).

Project 10: Employee Intranet with .NET.   This project brings together many of the technologies we learned in other projects to create a company intranet site. We have some nice features on this site, including the ability to view how much vacation you have available and make vacation requests, enter and review status reports, and review and modify your personnel information. We make use of ASP.NET, ADO.NET, Web security, and Web services for this project. It should be an exciting roundup of the technologies covered in other projects.

Setting Up Your Workbench

You will need some background knowledge and a small pile of software tools to complete the projects in this book. This section will detail exactly what those are.

Prerequisites

This book assumes that you can already create programs with Visual Basic 6.0 and are familiar with Visual Basic .NET. I am not going to teach you how to use the environment or do very basic things with the language. You should also be familiar with enterprise development concepts, such as distributed applications, and remote components.

Other knowledge will be helpful, too. Many of the projects use database access, so familiarity with SQL Server and SQL itself will be beneficial. If you are familiar with ASP development, Projects 6, 9, and 10 will go more smoothly. This knowledge is not required, however. You will pick up enough here to do the projects with relative ease.

On Your Machine

The projects in this book are focused on Visual Basic .NET, but we make liberal use of other tools as well. You will need to make sure the following items are available to you. If a particular tool is required for only one project, I'll let you know what it is. If possible, I'll also tell you where to get the tools.

Hardware

The projects in this book were built with a Pentium III 600 MHz Dell computer with plenty of hard disk space and 256 MB of RAM. I attempted to use 128 MB of RAM, but Visual Studio .NET spent a lot of time swapping and grinding; 256 MB of RAM was much smoother and faster. I recommend at least this base system for efficient performance.

If you want to test out Project 9, you'll also need a Web-enabled cell phone or other Web-enabled portable device. You can also use the Microsoft Mobile Emulator.

Operating System

You will need at least Microsoft Windows 2000 to build these projects. You can also use Windows XP Professional. I used Windows 2000 for the entire process, and it worked beautifully.

Software Tools

Quite a few software tools are required if you want to complete all the projects. Fortunately, you will already have most of them, and the others are free. They are:

Microsoft Visual Studio .NET Professional Edition. This version or higher of the development environment is required. I used the Enterprise Edition and enjoyed having all the extras around.

Microsoft SQL Server 2000. This database is used for at least half the projects. You could use another database engine as well, such as Microsoft Access. You'll just have to modify the code a little to do so (connection strings and the ADO.NET DB objects created). It will be easier to just use SQL Server if you have it available.

Internet Explorer 6.0. This should be installed for you when you install the Windows Component Update portion of Visual Studio .NET. You will need it for all the Web development projects.

Internet Information Server. Several projects make use of IIS. If you're using Windows 2000, you might have to install it because it is an option in the setup. This is easy to do.

Microsoft Mobile Internet Toolkit. This is a set of enhancements for ASP.NET that allow you to build Web applications for mobile devices. It contains additions to the ASP.NET language, as well as to the designers and help. It works like a champ and can be downloaded free from Microsoft's Web site. This is used for Project 9. The Mobile Internet Toolkit can currently be found at:

http://msdn.microsoft.com/downloads/default.asp?url=/downloads/sample. asp?url=/MSDN-FILES/027/001/516/msdncompositedoc.xml

Microsoft Mobile Explorer 3.0 or later. This is a cell phone simulator. It is a Web browser that emulates the Web browsers found on most Web-enabled cell phones and other portable devices. We use it in Project 9 as the test and debug execution environment. It is available for free download at Microsoft's Web site. You can find it at http://msdn.microsoft.com/downloads/. From this page, you can search for MME, and you'll jump right to it.

What's on the CD-ROM

The companion CD-ROM contains all the source code for every project in the book. It also includes any supporting files that might be needed, such as sample databases, diagrams, or graphics files. Anything you need for a project should be there. This is a good thing because you won't want to create all your own sample data, for example. It is much easier to import it right into SQL Server.

The CD-ROM is organized by project. There is a directory at the root called Projects. Underneath that is a folder for each project in the book that contains all the files for each project. For example, all the source for project 2 is located at:

```
\Projects\Project 2
```

The Web Site

A Web site was created for this book to keep you posted on any changes, to let you know about new developments, and to provide additional related information you might find interesting or useful. It will also be hosting some of the Web-based projects from the book that you can play around with in a production environment. Stop by and poke around for a while at http://www.wiley.com/compbooks/martin.

Time to Embark

You should have all you need to get started with the projects right away. As long as your development environment is configured properly and your tools are installed, any of the projects can be built. If you're a free spirit, go ahead and jump around. If not, the projects work very well in order.

The projects in this book are calling to you. Build them and enhance them, making them your own. You have your road map and requirements for your workbench. All the tools should be ready to go. The first project will help you get your feet wet and learn a few new things about the VB language capabilities. Dive into the rest at your leisure, but if you're anything like me, you'll be devouring them. The book will guide you through the forest of new technologies, making sure you're not embarking up the wrong tree.

Sorry. I couldn't help it. Have fun!

A WinForms Library

If you are an enterprise software engineer, writing applications for your company, you know that time is the one luxury that is most in demand. Everyone wants a special application completed yesterday and thinks his or hers is more important than all the others in your hopper. Shaving time off the top of all your projects could go a long way toward making your life easier and your internal customers happier. If we could write the common functionality once and use it for all of our upcoming projects, we might just achieve this.

In addition, we rarely have time to give thought to usability and consistency. Because our time is in high demand, we need to concentrate on functionality. Often we end up with applications that are inconsistent and look very different, making it diffi-cult for our customers to move easily from one to the other. However, if we could invest the time once to build in usability and consistency and then make use of that work on all our future projects, well, that would be a wise investment indeed.

THE PROBLEM:

We need to create all kinds of enterprise applications for our company, and they all need a similar look and feel and similar features and capabilities. However, we'd like to create the common functionality once and use it for all applications from then on.

THE SOLUTION:

Build a WinForms library containing common functionality and style that we can use as a starting point for all our future applications.

The Project

We will design and build a set of .NET WinForms classes using Visual Basic .NET that will encapsulate all the look, functionality, and consistency we need for our enterprise applications. There are six classes, or forms, in our collection, which you can use as a starting point for any future applications. It's easy to use, easy to add to your projects, and if we're careful, will even cut out a fair chunk of your development time.

You could certainly use trusty Visual Basic 6.0 to build a set of windows that you can load into your projects. However, using Visual Basic .NET and the .NET Framework makes this job a whole lot easier. One of the best things is being able to inherit functionality from other forms. For example, in this project we will be starting out with a base form that will contain some common functionality. If you want to create a new form with that same functionality, you can inherit your new form from the base form and get all that common functionality for free. Inheritance will save us time, both in creating the derived forms and when maintaining them in the future.

This project consists of six WinForms classes that we will create, followed by a simple test driver form. We'll be following these basic steps:

1. **Create the base form from which the other forms will be derived.**   It will contain common functionality that all our forms will need and use.

2. **Create the frmDialog class.**   This will form the basis of any dialog box we need to create.

3. **Create the frmMsgBox class.**   We will use this as a replacement for the Visual Basic MsgBox functionality.

4. **Create the frmWizard window class.**   This can be used as the basis for any wizard dialogs we need in our application.

5. **Create the frmApp window class.**   This can be used as the main window of any SDI application we want to create.

6. **Create the frmAbout class.**   We can use this as our application's About Box. This has been designed for use with only a single line of code.

7. **Detail how to base your own projects on these window classes.**   You can include the forms in your projects, or use a class library that includes the forms. You'll see how to do both.

8. **Create the test driver form that will allow us to test out the forms.**   This will also demonstrate how each should be used in code.

 ## You Will Need

✔ **Visual Basic .NET**

✔ **A basic knowledge of Visual Basic .NET and WinForms**

Let's Start the Project

If we were using Visual Basic 6.0 for this project, the whole idea of classes would not even enter the picture. We'd build a few forms, write a little code, and be done with it. Visual Basic .NET, as it does with almost every aspect of writing software, changes the game completely. All forms are now created as classes. And, with the addition of true inheritance and other object-oriented features, we can really add some power to our forms and the code we write. On the other hand, we also need to spend a little more time thinking about our design before we sit down to write code.

To develop a useful collection of windows as well as gain the most benefit from Visual Basic .NET's new features, we need to think at least a little bit about our needs and how to satisfy them with a decent design. The hierarchy of classes in this project is fairly simple but illustrates some of the benefits of a class hierarchy. Figure 1.1 shows the class organization.

Features of the Design

Our design incorporates a few interesting features that bear discussion. Some are related to the way the classes are designed, and some relate to the usability of the end result.

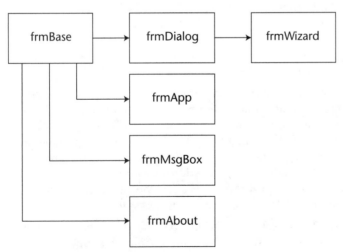

Figure 1.1 Class organization.

The Base Class

The most important part of our design is the use of the base class, *frmBase*. All our other forms are derived from the base class, meaning that those forms inherit all the controls, settings, and functionality of the base class. Build it once in the base class and all forms derived from it get everything it has.

This is even a great benefit during program maintenance. Assume, for instance, that you have three applications that you've built with this set of forms, and you need to add some functionality to all of them. Simply add it in the base class, once, and all forms and applications suddenly have access to the same functionality. This applies to bugs as well. Fix a bug in the base class, and all forms based on it get the same fix.

A fair amount of thought and functionality should be put into the base class. This is important because other forms not only inherit from it, but they also depend on it. If you get something wrong in the base class, it affects everything down the line. Your base classes make promises about functionality and reliability to the classes that are derived from it. And like a politician, if those promises are broken, it's unlikely they'll be in use after their current term.

Usability Features

One of the other goals of our project is to give our applications a common interface to help users move from one application to another without having to get used to a completely new interface. In addition, we are taking the opportunity to make the applications friendlier by incorporating some usability features. They include:

The modeless notification area.   A fancy name for a message area. This allows the program to provide feedback to the user in a modeless fashion so that it informs, but does not interrupt, the user's workflow. In the base form in Figure 1.2, there is a wide, single-line text box at the bottom. This should be used to notify users about anything important, such as a validation or error message, without popping up a message box that would interrupt their work. The form has properties that access this area and change its text.

The two-tier message box.   Often a simple message box appears with one large, ungainly paragraph in the middle that takes time to read and interpret. This impedes the users' work and wastes their time. Our alternative is to provide a message box that provides two message areas. The first, at the top, provides a one-line, easy-to-read message that summarizes the issue. The second area underneath the first contains additional, more detailed text that more fully explains the situation. This design allows users to get the gist of the message quickly and then read more detail if they feel this is necessary.

The custom About box.   This one, I admit, is personal. For years I have wondered why About Boxes don't tell you what the program is about. It traditionally has the name of the program, a version number, a huge pile of copyright information, and maybe a button to give you some system information. It never tells you what the program does or what it is for. Included in this form collection is my own About Box, which contains a section dedicated to a description of the application.

A Few Coding Notes

During the coding of these window classes, a few techniques were used that are worth pointing out. Some are just good practice, whereas others are compromises that need to be mentioned.

First, a technique for isolating constructor code has been used to prevent future difficulties. When generating form code for you, VB creates a default constructor called New(). It calls MyBase.New() and then InitializeComponent. These are fine and should be left as is. VB also puts a comment in at the end that reminds you to add in any initialization code that you might want to execute for your form. You could just put all the code inline. Instead, we've standardized on a method called InitForm() that we put in each form (as needed) and call it from the default constructor. This allows us to move the code somewhere else that's easier for us to maintain (in our User Code region; see the following tip for more information). It also keeps our modifications to the generated code to a minimum. This is important because, although VB generates this code for us and swears that it won't mess it up, history shows that this may not be true. If the region of generated code does change, all we have to do is add our single call to the InitForm() method and we're done.

Second, in the code, I make good use of the #Region directive to help organize it and make it easier to hide code we're not interested in. The standard regions defined are:

Class data and types.   This region contains any member data that the class may need, including variables, objects, user-defined types, and constants.

Properties.   All properties are located here, so they are grouped and easy to locate.

Event handlers.   Like properties, they're all in one place.

User code.   This contains everything else, including methods that are part of the class.

Debug code.   This is an optional section in which all self-contained debugging code is put. This makes it easier to track down and eliminate it from the final release.

> **TIP** **Microsoft has added a very useful directive to the Visual Basic .NET environment, called the #Region directive. You may have seen the #Region directive in your code, because VB encloses its generated code within it. Its purpose is pretty simple: It allows you to name a region of code and collapse or expand it within the editor. This is a great organizational tool that helps you keep related code together. It's easy to add your own by typing in the following statements in your code:**
>
> ```
> #Region "Some Name For Your Region"
> ...
> #End Region
> ```
>
> **Any code you place between these statements can be collapsed and hidden from view. This can help you focus on the code in which you're interested. In addition, it can help you organize your code into logical groupings.**
>
> **To make Regions more effective, it helps to adopt a standard for using them. If you and your programmers stick to your standard, your code will be more organized and more maintainable.**

Third is the use of protected data members. Normally class data is declared as private and accessed through methods or properties. This is the *encapsulation* mechanism, and it helps the class protect its data from unscrupulous or inexperienced programmers. However, there are times when declaring data members as protected is appropriate. The class itself as well as any classes inherited from it can access protected members. I decided to make the controls that are part of the form protected instead of private as VB generates them. This makes it easier for derived classes to access their many properties and methods. Making them private and writing properties for all the functionality of the controls would be wasteful and time consuming. An alternative would be to make the controls private and create a property that returns a reference to the control, but why bother? The protected controls work well and the additional properties would just mean more code to debug.

Constructing the Forms

My favorite part of any project is actually building it: writing code, testing it, debugging it, and making it do my bidding. Although concept, architecture, and design are fun, nothing beats writing code and seeing it work. The result is the famous programmer high that some of us live for. And here we are at that stage of Project 1.

I'll cover each form in the collection one at a time, providing an overview of it, code coverage, and details about the interesting parts. If you can't wait, and would like to see exactly what we're going to build, you can try it out now. On the companion CD-ROM you'll find a project called prj01. Load it into Visual Basic .NET and run it. The test driver form is set as the startup form and will give you access to all the forms in the collection. You'll be able to see them come up and can toy with them a bit. I'll cover the details of the test driver later in the project.

The frmBase Form

The base form for this collection of windows is in many ways the most important part of the project. Everything that follows will be based on it, so it has to be right. It will contain functionality that all the forms will use, so we need to carefully consider what we put in it. And, because we want to minimize our work in later forms, we need to cram as much into the base form as we can so that the other forms benefit from it. All this is a pretty tall order, especially for a class that will never be directly instantiated. However, the work invested in the base class window will pay off in later forms.

Take a look at the layout of the form in Figure 1.2. There are three controls on our form, all located at the bottom. The text box is our message line, which we call the mode-less notification area. It will be used to display any notifications to the user that the application needs to communicate. There are also two buttons, OK and Cancel. These are the controls that I decided almost every form would need, based on the applications we will be writing with the form collection.

Once these controls are dropped onto the form, VB generates .NET code to actually create and set up the controls. In VB 6.0, all this code was hidden from the user and not

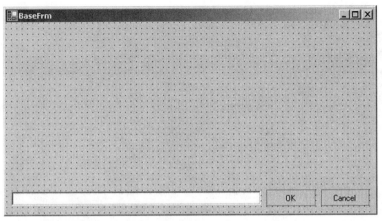

Figure 1.2   The frmBase form layout.

really necessary. With Visual Basic .NET, we're using the .NET WinForms library to create applications, just as we would if we were using C#, C++, or any other language based on the .NET Framework. The code it generates is all wrapped in a Region titled "Windows Form Designer generated code" and is hidden, so you don't have to worry about it. However, it's definitely worth knowing about what goes on in there. Not only is it interesting, but it also provides some insight into how the .NET Framework operates with WinForms. Examine this section of code that was generated for the simple base form:

```
#Region " Windows Form Designer generated code "

    Public Sub New()
        MyBase.New()

        'This call is required by the Windows Form Designer.
        InitializeComponent()

        'Add any initialization after the InitializeComponent() call
        InitForm()
    End Sub

    'Form overrides dispose to clean up the component list.
    Public Overrides Sub Dispose()
        MyBase.Dispose()
        If Not (components Is Nothing) Then
            components.Dispose()
        End If
    End Sub
```

```
'Required by the Windows Form Designer
Private components As System.ComponentModel.Container
Private WithEvents btnOK As System.Windows.Forms.Button
Private WithEvents btnCancel As System.Windows.Forms.Button
Private WithEvents txtNotify As System.Windows.Forms.TextBox

'NOTE: The following procedure is required by the
'      Windows Form Designer
'It can be modified using the Windows Form Designer.
'Do not modify it using the code editor.
<System.Diagnostics.DebuggerStepThrough()> _
      Private Sub InitializeComponent()
    Me.btnOK = New System.Windows.Forms.Button()
    Me.txtNotify = New System.Windows.Forms.TextBox()
    Me.btnCancel = New System.Windows.Forms.Button()
    Me.SuspendLayout()
    '
    'btnOK
    '
    Me.btnOK.Anchor = (System.Windows.Forms.AnchorStyles.Bottom _
      Or System.Windows.Forms.AnchorStyles.Right)
    Me.btnOK.FlatStyle = System.Windows.Forms.FlatStyle.Popup
    Me.btnOK.Location = New System.Drawing.Point(384, 240)
    Me.btnOK.Name = "btnOK"
    Me.btnOK.Size = New System.Drawing.Size(72, 24)
    Me.btnOK.TabIndex = 1
    Me.btnOK.Text = "&OK"
    '
    'txtNotify
    '
    Me.txtNotify.Anchor = (System.Windows.Forms.AnchorStyles.Bottom _
      Or System.Windows.Forms.AnchorStyles.Left)
    Me.txtNotify.Location = New System.Drawing.Point(8, 242)
    Me.txtNotify.Name = "txtNotify"
    Me.txtNotify.Size = New System.Drawing.Size(368, 20)
    Me.txtNotify.TabIndex = 0
    Me.txtNotify.Text = ""
    '
    'btnCancel
    '
    Me.btnCancel.Anchor = (System.Windows.Forms.AnchorStyles.Bottom _
      Or System.Windows.Forms.AnchorStyles.Right)
    Me.btnCancel.FlatStyle = System.Windows.Forms.FlatStyle.Popup
    Me.btnCancel.Location = New System.Drawing.Point(464, 240)
    Me.btnCancel.Name = "btnCancel"
    Me.btnCancel.Size = New System.Drawing.Size(72, 24)
    Me.btnCancel.TabIndex = 2
    Me.btnCancel.Text = "&Cancel"
```

```
'
'frmBase
'
Me.AutoScaleBaseSize = New System.Drawing.Size(5, 13)
Me.ClientSize = New System.Drawing.Size(544, 273)
Me.Controls.AddRange(New System.Windows.Forms.Control() _
    {Me.btnCancel, Me.btnOK, Me.txtNotify})
Me.Name = "frmBase"
Me.Text = "BaseFrm"
Me.ResumeLayout(False)

End Sub

#End Region
```

The first item of note is Sub New(). This is the classes' constructor and is called when an instance of the class is created. VB automatically puts code in there that is required. The first line,

```
MyBase.New()
```

calls the constructor of the base class. Even though this is a base class as far as we are concerned, it is automatically derived from System.Windows.Forms.Form, which contains the basic form functionality that we expect, such as a title bar and a control box. Therefore, this statement calls its constructor. We don't see the code for this constructor; it's down in the .NET Framework code.

 NOTE   **This default constructor, which VB created for us, takes no parameters. We can write our own constructors, with parameters, and we'll cover this later in this project.**

The second statement calls InitializeComponent(). The code for this method is just below New(). The InitializeComponent method contains the code that VB generates based on how we design the form in the Form Designer. Let's dissect this code a little bit. Consider this code section:

```
Me.btnOK = New System.Windows.Forms.Button()
Me.txtNotify = New System.Windows.Forms.TextBox()
Me.btnCancel = New System.Windows.Forms.Button()
Me.SuspendLayout()
```

The first three statements actually create instances of the controls we put on the form. They have to be created before we can use them. Every control is an object and has to be instantiated before it exists and can be used. What is this all about? We never saw this in VB6. Back in VB6, the VB runtime took care of creating controls through the Win32 API. We never saw this code, which, if you've ever written C++ Win32 API code to build Windows applications, you'll realize was a Godsend. So why are we seeing it now? Because VB now creates windows and other UI elements through the .NET Framework, it has to generate code to do this. Could Visual Basic .NET have hidden this code the way VB6 hid the API code? Probably. However, there was really no need to, and the code generation method held plenty of advantages, such as the language-independent runtime (see the sidebar regarding the common language runtime).

The last of the four statements, Me.SuspendLayout, prevents the window from being constantly redrawn while the code setting up the window and its controls are being executed. It is worth noting that as you make changes to the properties and settings of controls and other elements, they are put into effect immediately. If Suspend-Layout were not called, you would see each change as it was made, as if the form was actually being drawn on the screen (try it out if you like by commenting out the call). It runs more quickly with SuspendLayout active.

Now take a look at the statements generated for one of the controls. The following is the code for the OK button:

```
Me.btnOK.Anchor = (System.Windows.Forms.AnchorStyles.Bottom _
    Or System.Windows.Forms.AnchorStyles.Right)
Me.btnOK.FlatStyle = System.Windows.Forms.FlatStyle.Popup
Me.btnOK.Location = New System.Drawing.Point(384, 240)
Me.btnOK.Name = "btnOK"
Me.btnOK.Size = New System.Drawing.Size(72, 24)
Me.btnOK.TabIndex = 1
Me.btnOK.Text = "&OK"
```

Most of this code is self-explanatory. You can see that it all makes sense when you understand that VB now generates visible code to create a form on the screen. There are a couple of noteworthy statements, such as:

```
Me.btnOK.Location = New System.Drawing.Point(384, 240)
```

VB is simply setting the position of the button relative to the form itself. The fun part is the value it assigns to the Location property. The Location property does not take simple coordinates as you might think. Instead, it takes a *point* object. The point object is a class defined in the drawing portion of the .NET Framework, just like the Form class. If this sounds to you like a pain in chops, you would be right. However, you can do it fairly easily, as you can see, in one line of code. Simply use the New keyword followed by the object you want to create and any parameters the constructor might take. In this case, it takes the X and Y coordinates that the point represents.

> **Using objects as values and parameters, like setting the location with the Point object, is very common in the .NET Framework. The best thing TIP to do is to get used to it, accept it, and move on. It's just one of many things that is very different from VB6. The best technique for dealing with it is to create the object inline with the assignment and then pass its parameters in the constructor as necessary. The statement:**

```
Me.btnOK.Size = New System.Drawing.Size(72, 24)
```

illustrates the point perfectly. The New statement creates the System.Drawing.Size object with the passed-in constructor parameters (the width and height values). Don't worry about deleting the memory used by the Size object because VB's new and very efficient garbage collection mechanism will take care of it for you.

What's interesting is that whenever you make a change to a control setting or property in the Forms Designer and the Properties page, VB updates this code right away. For example, if you change the Text property of the button to something else and then check the code window, VB will have regenerated the code to reflect the property change.

That's a very important point to remember. All the code in the InitializeComponent method is regenerated any time a change is made to any property of any control or of the form itself. Therefore, don't put any of your own code in there, no matter how tempted you are. It will be wiped out as soon as the code is regenerated.

THE COMMON LANGUAGE RUNTIME

You've probably heard of the common language runtime that is part of Visual Studio .NET. Perhaps you've wondered, What's the big deal? or What's going on in that thing? Well, the point of the common language runtime is to allow any language to be added to the Visual Studio environment and easily generate binary programs. The goal is that the syntax of the language you use should be more or less a personal preference and in the end, have no effect on capability or performance of the applications you build.

For the most part, this has been achieved. There are over 20 languages being planned for the Visual Studio environment that work with the .NET Framework and the common language runtime. How do they do it? When you compile your VB program, the first thing it does is compile it into an intermediate form called Intermediate Language, or IL. It's very similar to assembly language. All languages in the Visual Studio environment do the same thing and end up as IL. It is then compiled to a local binary executable format.

The benefit? If you want to write a language that works in the Visual Studio environment, you only have to go as far as the generation of IL. This is much easier because you can use the final compiler that Microsoft already wrote, the IL compiler. In addition, you can switch around languages as you see fit, and your capabilities will be about the same.

However, there is an even bigger benefit: the seamless interoperability of components. Any language that works in Visual Studio with the common language runtime is called *managed code*. Any components written in managed code can easily call components written in other managed code languages. Write a function in Visual Basic and call it in C#. Create a class in C++ and use it in SmallTalk. It all works together because in the end, it's all IL. So you really can use any language you prefer. The language itself becomes mostly inconsequential and is often now referred to as syntax candy. Use whatever language you find to be the sweetest.

Our Part of the Code

I added a few interesting bits that bear explanation. Note that there are three controls at the bottom of the form: the OK button, the Cancel button, and the Notify text box. An important aspect of any dialog created from this base form is that you may not want or need all these controls. Therefore the form must be able to accommodate the removal of any of them. If the OK button, the Cancel button, or both are removed, the Notify text box needs to be resized to take up the available horizontal space along the bottom of the dialog. See Figure 1.3 for an example of the difference.

Although Visual Basic .NET has new features to take care of anchoring controls to the sides or corners of a form during a resize operation, it does not handle resizing the controls under custom circumstances, such as when one of the buttons is removed. To accommodate this need, a method called ShowControls() was added to the form. It is located in the User Code region of the source. This is what it looks like:

```
Protected Overridable Sub ShowControls()

    ' Local data
    Dim x As Int32    ' Stores calculated control locations
    Dim y As Int32

    ' Hide or show the controls as indicated by our flags.
    If m_bShowOK Then
        btnOK.Show()
    Else
        btnOK.Hide()
    End If
    If m_bShowCancel Then
        btnCancel.Show()
    Else
        btnCancel.Hide()
    End If
    If m_bShowNotify Then
        txtNotify.Show()
    Else
        txtNotify.Hide()
    End If

    ' Resize or move the controls based on which ones are visible.
    ' We do a lot of the moving around because the anchoring
    ' does not work correctly when designing an inherited form.
    ' Control positions get ALL messed up!

    ' Deal with the two buttons first, then the notify textbox.
    y = Me.Height - (btnCancel.Height * 2) - EDGESPACING

    ' The Cancel button...
    If m_bShowCancel Then
        x = Me.Width - btnCancel.Width - CTRLSPACING - EDGESPACING
```

```
        Else
            x = Me.Width - EDGESPACING
        End If
        btnCancel.Location = New System.Drawing.Point(x, y)


        ' The OK button...
        If m_bShowOK Then
            x = btnCancel.Location.X - btnOK.Width - CTRLSPACING
        End If
        btnOK.Location = New System.Drawing.Point(x, y)


        ' And our patented modeless notification area.
        If m_bShowNotify Then
            txtNotify.Width = Me.Width - (CTRLSPACING * 2) - EDGESPACING
            If m_bShowCancel Then txtNotify.Width = txtNotify.Width - _
                btnCancel.Width - CTRLSPACING
            If m_bShowOK Then txtNotify.Width = txtNotify.Width - _
                btnOK.Width - CTRLSPACING
        End If
        txtNotify.Location = New System.Drawing.Point(EDGESPACING, y + 2)


    End Sub
```

First of all, notice that we declared the method as Protected Overridable. The protected part allows subclasses, forms derived from this one, to see and call this method. The overridable part allows subclasses to replace this method with their own implementation. Most of the methods and properties in this class are declared as overridable because we can't anticipate every need of those who use these classes. Who knows if a programmer in the future might need to override this method to handle new controls?

The rest of the code in this method moves and resizes controls on the form based on the current size of the form. It is typically called when the form is resized or when one of the controls is hidden or unhidden. The actual calculations aren't that interesting (if you'd like to know more, feel free to cruise the code). It is slightly complicated by the fact that the size and position of the controls depend on which ones are visible at the time.

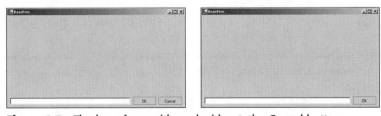

Figure 1.3 The base form with, and without, the Cancel button.

A perfect example of the usage of the ShowControls method is in the Show properties of the form. These properties, such as ShowOK, are Booleans that make the controls visible or hidden. When one of these properties changes, the spacing of the controls along the bottom of the form is no longer correct and needs to be redrawn. Therefore, as part of the Set portion of the property code, the ShowControls method is called. Following is the listing for the Show properties:

```
Public Overridable Property ShowOK() As Boolean
    Get
        ShowOK = m_bShowOK
    End Get
    Set(ByVal Value As Boolean)
        m_bShowOK = Value
        ShowControls()
    End Set
End Property


Public Overridable Property ShowCancel() As Boolean
    Get
        ShowCancel = m_bShowCancel
    End Get
    Set(ByVal Value As Boolean)
        m_bShowCancel = Value
        ShowControls()
    End Set
End Property


Public Overridable Property ShowNotify() As Boolean
    Get
        ShowNotify = m_bShowNotify
    End Get
    Set(ByVal Value As Boolean)
        m_bShowNotify = Value
        ShowControls()
    End Set
End Property
```

If you haven't had the opportunity to work with Visual Basic .NET properties yet, you can see that they're significantly different from those in VB. They are more structured, have a Get and Set section, and return a specific type. They're not really a problem, but it is one more difference between VB6 and Visual Basic .NET in a world of hundreds of differences.

DIGGING AROUND IN .NET

Someone recently asked me, "How big is the .NET Framework?" My answer? How wet is the ocean? How old is a trilobite? How annoying is Tom Green? It's big. There are all kinds of functionality in there, from graphics to multithreading, from Web services to remote networking. There are over 6,500 classes. There will be documentation that covers it all, eventually. However, the best and most interesting way to learn it is to prowl around in there yourself.

Sometimes, digging into the guts of a technical issue (even a huge one) uncovers extremely useful information that would be hard to discover otherwise (that's how authors write technical books like this one). Here's a good example. In VB6, you could determine the width of the display screen by using the Screen object, as in:

```
Screen.Width
```

Pretty easy? Try it in Visual Basic .NET. There is no screen object in Visual Basic .NET. Simply looking it up was not an option. After digging through the .NET Framework documentation, the answer was uncovered. The statement that returns the width of the screen is now:

```
System.Windows.Forms.Screen.PrimaryScreen.Bounds.Width
```

It was buried in the framework but was eventually unearthed. So dig a little and see what interesting capabilities you can discover.

The frmDialog Form

The first form we derive from frmBase is frmDialog. This form should to be used as the starting point for any modal dialog that you need to display in your application. It's not much different from frmBase. It adds a large dialog title at the top, as well as a frame around the dialog to contain the controls it needs. Figure 1.4 shows what it looks like.

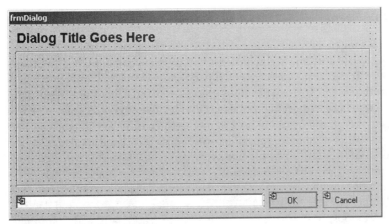

Figure 1.4   The frmDialog form.

We added a couple properties to the form class to make it easier to manipulate the large title at the top of the dialog. The first is simply the text of the title. The second allows the width of the title control to be adjusted. This is not normally a particularly useful attribute. However, it was put in there so that the frmWizard form class can adjust it. You'll see more about this in the frmWizard description.

```
Public Overridable Property Title() As String
    Get
        Title = lblTitle.Text
    End Get
    Set(ByVal Value As String)
        lblTitle.Text = Value
    End Set
End Property

Public Overridable Property TitleWidth() As Int32
    Get
        TitleWidth = lblTitle.Width
    End Get
    Set(ByVal Value As Int32)
        If Value < 0 Or Value > _
            System.Windows.Forms.Screen.PrimaryScreen.Bounds.Width Then
                Return
        End If
        lblTitle.Width = Value
    End Set
End Property
```

That's about it for frmDialog. Most of the work for this form has already been done in the base form.

The frmMsgBox Form

Is there something wrong here? Visual Basic already has a message box that works perfectly well. It's easy to use and pretty convenient. So why are we making another one? The big problem with the existing message box functionality is that you only get to put one type of text in there, and it's usually displayed as one big, ugly paragraph. The message box has been abused by trying to make it into an all-purpose display mechanism to tell the user everything from the time of day to the entire user manual for the program. There's usually too much information in it and it's difficult to read. Consequently, users will quickly adapt to its illegibility by not reading it. Not a good thing when you have something important to impart.

There is a usability technique you can use to make the message box more useful, easier to read, and a better benefit to the user. It's called a two-tier message box, and it looks just like Figure 1.5. The purpose is to create a large, easy-to-read headline that summarizes the issue you're trying to communicate quickly and easily and to follow it with a longer, more descriptive text block in smaller print that provides more details. This allows users to get the idea of the message quickly and read the details if they feel the need to. Also, our new message box looks much better than the cheesy VB message box.

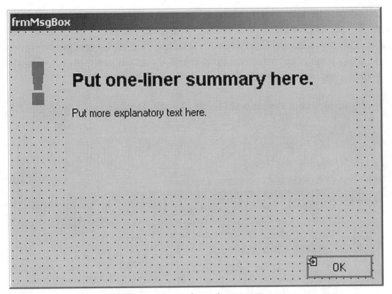

Figure 1.5   The two-tier message box, frmMsgBox.

One other thing I've done is to implement my own simulated icons using large colored text. I provide for an informational message box and an error message box and have chosen to eliminate the warning state because it typically just confuses users. When they see the warning icon, they typically think, "Was it actually an error? Do I need to take any action? What now?" The two states provided should work well.

One other design consideration that I feel is important is that it should be as easy to use for the programmer as the regular VB MsgBox. This means that the frmMsgBox must be usable in one line of code. I've done this and will show you how shortly.

So given all that, I built a message box of my own. Let's take a look at some of the code. First, we have the properties. The simple ones are:

```
Public Overridable Property OneLiner()
    Get
        OneLiner = lblOneLiner.Text
    End Get
    Set(ByVal Value)
        lblOneLiner.Text = Value
    End Set
End Property

Public Overridable Property Msg()
    Get
        Msg = lblMsg.Text
    End Get
    Set(ByVal Value)
        lblMsg.Text = Value
    End Set
End Property
```

These properties allow the user to set the large summary message text (OneLiner) and the potentially longer explanatory text (Msg). They are standard properties and are straightforward. The more interesting property is the TypeOfMsg property, which simply sets the message box to an informational message or an error message indicated by the large text-based icon. The property code looks like this:

```
Public Overridable Property TypeOfMsg() As MsgType
    Get
        TypeOfMsg = m_MsgBoxType
    End Get
    Set(ByVal Value As MsgType)
        Select Case Value
            Case MsgType.msgtypeINFO
                m_MsgBoxType = MsgType.msgtypeINFO
                lblIcon.ForeColor = System.Drawing.Color.Chartreuse
                lblIcon.Text = "i"
            Case MsgType.msgtypeERROR
                m_MsgBoxType = MsgType.msgtypeERROR
                lblIcon.ForeColor = System.Drawing.Color.Red
                lblIcon.Text = "!"
            Case Else
        End Select
    End Set
End Property
```

The Set portion is the fun part. It looks at the value of the parameter and sets the icon based on it. The value itself is an enumerated value I created as part of the class. The type, MsgType, has two possible values, one for an informational message and another for an error message. The code for the type follows:

```
Public Enum MsgType
    msgtypeINFO = 1
    msgtypeERROR
End Enum
Private m_MsgBoxType As MsgType
```

In the code for the property, notice that the value of the message type is specified with the type name and the value name, as in:

```
MsgType.msgtypeINFO
```

This fully qualifies the value to prevent confusion with any other type name that might be in scope at the time.

The really nifty part of using enumerated types with properties is twofold. First, Intellisense knows all about the types you create, and the possible values for a variable of type MsgType pop up automatically as you enter your code in the editor. Second, even the properties window picks up the possible enumerated values and allows you to set the property with appropriate values in the Forms Designer (see the following Tip for more information about properties and the Form Designer properties window).

Next we look at the best part of the frmMsgBox. This feature allows us to create the message box, set all its parameters, and display it, using one line of code, just like VB's message box. That feature is the user-defined constructor. If you recall, VB creates a default constructor for us, New(), with no parameters. We can overload the New constructor and make a new one that does what we want it to. Overloading a method with the same name is perfectly all right as long as the signature of the method (the combination of its name, its parameters, and its return value) is unique. We will be creating a constructor with parameters that allows the programmer to pass in all the necessary property values at the time of creation. Here's the code for our constructor:

```
Public Overloads Sub New(ByVal mType As MsgType, _
                         ByVal sOneLiner As String, _
                         ByVal sMsg As String, _
                         Optional ByVal bOK As Boolean = True, _
                         Optional ByVal bCancel As Boolean = False, _
                         Optional ByVal bShowNow As Boolean = True)
    ' Gotta call this
    MyBase.New()

    'This call is required by the Windows Form Designer.
    InitializeComponent()

    ' Call our own initialization code.
    InitForm()

    ' Now we do our own stuff. Set the attributes of this window
    ' based on the paramaters passed into this constructor.
    TypeOfMsg = mType
    OneLiner = sOneLiner
    Msg = sMsg
    ShowOK = bOK    'Note: ShowOK and ShowCancel are in the base class.
    ShowCancel = bCancel
    If bShowNow Then
        Me.Show()
    End If

End Sub
```

TIP **Overloading a method is a very powerful feature that allows you to provide multiple versions of the same functionality to suit different needs. For example, you might have a method that sorts an array of integers. Later you find a need within the same class to sort a list of names. You could create a second Sort method that overloads the first, taking an array of strings instead of integers. Visual Basic .NET provides the Overloads keyword to do this. What might not be obvious, though, is that the Overloads keyword has to be used on both methods, not just the second one. If you have two methods with the same name but different parameters, the Overloads keyword must be used on both. Don't forget to add it to your original method, or VB will gripe at you.**

The best part is the declaration of the constructor itself. It has the same name as the default constructor created by VB: New. However, we've loaded it with all sorts of parameters, including:

mType.   The type of message to display, informational or error.

sOneLiner.   The summary message to display.

sMsg.   The detailed message text to display.

bOK.   Indicates whether or not the OK button should be displayed.

bCancel.   Indicates whether or not the Cancel button should be displayed.

bShowNow.   Indicates whether or not the message box should be displayed immediately.

The first three parameters are what you would expect: the type of message, the summary text, and the detailed message. The remaining three are declared as optional and have default values. If these parameters are not specified when the object is declared, the default values are used. This is marvelously convenient because we can create a new message box with one line of code and as few as three parameters. For example, the following statement would give us a message box on the screen immediately:

```
Dim wMsg As New frmMsgBox(frmMsgBox.MsgType.msgtypeINFO, _
    "Sample Message Box", _
    "Some sort of interesting detailed message.")
```

It is sometimes difficult to get your programmers to use the in-house tools or code libraries you create for them, particularly if they are not simple to use. The slight extra effort put in to make this form as easy to use as the MsgBox function makes it much more likely that it will be put into daily use by your team.

The code for the constructor has some important calls in it, which are critical to put into your own custom constructors. They are:

```
MyBase.New()

InitializeComponent()

InitForm()
```

The first two are the same calls that VB puts in the default constructor that it generates. We need to mimic VB to make sure that those calls are in our own constructors. The last one is our own call, InitForm, which does our own initialization work. We put it in the VB-generated constructor, and we need it here as well.

The rest of the code in the constructor is basic setup stuff to get the form ready to display. We set the messages, make sure the correct buttons are displayed, and show the form if requested. Now you have no excuse to not use a friendlier, more informative message box in your applications.

TIP When you create properties in your window classes, they are real properties and are viewed as such by the VB IDE. They are treated as a property as much as Text, Name, and TabOrder are. The major benefit here is that once you create an instance of the form in the form designer, you can set your custom properties on the properties window just like the native properties are set. As soon as you set your properties through the property window, VB inserts code in the InitializeComponent method to take care of it.

There is one other important thing to remember about this. If your form has significant code in the property definition, that code will be executed as soon as the property value is set in the property window.

Properties	⫟ ✕
frmMsgBox prjCH01.frmBase	▼
Opacity	100%
RightToLeft	No
ShowCancel	**False**
ShowInTaskbar	**False**
ShowNotify	**False**
ShowOK	True
⊞ Size	**408, 296**
SizeGripStyle	Auto
SnapToGrid	True
StartPosition	WindowsDefaultLocation
Tag	
Text	**frmMsgBox**
TopMost	False

This can be a very powerful feature. In the frmDialog form, setting the ShowOK property to False will turn off the OK button and execute any code in the ShowOK property Set section. There is a call in there to Show Controls, which moves and resizes all the controls. The end result is that as soon as you turn off the OK button using the property, it will actually disappear and the Notify text box will resize. All this happens in the Form Designer. The danger is that if you forget this and put significant or inappropriate code in a property, it could execute when you don't want it to. For example, if you have code in there to contact a database and save the property data, you could cause all kinds of trouble. The database might not be available, or you might overwrite data you didn't mean to. So dive into this excellent feature of properties, but be careful!

The frmWizard Form

This is a pretty basic form and can be used as a starting point for any wizards you might need to create in your application. It is slightly different from the other forms in that it is derived from frmDialog instead of frmBase. It makes use of the title as well as the control frame. A few controls were added to the form, including a sidebar image on the left side of the dialog and the Next and Previous buttons. There's even a text label that tells users which step of the form they're currently viewing. There is no actual wizard functionality in the form, only the elements you need to make one yourself. Figure 1.6 shows what the dialog looks like.

The only code I added to the form is the InitForm method and a call to it in the constructor. We need to do a little work here to rearrange some of the controls from frmDialog to suit our wizardly needs. The control frame needs to be moved and resized to make room for the sidebar image. We also set the ShowNotify property of the Notify area (which is inherited from frmBase, two levels up the inheritance tree) to hide it. Here's the code for InitForm:

```
Private Sub InitForm()

        ' Tweak the base dialog so it will look like we want it to.
        Title = "Wizard Dialog"
        TitleWidth -= 150    ' Make room for the Step # label.
        ShowNotify = False   ' Don't need this.

        ' Shrink the group box to make room for the sidebar image.
        grpCtrls.SetBounds(grpCtrls.Location.X + 105, _
            grpCtrls.Location.Y, grpCtrls.Width - 105, grpCtrls.Height)

    End Sub
```

This is an example of reaping the rewards of putting a fair bit of the functionality that our forms need in the base class. We have a fairly nice wizard dialog with some functionality, and the preceding code is all we had to write.

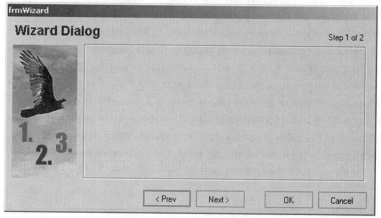

Figure 1.6 The frmWizard form.

The first three lines are pretty simple and make a few adjustments to the controls so that they fit better on our wizard dialog. We need to move the title over and shrink it a little so that it fits beside the sidebar image. The last statement is used to simultaneously move and resize the control frame on the dialog. The .NET method *SetBounds* is used and is the easy way to move and resize it using the framework. You pass it the new X and Y coordinates for the control first, followed by the new width and height values. It is worth noting that the Location.X and Location.Y properties are read-only. We are only changing the X coordinate and the width, essentially shrinking the size and shoving the control to the right to make room for the sidebar image.

The last detail to cover is that, like some of the controls on other forms, I changed their scope from private to protected. This will allow you to access the controls directly in derived forms instead of having to make properties for every little thing you want to do with them. And that's it for frmWizard.

The frmApp Form

Every application needs a main window, whether it's a word processor or a utility to help you decide where to eat lunch (don't laugh—I wrote one once). That's where frmApp helps out. It is derived from frmBase and is used for dialog-based applications. It was not designed for use with MDI applications, but you could modify it so that it could be.

I have taken frmBase and modified it so that it meets our corporate application needs. I added a sidebar image to give our applications identity and personality. I added a default menu to use a placeholder, which allows us to account for the menu in our control spacing calculations. Lastly, I hid all the default buttons because you rarely need them on a main application window. However, you can easily turn them back on by adjusting the ShowOK and ShowCancel properties in the Form Designer. We left the notification area in place because this is really where we need it. Figure 1.7 illustrates the frmApp form.

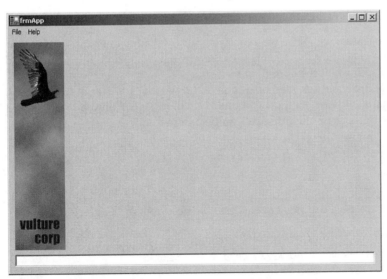

Figure 1.7   The frmApp form.

This form uses a Visual Basic .NET mechanism we haven't covered yet: *overriding* a method in a base class. This is done when we need to replace some functionality in the base class with new (but related) functionality in the subclass. In this case, the method ShowControls needs to do a little more work than it does in the base class. We have to make adjustments to the vertical position of the controls at the bottom of the screen. We have hidden the OK and Cancel buttons, but that doesn't mean a programmer won't turn them back on, so all three controls have to be positioned correctly. Here's the code for the new ShowControls method:

```
Protected Overrides Sub ShowControls()

    MyBase.ShowControls()

    txtNotify.SetBounds(txtNotify.Location.X, _
        txtNotify.Location.Y - MENUHEIGHT, _
        txtNotify.Width, txtNotify.Height)
    btnOK.SetBounds(btnOK.Location.X, _
        btnOK.Location.Y - MENUHEIGHT, btnOK.Width, btnOK.Height)
    btnCancel.SetBounds(btnCancel.Location.X, _
        btnCancel.Location.Y - MENUHEIGHT, btnCancel.Width, _
        btnCancel.Height)

End Sub
```

First, we use the Overrides keyword when declaring the method. This tells the compiler that when we call ShowControls, use this one instead of the one in the base class. Second, we still want the code in the base class version of the ShowControls method to execute. It does some good work for us that we still need. Once that executes, we just make a couple modifications of our own. Even through we've overridden the base class functionality, we still have access to it through the MyBase object. So calling

```
MyBase.ShowControls()
```

executes the base class code. Now we can make our own adjustments. We move the controls up a little to account for the height of the menu. If we didn't, the menu would push the controls almost off the bottom of the form.

Now that the ShowControls method is complete, we just have to make use of it. Create the standard InitForm method and put in a call to ShowControls. Don't forget to add the call to InitForm in the InitializeComponent method:

```
Private Sub InitForm()
    ShowControls()
End Sub
```

In this form, there are a couple of events that we need to handle. The following are the event handlers:

```
Private Sub MenuItem6_Click(ByVal sender As Object, _
    ByVal e As System.EventArgs) Handles MenuItem6.Click
    Me.Close()
```

```
End Sub

Private Sub frmApp_Resize(ByVal sender As Object, _
    ByVal e As System.EventArgs) Handles MyBase.Resize
    ShowControls()
End Sub
```

The first event handler simply ends the program if the Exit menu item is clicked. The second handles the resize event of the form. Visual Basic .NET adds features to handle some of your resizing issues, particularly the Anchoring feature. However, in this case, we need some custom handling. Because we've already written the new ShowControls method that takes care of our position and sizing, we just make a call to it when the resize event occurs.

The frmAbout Form

Our final form takes care of a small but useful part of application development: the About box. This window is often used to tell the users some information about the application they're using, such as the program version number, copyright information, and occasionally some details about their computer. Rarely, however, does it tell the user what the application is or does. My version of the form adds a section that describes that application itself. I also added a graphic on the left of the dialog and a link to the company's Web site. Figure 1.8 shows our prototype About box.

The form has some basic startup code in our standard InitForm method that centers the form on the display using our base class Center method. It also defaults any internal class data that needs it, in this case, the URL string. The InitForm code is as follows:

```
Private Sub InitForm()
    m_sURL = "http://www.wiley.com/compbooks"
    Center()
End Sub
```

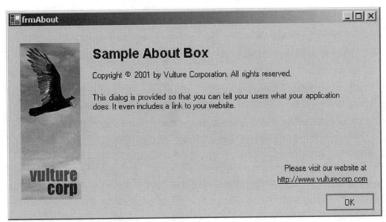

Figure 1.8 The frmAbout About box form.

In addition to making the form more useful, we also made it easier to use. Like our replacement for the message box, this form can be created and displayed in a single line of code. We created a new constructor that takes parameters for all the important properties, just like we did with frmMsgBox. Most of the parameters are defaulted and optional, so an About box can be created with as few as two parameters. The code follows:

```
Public Overloads Sub New(ByVal sTitle As String, _
                         ByVal sAbout As String, _
                         Optional ByVal sCopyright As String = _
                             "Copyright (c) 2001 ", _
                         Optional ByVal sImgPath As String = "", _
                         Optional ByVal sURL As String = "", _
                         Optional ByVal bShowNow As Boolean = True)
    ' Gotta call this
    MyBase.New()

    'This call is required by the Windows Form Designer.
    InitializeComponent()

    ' Call our own initialization code.
    InitForm()

    ' Now we do our own stuff. Set the attributes of this window
    ' based on the paramaters passed into this constructor.
    Title = sTitle
    About = sAbout
    Copyright = sCopyright
    If Len(sImgPath) > 0 Then
        SideImage = sImgPath
    End If
    If Len(sURL) > 0 Then
        URL = sURL
    End If
    If bShowNow Then
        Me.Show()
    End If

End Sub
```

The code includes the standard items required of a custom constructor, calling MyBase.New and InitializeComponent. It also calls our own InitForm method. It then uses all the passed-in parameters as values to its properties, preparing itself to be displayed. Its final task is to display itself if required to do so.

There are two interesting properties of this form. The first, URL, is as follows:

```
Public Overridable Property URL() As String
    Get
        URL = m_sURL
    End Get
```

```
        Set(ByVal Value As String)
            ' Set the internal URL, as well as the display of the
            ' URL on the dialog.
            m_sURL = Value
            llWebSite.Text = m_sURL
        End Set
    End Property
```

When the programmer sets the value of the URL, it not only stores it internally for use when the user clicks on it, but the property code also sets the text of the URL on the form itself. The control that we use to display the URL on the form is a new control in Visual Basic .NET called a LinkLabel. It simulates a Web link, as if it were on a Web page. However, it does not do any navigation for you. It only simulates the appearance of a Web link, changing colors when clicked and possessing an underline and other visual properties. If you want it to act as a Web link, opening a browser and launching a Web page, you'll have to do that yourself. This is done by trapping the click event that the LinkLabel fires. Here's the code for the event handler:

```
    Private Sub llWebSite_Click(ByVal sender As Object, _
        ByVal e As System.EventArgs) Handles llWebSite.Click

        llWebSite.LinkVisited = True
        If Len(m_sURL) > 0 Then
            System.Diagnostics.Process.Start(m_sURL)
        End If

    End Sub
```

Use the .NET Framework to start the browser process, specifically use System.Diagnostics.Process.Start. Just pass it a valid URL and it will know what to do with it.

The last part of frmAbout that bears mentioning is the SideImage property. It allows you to change the sidebar image displayed on the form. It takes a path to the image file as a value and then uses the .NET Framework to load it. The code looks like this:

```
    Public Overridable WriteOnly Property SideImage() As String
        Set(ByVal Value As String)
            ' Load the image if there is one. If not, clear the picture.
            If Len(Value) > 0 Then
                pbSidebar.Image = Image.FromFile(Value)
            Else
                pbSidebar.Image = Nothing
            End If
        End Set
    End Property
```

There is an object in the framework called System.Drawing.Image that you can use to load images (among other things). VB gives you a shortcut to it, so you can just use the Image object. The FromFile method simply loads an image from an image file on disk. There are several formats supported, including BMP, JPG, and GIF.

That's about it for frmAbout as well as for the collection of standardized forms. Now that you know how they're built, you'd probably like to know how to use them for your own applications.

Using the Forms in Your Projects

Creating forms as classes and building all sorts of elegant features into them is nothing more than a frivolous intellectual exercise, unless you can put them to work. In Visual Basic 6, we would have made copies of these forms, added them to the project, and then modified them to suit our needs. The process in Visual Basic .NET is a little different. In fact, there are two ways you can do it. The obvious way looks like this:

1. Create a new WinForms project.
2. Add our collection of forms to the project.
3. Create forms based on the collection by adding inherited forms to the project.

We'll be going over each step in detail, walking through the procedure for using the forms. After that, I'll show you the little test form we created to exercise and demonstrate the forms. Then I'll show you the second way to use them.

Creating Forms Using Our Collection

Create a new WinForms Project. Open Visual Studio .NET and create a new project, selecting the Windows Application project type. Name it what you like and store it where you want.

Build the project. Normally we wouldn't need to do this, but you can't add an inherited form to the project unless there is a valid assembly, created by building the project. The easiest way to build it is to just click the Play button on the toolbar.

Now remove the default form, Form1, which VB generates for you. You don't really need it and it will just get in our way. Besides, it's just a normal, peasant VB form, not an upperclass form derived from ours. Right-click on the form in the Solution Explorer and select Delete from the context menu. Of course, as yet there is no startup form or code for the project, so you have to set a new one. Once you have created the form you want to use as your startup form, select the project name in the Solution Explorer. Then, in the properties window, click the Property Pages button to display the Property Pages dialog, shown in Figure 1.9. Select the General category if it isn't already selected and then choose the form you built to act as your startup form in the Startup Object field.

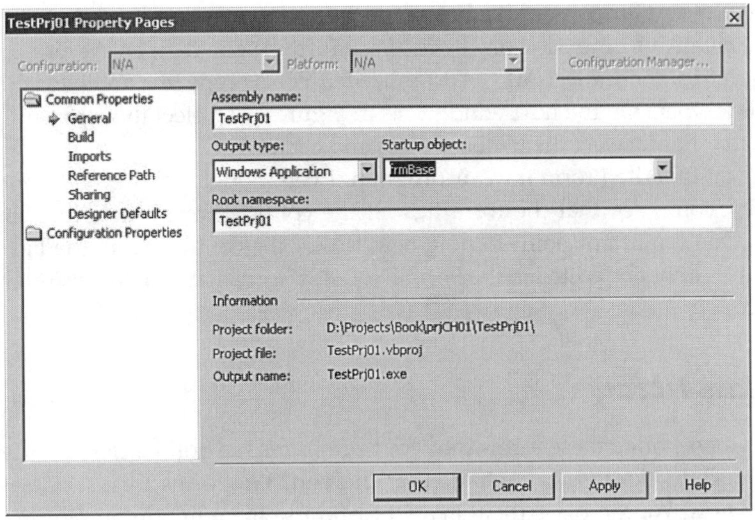

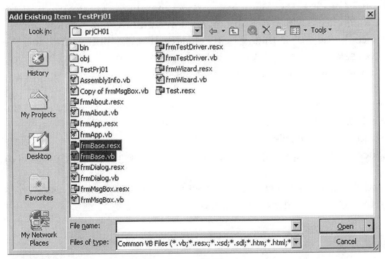

Figure 1.9   The Property Pages dialog.

Add in the forms from our collection that you might want to use. You don't have to add them all, and for now, just add the base form, frmBase. Right-click on the project name in the Project view and select Add/Add Existing Item. When the selection dialog opens, illustrated by Figure 1.10, select all the forms you want to use. Make sure you select both the .VB and the .RESX files for each form.

Figure 1.10   The Add Existing Item dialog.

Now you can add any forms you like based on the forms you just loaded. As an example, we will create a form based on the frmBase form. Right-click on the project name in the Project view and select Add/Add Inherited Form. Type in a name for the form and then click Open. On the next window, as in Figure 1.11, select the form from which you want to inherit. Select the frmBase form and click OK.

Now you have an inherited form in your program. Even though you haven't done anything to it yet, you'll see that the form has all the controls from the base form already in place. One important point to note here is that the controls from the base form are locked and cannot be edited in the Form Designer. You'll have to do it through properties or in code.

Creating a Class Library

The better way to incorporate these forms into your program is to build a class library that contains them. Didn't know you could do that, did you? WinForms are just classes like anything else now. We can place them in a DLL and use them in other programs. Here's the easy way to do it.

Create a new Class Library project in Visual Studio. Name it prj01classes. When the project creation is complete, delete the default class, Class1, from the project and add the form files to the project. Right-click on the solution name in the solution explorer, and from the context menu, select Add Existing Item. Select all the form .VB and .RESX files, and add them to the project. Build the project. When you're done, you'll have a DLL you can add to any project.

Want to try it out? Create a new WinForms project, naming it whatever you like. Right-click on the References section in Solution Explorer, and from the context menu, select Add Reference. In the dialog that appears click the Browse button and find the DLL we just created, select it, and click OK. Click OK on the original dialog. Now you can add a new inherited form to the project. When the Inherited Form dialog appears, type in a new name for the form and click Next. There will be nothing in the list, and you'll have to browse to the DLL again. When this is done, you'll see a list of all the forms in this project. Select the one you want, click OK, and you're done.

This is easier and more reusable than the first method. We'll be using the class library of forms, located on the accompanying CD-ROM, for several future projects in this book.

Now you're ready to go. You can create inherited forms like we just did as often as you like, through the Form Designer or through code.

The Test Driver

There is a test driver project on the CD-ROM that you can use to see how all the forms operate. Load the project prj01 into Visual Basic .NET and give it a run. I'll go over some of the code to illustrate some of the important usage points. It's a simple test form, consisting of a set of buttons you can click to launch samples of all the form classes. Figure 1.12 shows what it looks like.

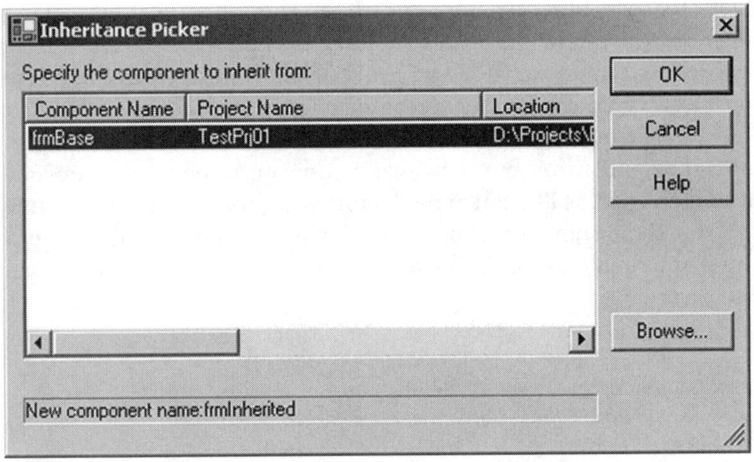
Inheritance Picker
Specify the component to inherit from:
Component Name
Project Name
Location
frmBase
TestPrj01
D:\Projects\
OK
Cancel
Help
Browse...
New component name:frmInherited

Figure 1.11 Specifying a form from which to inherit.

The code is not complex and is essentially just a set of event handlers, one for each button and window type. It illustrates how to use each type of form in code. Starting with the base form, you'll see the basic procedure for creating one of these windows in code. The base form was not meant to be created directly, but you can create any form derived from it:

```
Private Sub Button1_Click(ByVal sender As System.Object, _
    ByVal e As System.EventArgs) Handles Button1.Click

    Dim wBase As frmBase
    wBase = New frmBase()
    wBase.Show()

End Sub
```

frmT...
Base Form
MsgBox
Dialog
Wizard
App
About
See ya!

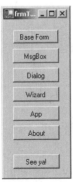

Figure 1.12 The test driver form, frmTestDriver.

Create a variable of the form type, in this case, frmBase. Then allocate a new instance of the form with New. Finally, show the form so that it ends up on the screen. You can follow the same procedure with frmDialog and frmWizard. Even frmApp can be created the same way. However, these forms are really designed be used as the basis for new forms that you derive from them.

The forms frmMsgBox and frmAbout, however, are meant to be used from code. They are forms of convenience, as illustrated by the following code, which shows how to use the frmMsgBox without showing the box immediately. In this example, we create the message box first and then make an adjustment to the height. It is then displayed using the Show method:

```
Private Sub Button2_Click(ByVal sender As System.Object, _
    ByVal e As System.EventArgs) Handles Button2.Click

    Dim wMsgBox As New frmMsgBox()
    wMsgBox = New frmMsgBox(frmMsgBox.MsgType.msgtypeERROR, _
        "What were you thinking?", _
        "Perhaps you had better take back what you just did." & _
        "I don't think it's in your best interest. Maybe you " & _
        "should take a vacation!", _
        True, False, False)
    wMsgBox.Height = 220
    wMsgBox.Show()

End Sub
```

The following example illustrates how to use the About box form in one line of code. Note that the second to last parameter, the path to the bitmap file to display on the dialog, will have to be changed before it works correctly. Point it to the actual location of the bitmap file on your computer:

```
Private Sub Button7_Click(ByVal sender As System.Object, _
    ByVal e As System.EventArgs) Handles Button7.Click

    Dim wAbout As New frmAbout("Sample About Box", _
        "This dialog is provided so that you can tell your users " + _
        "what your application does. It even includes a link to " + _
        "your Web site.", _
        "Copyright (c) 2001 by Vulture Corporation. All rights _
        "reserved.", _
        "vulturecorp.bmp", _
        "http://www.vulturecorp.com")

End Sub
```

The replacement constructor we built for frmAbout (and frmMsgBox) will show the form as soon as it's created.

Enhancing the Project

With a tiny bit of modification, you'll be able to use these forms in your own applications, giving them a consistent look and functionality, as well as saving yourself some time. Along the way, you will get a taste of the new .NET WinForms capabilities and using classes in Visual Basic .NET and will pick up a few advanced techniques.

There are all kinds of things you can do to make this project more useful and complete. Following is a list of just a few ideas you might try out if you feel like digging deeper:

Be less error-prone.   Add some error handling to the forms to allow them to protect themselves from bad inputs. By this, I mean complete, robust, structured error handling. Visual Basic .NET has a completely new error-handling mechanism using the Try..Catch..Throw standard. Now you can more reliably build error traps and throw your own errors very easily.

Make it MDI.   Create your own version of frmApp that acts as an MDI container. You'll be able to work with all kinds of windows and documents.

Create some wizardly magic.   Write some code in frmWizard to manage multiple control panels, making wizard creation easier. Start with multiple group controls, and hide or display them as the user clicks next or previous buttons.

Autosizing messages.   Add code to the frmMsgBox form to automatically size itself based on the size of the message content. Right now it just overflows, and longer text might get clipped. You'll have to figure out how tall to make the form and stretch the size of the lblMsg control.

More buttons.   Update the code in frmMsgBox to handle more button options. Right now it only supports OK. It probably needs, like VB's MsgBox, the capability of displaying various additional buttons, such as Yes, No, and Cancel. You could add another enumerated type to the code to specify the button types available, and Intellisense will pick them up and display them for the programmer. You could even override the ShowControls method from frmBase, like we did in frmApp, to handle the display of the various buttons.

WHAT'S COMING NEXT

If you're interested in databases, get ready to be excited. If you don't like databases, you'll be happy, too. We're covering ADO.NET next, and database people will really appreciate some of its new capabilities. Antidatabase people will be happy because it makes database work easier and more flexible than the old ADO did. When a programmer like me who has spent his life avoiding database coding enjoys it, you know it must be good.

Bug Tracking with ADO.NET

Database access has always been an important part of application development. It used to be extremely difficult, often requiring vendor-specific APIs to make it happen. After a period of darkness came ODBC, which allowed vendors to create a standardized implementation of their APIs. People could finally program for one interface and switch databases without changing all the code. But the ODBC interface was complex and difficult to learn. Microsoft's answer was DAO, a primitive object collection to make data access easier. DAO was an improvement, but it had problems and was incomplete. Finally ADO came along and really improved the whole mess. It became very popular and widely used. So why do we need another ADO?

With the advent Internet and complex Web-based applications that needed database access, ADO was fine if you had constant, direct access to the database. It had primitive disconnected functionality but was very difficult to send across an HTTP wire. Microsoft solved the problem by creating ADO.NET, a new ADO that is very Internet friendly and fits in with their new .NET framework. Its implementation is different; it has a new object model and a new paradigm.

THE PROBLEM:

Programmers write programs, and whether we like to admit it or not, those programs sometimes have bugs. Even super-humans make the occasional mistake. To correct those mistakes, we need to keep a list of them so that they don't fall through the cracks. Some IT shops use commercial software to track bugs, such as Microsoft SourceSafe. However, with the problems I've personally experienced with commercial bug-tracking software, I'm ready to write my own. Custom solutions give you more control over the software and features.

THE SOLUTION:

We're going to build our own bug-tracking solution, a simple front end to a database, using ADO.NET. It will show some of the ADO.NET techniques and objects and give you the basis for your own in-house bug-tracking system.

The Project

The project is a bug-tracking system, one that you can start with and expand as you need. We'll be following these steps to build the program:

1. **Set up the database.**   The database we will be using has several tables and one-to-many relationships. You can create them yourself or use the database provided.

2. **Construct the program form.**   The main form in the program has fields for all the fields in the database. Once it is created, we will attach code.

3. **Write the code.**   There is a fair amount of code in this project, from SQL statements to ADO.NET DataSets. We'll use it to make the connection between the fields on the form and the data in the database. You'll also see some data manipulations along the way, like loading list values into the UI from the database.

4. **Test it out.**   The best part of any project is running it and seeing the results. I'll take you on a quick tour of the functionality to see what you can do with it.

ADO.NET is fairly easy to work with once you use it a few times and get used to its new way of doing things. If you're database oriented, you'll find that it is much more capable than the old ADO.

 ## You Will Need

✔ **Visual Basic .NET**

✔ **A basic knowledge of Visual Basic .NET and WinForms**

✔ **Code from Project 1 (for the client portions)**

✔ **The prj02.mdb MS Access database from the accompanying CD-ROM**

ADO.NET Technology

ADO is probably quite familiar to most VB programmers. If you work in an enterprise environment, you probably have to access a database of some sort. ADO is the best way to do that from VB. Regardless of how familiar you are with ADO, chances are that the new ADO.NET will have you scratching your head for a few minutes. There are a few major differences in the way the two are designed, and understanding them is essential to quick productivity with ADO.NET.

The Primary Differences between ADO and ADO.NET

The best way to see the differences between the two ADO brothers is to do a side-by-side comparison. You'll see that the younger brother is the one that builds on the older brother's strengths, while taking a different path. Examine Table 2.1 and you'll see that although ADO.NET is a little different, it gets the same job done, and then some.

Table 2.1   ADO and ADO.NET Comparison

ADO	ADO.NET
ADO is primarily meant to work in a connected environment, with constant access to the database.	ADO.NET was designed from the ground up to work in a disconnected environment, such as the Internet (although it works connected just as well).
ADO's primary data container is the RecordSet. It can store one result set.	ADO.NET's primary data container is the DataSet. It can store as many result sets as you like.
ADO has many types of cursors for different purposes, each with its own specialized capabilities.	ADO.NET does not use cursors. It works in a disconnected environment that obviates the need for them.
ADO RecordSets are stored in their own proprietary binary format. They are difficult to send across firewalls, requiring marshalling. They are not useful to non-ADO-aware programs.	ADO.NET DataSets are stored internally as XML, an industry standard format. They are designed to be sent across a wire, and firewalls are not a problem. DataSets can be used in their XML form by almost any software.
ADO, being connected to the database most of the time, does not scale up very well and hogs connection resources.	ADO.NET, being designed to work as a disconnected data system, scales very well. It uses connections only when necessary, releasing resources for others to use.

There are a few other differences as well, but there are two big ones that stand out as the most important. First, ADO.NET works as a disconnected data system. This means that data is loaded from the database into the container, the DataSet, and then it is handed off to the application that needs to use it. The database connection is used only as long as absolutely necessary and is then released so that other applications can make use of the resources. In an environment such as the Internet, where many requests and users are involved at the same time, resources such as database connections are at a premium. The ability of ADO.NET to use a database connection for only a very short time and then release it makes it ideal for Internet-based applications.

The second big deal is that data in ADO.NET DataSets is stored internally as XML, an industry standard format. ADO RecordSets are stored in their own internal format. They are not particularly useful to an application that doesn't know about RecordSets. They cannot be used, for example, to pass to a Java applet on a Web page. However, the XML guts of an ADO.NET DataSet can be used by any client that understands XML, which, these days, can be just about anything.

These differences, along with being fairly easy to use, make ADO.NET an ideal database access mechanism for database work across the Internet. However, it also fulfills the job ADO does: working in a normal application environment. It has been designed to accommodate the needs of both environments.

ADO.NET Architecture

Like ADO, ADO.NET has its own collection of objects, and its own way of doing things. The basic architecture is illustrated in Figure 2.1. It shows the objects involved and their relationships to each other.

Let's take a brief look at the various objects and components of ADO.NET and what they do. We'll cover them in more detail later, but an overview will help establish the big picture.

The .NET data provider.   Any database provider can implement a .NET data provider, allowing normal ADO.NET access to its database. The provider has to provide its own implementation of the Connection, Command, DataAdapter, and DataReader objects. The very nice thing about the data provider is that you can create one yourself to access any sort of data, from Btrieve data to MP3 ID3 tag information. Anything you like.

The DataSet.   Arguably this is the most important object in the set. This is the ADO.NET equivalent of the RecordSet, with many improvements. It can store data from multiple queries, with each result set represented as a different table. The internal XML representation of the data makes it efficient and compatible with other sources of data and applications.

The DataAdapter.   This is the second most important object in ADO.NET. It is the component that acts as the bridge between the DataSet, a container, and the actual database. It houses commands for Select, Update, Insert, and Delete commands so that it can perform data operations. It is responsible for loading the DataSet with data and updating the database from changes made to the DataSet. This is a new concept for ADO.

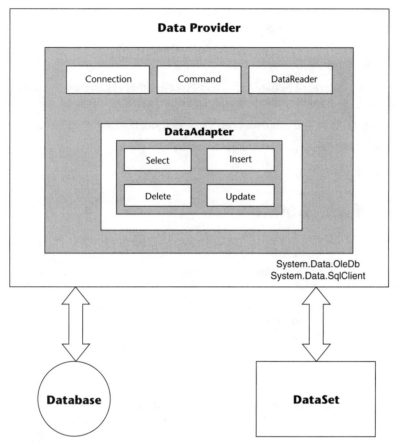

Figure 2.1 The ADO.NET architecture.

The DataReader. This object is an efficient forward-only data-streaming object. It's useful for large amounts of data that can't be cached in memory.

The DataRelation. This object is a stand-in for the SQL JOIN clause. It allows you to set up relationships between tables that would normally require a JOIN clause.

The Connection. This object works a lot like the older ADO connection object. It establishes a connection to the database so that the DataAdapter can communicate with it.

The Command. The Command object allows the DataAdapter to issue commands to the database in order to operate on the data. The DataAdapter can contain four of these commands.

These components and objects all work together rather nicely. A basic usage scenario goes something like this:

1. Create the basic objects first: an instance of the Connection, a DataSet, a DataAdapter, and a Command object.

2. Give your Connection object a connection string and open it. You can stuff the connection object into the DataAdapter.

3. Then add a select statement to the Command object so that it knows what data to pull out. Add the command object to the DataAdapter.

4. Load the data by calling the DataAdapter's Fill method, passing it the DataSet.

5. Do what you will with the data now in the DataSet.

There are, of course, other things you can do, but you get the idea.

Getting Started with ADO.NET

You've had a taste of ADO.NET to whet your appetite. If you're like other programmers I know, you'll be pretty hungry for more by now. Details are important, as those who have forgotten to use *Option Explicit* in their code can attest. So now we find out the details of ADO.NET operation.

The basic steps we'll cover include setting up for data access, actually getting some data, how to use the data once you have it, and finally, a few of the other nonquery operations you can perform.

Setting Up

Getting ready for ADO data access involves two parts. First, you must give your program access to the ADO.NET functionality. Do this by adding an Imports statement to your code. You can import one of two packages, depending on the type of data access you require:

System.Data.OleDb.   This package gives you access to SQL Server, Microsoft Access, and Oracle. Its main attraction is its ability to access more than one type of database. We'll be using this data provider for all the code in this project.

System.Data.SqlClient.   This package gives you access to Microsoft SQL Server. It is streamlined and optimized to give you the most efficient performance to that database. It's faster and smaller than using the full-blown OleDb provider.

Once you have imported the appropriate package, it's time to connect up. You need to create a connection object and supply it with a connection string in order to use it. The connection object has a number of constructors you can use. Usually you will want to pass it the connection string when you create it, something like this:

```
Private conn As New OleDbConnection(sConnStr)
```

You can connect to the database anytime using the Connection object's Open and Close methods. When doing this, it is important to remember to open a connection as late as possible, that is, only when you need it, and to close it as soon as possible, or as soon as your data operation is complete.

Getting Data

Once you are connected, you can start working with the database. To do this, you need a Command object to tell the database what you want to do, a DataSet to hold the returned data, and a DataAdapter to do the work for you. Create them like you would any other object:

```
Private objCommand As New OleDbCommand()
Private objDS As New DataSet()
Private objDA As New OleDbDataAdapter()
```

Continue by adding your SQL command to the Command object and telling the DataAdapter to use the command:

```
objDA.Connection = objConn
objCommand.CommandText = "SELECT SupplierName FROM Suppliers"
objDA.SelectCommand = objCommand
```

Open the connection and fill the DataSet using the DataAdapter. Close the connection right away to free up the connection resource for other needs:

```
objConn.Open()
objDA.Fill(objDS, "Suppliers")
objConn.Close()
```

This code tells the DataAdapter to get the data specified by the SelectCommand stored within it and put it into the supplied DataSet, in this case, objDS. But we're not done yet. We get a chance to see one of the most useful features of the DataSet and understand another very good reason why it was implemented using XML.

There is currently a single result set in the DataSet, the results from a single query. With ADO, if you wanted another result set, you'd have to create another RecordSet and issue another query. If you wanted to send both result sets to a client, you would have to send both RecordSets, either as two parameters or in two separate calls. With ADO.NET, that all changes. You can add multiple result sets to the same DataSet by simply changing the query and calling Fill again:

```
objDA.SelectCommand.CommandText = "SELECT * FROM Products"
objDA.Fill(objDS, "Products")
```

You can do this as many times as you like. Read on to see how to get at the data, including the data from multiple queries.

The DataSet: Getting at Your Data

Those of you who are familiar with ADO would now be ready to access data by using such methods as MoveLast and MovePrevious methods. Well, you can forget that. Things work a little differently now, and they work better than they used to. The DataSet has new methods and collections of objects that make record access, including direct record access, pretty easy.

Take a look at Figure 2.2. It illustrates the objects and collections contained within the DataSet object. As you can see, there's quite a bit there, but it's all useful. The most important items here are the three collections: Tables, Rows, and Columns.

As we mentioned earlier, the DataSet can contain multiple result sets from more than one query. Each set of results is represented in the DataSet as a table. The Tables collection contains them all. You can navigate them using standard collection iterators and access methods, such as the For..Each loop and referencing them as an array with numeric or named indexes. Using our preceding example, you could access the two different tables like this:

```
Dim table As DataTable
For Each table In objDS.Tables
     MsgBox( table.TableName )
Next
```

Or, you could reference them directly:

```
MsgBox( objDS.Tables(0).TableName )
MsgBox( objDS.Tables("Products").TableName )
```

Each table has a Columns and Rows collection that can be used to access data for each row returned in the table. An example is:

```
Dim row As DataRow
For Each row in objDS.Tables("Suppliers").Rows
     row.Delete
Next
```

You can access the columns stored in a row in a similar fashion:

```
For Each row In objDS.Tables("Suppliers").Rows
    MsgBox( CStr(row("SupplierName")) & ", " & _
  CStr(row("SupplierID")) )
Next
```

If you want to display the name of the supplier in the fourth row of the Suppliers table, here's how you do it in a single line:

```
objDS.Tables("Suppliers").Rows(3).Columns("SupplierName")
```

TIP **DataTable names are *conditionally case sensitive*. This means that if there are two tables with the same name, they are distinguished by the case. If there is only one table of a given name, referencing its name is a case-insensitive operation. This can cause problems, of course. The best way to handle this is to treat everything as case sensitive and make sure you get the case right.**

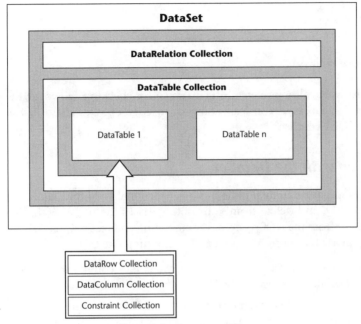

Figure 2.2   The contents of the DataSet object.

Within the DataSet, there is no concept of current record, next record, last record, or EOF. You simply access the data you want directly; it's all there for the taking. However, if you're using data binding, you will use the concept of current record and record position. I'll talk about that later when I introduce the BindingContext object.

Creating, Updating, and Deleting

You can read and navigate a DataSet, but how do you manipulate data in other ways? SQL lets you also delete, update, and insert new rows. ADO.NET also lets you do this through the Command object. The key is a combination of the right SQL statement and a single method: ExecuteNonQuery. Three short examples follow, one each for the create, update, and delete operations. Notice that each one uses the same method call, ExecuteNonQuery, to make it happen.

```
Dim sSQL As String
sSQL = "INSERT INTO Suppliers (SupplierName, SupplierID) " & _
       "VALUES ('Rotten Potatoes, Inc.', 1)"
objCommand.CommandText = sSQL
objCommand.ExecuteNonQuery()
objCommand.CommandText = "UPDATE Suppliers SET SupplierName = " & _
```

```
        "'Rotten Tomatoes, Inc.' WHERE SupplierID=1"
objCommand.ExecuteNonQuery()
objCommand.CommandText = "DELETE FROM Suppliers WHERE " & _
        "SupplierID=1"
objCommand.ExecuteNonQuery()
```

It is pretty straightforward, although we didn't do any error checking. However, the techniques you've seen so far require at least some knowledge of SQL. How do you manage data without SQL expertise?

Data Manipulation with the DataSet

You can make changes to your data using the built-in functionality of the DataSet. It allows you to add, modify, and delete from your data without the use of SQL. The process is a little different from the ADO process for managing changes because we are always using the data in a disconnected state. It goes something like this:

1. Once you have your DataSet populated, make any changes you like to the data using the collections and methods in the DataSet.

2. When you're ready to update the data, create a second DataSet using the GetChanges method. This will return only the records that have changed since the DataSet was populated. This second DataSet is more optimized to check for errors or to perform your own validations.

3. Check the new DataSet for errors using the HasErrors methods on the DataSet, the DataTable(s), and the DataRows. Use each in succession if the previous one returned an error state. Also take this opportunity now, if appropriate, to perform your own validations on the changed data.

4. Once everything is okay, call the DataSet's Merge method to merge the two DataSets back together, creating one DataSet with correct, validated data that contains all the edits you made to the data.

We start with editing the data once we have it. Primarily the objects contained in the DataSet provide this functionality, such as the Rows and Columns collections. The basic operations and the methods used are detailed in Table 2.2.

Table 2.2   Dealing with Changes to Data Using ADO.NET Objects

OPERATION	METHOD
Add a new row	objDS.Tables("Suppliers").NewRow()
	objDS.Tables("Suppliers").Rows.Add(RowObject)
Delete a row	objDS.Tables("Suppliers").Rows.Remove(RowObject)
	objDS.Tables("Suppliers").Rows(index).Delete()
Update a row	Nothing specific; just make edits directly to the row/column values

To add a new row, you have to create a new DataRow object. However, for it to be useful, it needs the correct schema (columns and types) for you to fill in. You do this by using the destination table to create the row, then add the data to the DataRow, and finally add it back into the table. The following code illustrates the process:

```
Dim aRow As DataRow
aRow = objDS.Tables("Suppliers").NewRow()
aRow("SupplierID") = 1
aRow("SupplierName") = "Rotten Eggs, Ltd."
objDS.Tables("Suppliers").Rows.Add(aRow)
```

And voila! You have a new row in your table. To delete a row, you have two options available to you. First is the direct way, which deletes the row's data immediately. It's a little odd, but here's an example that deletes the first row in a table:

```
Dim aRow As DataRow
aRow = objDS.Tables("Suppliers").Rows(0)
objDS.Tables("Suppliers").Remove(aRow)
```

Why select the row out and then pass it back into the Remove method? Good question. One scenario where this is useful is when the Find method is used. The Find method searches a table for a row and returns a DataRow object. That object can then be passed into the Remove method. There is a more direct method, but it has a quirk of its own:

```
objDS.Tables("Suppliers").Rows(0).Delete()
```

This method only marks the row for deletion. It is not physically removed from the table until you call the AcceptChanges() method.

After your updates are complete, you might want to review the data for errors or validate the changes that have been made. To make this easier, you can extract only the records that have changes into a new DataSet. It goes like this:

```
Dim objMergeData As DataSet
objMergeData = objDS.Tables("Suppliers").GetChanges()
```

Now you can cruise through the contents of objMergeTable, looking for errors or validating it using your own code. You can make use of the HasErrors methods on the table and rows or perform your own checks. Once you're done, it's time to merge the data back into the original DataSet, like this:

```
objDS.Merge(objMergeData)
```

That's all. Your changes are complete, checked, and merged back into the main DataSet. You can now send it all back to the physical database. The DataAdapter comes back into the picture for this step. Use its Update method to send the contents of the DataSet back to the database. You should also call AcceptChanges on the DataSet if you plan to continue using it. This flags all the data to an unchanged state:

```
objDA.Update(objDS)
objDS.AcceptChanges()
```

If you found errors, or changed your mind about updating the database, skip the Update call and instead of calling AcceptChanges, call RejectChanges. This will reset the state of the data back to the way it was when it was either loaded or the last time AcceptChanges was called.

The DataRelation Object

The DataRelation object is used to represent relationships between two tables. For example, assume we have a database that has a Computer table, each row of which represents a single complete computer. Associated with this table is another one called Parts, which represents all the parts in all the computers you have in your database. There is a one-to-many relationship between the two tables. For a single row in the computer table, there may be many records in the Parts table. It would be nice, when retrieving a computer record, to also get all the associate parts with it. The DataRelation can help with this. Let's look at how we can make this example happen using the DataRelation and other ADO.NET objects.

First you have to set up the DataRelation. This involves linking the tables with the two matching columns in the tables. In our case, we have a ComputerID field that exists in both tables to link the records together. Start by creating a DataRelation object variable to hold our relationship.

```
Dim objDR As DataRelation
```

Now set up the relationship. Use the two columns we're interested in from the DataSet:

```
objRA = New DataRelation("ComputersAndParts", _
        objDS.Tables("Computers").Columns("ComputerID"), _
        objDS.Tables("Parts").Columns("ComputerID"))
```

Now that we have the relationship defined, you can use it to get a computer record and a complete list of the parts that make it up. We'll get them all and create a string that can be placed into a multiline text box. Iterate through all the rows in the Computers table, and for each one, loop through all the Parts rows that are related to it using the DataRelationship. The code looks like this:

```
Dim rowComputers As DataRow
Dim rowParts As DataRow
Dim sComputer As String

For Each rowComputers In objDS.Tables("Computers").Rows
    sComputer = rowComputers("ComputerName") & vbCrLf
```

```
      For Each rowParts In rowComputers.GetChildRows(objRA)
          sComputer &= "- " & rowParts("PartName") & vbCrLf
      Next
  Next
```

What we've done is set up a link between the two tables and passed that link, the DataRelation, to the GetChildRecords method. It will use the information in the DataRelation to pull back only records that the relationship defines. In our case, a single row from the Computers table will contain a single ComputerID. The GetChildRecords method will find all the Parts records with the same ComputerID because that's the relationship we set up.

There is more to using DataRelations, but you can dig in and discover the rest when you have a spare moment. For now you can see their potential, and even this small example can be useful in daily programming life.

Data Binding

Data binding, in case you're new to the concept, allows you to bind a collection of data (previously a RecordSet) to the controls on a form. Changes to the data on the form would be reflected in the attached, or bound, data. It was a big leap forward for simple data access forms and was very popular. Data access programs could be whipped up in almost no time and with very little programming.

Microsoft has not forgotten about data binding with ADO.NET. There are tools and wizards aplenty to keep the impatient database programmer happy. You can use the automated tools in the Visual Studio .NET environment to help you along or use your own brain to do it programmatically. We're going to go through both techniques here because they each have their place.

Automated Data Binding with Visual Studio .NET

I'm going to show you how to build a database application with as little coding as possible using the Visual Studio .NET automated tools to create data-based projects. If you like, you can use the sample Microsoft Access database, called prj02test.mdb, on the accompanying CD-ROM. It has a single table called Suppliers that has a few columns in it. The examples and screen shots used in this section are based on it.

Fire up Visual Studio .NET, and create a Windows Forms project. When everything has been created, right-click on the project name in the Solution Explorer and select *Add Item* from the context menu. When the dialog appears, select DataForm wizard and click OK. This will launch a wizard that will ask you to specify a data connection to a database and, from it, a form will be generated that has fields and navigation functionality based on that database. Table 2.3 illustrates the settings you should choose in each panel of the wizard.

Table 2.3 Settings for Each Wizard Panel in the Data Form Wizard

PANEL #	PANEL FUNCTION	SETTINGS
1	Choose or Create a DataSet	Specify Create a DataSet and enter the name dsSuppliers.
2	Choose a Data Connection	Click the New Connection button and set up a Jet 4.0 connection to the MS Access database.
3	Choose Tables or Views	Select the Suppliers table on the left and click the right arrow to move it to the right side.
4	Choose Tables for the Form	Make sure all the fields from the Suppliers table are checked.
5	Choose Display Style	Select the *Single record in individual controls* options, and accept the other defaults. Click Finish to generate the form.

When you click the finish button, the wizard will create the form and code to do the basic work. The form we created is displayed in Figure 2.3. Looking at the form, you can see that the wizard not only created controls for each column in the database table, but it also added navigation controls that look suspiciously like the deceased Data-Control from VB6. There are also controls to Load data, Update data, and Add and Delete records. The wizard also generated a fair amount of code for us. It created a DataSet, a Connection, and a DataAdapter, complete with commands for Update, Select, Insert, and Delete. Everything is data bound for us, and if compiled, this program will work as is.

Sounds pretty powerful, doesn't it? Unfortunately, it is only suitable for simple projects and examples. Complex multitable queries are beyond it, and if you need to do any special processing with the database on your own, it can be difficult to modify. If you want a basic data editor, go for it or use it as a starting point for more complex applications. You could also use it as the basis for some programming tools. However, it is usually better to create your own application from the ground up, planning it carefully and doing your own design work. This has many benefits, including:

- Data access functionality is better organized and tuned to suit your specific needs.

- You don't have to work with a generated framework that might compromise your own design needs.

- The wizard's data access and manipulation capabilities are limited.

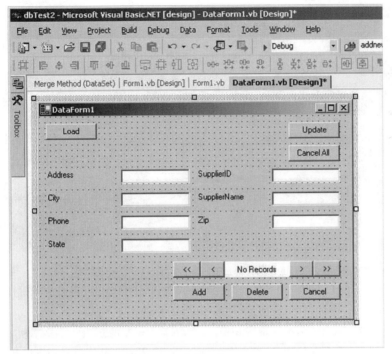

Figure 2.3   The wizard-generated data form.

You can also use some of the built-in data wizards and tools at a lower level. For example, there is a wizard to create a DataAdapter for you and the code to support it. From that DataAdapter, you can create a DataSet and add it to your code. These can be small, useful timesavers when used individually. Give this a try when you have some time to play with it.

For example, perhaps you would like to automate the process of adding the standard ADO.NET objects to your program, after which you will take over using skillfully handcrafted code. Here's a walkthrough. Because this is intended to make our lives easier, and we might actually make use of it, we'll examine each panel of the wizard.

Start by creating a DataAdapter. From the Data Toolbox in Visual Studio, drag an OleDbDataAdapter onto your data form. Figure 2.4 shows the data toolbox. This will start the DataAdapter wizard, which makes it very easy to get going.

The DataAdapter wizard begins by asking you which data connection you would like to use. If you don't have one in your project already, click the New Connection button to create one. I have already filled it in, as shown in Figure 2.5.

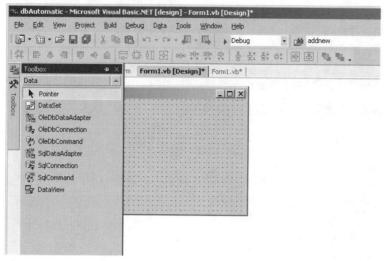

Figure 2.4   The Data Toolbox in Visual Studio.

In the second panel we need to decide how we want the DataAdapter to retrieve our data. We can either enter a SQL statement (if you have an aversion to SQL, there is hope. Keep reading) or use stored procedures in the database. Stored procedures are a little beyond the scope of this project, so we'll use a SQL statement. Make that selection, shown in Figure 2.6, and click Next.

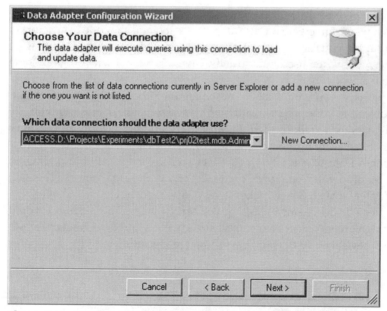

Figure 2.5   The DataAdapter wizard: Selecting a database connection.

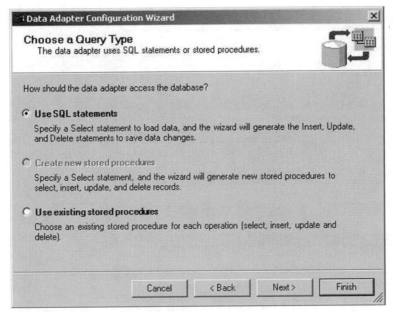

Figure 2.6   The DataAdapter wizard: Select a query type.

This is where we tell the DataAdapter what data to retrieve. Enter a SQL Select statement, as shown in Figure 2.7, or if you sneeze whenever someone mentions SQL, you can use the Query Builder. Click the Query Builder button to create your query graphically instead of syntactically. The Query builder looks just like Figure 2.8 and reflects the same query we entered as SQL.

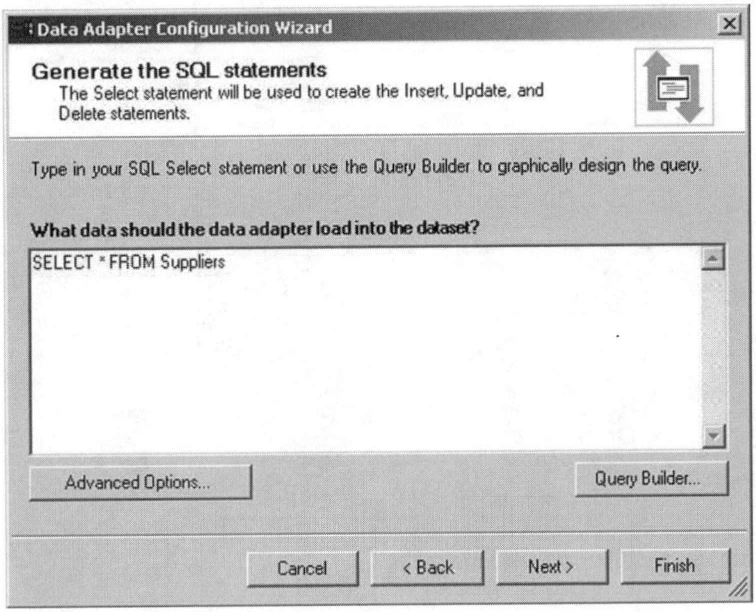

Figure 2.7   The DataAdapter Wizard: Create SQL statements.

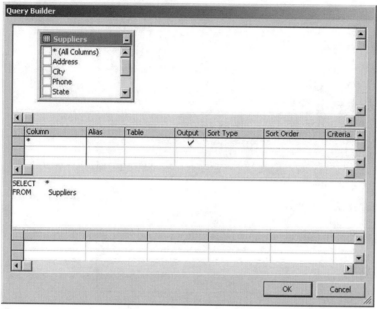

Figure 2.8 The DataAdapter Wizard: The query builder.

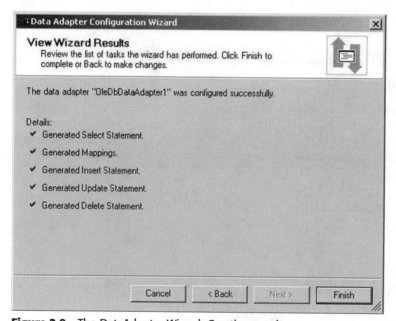

Figure 2.9 The DataAdapter Wizard: Creation results.

The next wizard panel requires no interaction. It simply informs us that everything was created successfully. The really interesting part is that we see that it has generated commands for Selecting, Inserting, Updating, and Deleting data. This is pretty handy. Figure 2.9 shows the results.

That's it for the DataAdapter. If you examine the area of the Visual Studio window just below the form design window, you'll see that the wizard not only created a DataAdapter for us, but it also created a Connection object. The only thing left is the DataSet. You can create one of these the same way you started the DataAdapter: by dragging a DataSet object from the data toolbox onto the form. It will respond with a single dialog, shown in Figure 2.10.

For the purposes of this example, select Untyped DataSet on the dialog. All you have to do is click the OK button and you're done. Code has been generated for three objects by simply dealing with a few wizard panels. That's the good news. The bad news is that this only works well for simple single-table queries. The DataAdapter wizard allows you create some complex multitable queries, but it will not generate correct commands for you in the code. For example, we created a two-table query, shown in the Query Builder in Figure 2.11. The figure also shows the SQL with a simple JOIN involved. However, when you return from the Query Builder and click next to finish up, it responds with the warning message shown in Figure 2.12. It could not generate a Select statement for the SQL that it generated itself. This seems a little odd, and perhaps it will be upgraded in the future.

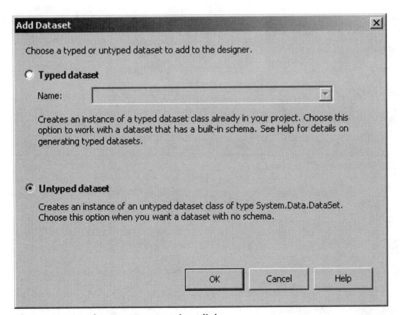

Figure 2.10 The DataSet creation dialog.

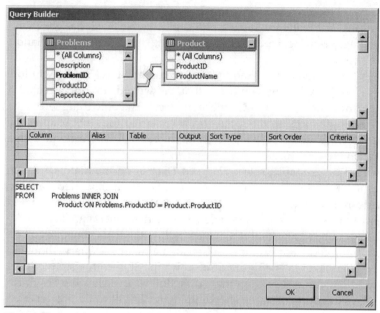

Figure 2.11 The Query Builder with a JOIN.

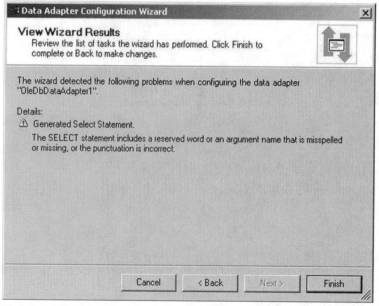

Figure 2.12 The Select generation warning message.

This technique is not useless for more complicated queries. It remains a nice short-cut for creating all the objects for us. All you'll have to do is replace the generated SQL with the code to do what you really want it to.

Programmatic Data Binding with Visual Basic

That didactic, overbearing wizard is not the only way to implement data binding and make it useful. You can do it yourself in code. There are some nice benefits of doing it this way:

- It's not hard.
- It gives you more control, and you can easily fit it into your own design.
- You can use just as much as you like without going overboard.

When you write your own code to bind data from a DataSet to controls on your form, there are a couple basic things you need to do:

1. Create all the standard ADO.NET objects: Connection, DataSet, Command, and DataAdapter.
2. Set up the bindings between the controls and the columns in your DataSet.
3. Implement your own record navigation.
4. Implement your own database operations.

Let's take a brief walk through each one to see how it's done. We already know how to create ADO.NET data objects, so we'll skip over that part. Setting up the data bindings is all new. We are now introduced to the DataBindings object on each control. We'll use the same basic controls for data as those generated in the foregoing.

To create data bindings, you add a new Binding object to the control's DataBindings collection. The Binding object is found in System.Windows.Forms, and the code for creating them looks like this:

```
Me.txtSupplier.DataBindings.Add( _
    New System.Windows.Forms.Binding( _
    "Text", Me.objDS, "Suppliers.SupplierName")
Me.txtSupplierID.DataBindings.Add( _
    New System.Windows.Forms.Binding( _
    "Text", Me.objDS, "Suppliers.SupplierID")
Me.txtAddress.DataBindings.Add( _
    New System.Windows.Forms.Binding( _
    "Text", Me.objDS, "Suppliers.Address")
Me.txtCity.DataBindings.Add( _
    New System.Windows.Forms.Binding( _
    "Text", Me.objDS, "Suppliers.City")
Me.txtState.DataBindings.Add( _
    New System.Windows.Forms.Binding( _
    "Text", Me.objDS, "Suppliers.State")
```

```
Me.txtZIP.DataBindings.Add( _
    New System.Windows.Forms.Binding( _
    "Text", Me.objDS, "Suppliers.Zip")
Me.txtPhone.DataBindings.Add( _
    New System.Windows.Forms.Binding( _
    "Text", Me.objDS, "Suppliers.Phone")
```

Each statement adds a new Binding object to the control's DataBindings collection, passing in the name of the property to which the data is bound (in this case, the Text property), the DataSet to which we are binding, and the column name that is being bound. We have now established a link between the data and the controls on the form. Now what? How do we use that?

An important object is part of the Windows Form that we use to move data around when it is bound. It's called the BindingContext, and we'll use it quite a bit. If we examine some code to move the data around from record to record on the form, you'll see why. The following code is inside a click handler function on a Next button that will move the data on the form to the next record:

```
Me.BindingContext(objDS, "Suppliers").Position += 1
```

This single line of code will move the data on the screen to the next record, handing display as well. We can also move to the last record with a single line of code, like this:

```
Me.BindingContext(objDS, "Suppliers").Position = _
    Me.BindingContext(objDS, "Suppliers").Count - 1
```

Those two properties of the BindingContext, Position and Count, are very useful when dealing with data binding on your own. This, combined with the standard techniques already described for manipulating data through the DataSet, DataAdapter, and Command objects, will let you do just about anything you need to with data binding on a form.

The good thing is that you can use as much or as little of the ADO.NET features as you like. If you want it to automate everything you do, it can handle most of this for you. If you prefer to write SQL statements for more control, you can do that as well. Use data binding to simply move records around the screen or to handle data updates as well. It all depends on how much control you want or need.

Let's Start the Project

Putting ADO.NET to work is the best part. Reading about the way it works or seeing a few code fragments is all well and good, and educational. However, the real fun comes with building something substantial. We're building a simple bug-tracking system that will let us use a significant portion of what we've learned so far.

Overview

Our bug-tracking system will be using ADO.NET in several respects. The ADO.NET objects will be used to load and save data, and the ubiquitous DataSet will be there as well to hold onto data for us. We have made a design decision to use our own SQL statements in the code to get data work done rather than using intrinsic data object methods.

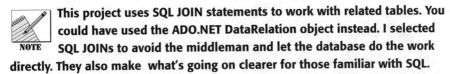 **This project uses SQL JOIN statements to work with related tables. You could have used the ADO.NET DataRelation object instead. I selected SQL JOINs to avoid the middleman and let the database do the work directly. They also make what's going on clearer for those familiar with SQL.**

In addition, we'll be following standard operating procedures that comply with scalability guidelines. In other words, we'll be connecting to the database as late as possible and disconnecting as soon as possible. Although this implementation does not particularly need to be very scalable, a derived, more fully functional version just might. It's better to build it in early rather than later.

Our bug-tracking application is a single-form affair that displays data fields on the screen and allows the user to navigate, edit, and save information in the database. It's a classic data application, and I've left plenty of room to customize it for your own needs. I used the forms class library from project 1 as a basis for the main window.

Basic Usage

The application itself is pretty simple to use. The operations that you can perform, and instructions for doing so, are listed in Table 2.4.

Table 2.4   Instructions for Using the Bug-Tracking System

OPERATION	INSTRUCTIONS
Add New Bug	Click the New button. This will create a blank record in which new data can be entered.
Save Bug Data	Click the Save button. This will save either a new record or edits made to an existing record.
Delete Bug	Click the Delete button. This will delete the bug that is currently displayed.
Navigate Bug Data	Use the First, Last, Next, and Previous buttons to move through the data.

Our Database

We'll probably need some place to store and retrieve data from, so we may as well create a database. We decided to create a Microsoft Access database for two reasons. First, because everything is stored in a single file, the database is very portable, and it was easy to include it on the accompanying CD-ROM. Second, we can use it directly without any import process. In the next project, we'll use an Access database and import it into SQL Server.

Database Design

We do need to design a decent database schema, even though we have relatively simple needs. Take a look at Figure 2.13 to see our schema. We have four tables. The primary table, Problems, is where actual bug data is stored. The Users table contains the names and contact information about all the users allowed to access the bug reporting system. Both of these are pretty straightforward and are linked by a one-to-many relationship through a UserID.

The remaining tables, Product and Severity, are simple lookup lists of values that we need to make available for the bug system. They contain the names of the products for which bugs can be reported and the various severity ratings a user can assign to a bug.

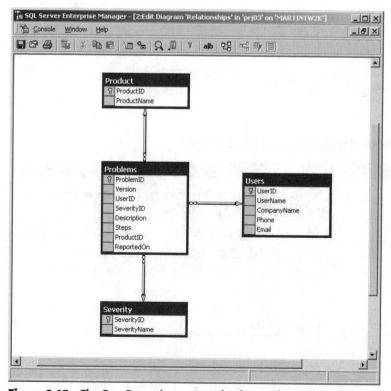

Figure 2.13   The Bug Reporting system database schema.

They are linked to the main table using an ID and a one-to-many relationship. These two tables make it much easier to customize the bug-reporting system to suit our needs. This allows us to make changes to the Products or Severity ratings by simply updating the data in these tables. The UI will be taken care of automatically.

The Sample Database

I have included a sample database on the CD-ROM that accompanies this book. It has been stored, for the sake of convenience, as a Microsoft Access database. It contains all the tables and relationships and a handful of actual sample data. You can, if you feel industrious and are conversant with Microsoft Access, create the database yourself manually. We will be using the Access database directly, providing a connection string for it. Because the database is not a SQL Server database, we'll have to the use OleDb data provider instead of the SqlClient data provider.

The Access database on the CD-ROM is called prj02.mdb, and it is located with the Project 2 source code files. To use the database, you'll have to change the connection string in the code to point to the actual location of your database. I'll point that out in the code when we get there.

The Main Form

Start by either loading the project from the accompanying CD-ROM (prj02) or by creating a new project in Visual Studio .NET. A standard Windows Forms project is our starting point. The only form in our project is the main form. It is derived from frmApp in the prj01classes library from Project 1. It contains all the controls that we need to display and operate on the data. Figure 2.14 shows what the form looks like.

Figure 2.14   The main application form.

Table 2.5 The Controls on the Main Form

CONTROL NAME	TYPE	SETTINGS
Label1	Label	Text: "Bug Tracking System" Font: 14pt, Bold
Label2	Label	Text: "BugID:"
Label3	Label	Text: "Product:"
Label4	Label	Text: "Version:"
Label5	Label	Text: "Severity:"
Label6	Label	Text: "Description:"
Label7	Label	Text: "Steps to reproduce:"
Label8	Label	Text: "User:"
Label9	Label	Text: "Date:"
lblDate	Label	Text: "—"
lblBugID	Label	Text: "—"
btnLast	Button	Text: "> |"
btnFirst	Button	Text: "| <"
btnNext	Button	Text: ">"
btnPrevious	Button	"<"
btnNew	Button	Text: "New"
btnUpdate	Button	Text: "Save"
btnDelete	Button	Text: "Delete"
TxtSteps	Textbox	Multiline: True ScrollBars: Vertical
TxtDesc	Textbox	Multiline: True ScrollBars: Vertical
txtVersion	Textbox	(None)
txtRecord	Textbox	Enabled: False
cmbProduct	ComboBox	Style: DropDown
cmbUser	ComboBox	Style: DropDown
cmbSeverity	ComboBox	Style: DropDown

There are many controls here, so examine Table 2.5, which gives a listing of all the controls to find out what their names are and what they do. Using Figure 2.15 and Table 2.5, you can create the form by adding an Inherited Form to the project. Right-click on the project name in Solution Explorer and select *Add Inherited Form* from the context menu. A dialog will appear, one that you've seen before, where you can enter the name of the form. When you click OK, you will be presented with a window in which you must select the form's parent, from which it will be inherited. You'll notice that none of the forms from Project 1 are listed. You'll have to browse to the DLL to make them show up in the list. See Figure 2.15 to make sure you're looking at the right dialog. When you have the correct list, select the frmApp item and click OK. You should see a nice, new, empty dialog that looks just like the frmApp. You can proceed to add the controls to it.

The Code

Time to dive in. We'll be covering all the code that we write and skipping the generated code. You can cruise through that if you like, but it's fairly simple and straightforward. We will peek at the constructor briefly, but that's it.

Defining Ourselves

There are a few items to define and set up before we get to actual functionality, including Imports, constants, and other data items we'll need across the entire form class. So start by adding the following code to the top of the listing:

```
Option Strict On
Option Explicit On

' Make sure we can use the generic data access functionality in the
'framework.
Imports System.Data.OleDb
```

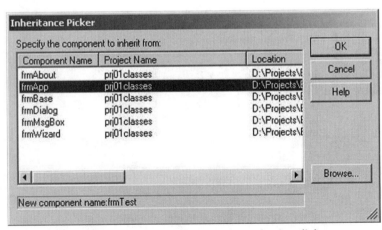

Figure 2.15 The Inherited Form Component Selection dialog.

The Options help to ensure that our code is solid, and the Imports statement provides us with access to the OleDb functionality. If you wanted to use the SQL Server data provider instead, you could change the Imports statement so that it instead includes System.Data.SqlClient.

Now move past the Class definition line and add the following code to define some preliminary constants and other goodies:

```
#Region " Class Data and Types "

    ' The DB connection string. This is a little ridiculous,
    ' but was generated.
    Const sConnStr As String = _
                    "Provider=Microsoft.Jet.OLEDB.4.0;Password="""";" & _
                    "User ID=Admin;" & _
                    "Data Source=D:\Projects\Book\prj02\prj03.mdb;" & _
                    "Mode=Share Deny None;Extended Properties="""";" & _
                    "Jet OLEDB:System database="""";" & _
                    "Jet OLEDB:Registry Path="""";" & _
                    "Jet OLEDB:Database Password="""";" & _
                    "Jet OLEDB:Engine Type=5;" & _
                    "Jet OLEDB:Database Locking Mode=1;" & _
                    "Jet OLEDB:Global Partial Bulk Ops=2;" & _
                    "Jet OLEDB:Global Bulk Transactions=1;" & _
                    "Jet OLEDB:New Database Password="""";" & _
                    "Jet OLEDB:Create System Database=False;" & _
                    "Jet OLEDB:Encrypt Database=False;" & _
                    "Jet OLEDB:Don't Copy Locale on Compact=False;" & _
                    "Jet OLEDB:Compact Without Replica Repair=False;" & _
                        "Jet OLEDB:SFP=False"

    ' Our SELECT statement that will be used to fill our DataSet
    ' whenever we need to do so.
    Const sSELECT As String = "SELECT Problems.ProblemID, " & _
        "Problems.ReportedOn, " & _
        "Users.UserName, Product.ProductName, Problems.Version, " & _
        "Severity.SeverityName, Problems.Description, Problems.Steps " & _
        "FROM Severity INNER JOIN (Product INNER JOIN " & _
        "(Users INNER JOIN Problems ON " & _
        "Users.UserID = Problems.UserID) ON Product.ProductID = " & _
        "Problems.ProductID) ON " & _
        "Severity.SeverityID = Problems.SeverityID " & _
        "ORDER BY Problems.ProblemID"

    ' Create all our data objects.
    Dim conn As OleDbConnection
    Dim cmd As OleDbCommand
    Dim daBugs As OleDbDataAdapter
    Dim dsBugs As DataSet

    ' Other class data
    Private bNewMode As Boolean = False

#End Region
```

The connection string we need to use is long and ugly. It was generated, so there are some details in it that we probably don't need, but we will leave them in for safety. Most of those "JET OLEDB" parameters can be removed, and everything will work properly. Make sure you change the DataSource property so that it points to the actual location of your copy of the database. If necessary, change the UserID property as well.

The Select statement we use to load the data from the database never changes throughout the program, but it is used all the time. Therefore, we're defining it here once and then using the constant reference when we need it. It's also rather lengthy, so defining it once is a good idea. Take a look at it carefully. It uses JOINs to reference the relationships between the tables and load the data correctly. If you don't know about JOINs, you might want to look into them. JOINs are pretty easy to understand and very powerful. You could also use an ADO.NET DataRelation object instead, but that's just a crutch that hides the details and restricts your control over the JOIN.

TIP **Want an easy way to get SQL into your code? Fire up any query designer, such as Microsoft Access, and build your query visually by dragging tables and fields around. Set everything up the way you want it, and then switch to the SQL view. You can then copy the generated SQL and use it in your code. This is particularly useful with complex queries.**

Next, we create placeholders for the primary ADO.NET data objects we'll be using across the program code. There's a Connection, a Command, a DataAdapter, and a DataSet. We'll create the actual instances with New later. For now, note their names, because you'll be seeing a lot of them.

Lastly, we create a boolean variable that tracks whether or not the user is editing a new bug record. We will use this later when we need to save bug data. Note that we defined our own Region for class data and types. These handy regions make managing and editing your code much easier.

Initialization

We need to perform some setup tasks when the application starts, including setting up the data objects, loading the data, and getting the UI ready to use. We put all our initialization code in a single method called InitApp(). Of course, InitApp has to be called somewhere. In the olden days of VB6, you would probably use the Form Load event to do this. You can still do that if you like. However, there is a better place now: in the form's constructor. Pop open the region labeled "Windows Form Designer Generated Code" and look for the *New* method. This is the form class's constructor. It calls its own initialization method called InitializeComponent and then leaves a comment informing you that you should add your own initialization code here. In that part of the code, add a call to InitApp, like this:

```
Public Sub New()

    MyBase.New()
    'This call is required by the Windows Form Designer.
    InitializeComponent()

    'Add any initialization after the InitializeComponent() call
    InitApp()

End Sub
```

This code will execute better if we define InitApp and add some code to it. The listing follows and does quite a bit of work for us. Enter all this code in a new region labeled "User Code."

```
' Take care of any application-level initialization. This method is
' called from the VS-generated "New" constructor.
Private Sub InitApp()

    ' Create our data objects for use throughout the app.
    conn = New OleDbConnection(sConnStr)
    cmd = New OleDbCommand()
    daBugs = New OleDbDataAdapter()
    dsBugs = New DataSet()

    ' Load some data.
    cmd.CommandText = sSELECT
    cmd.Connection = conn
    daBugs.SelectCommand = cmd
    conn.Open()
    RefreshBugData()
    conn.Close()

    ' Create some data bindings between our controls and our
    ' DataSet.
    Me.lblBugID.DataBindings.Add(New _
        System.Windows.Forms.Binding("Text", Me.dsBugs, _
        "Problems.ProblemID"))
    Me.lblDate.DataBindings.Add(New _
        System.Windows.Forms.Binding("Text", Me.dsBugs, _
        "Problems.ReportedOn"))
    Me.cmbUser.DataBindings.Add(New _
        System.Windows.Forms.Binding("Text", Me.dsBugs, _
        "Problems.UserName"))
    Me.cmbProduct.DataBindings.Add(New _
        System.Windows.Forms.Binding("Text", Me.dsBugs, _
        "Problems.ProductName"))
```

```
Me.txtVersion.DataBindings.Add(New _
    System.Windows.Forms.Binding("Text", Me.dsBugs, _
    "Problems.Version"))
Me.cmbSeverity.DataBindings.Add(New _
    System.Windows.Forms.Binding("Text", Me.dsBugs, _
    "Problems.SeverityName"))
Me.txtDesc.DataBindings.Add(New _
    System.Windows.Forms.Binding("Text", Me.dsBugs, _
    "Problems.Description"))
Me.txtSteps.DataBindings.Add(New _
    System.Windows.Forms.Binding("Text", Me.dsBugs, _
    "Problems.Steps"))

' Fill our combo boxes with data
FillCombos()

' First record, please.
Me.BindingContext(dsBugs, "Problems").Position = 0
UpdateRecordNumber()

End Sub
```

The first step is to create actual instances of all our ADO.NET objects. This is a good place to do this, at the beginning of the application, because you don't want to forget to do it. Having them hang around in memory isn't a big deal these days (I just bought a 256-MB RAM DIMM for my computer. Cost? $45. Amazing.). The only constructor we need to pass a parameter to at this point is the Connection object: We send it the connection string we defined earlier.

Next, we actually load the bug data into our DataSet from the database. The code for this operation looks very small, which it is. A few lines of code are all it takes. We set up our SQL command and the database connection. Then we open the connection and call RefreshBugData, which we'll see shortly. This method actually loads the data and was put into a method of its own because it's called all over the place. Following our rules of improved scalability, we close the database connection as soon as the data is loaded.

Now comes the most interesting part. We are doing our data binding manually, so we need to set up the links between the columns in the table with the controls on the form. Look at one of them as an example:

```
Me.lblBugID.DataBindings.Add(New _
    System.Windows.Forms.Binding("Text", Me.dsBugs, _
    "Problems.ProblemID"))
```

This code creates a data binding for the BugID control and ties its Text property to the Problems.ProblemID column in the dsBugs DataSet. Then we do it seven more times for the rest of the controls and data columns.

At this point we have data loaded and it is properly tied to the controls on our form. However, our combo boxes need valid items from which the user can select. All these values come from the database in our small auxiliary tables. I created a method to handle this called FillCombos. I'll cover it in just a moment.

Our final initialization task is to set the UI to show the first record in the DataSet. We use the BindingContext object, part of the form, to navigate through the bound data. Setting its *Position* property to zero will move it to the first record. The UpdateRecord-Number method was created to display the correct record number in the record navigation area of the form, and I will cover it in just a second.

Supporting Methods

There are four supporting methods that have been created to help out with some of the repetitious tasks that we perform in the code. The first is a simple one called ClearForm that is used when a new record is created and empties out the controls on the form:

```
' A simple utility to clear the fields on the form.
Private Sub ClearForm()

    lblBugID.Text = ""
    lblDate.Text = ""
    cmbUser.Text = ""
    cmbProduct.Text = ""
    txtVersion.Text = ""
    cmbSeverity.Text = ""
    txtDesc.Text = ""
    txtSteps.Text = ""

End Sub
```

There's not much to explain here, so let's look at the second one, UpdateRecord-Number. This method is used when the user navigates to a new record using any of the navigation functions:

```
' Update the current record displayed in the UI based on the
' actual current position in the DataSet.
Private Sub UpdateRecordNumber()

    Dim iRec As Int32
    iRec = Me.BindingContext(dsBugs, "Problems").Count

    If iRec > 0 Then
        txtRecord.Text = CStr(Me.BindingContext(dsBugs, _
            "Problems").Position + 1)
    Else
        txtRecord.Text = ""
    End If

End Sub
```

We see the use of the BindingContext object two more times. We use its *Count* property to first determine the highest record number in the DataSet to see if there are any records at all. If not, we clear out the record number display. If so, we use its *Position* property to find out what the current record is. Although the Count property returns an actual number of records, the Position property is zero based. We add 1 to its value to account for this.

Any time that the data has been changed in the database, we refresh the data in the DataSet so that we have an accurate representation of what's been done to it. This operation has been encapsulated in single method called RefreshBugData. Its code is as follows:

```
Private Sub RefreshBugData(Optional ByVal iRecToShow As Int32 = 0)

    ' Clear the DataSet first. If we don't, the data from the 'Fill'
    ' method call will append, not replace.
    dsBugs.Clear()
    Try
        cmd.CommandText = sSELECT
        ClearForm()
        daBugs.Fill(dsBugs, "Problems")
        Me.BindingContext(dsBugs, "Problems").Position = iRecToShow
    Catch ex As OleDbException
        MsgBox("RefreshBugData(): " & ex.Message)
    End Try

End Sub
```

This method accepts a single parameter, a record number that indicates which record should be displayed when the update takes place. If a record is simply saved, it should be the same record. However, if a record was deleted, you'll need to display a different one. It is also important to note that this method does not open or close the database connection. This is up to the caller, which makes sense in this application.

First, this method calls the Clear method on the DataSet. This is an important step. If it didn't, the call to Fill would append the data to the DataSet, resulting in duplication of data. Next, the Fill method is called from the DataAdapter to reload the updated data from the database. The last step is the display of the specified record, which is handled by the BindingContext object.

> **NOTE** This design makes a fair number of calls to the database; it makes one every time the data is changed. You could easily change the operation of this program so that the updates only occur occasionally, improving its scalability. Using the ADO.NET data operations instead of SQL statements to track changes would help out with this. The only trick is deciding when to perform the update. You'll have to decide not only what mechanism to use to determine when the update occurs, but how often as well. The less frequently you update the database, the more scalable the application is. However, the less often you update the database, the less safe the data is. If something happens to the program (a crash, a power outage, whatever) before you update the data, any pending changes will be lost. The best way might be to allow users to decide, updating the database only when they tell you to.

Our last but most interesting support method is the FillCombos method. The code is as follows:

```
' Load data from the database tables into our combo boxes. This is
' done like any other query, except that we are putting the results
' of three queries into a single DataSet.
Private Sub FillCombos()

    ' Load the data from the database
    Dim sSQL As String
    conn.Open()

    ' Priming SQL statement, for the data adapter.
    sSQL = "SELECT * FROM Users"

    ' Get the DataAdapter and DataSet ready to go.
    Dim da As New OleDbDataAdapter(sSQL, conn)
    Dim ds As New DataSet()

    ' Load the data into the DataSet.
    Try
        da.Fill(ds, "Users")
        da.SelectCommand.CommandText = "SELECT * FROM Severity"
        da.Fill(ds, "Severity")
        da.SelectCommand.CommandText = "SELECT * FROM Product"
        da.Fill(ds, "Product")
    Catch ex As OleDbException
        MsgBox("Error initializing application during " & _
            ""FillCombos()."" Error: " & ex.Message)
    End Try

    conn.Close()

    ' Now fill the combo boxes with the retrieved data.
    ' Fill the users list.
    Dim aRow As DataRow
    For Each aRow In ds.Tables("Users").Rows
        cmbUser.Items.Insert(CInt(aRow("UserID")) - 1, _
        CStr(aRow("UserName")))
    Next

    ' Fill the Severity list.
    For Each aRow In ds.Tables("Severity").Rows
        cmbSeverity.Items.Insert(CInt(aRow("SeverityID")) - 1, _
            CStr(aRow("SeverityName")))
    Next

    ' Fill the Products list.
    For Each aRow In ds.Tables("Product").Rows
        cmbProduct.Items.Insert(CInt(aRow("ProductID")) - 1, _
```

```
                    CStr(aRow("ProductName")))
        Next

    End Sub
```

All the values for our combo boxes come from the database, making it much easier to update the available choices without changing the program code. We're doing this manually rather than using the DataSource and DisplayMember properties of the control. When we send a bug record back to the database, we need to send it the IDs of the related values, not the actual text. For example, if the user selects a User value of "Tony Martin," we don't want to send that value back, but instead its ID value of 1. We make this easy by adding the associated ID value into the combo box as the Index value of the item in the combo box.

The FillCombos code does some basic ADO.NET data access. It opens our connection, sets up the SQL Select statement, and creates a new DataSet and DataAdapter. It then loads the list of Users into the DataSet. However, it then changes the SQL and loads two more hunks of data into the DataSet: Severity and Product values. This results in three table objects in the DataSet's Tables collection. Each can be referenced by name or index value (name is safer).

The last part of the method uses three For..Each loops to load the returned data into the corresponding combo boxes. Examine the Insert calls to see the usage of the Rows collection and how to index into it using a column name.

Navigating the Data

Getting around the data is pretty easy thanks to the data binding we already set up. The BindingContext object does most of the work. We just have to do a little book-keeping. The code for the primary navigation methods looks like this:

```
    ' Moves to the next record in the DataSet
    Private Sub btnNext_Click(ByVal sender As System.Object, _
        ByVal e As System.EventArgs) Handles btnNext.Click

        Dim iPos As Int32
        Dim iCount As Int32

        ' Find out the position in the dataset and count of records
        iPos = Me.BindingContext(dsBugs, "Problems").Position + 1
        iCount = Me.BindingContext(dsBugs, "Problems").Count

        ' Moves to the next record
        If iPos < iCount Then
            Me.BindingContext(dsBugs, "Problems").Position += 1
            UpdateRecordNumber()
            bNewMode = False
        End If

    End Sub
```

```
' Moves to the previous record in the DataSet
Private Sub btnPrevious_Click(ByVal sender As System.Object, _
    ByVal e As System.EventArgs) Handles btnPrevious.Click

    Dim iPos As Int32

    ' Find out the position in the dataset and count of records
    iPos = Me.BindingContext(dsBugs, "Problems").Position + 1

    ' Moves to the previous record
    If iPos > 0 Then
        Me.BindingContext(dsBugs, "Problems").Position -= 1
        UpdateRecordNumber()
        bNewMode = False
    End If

End Sub

' Moves to the first record in the DataSet
Private Sub btnFirst_Click(ByVal sender As System.Object, _
    ByVal e As System.EventArgs) Handles btnFirst.Click

    ' Moves to the first record
    Me.BindingContext(dsBugs, "Problems").Position = 0
    UpdateRecordNumber()
    bNewMode = False

End Sub

' Moves to the last record in the DataSet
Private Sub btnLast_Click(ByVal sender As System.Object, _
    ByVal e As System.EventArgs) Handles btnLast.Click

    ' Moves to the last record
    Me.BindingContext(dsBugs, "Problems").Position = _
        Me.BindingContext(dsBugs, "Problems").Count - 1
    UpdateRecordNumber()
    bNewMode = False

End Sub
```

The Next and Previous methods both use the BindingContext object to determine the current record and the current count of records. They check to see if the current position is at their maximum limit, the beginning record in the case of the Previous method and the last record in the case of the Next method. Then each makes sure that we do not try to move beyond those maximums. If we have not, we use the Binding-Context's Position property to move to the new record. The First and Last methods do not need to perform these checks. They simply move absolutely to the first or last record currently in the DataSet.

Note that all the methods call the UpdateRecordNumber method if the navigation operation is successful. This makes sure that the record number indicator properly reflects the current record.

Creating a New Record

Adding a new record only makes room for the user to enter new data. It does not save the record when the user is done editing. That is handled by the Save functionality, to be covered shortly. The code for the New Record functionality is fired when the user clicks the New button, and it looks like this:

```
' Create a new blank record for the user to enter bug data.
Private Sub btnNew_Click(ByVal sender As System.Object, _
    ByVal e As System.EventArgs) Handles btnNew.Click

    Me.BindingContext(dsBugs, "Problems").AddNew()
    txtRecord.Text = "New"
    bNewMode = True
    Me.NotifyText = "New record created."

End Sub
```

Not much too it is there? We use the BindingContext to create a new record using its AddNew method. This makes room on the screen as well as in the DataSet. Once called, the user can start entering bug data right away. We just have to take care of a few more details before entry is allowed.

The record indicator is updated to say "New" to make sure users know that they're in new mode. We set our internal boolean flag to true so that our own code knows we're creating a new record (used later when we save the data). Lastly, we update the application's status line to indicate that a new record was successfully created and is ready to edit.

Saving Changes: Update or New

The real trick in this application is saving changes to the data. We have a single method, an event handler hooked up to the Save button, that takes care of saving data for both a new record and a changed existing record. First, take a look at the code:

```
' This method handles the saving of a new record as well as
' updates to existing records.
Private Sub btnUpdate_Click(ByVal sender As System.Object, _
    ByVal e As System.EventArgs) Handles btnUpdate.Click

    Dim sSQL As String
    Dim dbCmd As New OleDbCommand()
    Dim iRecToShow As Int32

    ' Determine the record to display AFTER the Update has
```

```vb
' completed successfully, in this case, the same record.
iRecToShow = Me.BindingContext(dsBugs, "Problems").Position

conn.Open()

' If there are any single quotes (apostrophes) in the string
' that the user entered, replace them with two so the SQL won't
' blow up (I mean "won''t")
txtSteps.Text.Replace("'", "''")
txtDesc.Text.Replace("'", "''")
txtVersion.Text.Replace("'", "''")

If bNewMode Then
    ' In NEW mode, so do an INSERT.
    bNewMode = False
    sSQL = "INSERT INTO Problems (ReportedOn, UserID, " & _
        "ProductID, Version, SeverityID, Description, Steps) " & _
        "VALUES ('" & Now & "', " & cmbUser.SelectedIndex + 1 & _
        ", " & cmbProduct.SelectedIndex + 1 & _
            ", '" & txtVersion.Text & "', " & _
            cmbSeverity.SelectedIndex + 1 & _
            ", '" & txtDesc.Text & _
            "', '" & txtSteps.Text & "')"
    cmd.CommandText = sSQL

    Try
     ' Prevent duplicate record.
        Me.BindingContext(dsBugs,"Problems").CancelCurrentEdit()
        cmd.ExecuteNonQuery()
        RefreshBugData(iRecToShow)
        UpdateRecordNumber()
        Me.NotifyText = "New record saved."
    Catch ex As OleDbException
        MsgBox("Saving the bug record (insert) did not work. " & _
            "Error: " & ex.Message)
    End Try
Else
    ' Not in NEW mode, so perform an UPDATE instead of INSERT.
    sSQL = "UPDATE Problems SET UserID=" & _
        cmbUser.SelectedIndex + 1 & ", " & _
        "ProductID=" & cmbProduct.SelectedIndex + 1 & ", " & _
        "Version='" & txtVersion.Text & "', " & _
        "SeverityID=" & cmbSeverity.SelectedIndex + 1 & ", " & _
        "Description='" & txtDesc.Text & "', " & _
        "Steps='" & txtSteps.Text & "' " & _
        "WHERE ProblemID=" & lblBugID.Text
    cmd.CommandText = sSQL
```

```
        Try
            cmd.ExecuteNonQuery()
            RefreshBugData(iRecToShow)
            UpdateRecordNumber()
            Me.NotifyText = "Record updated."
        Catch ex As OleDbException
            MsgBox("Saving the bug record (update) did not work. " & _
                "Error: " & ex.Message)
        End Try
    End If

    conn.Close()

End Sub
```

The basic idea behind the code is that if we are in New mode, we perform an Insert on the database to store the data for the current record. If we're not in New mode, we perform an Update instead. This will prevent duplicate records from being entered in the database.

The code first determines which record should be displayed when the database update is complete and saves the record number in iRecToShow. This record number will always be the current record number because we're not removing anything from the database. It uses our best friend, the BindingContext object, to make this happen. Next we replace all single quotes (apostrophes) that the user may have entered in text fields with two sequential single quotes. This will prevent errors with prematurely terminated SQL strings.

Then we open our connection and decide what to do. If we're in New mode, we branch to the Insert. Our Insert statement is created next and is fairly straightforward if you are conversant with SQL. The values we are inserting into the database are pulled from the UI fields and placed into our Insert string.

Now we enter our Try..Catch block in which we actually execute the SQL. This code first calls the BindingContext method CancelCurrentEdit. This fixes a quirk in the system that results in a duplicate record in the DataSet after we update the data. Even though we clear the DataSet and reload the data in the RefreshBugData method, we get a duplicate if we don't cancel the edit first. Note that the duplicate record only appears in the DataSet and never in the database itself.

We use the Command object's ExecuteNonQuery method to execute the Insert statement. If all goes well, we refresh the data in the DataSet from the database to make sure it's current, update the current record number on the display, and tell the user through our status line that everything is done.

The Update branch, which saves edits to an existing record, works pretty much the same way. We do not have to call CancelCurrentEdit, and our SQL statement is an Update instead of an Insert. Everything else is similar. At the end of the method, we close the connection.

Deleting a Record

There's nothing complex about deleting a record. It follows the same basic steps as any other database operation, and the SQL is simple. The code for our Delete button event handler follows:

```
' Delete the current record.
Private Sub btnDelete_Click(ByVal sender As System.Object, _
    ByVal e As System.EventArgs) Handles btnDelete.Click

    Dim sSQL As String
    Dim iRec As Int32
    Dim iRecToShow As Int32

    ' Determine the record to display AFTER the Delete has
    ' completed successfully, in this case, the previous record.
    iRec = Me.BindingContext(dsBugs, "Problems").Position
    If iRec > 0 Then
        iRecToShow = Me.BindingContext(dsBugs, _
            "Problems").Position - 1
    Else
        iRecToShow = 0
    End If

    sSQL = "DELETE FROM Problems WHERE ProblemID=" & lblBugID.Text
    cmd.CommandText = sSQL

    conn.Open()

    Try
        cmd.ExecuteNonQuery()
        RefreshBugData(iRecToShow)
        UpdateRecordNumber()
        Me.NotifyText = "Record deleted."
    Catch ex As OleDbException
        MsgBox("Deleting the bug record did not work. " & _
            Error: " & ex.Message)
    End Try

    conn.Close()

End Sub
```

This code goes through all the steps we've already seen. First determine which record to display after the delete operation is complete. In this case, we display the previous record or the new first record if the first record was just deleted. Then our SQL statement is prepared and the connection to the database is opened. A standard Try..Catch block encapsulates our attempt to delete the record, and if successful, updates the bug data and the record number displayed on the screen. Our connection is finally closed at the end.

Running the Program

Our application is a basic WinForms application with some database access thrown in. You can run it from the environment or once the EXE is compiled. Make sure that if the location of the database changes, you update the connection string to reflect the move.

With a small- to medium-sized bug count, this program should hold up well. Even with the database located on another server, it should not be a performance problem. However, if your bug count gets large, you might want to look into ADO.NET's data paging capability. This will move data in pages so that you don't have to hold a huge DataSet in memory or, more importantly, pass a large amount of data over a wire.

Enhancing the Project

This overview of ADO.NET has covered most of the basics, but there are more features you might want to look into. The data paging capability can be very useful for large DataSets. Also, the DataReader can help with large DataSets, although it has some limitations. It is particularly useful in Web sites and will be covered in Project 6. You can also explore the use of DataRelations to handle your JOIN needs instead of using SQL.

This project, which illustrates ADO.NET concepts and provides basic bug-tracking functionality, is wide open for extra features. Here are few suggestions, in case you're eager to dive in and explore some more on your own:

Add more fields.   There are plenty of additional data fields you might want to add, such as the status of a bug (Reviewed, Corrected, Returned, etc.) or the functional area of the program in which the bug occurred (an opportunity to add another related table to the database).

Add a report or two.   Visual Studio .NET comes with Crystal Reports, which you can use to generate a bug-listing or a bug-status report. You could also do it manually. Either way, a report would be very useful.

Add a search feature.   When your bug count gets beyond 30 or 40, you're going to be begging for a search feature. Use ADO.NET's Find method to look for records in the DataSet.

Try it with all ADO.NET functionality.   Rewrite the SQL sections of the application to use ADO.NET's built-in functionality instead of SQL statements. This would allow you to reduce the number of updates to the database and let the user decide when to update.

WHAT'S COMING NEXT

The next project deals with Web services, one of the hottest new topics in the software development world. I'll cover the .NET way to build Web services and will do it by creating some companion functionality to the bug-reporting system that we just built. Think about this: How would you feel about not having to enter your own bugs but could instead rely on your users to do it for you?

Move on to Project 3 to discover how, and catch the Web services wave.

Bug Reporting with Web Services

Web service hype is almost as ubiquitous as the cell phone commercials on television. It promises to open new frontiers in B2B services and communications and provide application interoperability with unparalleled ease and reusable functionality for all. We've all heard things like this before from technology companies, Microsoft included. This time, however, there's a significant difference. It's all true, at least so far.

Web services will make functionality of all sorts available to anyone with an Internet connection, from checking for local concert tickets to adding this capability to your own applications. And Web services don't have to travel far and wide on the Internet to be useful. They can provide reusable capabilities across an intranet within a single company as well.

In this project, we will be creating a Web service and some client code that will allow you to add bug-reporting capabilities to any program (or even a Web site) that you like. Along the way, we'll discover some more information about Web services and see a demonstration of accessing data from Web services.

THE PROBLEM:

We need to collect information from users about bugs in the software we create for them, but without annoying direct phone calls to the engineering and IT staff from frustrated users. The problem reports need to be logged and recorded so that they don't get lost or slip through the cracks. This needs to happen with minimal time impact to the engineering and IT staff.

THE SOLUTION:

Build user error reporting into the programs we create. This will allow users to report the bugs, which get stored automatically into a database that IT can review at its leisure. Which of the new toys that Microsoft has created for us should we use? Why, Web services, of course. We'll see why Web services are the perfect solution to the problem in this project, as well as why Web services are going to be a big hit in many diverse businesses.

The Project

Our bug-tracking Web service works by itself for your programs, or it can work in concert with the bug-tracking system built in Project 2. This project will provide you with a complete solution to let your users tell you all about the problems they are having with your software. We'll be doing the following:

1. **The Web service.**   First we'll build the Web service that allows any program to save bug-report records to your database. It also provides some basic reporting and supporting functionality. You'll see how to get a Web service configured and functional on your server as well.

2. **The client side.**   We will also develop a collection of forms and code to easily add the capability to report bugs through the Web service to any client program. You'll see how to access the Web service, deal with proxies, and get returned data from Web services.

 ## You Will Need

✔ **Visual Basic .NET**

✔ **A basic knowledge of Visual Basic .NET and WinForms**

✔ **Code from Project 1 (for the client portions)**

✔ **SQL Server**

✔ **Functional IIS installation**

What Exactly Are Web Services?

Put simply, Web services are components of functionality that can be accessed across the Internet or other network. A few examples will illustrate their utility.

Imagine that you are a programmer in an IT shop that maintains many applications, some of which have overlapping data. A customer database, for example, might be used by many different applications, as might a products database. You could create a general data access Web service that returns (and updates) customer and product data. Any application could use it and retrieve and exchange the data it needed. This data could be accessed by users in the field using Internet connections; it could also be used by remote locations, such as car dealers or storefronts.

You work for a marketing company that has mailing lists and other data about customers. You want to create a Web service that would allow anyone (who paid you gobs of money) to access the query functionality in your service to return lists of potential customers that might be interested in their products.

You might also be a programmer who has created a library of functionality that your company would like to sell to other development companies, perhaps a graphics library or an engine that estimates construction costs. Instead of selling that package, making disks and paying for distribution costs, you could host it as a Web service. Your customers could access the functionality across the Internet as needed.

By now you should be getting the idea. Web services provide all kinds of services without distribution issues, for both internal and external purposes. Here are some of their benefits:

Provide functionality to the world.   Got some functionality that you want to sell to the masses? Create it and publish it as a Web service, and they can easily access it.

Provide functionality to your company.   Create an employee database, a library of company-standard financial calculations, or a parts inventory system as a Web service. Put it on your intranet and everyone can use it.

Write functionality once and use it in any program.   Our project, the bug-reporting system, is a good example. Once created, we can easily add it in to any application we create. All users get the same functionality and we get much better bug reporting.

Interoperate.   Web services are the perfect mechanism for businesses to exchange information, provide each other with services, or sell products to each other.

Use them in applications, not just Web sites.   Although Web services operate across an Internet connection, any application can use them: Win32, Web, and even UNIX applications.

Based on .NET.   This means that Web services are based on a set of standards, and you have many choices for creating your Web services. Build them with any language that .NET supports (at last report there were over 20 languages being built for .NET). I even saw code for a Web service that was written in COBOL. As scary as that might be, it's also amazing.

There are also things to be wary of. Web services, though useful, are not right for everything. For example, Web services require network (usually Internet) connectivity. If your users might not have this, Web services are not appropriate. Web services are also based on standards that are still emerging, and if you jump the gun, you may end up with a fair amount of rework to do on your code. For example, at the time this was written, there was still no standard for dealing with user security or how to validate a user.

How Web Services Work

On the surface, Web services seem like a simple idea. We've always written functionality that was remotely accessible one way or another. However, Web services are based on new technologies that are, in some cases, still gelling. These technologies include:

The Internet.   This one has been around for a while and is really the reason that Web services were created. It is the environment where Web services live and breathe.

HTTP.   This is the language of the Web. It is the mechanism by which requests for functionality and data travel from clients to Web services and back again. It's already there and very convenient if we can just use it.

XML.   If there's one thing that has received more hype than Web services, this is it. XML allows generic and portable packaging of data and descriptive schemas. XML is the mechanism used by Web services to format requests and return data. It is still a standard in fluctuation, but it is fairly stable. I'm sure the .NET architecture will keep up with any changes made here.

SOAP.   This is a convenient acronym that stands for Simple Object Access Protocol. Although XML is the mechanism used to send and receive requests for functionality, SOAP defines the format of those requests. It is a standard to which requests must adhere if they are to be handled in a generic fashion by any Web service or client. SOAP is fairly new and still undergoing changes.

The Basic Idea

All of these technologies come together to allow Web services to offer functionality across the Internet. How, you might ask, do they fit together exactly? A generalized description of a Web service call will illustrate this. Here's the blow-by-blow account:

1. The client program needs the functionality of a Web service. It makes the call by formatting a SOAP request (in practice, a *proxy* does this for you; more on this in a moment).

2. The SOAP request contains the name of the Web service, the method it wants to use from the service, the URL where the Web service is located, and any parameters that might be required. The SOAP request is all XML.

3. The XML containing the SOAP request is sent across the Internet to the Web service using HTTP.

4. Once received, the request is unpacked and parsed, and the appropriate method is called.

5. Any results from the request are packaged into XML for the return trip. The XML is shipped down the wire to the client.

6. The client then has the returned results, which can be extracted from the XML (this is also done for you by the proxy).

In the end, the whole mechanism is similar to DCOM, where you can call components and their methods remotely. However, instead of DCOM (or the lesser-known tunneling DCOM), the Web service mechanism uses HTTP and SOAP to make the call and return the result.

A Quick Example

By now you're probably ready to dive into a little code. Let's build a simple Web service just to see the whole thing in action. I'll skip the client part for now and show you the easy way to test out your service methods without all the fuss of making a client.

Our little Web service will offer a method that returns a random vocabulary word and its definition. If it were posted publicly, those who wanted to display a vocabulary word on their Web site or application would simply point to the service and make a call. Although the code is very short and simple, you may prefer to load the project from the CD-ROM included with the book, rather then typing it in.

We start the process by firing up Visual Studio and creating a new project. Select the ASP.NET Web Service project type and call it Vocab, as illustrated in Figure 3.1. Click OK and let Visual Studio create it for you.

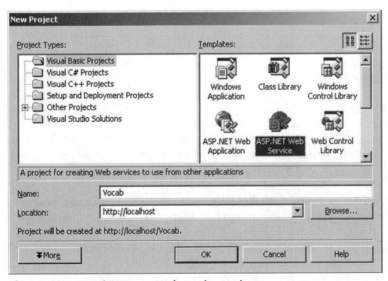

Figure 3.1 Creating a new Web service project.

There are a couple of details that you might want to take care of on any Web service you build. First, the default name of the source file for the service is Service1.asmx. Right-click on this to rename it to something more meaningful, in this case, Vocab. Now view the source code for this file. At the top of the source listing is the statement that declares the class representing your Web service, which is named Service1:

```
Public Class Service1
    Inherits System.Web.Services.WebService
```

Delete that name and replace it with something that matches what you named your source file. Call ours Vocab.

Now we can have some fun. You will notice some commented sample code that Visual Studio created for you called HelloWorld. Remove all that junk and replace it with the following listing:

```
<WebMethod()> Public Function GetVocabWord() As String

    Dim i As Int16

    Randomize(Timer)
    i = Int(Rnd(1) * 4) + 1

    Select Case i
        Case 1
            GetVocabWord = "Diffident (adj): Timid; lacking " + _
                "self-confidence"
        Case 2
            GetVocabWord = "Ascetic (adj): Hermit-like; " + _
                "practicing self-denial"
        Case 3
            GetVocabWord = "Remonstrate (v): To argue against; " + _
                "to protest; to raise objections"
        Case 4
            GetVocabWord = "Foment (v): To stir up; to instigate"
        Case Else
            GetVocabWord = ""
    End Select

End Function
```

It looks just like a normal VB function, with the exception of the *<WebMethod()>* directive in front of the function declaration. That's enough for now to make this a functional Web service with one method called GetVocabWord.

Build the code, and everything should work properly. Now we need to test it and make sure everything is connected up properly between your Visual Studio, IIS, and your service. There is a mechanism built into the system that allows you to run your Web service without the use of a client, which Visual Studio uses automatically to run your service. Access it through your browser by right-clicking on the file *Vocab.asmx* in the Visual Studio Solution Explorer, and select View In Browser from the context menu. IE will load, or it will load in the environment, depending on how you have configured Visual Studio. In either case, you'll see a Web page similar to the one represented in Figure 3.2.

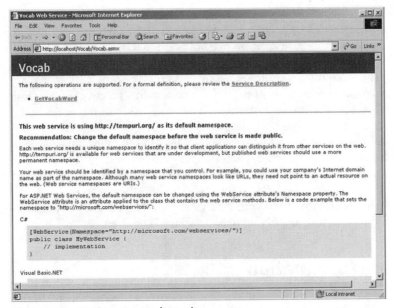

Figure 3.2 Testing your Web service.

At the top will be a listing of all the methods described in your Web service. In our case, we have only one, GetVocabWord, which is displayed as a link. Click the link to invoke (or at least prepare to invoke) the method. The page will be replaced with a new one, displayed in Figure 3.3.

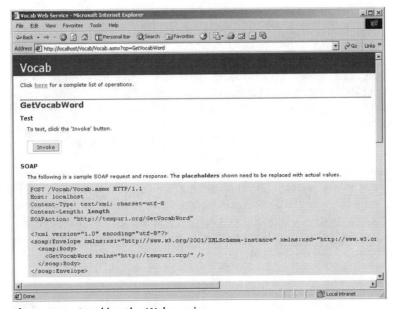

Figure 3.3 Invoking the Web service.

In our case, this page displays only a single button, labeled Invoke. If your method required input parameters, this page would allow you to enter values for each parameter before invoking the service. Click the invoke button to execute the method. You'll see a result similar to that in Figure 3.4.

You'll notice that the results are returned as XML. As we've seen, XML is the language of Web services, as well as most of the .NET functionality. I'll cover that later in more detail. If you like, try the Invoke button a couple times to see different results.

This Web service clearly contains only simple functionality for demonstration purposes. However, were someone to create a much larger list of useful vocabulary words, put them in a database, and then add database access functionality to the service to read that list, you would have a very useful Web service indeed. In fact, you could add a simple client and a service method that allows users to add their own words to the master list, and it would grow without your intervention. When I think of things like this, I have a hard time resisting just diving in and making it happen.

A Little More Information

There are more details about Web services that will be helpful. There could eventually be a huge pile of Web services out there that you could potentially use in your own code, or you might create a service that you'd like to make available to the world. You can find out what's out there or tell people about your service through UDDI. You also need to know about the proxy, a chunk of code that encapsulates the SOAP work for you and that bears some scrutiny. Web References in VB projects will help you out with proxies. The Web Service Description Language, or WSDL, is important to know about, as is the WSDL.EXE utility.

UDDI

UDDI stands for Universal Description, Discovery, and Integration. It sounds elaborate, but it really is just a Web service directory, sort of a Yellow Pages for Web services. It is a series of Web sites, hosted by Microsoft, IBM, and Ariba, that contain XML descriptions of all the Web services that have been registered with it. You can even register your own Web services there by creating some appropriate XML and posting it. This process is too elaborate to cover here, but you can find out how to do it easily enough when you become a Web service expert. Of course, hosting the service and providing access to it for the rest of the world is up to you.

You can also browse the contents of the UDDI directory to see what's there, components you might want to use yourself. Try it by attempting to add a Web reference to any Visual Studio project. From the Project menu, select *Add Web Service*. You'll see a dialog split in two. Click either UDDI link on the left side. You'll see a search page that lets you enter the name of a business that offers Web services. Type in just one letter and click search. Figure 3.5 shows the results.

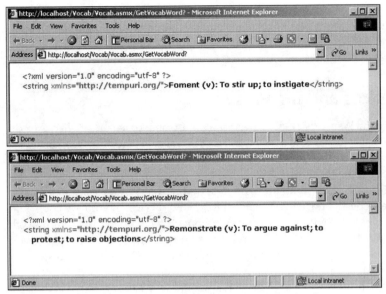

Figure 3.4   The results of the GetVocabWord() method call.

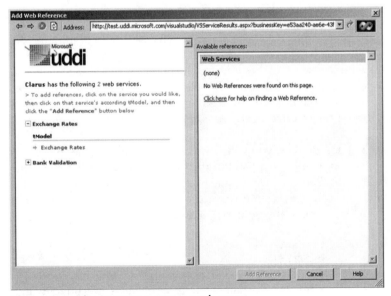

Figure 3.5   The UDDI company search page.

Click on one of the displayed links and you'll be able the see the XML contract, which describes the services available (see Figure 3.6). If everything is set up correctly, you will be able to add a reference to that service to your project and use the functionality it provided.

Web References and the Proxy

Once you create your Web service, you need to call it from some sort of client. To do this manually, you'd need to know all about SOAP calls, where the Web service is hosted (its URL), and possibly format the request XML yourself. However, there's an easier way.

The Web Service Proxy is a small piece of code that performs a translation between a standard VB method call and a SOAP request for a Web service. In your VB code, you create an instance of the proxy object, which will contain all of the method in the Web service. It's very much like having the Web service on your own machine so that you can call its functionality. However, the proxy stands in for the Web service, because it can't be there itself.

The proxy comes from two places. The more manual way to get a proxy is to use a command line utility called WSDL.EXE (which we'll cover next). The easier, automatic way, which prevents you from ever having to see any proxy code, is to let VB generate it for you. You do this by adding a *Web reference* to your project.

Let's assume that you are creating a simple client that will use the Vocab Web service we created earlier. To call the service, you need to add a reference to it, much like you would add a reference to any external COM component. The process is a little different, however. Let's walk through it and see what it's like.

From the Project menu in Visual Studio, you would select the Add Web Reference... item. This brings up a dialog that gives you some options for where to look for the Web service. If you know the URL, you can just type it in. If you need to browse for it, you can use the UDDI directory (which we've seen). If it's on your local machine, as it probably will be for these examples, click on the Web References on Local Web Server link. Once you do so, you should, on the right side of the dialog, see a listing of all available Web services on the selected host. See Figure 3.7 for an example of what it should look like.

In your Solution Explorer window, you will now have a new folder called Web References. If you pop it open, you'll see a listing called Localhost (assuming that your service is on your localhost). Rename this to something meaningful, in our case, Vocab-Svc. This is the name you will use in your client project to create an instance of the proxy and access your Web service. It would look like this:

```
Dim svc As New VocabSvc.Vocab()
Label1.Text = svc.GetVocabWord()
```

One Web reference and two lines of code later, you have called the functionality in a Web service. The proxy was generated for you behind the scenes by VB, and you never had to see it.

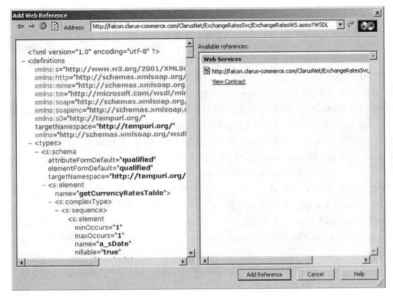

Figure 3.6   A Web service contract.

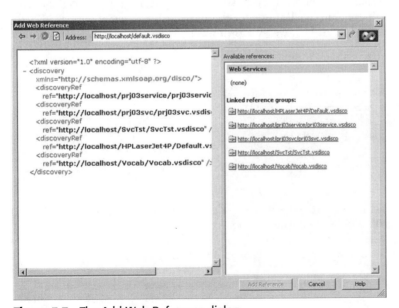

Figure 3.7   The Add Web Reference dialog.

WSDL

Clearly, the easier route to Web service proxies is the automatic way. However, there are occasions when you will want more control over the process (perhaps you're making your service in another language or outside of the Visual Studio environment). Before we launch into how to do this, a little background on WSDL is in order.

WSDL is essentially a standard XML grammar that allows you to describe the functionality that a Web service offers. In order for a Web service (or any sort of component) to understand the requests made of it, the request must be in a standard format. This format is specified by WSDL. When you create a proxy to interface with your Web service, it uses the WSDL specification to communicate with the service.

Although you probably won't need to mess with WSDL specifications themselves (they are usually generated for you), you might need to use the WSDL utility to generate a proxy for you. Normally, Visual Studio will create a proxy for you in the environment. However, if you do not have direct access to the Web reference machine, you can create one manually using the URL to the Web service. Once it is generated, the proxy can be added to your client project and called from your code. Generating a proxy with WSDL.EXE is also a good way to get a look at proxy code, so let's do that.

The command line to create a proxy for our simple Vocab service looks like this:

```
Wsdl.exe /out:VocbProxy.vb /language:VB
    http://localhost/Vocab/Vocab.asmx?wsdl
```

The */out* parameter specifies the name of the source code file to write. The */language* parameter specifies in which language to generate the proxy. The URL points to the asmx file of the Web service, wherever it is hosted. In our case, it's on the localhost. The wsdl parameter will generate wsdl input for the wsdl utility. Once it's finished, you can look at the proxy code, and because we promised you a peek at it, here you go:

```
Imports System
Imports System.Diagnostics
Imports System.Web.Services
Imports System.Web.Services.Protocols
Imports System.Xml.Serialization

'
'This source code was autogenerated by wsdl, Version=1.0.2914.16.
'

<System.Web.Services.WebServiceBindingAttribute(Name:="VocabSoap", _
    [Namespace]:="http://tempuri.org/")> _
Public Class Vocab
    Inherits System.Web.Services.Protocols.SoapHttpClientProtocol

    <System.Diagnostics.DebuggerStepThroughAttribute()> _
    Public Sub New()
        MyBase.New
        Me.Url = "http://localhost/Vocab/Vocab.asmx"
    End Sub
```

```
    <System.Diagnostics.DebuggerStepThroughAttribute(), _
     System.Web.Services.Protocols.SoapDocumentMethodAttribute( _
           "http://tempuri.org/GetVocabWord", _
           Use:=System.Web.Services.Description.SoapBindingUse.Literal, _
           ParameterStyle:= _
               System.Web.Services.Protocols.SoapParameterStyle.Wrapped)> _
    Public Function GetVocabWord() As String
        Dim results() As Object = Me.Invoke("GetVocabWord", _
            New Object(-1) {})
        Return CType(results(0),String)
    End Function

    <System.Diagnostics.DebuggerStepThroughAttribute()>  _
    Public Function BeginGetVocabWord( _
        ByVal callback As System.AsyncCallback, _
        ByVal asyncState As Object) As System.IAsyncResult
        Return Me.BeginInvoke("GetVocabWord", New Object(-1) {}, _
            callback, asyncState)
    End Function

    <System.Diagnostics.DebuggerStepThroughAttribute()>  _
    Public Function EndGetVocabWord( _
        ByVal asyncResult As System.IAsyncResult) As String
        Dim results() As Object = Me.EndInvoke(asyncResult)
        Return CType(results(0),String)
    End Function
End Class
```

There are several things of interest in here. There is a Begin and End method for starting and ending each function invocation. More interesting, though, is the proxy for the method we put in there, GetVocabWord. It uses an Invoke method to generate a SOAP request, telling it the name of the method. It would also pass along parameters, if we had any. A bunch of SOAP junk precedes this, which defines the location of the method and how to form the SOAP message. The constructor (New) defines the location, or URL, of the Web service itself.

The bottom line is that it's a good thing that there are automated ways to create this code rather than having to do it manually. Use the Web reference in the environment when you can, and WSDL.EXE when you have to.

All of Them Together

Now that you have the pieces, here's the big picture. UDDI takes care of making Web services available to the world. It's not a hosting service, but a big directory. Once you know that a Web service is there through UDDI, you need to know how to use it. The methods available in a Web service, as well as directions for using them, are described in WSDL. Visual Studio or the WSDL utility consumes the WSDL and uses it to create a proxy class that makes it easy and convenient for you to call the methods of the Web service. Figure 3.8 illustrates how UDDI and WSDL work to provide you and your client with Web service resources.

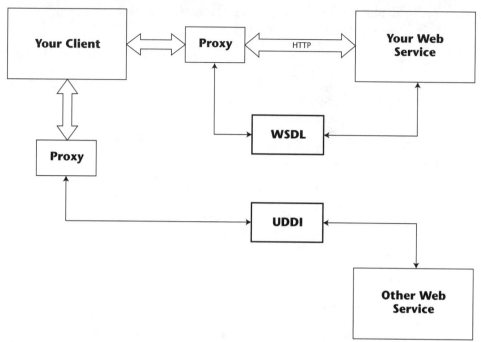

Figure 3.8   UDDI, WSDL, and Proxies working together.

Let's Start the Project

The real meat of using Web services is, of course, doing something useful with them, and we've come to that part. We will be constructing a system, meaning a Web service and a client, that allows you to build a bug-reporting system into all your applications or even Web sites.

Overview

The Web service itself will be taking care of the backend, accepting requests and sending back results. The client portion is where the user interacts with the service, and it is constructed as a pair of WinForms that you can include in any project. There is a little database work involved as well, but it's pretty basic. We're building on what we covered in the first two projects and throwing in the Web service.

In practice, you would host the Web service on a Web server of your own. For each application you release, for paying customers or internal customers, you would build the client portion into it. The user, upon running across a bug or other problem, could access the bug-reporting functionality. There they enter information about the bug and click an OK button. The information zips off to the Web service, which stores it in a database for your perusal at a later time.

The Web Service

The Web service is responsible for accepting requests, processing them, and sending back results. We have three things related to bug reporting that it needs to do for us:

Accept information from a user about a bug and save it in the database.   Only a success or failure indicator is returned.

Return information for the UI in the form of lists.   This information consists of a list of valid user names, a list of products for which bugs can be reported, and the list of severity ratings the user can use when reporting a bug.

Return a list of bugs reported by the user.   Users will periodically need to see a list of the bugs they've reported. This will help prevent them from reporting the same bug twice and will allow them to review what they've reported.

The three methods we are exposing in our Web service to take care of these needs are:

```
SumbitProblem
GetLists
GetBugList
```

The Database

Most of the work that the Web service will be doing for us is related to the database: storing bugs, retrieving bugs, and retrieving list values. Most of the database techniques we use were covered in Project 2. We will be using the new ADO.NET DataSets and DataAdapters to retrieve and contain data, and in the code you'll see how they're put to work.

The really interesting part of using DataSets here is how they're implemented. Internally, DataSets are just XML. If you return a DataSet to a .NET-savvy client, one that understands DataSets, you can access it just like DataSet objects. This is what we'll be doing; however, you could just as easily send DataSets to any sort of client: a Web page, a Unix application, whatever. As long as they understand XML, they can consume the data. This makes life very easy for the creators of data-oriented Web services because they can work with DataSets and not worry too much about the clients' compatibility. This is what basing your tools on open standards is all about.

Note that the database used for this project is Microsoft SQL Server 2000. All the instructions are based on this, but I'll try to point out where there are differences in the code that you need to be aware of. The most important one is the connection.

Database Design

The database we'll be using is the same one we used in Project 2, the bug-tracking system. That project and this one will work together to provide a complete bug-reporting solution. Project 2 allows you as engineers to track your own bugs, whereas this project gets your users in on the act. Let them do some of your work.

The primary table in use by this project is the Problems table. We will also return the lists of users, severities, and products from the other tables for use in the user interface. Run through the next section to see how to import the Microsoft Access database we've provided into SQL Server.

The Sample Database

We have included a sample database on the CD-ROM that accompanies this book. It has been stored, for the sake of convenience, as a Microsoft Access database. It contains all the tables and relationships and a handful of actual sample data. You can, if you feel industrious and are conversant with SQL Server, create the database yourself manually. However, for those who have actual work to do, I have included instructions here for importing the data into SQL Server. You could also just use the Access database directly, but you'll have to come up with a new connection string in the code.

The Access database on the CD-ROM is called prj03.mdb and is located with the Project 3 source code files. To use the data with SQL Server, we'll have to import it into SQL Server. It should only take a couple of minutes. Make sure you know where your SQL Server is and that you have access to it.

Fire up the SQL Server Enterprise Manager and open up the tree view so that you can see all your databases. First create the target database into which our data will be imported. Right-click on the Databases item in the tree view, and select New Database from the context menu. In the dialog that appears, enter the name *prj03* in the Name field. Click OK. The empty database is now ready to hold our tables of data.

Now we need to import the data. Right-click on the Databases item in the tree view, and select Import from the All Tasks flyout menu. You'll see the Data Transformation Services (DTS) wizard. Click Next to move to the important stuff. Figure 3.9 shows what this looks like and how it should be filled in. Change the Data Source to Microsoft Access and then fill in the filename of the sample database. Click Next.

Part two of the wizard is shown in Figure 3.10. This is where you specify the destination database information. Make sure the correct server is selected, as well as the correct security option. The connection strings used in this project are based on the use of SQL Server authentication, so that is what you should select. Lastly, select the *prj03* database that we created from the list of databases at the bottom of the dialog. Click Next.

On the next wizard panel, make sure the option labeled "Copy Tables and Views from the source database" is selected and click Next. The resulting wizard panel, shown in Figure 3.11, allows you to select which tables and views to import. Check them all, as illustrated, and click Next.

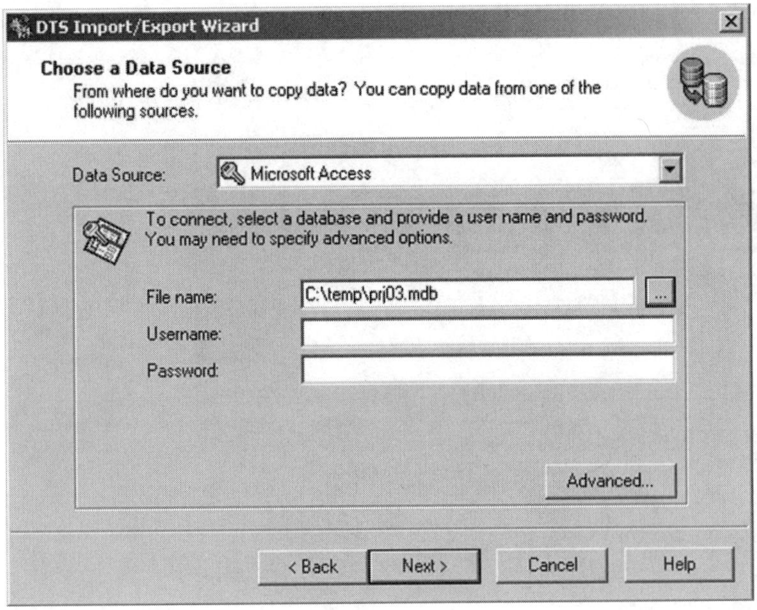

Figure 3.9 The Import/Export wizard, part 1.

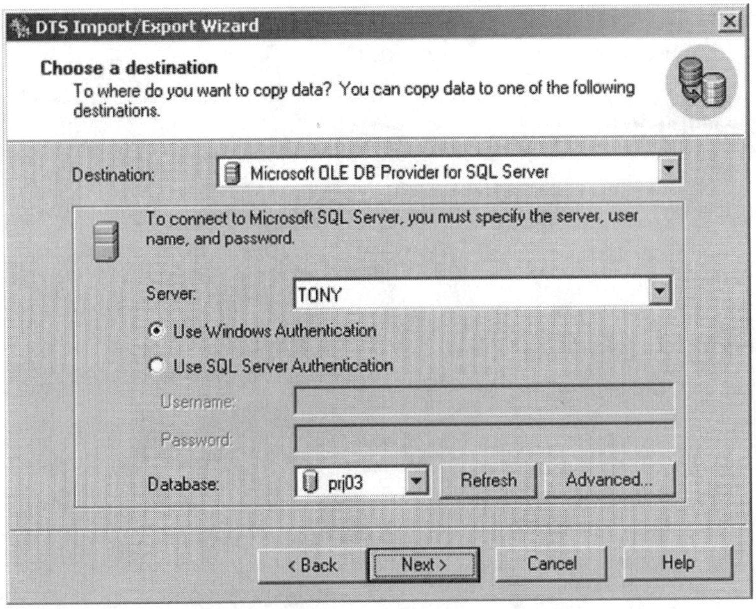

Figure 3.10 The Import/Export wizard, part 2.

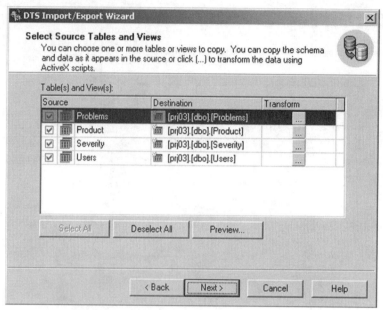

Figure 3.11   The Import/Export wizard, part 3.

In this next panel, make sure the Run immediately item is selected and click Next. In the final panel, make sure everything looks all right, and click Finish. The import process will run, and the results should look something like Figure 3.12.

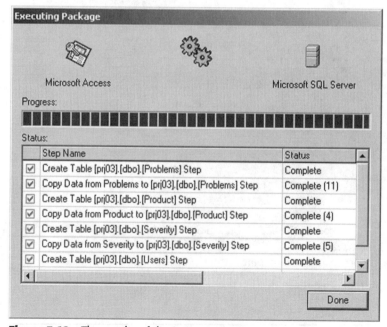

Figure 3.12   The results of the Import process.

There's one more step we need to perform manually. Open the database table *Problems* in design mode by right-clicking on it and selecting *Design Table*. Once the window opens, select the *ProblemID* field. At the bottom of the window are some options for that field. We are interested in the one that says *Identity*. Change its value to Yes. Make sure that the *Identity Seed* and *Identity Increment* values are set to 1. This will force our ProblemID field to act like an Access Autonumber field and will automatically increment by 1 every time we add a row to the database.

Your data should now be ready to roll. Hop back into SQL Server Enterprise Manager and make sure it all looks okay. Open up the prj03 database, and then open the Tables item. You should see something like Figure 3.11, which lists the tables. In addition to all the system tables, make sure that the tables called Problems, Product, Severity, and Users are all there. Feel free to check out the data, too.

The Web Service

It's time for the real fun. You can either load the code from the CD-ROM (prj03) or enter it yourself to get the feel of it all. Let's start by covering a couple of Web service coding concepts.

Web services, like almost everything in .NET, are classes. They inherit from System.Web.Services.WebService, and they're created like any other class, with one minor but important exception. The declaration for each method in the class is preceded by the attribute:

```
<WebMethod()>
```

This attribute can handle more than simply telling the compiler that we want to expose this method as part of the Web service. See those empty parentheses? There is a handful of parameters that you can put in there to control its behavior. Most are very low level and will not be covered here (for example, one of them lets your Web service participate in a session), but one is useful for everyone: *Description*. Fill in a description for the Web service, and it will help with the discovery part of your Web service. Here's an example:

```
<WebMethod(Description = "A method that returns a random vocabulary word
    and definition from the largest vocabulary database in the world.")
```

Once you have the <WebMethod()> attribute in front of your method, which VB does for you, you're ready to code.

> **TIP** There are two schools of thought when it comes to planning and implementing your Web services for performance. One says to keep in mind that Web services are remote components and that you have to account for connection and information travel time. Try to minimize the amount of work done by a given Web method so that the return trip will be quick.
>
> The other school says that you should get as much done while you're at the server as possible, for the same reasons: The round trip is expensive. The

internal execution of the service, compared to the communication time, is relatively fast. In this way, you minimize the number of round trips you need.

In reality, both are right. You need to strike a balance between making the user wait for a particular call to complete, while minimizing the number of times the user has to wait. With Web services, the first time you call the service, when it is activated, takes the longest. It's a good idea to do this early, at a time when the user expects to wait anyway. Subsequent calls to the service, as long as they're within the timeout period, are fast.

The Code

To start off, we add a couple important lines at the top of our code. They are:

```
Option Strict On
Option Explicit On

Imports System.Web.Services
Imports System.Data.SqlClient
```

The Option Explicit and Option Strict are standard. However, we need to make sure that we import both the Web services library and the database client. So that's done.

When you create a new Web service in the Visual Studio environment, it automatically names the new service *Service1*. This will work, but it is not terribly useful or descriptive (I wonder how many Service1's will end up out there by accident?). Change the name in the code (and in the Solution Explorer) to something meaningful, in our case, *prj03svc*:

```
Public Class prj03svc
    Inherits System.Web.Services.WebService
```

We also define a single class constant that holds our connection string. You will need to change this to match your own database and server:

```
Private Const CONNSTR As String = "PERSIST SECURITY INFO=False;
    DATA SOURCE=tony; INITIAL CATALOG=prj03; UID=sa; PWD=;"
```

The *data source* item needs to be changed to match your database server name, and the *initial catalog* should match the name of the database that has the bug data. Our connection string is set up to use SQL Server and the SQL Server integrated security. If you have other needs, change the string accordingly.

GetLists

As mentioned, there are three methods in this Web service. First we'll cover *GetLists*, a fairly simple method that returns a list of values for potential use in the UI. It pokes its head into the database and digs out all the users, severities, and product names that are defined there. Here is the complete code list for the method:

```
' This method returns lists of items from the auxilliary tables,
' such as the Users in the system, the products available, and
' the possible problem severities. All of the result sets are
' returned in a single dataset.
<WebMethod()> Public Function GetLists() As DataSet

    Dim sSQL As String
    Dim bSelectsWorked As Boolean = True

    ' Set up and open the connection to our database.
    Dim connection As SqlConnection = New SqlConnection(CONNSTR)
    connection.Open()

    ' Define our first query.
    sSQL = "SELECT * FROM Users"

    ' Set up a data adapter and dataset to store our lists.
    Dim da As SqlDataAdapter = New SqlDataAdapter(sSQL, connection)
    Dim ds As DataSet = New DataSet()

    ' Load all the data. If anything goes wrong, we will handle it
    ' by aborting the whole thing.
    Try
        da.Fill(ds, "Users")
        da.SelectCommand.CommandText = "SELECT * FROM Severity"
        da.Fill(ds, "Severity")
        da.SelectCommand.CommandText = "SELECT * FROM Product"
        da.Fill(ds, "Products")
    Catch
        bSelectsWorked = False
    End Try

    ' Clean up and return the results.
    connection.Close()
    If bSelectsWorked Then
        Return ds
    Else
        Return Nothing
    End If

End Function
```

The first interesting element is that we are sending back a DataSet as a return value. This will be great for .NET clients that know about DataSets because they get all the extended DataSet functionality. This will be fine for non-DataSet-aware clients, too, as long as they understand XML. If they don't understand XML, they shouldn't be fooling around with Web services anyway.

Next we do the basic database stuff: create a connection, open it, and define the simple SQL we need to retrieve the information from our first query. Then we have to create a DataAdapter to serve as a mechanism that stands between the database itself and our DataSet. It's kind of like a runner: The SQL tells the DataAdapter what to go get, and it shoots off to the database, gets it, and then runs back and hands the data off to the DataSet. Once the DataSet and DataAdapter are created and properly fed with information, we can start loading data. The following code does just that:

```
da.Fill(ds, "Users")
da.SelectCommand.CommandText = "SELECT * FROM Severity"
da.Fill(ds, "Severity")
da.SelectCommand.CommandText = "SELECT * FROM Product"
da.Fill(ds, "Products")
```

This code executes three separate queries and stashes the data away in the same DataSet. This is one of the best benefits of DataSets and XML: being able to store heterogeneous data in the same structure. If we were using RecordSets, we'd have to pass back three different queries or force the client to issue three calls. Note also that this functionality is wrapped inside the Try..Catch error-handling mechanism. You should get used to using Try..Catch because it pretty much replaces the old error objects and mechanisms.

Lastly, we close the connection and return the DataSet if everything worked out all right. Pretty basic stuff so far, with a little .NET data access thrown in. Later, when we cover the client portion of our solution, we'll see how to get the various result sets data stored in the DataSet.

GetProblems

The GetProblems method accepts a user name from the client and uses it to retrieve all the rows in the Problems table that match the name. This functionality is supplied so that users can review what they've reported so far. The code for the method follows:

```
' This method will return a dataset that contains all the problems
' reported by a specific user by name.
<WebMethod()> Public Function GetProblems(ByVal sUserName As String)
    As DataSet

    ' Set up and open the connection to our database
    Dim connection As SqlConnection = New SqlConnection(CONNSTR)
    connection.Open()

    ' Define the query that will get displayable data for the user.
    ' We want all user-understandable data, so we have a join on our
    ' auxilliary tables to get the names of things instead of their
    ' IDs.
    Dim sSQL As String
    sSQL = "SELECT Problems.ProblemID, Problems.Version, " & _
        "Product.ProductName, Users.UserName, " & _
        "Severity.SeverityName," & _
        "Problems.Steps, Problems.Description " & _
        "FROM Problems INNER JOIN " & _
        "Product ON Problems.ProductID = Product.ProductID " & _
```

```
        "INNER JOIN " & _
        "Severity ON Problems.SeverityID = Severity.SeverityID" & _
        "INNER JOIN " & _
        "Users ON Problems.UserID = Users.UserID "


    ' If the username is omitted, return all records. Otherwise,
    ' add a where clause based on the user name.
    If Len(Trim(sUserName)) > 0 Then
        sSQL += "WHERE (Users.UserName = '" & Trim(sUserName) & "')"
    End If


    ' Set up a data adapter to get our data and fill a data set
    ' with it.
    Dim da As SqlDataAdapter = New SqlDataAdapter(sSQL, connection)
    Dim ds As DataSet = New DataSet()
    Dim bSelectWorked As Boolean = True
    Try
        da.Fill(ds, "Problems")
    Catch exception as SqlException
        bSelectWorked = False
    End Try


    ' Clean up and return the results
    connection.Close()
    If bSelectWorked Then
        Return ds
    Else
        Return Nothing
    End If

End Function
```

We start out with the usual creation and opening of a database connection. Then we create the SQL statement that will retrieve our list of matching bug reports. The SQL is a little complicated. This is because we get a user name, a string, with which to match Problem rows, but the user names are stored in a separate table, connected with an ID key. So we need to use a couple inner JOINs to solve the problem. If this doesn't make sense to you, trust me for the moment and consult your local SQL guru later. It does actually retrieve the list we want.

Once the SQL is defined, the rest looks a lot like the GetLists method, except that we're only issuing a single query. We set up the DataSet and DataAdapter, and then make the call in a Try..Catch block. If it works, we return the list. If not, we return nothing.

SubmitProblem

This is the big guy, the one that sends users' woes back to our database so that we can alleviate their suffering. It accepts a pretty good handful of parameters, all the information the user entered about the bug, and ships it off to our database to be stored for later review. The code for it follows:

```
' This method allows a user to submit information about a bug,
' which will then be saved in our Problems database.
<WebMethod()> Public Function SubmitProblem( _
        ByVal iUserID As Int64, _
        ByVal sDesc As String, _
        ByVal sSteps As String, _
        ByVal iSeverityID As Int32, _
        ByVal sVersion As String, _
        ByVal iProductID As Int64) _
        As Boolean

    ' Validate incoming parameters.
    If sDesc = "" Or sSteps = "" Or iUserID < 1 Or iProductID < 1
Then
        Return False
    End If

    ' Fix any apostrophes in the passed-in strings. They'll mess
    ' up our SQL if they're not handled correctly.
    sDesc = sDesc.Replace("'", "''")
    sSteps = sSteps.Replace("'", "''")

    ' Set up and open the connection to our database.
    Dim connection As SqlConnection = New SqlConnection(CONNSTR)
    connection.Open()

    ' Create the SQL insert command we need.
    Dim sSQL As String
    sSQL = "INSERT INTO Problems(Version, UserID, SeverityID," & _
            "Description, Steps, ProductID, ReportedOn) " & _
            "VALUES(" & _
                "'" & Trim(sVersion) & "'" & _
                ", " & CStr(iUserID) & _
                ", " & CStr(iSeverityID) & _
                ", '" & Trim(sDesc) & "'" & _
                ", '" & Trim(sSteps) & "'" & _
                ", " & CStr(iProductID) & _
                ", '" & Now & "'" & ")"

    ' Create the command object we'll use to execute the insert.
    Dim cmd As New SqlCommand(sSQL, connection)

    ' Attempt the insertion.
    Dim bInsertWorked As Boolean = True
    Try
        cmd.ExecuteNonQuery()
    Catch
        bInsertWorked = False
```

```
End Try

' If it worked or didn't, let the caller know.
If bInsertWorked Then
    Return True
Else
    Return False
End If

End Function
```

There are a lot of parameters, but most are self-explanatory. Note that our User and Severity values come back as IDs. The user, or course, selects by name. We left it up to the client to translate between the IDs and the text names to make it easier on the service. Some basic error checking of the parameters follows. However, we also need to remove any single quotes from the user's description and steps-to-reproduce strings that they typed in. They will mess up our SQL because internally it uses single quotes as a string delimiter. The code to do this is simple and much easier than it would have been in VB6. We finally have an intrinsic replace function for strings.

```
sDesc = sDesc.Replace("'", "''")
sSteps = sSteps.Replace("'", "''")
```

Next we create our connection object and our SQL statement. The SQL is a straightforward Insert statement that puts all the data into the Problems table. In this method, because we're not using a Select statement to return data, we can't use the DataAdapter's *Fill* method. Instead, we use a SqlCommand object, which will allow us to execute a nonquery statement using, oddly enough, the ExecuteNonQuery method. We do this, as usual, in a Try..Catch block. Whether the Insert works or not, we inform the client of the result.

Pretty simple, huh? The code inside the Web service itself is not astoundingly complicated. There are some new .NET things in there, but nothing complex. VB takes care of most of the difficulties for us.

Test It Out

You can test the Web service much like we tested the little vocabulary word service we created earlier. In the Solution Explorer, right-click on the file ProblemLogger.asmx and from the context menu, select View in Browser. A page will be displayed that lists all the methods available in the Web service. Click on any that you'd like to try out. For example, select the GetProblems method. A page will be displayed that allows you to enter any parameters that the method requires, much like the one in Figure 3.13.

Type in a valid name, click the Invoke button, and you get your results. Because this method returns a DataSet, you'll see the XML contents of the DataSet, wrapped in the XML of the returning result set. It will look something like Figure 3.14.

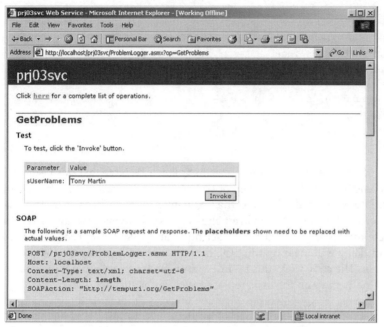

Figure 3.13   Entering parameters for a Web service method.

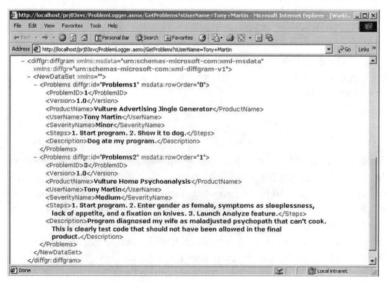

Figure 3.14   The results from the GetProblems method.

You can do the same thing with any of the methods in any Web service you create. Test drivers are no longer required to run your components.

The Client

Although Web services are exciting and fun, they pretty much need a client of some sort to be useful. The second half of this project is a pair of client dialogs (and a third test container) that you can add to any application that you want to have bug-reporting capabilities. You will just add them, customize them to suit your needs, and build the client. The connection to the Web service will be handled through a proxy that we don't have to create or even look at.

There are two primary windows that we will use to provide the bug-reporting functionality:

frmBug.   The user will enter bug information in this form and use it to submit the bug report to the server.

frmSeeBugs.   Users can retrieve a list of all the bugs that they have reported so far, and the information will be displayed in this form.

Note that all the forms for this project are inherited forms based on the forms library that we created in Project 1. We make use of frmApp for the main application container, frmDialog for the two dialog boxes we create, and frmMsgBox to let the user know what's going on. You can add this as a reference to your project; I'll point out where and how later.

The code for the project is on the accompanying CD-ROM and is called *prj03client*. Load it from there or type along with us. Start by creating a VB Windows Forms project in Visual Studio. Name it prj03client. Then add a reference to the class library DLL that we created in Project 1. Right-click on the References item in the Solution Explorer and select Add Reference (or you could select Add Reference from the Project menu). Find the DLL from Project 1 and click OK.

The Web Reference

To access the functionality of the Web service, we need to create the proxy that we've spoken of so highly. You do this in VB automatically by adding a Web reference. If you were looking for an external Web service, you could use the UDDI directory to find the service. In our case, the service is probably on localhost, and that makes it easier.

This time we'll use the menu. From the Project menu, select *Add Web Reference*. The dialog that comes up is split in half. On the left side, there should be a link at the bottom of the page that says Web references on the local machine. Click this option. The right side of the window should now contain a list of the Web services on your computer. Click on prj03svc in the right side of the window.

One last step. In the Solution Explorer, open up the Web References item. Right-click on the first item under it, which should be *Localhost*. Select the *Rename* option and give it a new name. Ours is called *prj03SvcProxy*. Once that's done, you can create an instance of *prj03SvcProxy.prj03svc* in your code and use it like any other object with functionality.

The frmBug Form—I Found a Bug!

The frmBug form is where most of the work will be done. It is based on the frmDialog form created in Project 1. To create it, right-click on the project name in the Solution Explorer and select Inherited Form from the list. A dialog will appear, one that you've seen before, where you can enter the name of the form. When you click OK, you will be presented with a window in which you must select the form's parent, from which it will be inherited. You'll notice that none of the forms from Project 1 are listed. You'll have to browse to the DLL, and then they will show up in the list. See Figure 3.15 to make sure you're looking at the right dialog. When the forms are shown, select the frmDialog item and click OK. You should see a nice, new, empty dialog that looks just like the frmDialog.

Now we need to create the controls that the user will interact with to tell us what's wrong with our application. Table 3.1 details the controls, and Figure 3.16 shows you where they go. Your form won't look quite like Figure 3.16 yet, but we're almost there.

Table 3.1   The Fields (Controls) on frmBug

CONTROL NAME	CONTROL TYPE	DESCRIPTION
CmbUserID	Combo Box	A list of valid user names from which users select their own
CmdSeverity	Combo Box	A list of valid severity values for the bug
TxtDesc	Text Box	A large text box in which users can complain all they like about the problem they found
TxtSteps	Text Box	A large text box in which users should enter any steps to reproduce the bug, making it easier for engineers to diagnose

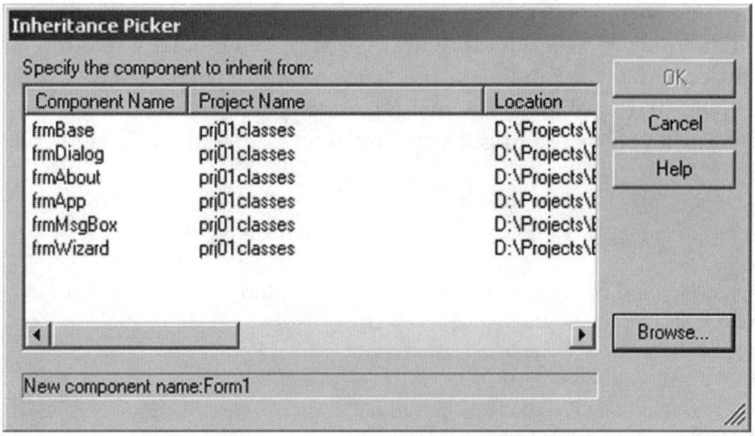

Figure 3.15   The Inherited Form Component Selection dialog.

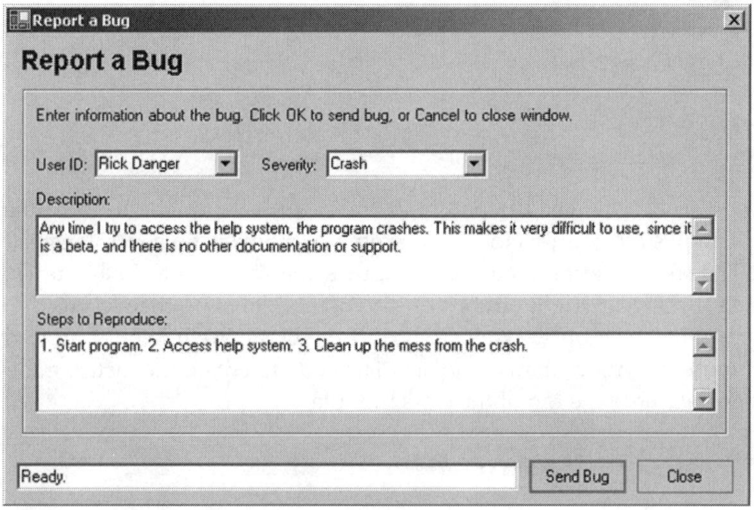

Figure 3.16   The layout of frmBug.

Now that we have the form created, we need to make it do something. It will have to accept and validate input and send it off to the Web service. First, let's take care of some issues with the control layout and make the dialog look like we want it to. Under the section of code in the region labeled Windows Form Designer generated code, there is a comment that shows you where to put your own code. Add the following code after that:

```
Me.FormBorderStyle = FormBorderStyle.FixedDialog

' Re-parent the controls so they actually show up on the form.
Me.txtSteps.Parent = MyBase.grpCtrls
Me.Label4.Parent = MyBase.grpCtrls
Me.Label5.Parent = MyBase.grpCtrls
Me.txtDesc.Parent = MyBase.grpCtrls
Me.cmbUserID.Parent = MyBase.grpCtrls
Me.Label1.Parent = MyBase.grpCtrls
Me.Label2.Parent = MyBase.grpCtrls
Me.Label3.Parent = MyBase.grpCtrls
Me.cmbSeverity.Parent = MyBase.grpCtrls

' Make sure the controls we want are visible
Me.ShowCancel = True
Me.ShowOK = True
Me.ShowNotify = True
Me.OKText = "&Send Bug"
Me.CancelText = "&Close"
MyBase.ShowControls()
```

The first section of code changes the parent of the controls from the form to the group control. This allows the controls to show up on top of the group control instead of underneath it. The second section simply configures the window to look like we want it to, including turning the right buttons on and off and labeling them correctly.

Next add a private instance of the Web service to the class. We'll keep it around because we have to use it in more than one place. The code to create the instance follows. Place it somewhere near the top of the class module.

```
Private svc As New prj03svcProxy.prj03svc()
```

This form has to do two primary things with the Web service in the background. First, it has to get a list of users and severity values from the Web service, which pulls that information from the database. Second, it must take the data the user enters and send it to the server for safekeeping.

We load the information for the combo boxes in the Form Load event. When the form appears, the combo boxes are populated. The code to do this is not complex, but it shows us how to navigate through a DataSet that has multiple result sets stored in it. Take a look:

```
Private Sub frmBug_Load(ByVal sender As Object, _
                ByVal e As System.EventArgs) _
```

```
                    Handles MyBase.Load

    ' Now populate the UI lists with data from the Web service
    Dim d As New DataSet()
    Dim aRow As DataRow
    Dim s As String

    ' It can take a few seconds to get results back from the
    ' Web service, so tell the user.
    Me.NotifyText = "Loading list data..."

    ' Call the Web service and get the lists of data.
    d = svc.GetLists()

    ' Fill the users list.
    For Each aRow In d.Tables(0).Rows
        cmbUserID.Items.Insert(CInt(aRow("UserID")) - 1, _
            CStr(aRow("UserName")))
    Next

    ' Fill the Severity list.
    For Each aRow In d.Tables(1).Rows
        cmbSeverity.Items.Insert(CInt(aRow("SeverityID")) - 1, _
            CStr(aRow("SeverityName")))
    Next

    Me.NotifyText = "Ready."

End Sub
```

Notice how simple it is to use a Web service once you have a Web reference to it and a proxy that you didn't have to make. It looks just like any other component. We simply call the service method and the return result is stuffed into our DataSet.

Take a look at the DataSet navigation, specifically the two For..Each loops. The object we're iterating through is the DataSet's Rows collection for each individual table. Each table is a result set from a query issued and stored in the DataSet. Each table has a collection of rows and columns. We simply use an index to tell the DataSet which table we want to reference. Inside the loops, we use the current row object, specified by the loop, and we tell it, by name, the column in which we are interested. In this case, we need two columns. The ID field is first; it is used as the index value in the combo box and the actual text string that gets displayed (either UserName or SeverityName). We have to adjust the index by 1 because the index values in combo boxes are zero based.

That's all there is to part one. After this, the form displays and users can interact with it. Once users have completed their data entry, they click the OK button and we kick off part two, saving the data to our database.

The data-saving code is connected to the OK button click event and looks like this:

```
    ' Handle the OK button click, which is where the real work is. Do
    ' some error checking, then try to submit the bug to the server
    ' using the Web service.
```

```
Public Overrides Sub btnOK_Click(ByVal sender As System.Object, _
                                 ByVal e As System.EventArgs)

    ' Get one of our custom message boxes ready. We'll probably
    ' have to display something.
    Dim fMsg As New prj01classes.frmMsgBox( _
        prj01classes.frmMsgBox.MsgType.msgtypeERROR, _
        "There was a problem submitting the bug.", "", True, False,_
        False)

    ' Do some basic error checking to make sure we have
    ' enough information.
    If Len(Trim(txtSteps.Text)) = 0 Then
        fMsg.Msg = "Fill in some information in " & _
            "the ""Steps To Reproduce"" field please. " & _
            "This will help our engineers reproduce the bug."
        fMsg.ShowDialog()
        Return
    End If
    If Len(Trim(txtDesc.Text)) = 0 Then
        fMsg.Msg = "Fill in some information in " & _
            "the ""Description"" field please. " & _
            "This is the only way we can identify the problem. " & _
            "Please be specific and detailed."
        fMsg.ShowDialog()
        Return
    End If
    If Len(Trim(cmbUserID.Text)) = 0 Then
        fMsg.Msg = "Please select your user name in " & _
            "the ""User ID"" field. " & _
            "We need to know which user filed the bug so we can " & _
            "contact him or her if we have questions."
        fMsg.ShowDialog()
        Return
    End If
    If Len(Trim(cmbSeverity.Text)) = 0 Then
        fMsg.Msg = "Please select a value from " & _
            "the ""Severity"" field. " & _
            "This will help our engineers prioritize the bugs " & _
            "they have to fix."
        fMsg.ShowDialog()
        Return
    End If

    ' If we got this far, file the data using the Web service.
    ' The call to SubmitProblem is all there is to it!
    Dim bWorked As Boolean
    bWorked = svc.SubmitProblem(CLng(cmbUserID.SelectedIndex) + 1, _
        Trim(txtDesc.Text), _
        Trim(txtSteps.Text), _
```

```
            CInt(cmbSeverity.SelectedIndex) + 1, _
            frmMain.Version, _
            frmMain.ProdID)


    ' If the databse insert worked, tell the user and clear
    ' the form. If not, also tell the user, but leave the form.
    If bWorked Then
        Me.NotifyText = "Bug was successfully submitted."
        ClearForm()
    Else
        fMsg.Msg = "Bug submission did not work. " & _
            "There was a problem submitting the bug information " & _
            "to the server.  " & _
            "The database or the Internet " & _
            "connection could be down. Please " & _
            "try again later."
        fMsg.ShowDialog()
    End If

End Sub
```

At least half the code in this method is dedicated to checking that the user has entered all the values on the form and to displaying appropriate messages if there's anything missing. We did use the custom message box that we created in Project 1, just because it's there. After that, we make the call to the Web service to pass on the user's bug data. It's a single call with a handful of parameters.

Note that the last two parameters, the program version and product ID, are part of the application. The user does not need to be concerned with them. The values are defined as part of the application, in our case, the frmMain application class. You will learn more about those special values later when we cover frmMain.

If the call worked, we tell the user and clear the form so the user can enter more bugs if necessary. If not, we leave the data on the form alone and tell the user that there was a problem.

The frmSeeBugs Form—What Have I Done?

Perhaps your users would like to review the bugs they've entered so far. Perhaps the engineers would like to encourage the users to review the bugs others have entered before they enter one of their own. These are very good reasons to include functionality that allows users to see the bugs, by user, that have already been reported. So we have, using the frmSeeBugs form and the GetProblems method of the Web service.

The form is very simple, and includes only two real controls, listed in Table 3.2. Figure 3.17 shows what it should look like. This form is also inherited from proj01classes.frmDialog. And again, as we did in frmBug, add a Web reference to our prj03svc Web service, including renaming it to prj02SvcProxy.

Table 3.2   The Controls for frmSeeBugs

CONTROL NAME	CONTROL TYPE	DESCRIPTION
CmbUsers	Combo Box	Selection list for user name
TxtBugs	Text Box	Display area for the bug listings

We'll take care of some basic housekeeping first. Import the SqlClient package so that we can use the DataSet functionality. Then add an instance of our Web service proxy, and add a simple event handler for the OK button that closes the dialog:

```
Imports System.Data.SqlClient

' Create a reference to the Web service proxy that we can keep around.
Private svc As New prj03svcProxy.prj03svc()

Public Overrides Sub btnOK_Click(ByVal sender As Object, _
                                 ByVal e As System.EventArgs)
    Me.Close()
End Sub
```

In the constructor, add some code to rename our window and turn on the OK button:

```
'Add any initialization after the InitializeComponent() call
MyBase.InitForm()
MyBase.Title = "See My Bugs"
MyBase.Text = "See My Bugs"
MyBase.ShowOK = True
```

Now we need to populate the list of user names with values from the service, so we'll add some code to do that. It is very much like the code we wrote in frmBugs to fill in the Users list:

```
' Load the user list.
Dim d As New DataSet()
d = svc.GetLists()

Dim aRow As DataRow
Dim aColumn As DataColumn

' Fill the user list combo box.
For Each aRow In d.Tables(0).Rows
    cmbUser.Items.Add(aRow("UserName"))
Next
' Add all the new controls to the inherited group box so they
' actually show up.
grpCtrls.Controls.Add(cmbUser)
grpCtrls.Controls.Add(Label1)
grpCtrls.Controls.Add(Label2)
grpCtrls.Controls.Add(txtBugs)
```

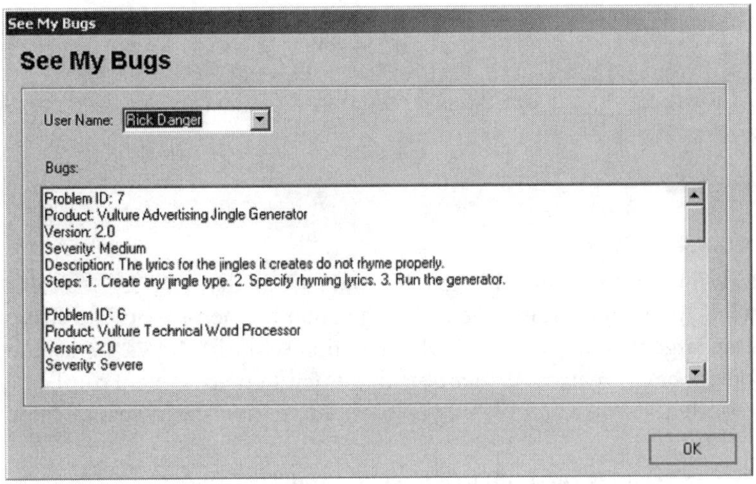

Figure 3.17   The layout of frmSeeBugs.

Now we have the list populated with user names. The dialog will come up blank. When the user changes the name selection in the combo box, we want to reload the bug information for that user. We wired the code to retrieve the bug data into the Selected-IndexChanged event for the combo box. The code looks like this:

```
' When users select their user name, load the list of their bugs.
' In this implementation, the user can see other user's bugs. You
' can add integrated security later to restrict the bugs viewable.
Private Sub cmbUser_SelectedIndexChanged( _
    ByVal sender As System.Object, _
    ByVal e As System.EventArgs) Handles cmbUser.SelectedIndexChanged

    Dim d As New DataSet()
    Dim aRow As DataRow
    Dim s As String

    ' It can take a few seconds to get results back from the _
    ' Web service, so tell the user.
    txtBugs.Text = "Retrieving bug information...hang on..."

    ' Call the Web service and get the bug list.
    d = svc.GetProblems(cmbUser.Text)

    ' Populate the list with a reasonably formatted version _
    ' of the data.
    txtBugs.Text = ""
    For Each aRow In d.Tables(0).Rows
        s = "Problem ID: " & CStr(aRow("ProblemID")) & vbCrLf
        s += "Product: " & CStr(aRow("ProductName")) & vbCrLf
```

```
            s += "Version: " & CStr(aRow("Version")) & vbCrLf
            s += "Severity: " & CStr(aRow("SeverityName")) & vbCrLf
            s += "Description: " & CStr(aRow("Description")) & vbCrLf
            s += "Steps: " & CStr(aRow("Steps")) & vbCrLf & vbCrLf
            txtBugs.Text += s
        Next

    End Sub
```

The code is fairly straightforward. We get the data from the service, which is returned in a DataSet. We navigate it like we did in the other methods to build a string we can display in the large text box. So the implementation we built allows the user to see the bugs that others have created. As mentioned, this could help prevent duplicate bugs from being reported. If you don't like it, you can add security to the service later.

 TIP **If you haven't seen it yet, notice that we use the "+=" operator added to VB, a plagiarism from C. It's a shortcut for adding something to itself. The code**

```
txtBugs.Text += s
```

is equivalent to

```
txtBugs.Text = txtBugs.Text + s
```

There are other shortcut operators, including *=, ^=, /=, \=, -=, and &=. Each one performs the operation indicated using the operand on the right and the value in the operand on the left and assigns the result to the operand on the left. These are nice shortcuts, one of the better mechanisms of C, now available to VB programmers.

That's it for the forms. You can include them in your own application directly, or as we did with Project 1, build them into a class library that you can include by adding a reference to your project. Either way, you get bug-reporting functionality with very little work. We still need to cover the main form a little, just to go over a few details about adding the bug form to your own applications.

The frmMain Form—Wiring It Together

Our test program, an application shell that would normally be your real program, is frmMain. It is derived from the pro01classes.frmApp form, which sets up a basic application window. The only thing we did to the UI was to add a menu to it. In the Help menu, we added two items: *Report a Bug* and *See My Bugs*. These are wired in the code, respectively, to frmBug and frmSeeBugs. All they do is load the forms and kick them off. Here is the code for one of them; the other is essentially the same:

```
' Handle the menu selection for viewing a list of bugs.
Private Sub MenuItem5_Click(ByVal sender As System.Object, _
```

```
        ByVal e As System.EventArgs) Handles MenuItem5.Click

        Dim f As New frmSeeBugs()
        f.ShowDialog()

    End Sub
```

The more interesting part is the technique used to store and expose the class values Version and ProdID. Presumably these are items you might want to be available all over the program, for such things as the About box, export file version identification, or in our case, bug reporting. We use the VB Shared Properties mechanism, which makes only one copy available for every instance of the containing class that is created. See the sidebar entitled "Shared Class Members" for details on how this mechanism works. For now, take a look at the code. First we declare the private class values, and then we make them available through the shared properties.

```
        ' Set up some constants for the product version and product ID.
        ' These are needed by the Web service to submit a new bug, but
        ' there's no need to bother the user with them.
        Private Const sVersion As String = "1.5"
        Private Const lProdID As Long = 3

        ' Make the Version and Product ID available as properties. They're
        ' shared properties, to make them easier to access.
        Public Shared ReadOnly Property Version() As String
            Get
                Return (sVersion)
            End Get
        End Property

        Public Shared ReadOnly Property ProdID() As Long
            Get
                Return (lProdID)
            End Get
        End Property
```

The constant definition is simple. The properties are set up as read-only because they will not be modified programmatically. Change the values of the constants to suit your own needs. The best part of this mechanism is that other classes—specifically frmBug, but any class could use them—and that you can reference the properties without creating an instance of the class. In frmBug, we pass these values to the Web service, even though frmBug know nothing about the instance of frmMain. The code is:

```
    frmMain.Version
    frmMain.ProdID
```

Simply precede the property name by the name of the class that contains the shared property. Look back at the code for frmBug, and you'll see the same code being passed into the Web service as for the last two parameters.

SHARED CLASS MEMBERS

Shared class members, including shared values, properties, methods, and variables, are a valuable mechanism to have in your repertoire if they are used properly. The basic idea behind them is that for every instance of a class created from one with a shared property, only one instance of the member is maintained. Here's an example.

We have created a class that accumulates a total called Accumulate. It adds to a shared variable called iTotal. The code would look something like this:

```
Public Class Accumulator

Private Shared iTotal As Int64

Public Shared Property Accumulate(ByVal iValue As Int64) As Int64
   Get
      Return iTotal
   End Get
   Set (ByVal Value As Int64)
      ITotal += Value
   End Set
End Property

End Class
```

Each instance of the class can add to the same total. We create two instances of the class, clsA and clsB. Then we make the following calls:

```
clsA.Accumulate = 50
clsB.Accumulate = 75
```

If we then display the Accumulate property (Get version) for each instance of the class, we will get the same result for both: 125. The actual storage of the shared properties and data is not directly associated with the class but is stored elsewhere. You simply access them through a class name. This mechanism is essentially what COM uses for its internal reference counting.

There is one other nice feature of shared members. They can be used without creating an instance of the class in which they are defined. For example, we could add something to that total in our example without using a class instance, and instead using only the name of the class, like this:

```
Accumulator.Accumulate = 100
```

If we did this after the other calls we listed, the total of the Accumulate property would be 225, regardless of who reported it.

This feature has many possibilities and is much like static members in C and C++. Use it carefully though; it's very easy to get this sort of thing messed up, resulting in unpredictable results and bugs that are hard to track down.

Try It Out

Now that everything is in place, make sure that frmMain is the starting point for the project by right-clicking on the project in the Solution Explorer. From the context menu, choose Properties. When the Properties window opens, select the frmMain item in the *Startup Object* combo box and click OK.

When that's done, click the VB Play button or press F5. The main form will display and look a great deal like Figure 3.18. Exercise it a little by selecting our bug-reporting services from the menu. The sample database on the CD-ROM had some example bugs in it, so you can use the features right away. If you're properly amazed and satisfied, you can walk around looking smug for a while. Tell people you know how to build Web services, and they'll either be duly impressed or look at you strangely. Whatever the case, you can now inflict your own Web services on the world.

Debugging Web Services

There are two ways you can debug a Web service using Visual Studio. Both are useful in different circumstances, and it's good to know them. You can either debug the service directly while you're working on it, or you can do it from the client while you're testing its interaction with the service.

Figure 3.18 The main form in action.

Debugging Web Services
the Really Easy Way

This is very simple; however, it puts the other method in context. While your Web service project is open (you can try it with the Vocab example we used earlier just to make it clear), set any breakpoints you might like to use. Then click the run button. This works much like any other project you might debug. VB loads your Web service into the browser. Once you click the Invoke button, the code is run and the breakpoints will cause execution to pause. This is pretty easy, but what do you do when you have the client project loaded? Read on.

Debugging Web Services
the Mostly Easy Way

The first step is to enable ASP.NET debugging ahead of time while your Web service project is open. The following steps explain how to do this:

1. Right-click on the project in Solution Explorer and select Properties.

2. In the Properties dialog, select *Debug* from the Configuration list box.

3. In the list on the bottom left, select the *Debugging* item.

4. Under *Debuggers*, make sure *ASP.NET Debugging* is checked.

Once this is done, save and build your project. Then load your client project into Visual Studio. At this stage, you can put a breakpoint on your call to any Web service method. When execution stops there, you can step into the Web service method (F10). The debugger will follow the SOAP request message to the Web service and actually load the code for the Web service and let you continue tracing execution.

This is really cool. When you consider how much of a pain it was to debug DCOM components from the client, you'll realize what an improvement this is. When I tried it, it worked the first time (pretty amazing for Beta software). I plan to be using it a great deal in the future.

Enhancing the Project

Web services are not only blindingly useful, they are also fun to work with, either using those that exist or building your own. You've had the 25-cent tour, and you've seen it applied to a complete project, including client code you can add to your own applications. Although the bug-reporting system is pretty nifty, there is plenty you could do to improve it.

This project could certainly be used as is, but there are things you can add to it to make it more robust and useful in a production environment. Here are some suggestions:

Add security.   When you complete Project 8, which deals with security, come back here and add integrated security to the Web service. This will prevent unauthorized reporting of bugs using someone else's name.

Make a class library for the client.   As we did with the first project, you can package up all the client code into a class library. This would make it much easier to include the client portion of the project in your application and would make it self-contained for easier distribution.

Fit your needs.   You can change the data fields around to suit your own needs. The fields included are obvious and general. It is likely, however, that you will have additional needs.

Keep users informed.   Add some functionality and data fields to keep track of the status of reported problems. As engineers make updates to the problems, they can update the data to reflect that. For example, as a bug is reviewed, you could set its status to Under Review and then later to Being Repaired or Deferred. Then allow the users to check on the status of the reports they have created.

Write an import/export.   If you already use a defect-tracking system, perhaps you could write an import/export module to move bugs reported by users in and out of a system that is already in place.

WHAT'S COMING NEXT

The next project will cover the .NET Remoting technology and use it in a project. Remoting is a server-based replacement for DCOM. It allows you to make calls to components across servers when Web services are not required or not appropriate. We'll also cover when to use it and when to use something else. The project will be fun as well.

Performance Testing with Remoting

Accessing functionality on other machines has always been a daunting challenge for the enterprise programmer. It is something that we need to do because there are many benefits to hosting functionality on a server and calling it from client computers. Better management and sharing of resources, easier deployment and maintenance, and improved performance, among others, are on the list. However, there are all kinds of problems that need to be overcome in order to call functionality across wires.

Microsoft has given us two major new mechanisms that allow you to call remote functionality. We just covered one of them, Web services, in the previous project. The other is called Remoting and is the topic of this project. We'll cover its benefits as well as its drawbacks.

THE PROBLEM:

All the programs you write, especially distributed programs, need to perform to your users' expectations. A slow program will never be used and your development efforts will be wasted. You can analyze performance yourself or using third-party tools. Many of the tools are expensive and take time to learn. You could also do your own performance testing, instrumenting your code, storing and tracking the results, and doing your own analysis. This also takes lots of time, but it has the advantage of allowing you to tune the kinds of performance testing you do.

To get sufficient performance data to be significant, you need a fair amount of data. Typically, you need to get a bunch of people working on the program to generate more performance data. This makes the problem of managing, collecting, and analyzing the performance data worse, now that you have many people creating it. How do we generate, collect, and analyze the performance data generated by a bunch of test personnel?

THE SOLUTION:

Our solution solves two problems. We reduce the time it takes to create the testing and instrumentation code by letting someone else do most of it. I did it for you by creating this project. Second, we manage the creation, storage, and analysis of the performance data by creating a remote component that your program can call in order to store the performance data in a remote database. The remote component will also do some analysis of the data for you. Our client program, included as part of this project, will retrieve and present this data for your review.

The Project

In this project, we'll be covering techniques that will allow you to call remote objects across wires from client to server. In the process, we might even help you test the performance of your applications. The project actually consists of the following components:

1. **The Remote Component.**   This little guy will sit on the server, allowing you to call it and make use of its services. This includes the ability to save performance data to the database, selectively retrieve performance data, and get some basic performance analysis.

2. **The Client Component.**   Once your own program has generated and stashed away all kinds of performance data, you'll have to do something with it. The client program we will build in this project will retrieve performance data and analysis information from the remote component and display it for you in useful ways.

3. **The Test Program.**   We will also create a test program that will stand in for your own applications that need performance testing. I will show you how to create a class that your programs can use to take care of most of the work of instrumenting your program with code to track performance data. You can use the class we create directly in your own applications.

By the time we're done, you'll be able to create your own remote components and test the performance of your applications.

You Will Need

✔ **Visual Studio .NET**

✔ **SQL Server (or other database)**

✔ **Internet Information Server**

✔ **The Microsoft Chart control version 2.0 (mschrt20.ocx)**

Remoting Overview

We've seen how Web services allow you to call remote functionality through the Web over HTTP wires. It's all very cool and fun, but it can't solve all our problems. When you aren't using the Web, you still need a way to call remote functionality. We used to have this in the form of DCOM, which would allow you to call components on another machine or in another process space. It worked, but it was a real pain to get the proxy portion of the component distributed properly. It also had real issues if you wanted to cross a firewall.

Remote Components

Building remote components is a little different from building DCOM components. Remote components, called *remotable objects*, are more flexible than DCOM components. They can work across different kinds of connections and share their resources better. Theoretically, remotable objects can work across diverse networks and even different operating systems. Remoting also supports the capability to tear down a component that is executing on one system, serialize it, ship it off to a component on another machine, reconstitute it, and continue execution. We'll talk about this more later.

If we were to simplify the architecture of Remoting to a mere paragraph, it might read something like this. A remote object sits over on a server somewhere. When your client creates an instance of the remote object, it is actually creating a proxy for the component. It is a stand-in component that looks exactly like the remote component to your program, but this component knows how to package your request and send it off to the actual remote component. It does this using a channel, which is a communication channel that you specify. The channel sends the request and any accompanying data across to the remote component, where it is reconstituted and interpreted for execution by the real component. The process is reversed to return data. The concept is not difficult, but it requires a fair amount of configuration to make it work. We'll be covering that later.

So how do you make a component remotable? There are two ways, one of which you will use more often as a VB programmer. First, your object can inherit from the *MarshalByRefObject* or *MarshalByValueObject* component. This is a standard part of the .NET namespace. The other way is to implement the ISerializable interface. Objects must be serializable in order to be sent through the Remoting system. Both of these techniques result in serializable objects.

TIP For objects to be remotable, or passed back and forth by the Remoting system, they must be serializable. These are also the only types of objects, besides intrinsic types, that can be returned to the client by remote functionality. However, one of the best objects for returning data of varying types and quantities is by passing back a DataSet. Can we still do this? Will we be hamstrung by this restriction? The answer is a pleasant No. The DataSet object inherits from MarshalByValueObject, which creates an object that can be serialized. So feel free to pass DataSets back from your remote objects, as we do it in this project.

As a VB programmer, the easiest way to create remotable objects is the inheritance route. For example, you could create a new remotable class like this:

```
Public Class RemoteMe
    Inherits MarshaByRefObject
```

Classes created in this way can be hosted as remote components and can also be passed around through the Remoting system.

Remoting Mechanics

Remoting involves several mechanisms and objects to make the whole thing work, including proxies, channels, configuration files, and a couple protocols. It seems complicated because there are several steps, but once it's explained, it becomes relatively easy. Here are the basic parts of the remote object creation process:

1. Build your remote component, inheriting from MarshalByRefObject.
2. Compile the component.
3. Create a configuration file for the component that defines the way the component will be called and activated.
4. Configure the component in IIS to make it available over HTTP.

Once these steps are complete, you can create clients to use the component.

Proxies

The proxy is a component that is called from your client on behalf of the remote component. It allows you to interact with the remote component as if it were right there on the local machine. You do not have to create the proxy yourself. It is handled by the Remoting system. The actual proxy that executes is generated when you create a new instance of the remote object, using New. Once the proxy is active, you can use the component like any other local component.

The proxy handles all sorts of details for you that you won't have to worry about but are necessary for Remoting to work properly. It deals with converting data to a form that can be marshaled, packaging your request into the correct format (using SOAP;

more on that shortly), identifying the channel to use, and sending your request to the right place. It also handles the reverse process, receiving the results and data from requests that have been sent out. You should only have to worry about the proxy if you need to do low-level remote programming, managing channels and requests yourself.

Channels

Channels are the communication mechanisms used by Remoting to pass requests and data back and forth between clients and remote objects. Using channels, you can specify which protocol and port should be used for remote communication. You'll deal with channels when creating configuration files, which I'll cover shortly.

Channels have to be created and registered with the Remoting system before any remote objects are called across them. You can do this manually, using a series of calls and figuring out all the correct information to send them, or you can make a single call to a very handy method in the .NET framework called *RemotingConfiguration.Configure*. You pass this method the name of a configuration file that contains information about how to set up channels and where the remote object is located. It takes care of channel registration and other details that we don't want to mess with. Once this method is called, you can use your remote objects.

SOAP

How do all these request messages get passed around, and in what form? The raw format is XML, but the context of the XML is defined by SOAP. It defines a protocol for formatting requests for functionality, and related data, into a standard form that can be understood by anyone who knows SOAP.

When using the HTTP channel for transporting remote messages, SOAP is the protocol used. You don't have to worry about creating your own SOAP messages; the proxy takes care of this for you. You also have the option of using a separate binary formatter for your messages, but the SOAP method handles most situations.

Single Call versus Singleton

Remote components can operate under two modes: Single Call and Singleton. Pick the one that best suits your needs, though Single Call will be the most prominent.

Single Call components are called, hang around for a while, usually long enough to do their job, and then expire. They are then garbage collected and removed from memory. This is perfect for service-oriented functions that do a job for you and are no longer needed.

Singleton components are just like the singleton design pattern they teach in computer science. They are single-instance components. Only one instance is ever created at a time and is shared by various callers. Singleton components are ideal for components that have an ongoing job to do, regardless of who is calling it. For example, you might have a component that constantly accumulates a value from many different callers. This component would have to stick around, maintaining the count and adding to it when another caller had something to add.

Both of these types of components are supported by Remoting and are specified in a configuration file. Although you can change a component's mode in a configuration file, you will certainly have to decide what mode it will operate in before it is created. This sort of decision happens at design time.

> **TIP**
> If you make a remote singleton class, you will potentially have more than one client trying to execute the same code simultaneously over the same thread. This is bad. It could easily corrupt what your class is trying to do. Microsoft thought of this already and made it easy to allow only one caller access to the sensitive code at a time. You use a statement called SyncLock to keep others out, like this:

```
SyncLock Me
      ' Sensitive code
End SyncLock
```

Any code within the SyncLock will only be executed by a single process at a single time. Use it for safety.

Configuration Files

You will need to create two configuration files when developing remote components: one for the remote component, and another for the client program. They are both formatted as XML, which we'll see a great deal of in Project 7, but for now, think of them as text files. Let's take a look at each one.

The Remote Component Configuration File

The component itself requires a configuration file that tells the server how to create and execute the component. You define the name of the component and assembly here and specify its mode, Single Call or Singleton. A simple example looks like this:

```
<configuration>
    <system.runtime.remoting>
        <application>
            <service>
                <wellknown mode="SingleCall"
                 type="prj04.ExampleSvc, prj04ex"
                 objectURI="prj04.soap">
            </service>
        </application>
    </system.runtime.remoting>
</configuration>
```

The part where the mode is specified is obvious. You could also specify Singleton here. The *type* attribute specifies two things separated by a comma: the type of the service/component and the assembly name. For the objectURI, which is what remote objects connect to, you can insert the name of the assembly with a .soap extension.

This file is located in the virtual directory where the component will be located and is always called web.config. We'll see an example of this shortly.

The Client Configuration File

The client also needs to know how to set up channels and communicate with the remote component. A configuration file is used for this. It is typically named using the assembly name and a .config extension. For example, a client program called prj04.exe would have a configuration file named prj04.exe.config. An example of a client configuration file looks like this:

```
<configuration>
    <system.runtime.remoting>
        <application name="prj04">
            <client url="http://localhost/prj04">
                <wellknown type="prj04.ExampleSvc, prj04"
                url="http://localhost/prj04/prj04.soap" />
            </client>
            <channels>
                <channel type="System.Runtime.Remoting.Channels.
                Http.HttpChannel, System.Runtime.Remoting />
            </channels>
        </application>
    </system.runtime.remoting>
</configuration>
```

The client section of this file specifies the URL to the remote component, as well as its type and assembly name. The channels section specifies which channel types should be configured for use by the program. You can change the URLs to match those that you set up for your own components. The channel statement can be used directly, as long as you want to use the HTTP channel.

A Remoting Walkthrough

I'm going to take you through the steps of creating a simple remote component and client example and making it work. We will:

1. Create the remote component.
2. Create the remote component configuration file.
3. Configure the component in IIS.
4. Create the client program.
5. Create the client configuration file.
6. Run it.

The Remote Component

Our component is very simple. It will contain a single method that will return a random fortune to help guide you through your day. Create a new Class Library project in Visual Studio, and name it prj04fortune. Change the name of the class to FortuneSvc. Add code to make sure it inherits from MarshalByRefObject. Add the code to return a random fortune. The listing should look like this:

```
Public Class FortuneSvc
    Inherits MarshalByRefObject

    Public Function Fortune() As String

        Dim i As Integer
        Randomize(Timer)
        i = Int(Rnd(1) * 4) + 1
        Select Case i
            Case 1
                Fortune = "You will be a great artist one day. " & _
                          "At least, that's what all had hoped."
            Case 2
                Fortune = "Stay away from dogs. They think you look " & _
                          "like dinner."
            Case 3
                Fortune = "You will soon meet a tall, dark stranger. " & _
                          "From Neptune."
            Case 4
                Fortune = "Stay in and watch videos tonight. " & _
                          "Danger lurks at the singles bars."
        End Select

    End Function

End Class
```

Compile the component and you're done with that step.

The Remote Component Configuration File

We need to create a file named web.config in the directory *above* the bin directory. This will be used by IIS and the Remoting system. The file should look like this:

```
<configuration>
  <system.runtime.remoting>
    <application>

      <service>
        <wellknown mode="SingleCall"
```

```
        type="prj04fortune.FortuneSvc, prj04fortune"
        objectUri="prj04fortune.soap" />
    </service>

  </application>
 </system.runtime.remoting>
</configuration>
```

Configure the Component in IIS

The last step for the component is to get it set up in IIS so that it can function over HTTP. Open up the Internet Services Manager and select the Default Web Site. From the Actions menu, add a new virtual directory. Name it prj04fortune and on the next wizard panel, enter the path to the DLL we just built, up to but not including the BIN subdirectory. Finish off the wizard with defaults. When it is complete, you should be able to see the contents of the directory, including the web.config file we just created. And that takes care of that.

Create the Client Program

We need a little client program to test out our component. Create a new WinForms project in Visual Studio and name it whatever you like. The first step is to add a reference to the remote component. Point to your local copy and add the reference to the project.

Next, create a form with two buttons, one to get a fortune and one to quit. Add a label to the form that will display our fortune once we get it. Add the following method to handle the Fortune button click, which will do most of our Remoting work.

```
Private Sub btnFortune_Click(ByVal sender As System.Object, _
    ByVal e As System.EventArgs) Handles btnFortune.Click

    Try
        Dim svcFortune As New prj04fortune.FortuneSvc()
        lblFortune.Text = svcFortune.Fortune()
    Catch ex As Exception
        MsgBox(ex.Message())
    End Try

End Sub
```

The code creates an instance of our remote component, which actually creates a proxy to the remote component. The program doesn't care, however. It just makes the calls. Once the object is created, we call the Fortune method and assign the return value to the label. We still need another call. Before any of this will work, we need to set up the Remoting environment. Do this in the Form Load event, like this:

```
Private Sub Form1_Load(ByVal sender As System.Object, ByVal e As
System.EventArgs) Handles MyBase.Load

    Try
        Dim sCfgFilename As String = "prj04fortune.exe.config"
        RemotingConfiguration.Configure(sCfgFilename)
    Catch ex As Exception
        MsgBox(ex.Message())
    End Try

End Sub
```

We pass the name of our configuration file (which we will create momentarily) to the RemotingConfiguration.Configure method. This takes care of our channels and other configuration issues. We are almost ready to run the program.

The Client Configuration File

Create a text file in the same directory as your assembly (executable). This should be the BIN subdirectory under your project directory. The file should contain the following:

```
<configuration>
  <system.runtime.remoting>
    <application name="prj04fortune">
      <client url="http://localhost/prj04fortune">
        <wellknown type="prj04fortune.FortuneSvc, prj04fortune"
        url="http://localhost/prj04fortune/prj04fortune.soap" />
      </client>
      <channels>
        <channel
         type="System.Runtime.Remoting.Channels.Http.HttpChannel,
         System.Runtime.Remoting" />
      </channels>
    </application>
  </system.runtime.remoting>
</configuration>
```

Once this file is in place, we should be all set.

Run It

If everything is configured correctly, you should be able to run the client program now. As soon as it is run, the Remoting environment will be configured. Then the form will be displayed and you can click the Fortune button. Your results should resemble Figure 4.1.

Figure 4.1   The fortune example executing.

Is It Really Working?

Notice that a copy of the remote component is sitting inconspicuously in the BIN directory for the client. It was placed here when you added a reference to the remote component to your client project. In fact, if you delete or rename it, the client program will no longer work. Why is this, and what's going on?

During both compilation and runtime, the client needs this for type information. It actually executes the remote component. Try these steps to verify that the remote component is being called and not the local one:

1. Rename the copy of the remote component in the client's BIN directory to something else so that it won't get overwritten later.

2. Open the component project and change the functionality to something different. I commented out the functionality inside the Fortune method so it wouldn't do anything, just return an empty string. Feel free to return something else. Rebuild the component.

3. Open the client project again and rebuild it. This will create a new copy of the new remote component in the local client BIN directory.

4. Delete the new copy of the DLL in the BIN directory and change the old one back to its original name. Now you have the original client DLL, which works correctly in the client BIN directory, and the new version of the client DLL in the remote Web directory, which does nothing.

5. Run the client. You should *not* get a normal fortune string when you click the Fortune button.

This process verifies that the remote component is being called. If you are having any doubts about your setup or think that the components are not configured correctly, you can use this process to test them out.

Let's Start the Project

We will be constructing a remote component that is used for tracking performance data and a client to review and present that data; we will also create a test application to illustrate usage and timing techniques. The following subprojects are involved:

The remote component, prj04remote.   This is the remote part. It has three methods. The first allows your client to submit a record of performance data, which will be saved to the database. The second retrieves all or selected performance data based on parameters you pass to it. The third is the most interesting; it loads performance data and does some basic analysis on it.

The client program, prj04client.   This program is used once you have some performance data piled up, and it helps you analyze the data. It allows you to review the raw data, and it presents the data in text form, as well as in a nice graph. This will illustrate the client usage of part of the remote component's functionality. It should also make short work of analyzing your performance data.

The client test program, prj04app.   This program will act as a stand-in for your own applications. It simulates functionality of varying durations and illustrates how to use the logging portions of the remote component. As part of the application, we will also build a local class that will make it very easy to do the timing and log the results. This class could be used by any of your own applications. It's very cool indeed.

The Database

Before we dive into the actual program, we need to get our database set up. There is a version of the database, along with some sample data, on the accompanying CD-ROM. It is called prj04.mdb and is a Microsoft Access database. You can easily import it into SQL Server using techniques described in previous chapters.

The database is very simple and consists of only one table, PerfData. It has columns defined to hold various data related to application performance. Table 4.1 describes the fields and their purpose.

Table 4.1   Database Columns and Their Purpose

COLUMN NAME	DATA TYPE	PURPOSE
ID	bigint	Assigns a unique ID to the row. This is set up as an Identity column, so we don't have to supply it ourselves. It will increment automatically. It is also the primary key on the table.
SessionID	char(50)	When an application executes, and performance data is collected, we want to associate all the performance data with that same run of the application. We use a GUID for this session ID, which the client generates and passes to the database.
Username	char(20)	This is the user name extracted from the operating system on the client, and it is passed to the database. We use it for recordkeeping purposes.
FunctionName	char(50)	This is a string that describes the function being timed. It is used to aggregate data based on what is being tested.
CompletedDate	datetime	The date and time that the function completed its timing run are stored here. They can be used to help group performance data based on similar timeframes.
ElapsedMillisecs	bigint	The actual performance data. It is the elapsed time, in milliseconds, that the function took to execute.

The Remote Component

As mentioned, this component is the remote part and takes care of logging, data retrieval, and data analysis. You can begin by creating a new Class Library project and naming it prj04remote. Rename the default Class1 to prj04svc and add code to make it inherit from MarshalByRefObject. Now we're set up to add real code.

We'll be working with the database, so we'll import the SqlClient namespace and put in a connection string. The code follows; make sure you change the connection string to match your own server.

```
Imports System.Data.SqlClient

Public Class prj04svc
    Inherits MarshalByRefObject

    Private Const CONNSTR As String = "PERSIST SECURITY INFO=False; " & _
        "DATA SOURCE=tony; INITIAL CATALOG=prj04; UID=sa; PWD=;"
```

Next we'll save a performance data record sent to us by the client. The client will be passing the fields to us as method parameters. It's pretty straightforward ADO work, but I'll show you all the code and then discuss any interesting points.

```
Public Sub SavePerfData( _
    ByVal sUser As String, _
    ByVal sFunction As String, _
    ByVal dtExecDate As Date, _
    ByVal iElapsed As Int32, _
    ByVal sSession As String)

    ' Accept the data and load it into the database. Simple.
    Dim conn As New SqlConnection(CONNSTR)
    Dim sSQL As String
    Dim cmd As New SqlCommand()

    ' Define our INSERT statement using the passed-in parameters
    ' as values.
    sSQL = "INSERT INTO PerfData (SessionID, Username, " & _
        "FunctionName, CompleteDate, ElapsedMillisecs) " & _
        "VALUES ('" & sSession & "', '" & sUser & "', '" & _
        sFunction & _
        "', '" & dtExecDate & "', " & iElapsed & ")"
    Try
        cmd.Connection = conn
        cmd.CommandText = sSQL
        conn.Open()
        cmd.ExecuteNonQuery()
        conn.Close()
    Catch ex As SqlException
        conn.Close()
        Throw ex
    End Try

End Sub
```

We construct a SQL INSERT statement from the parameters passed in to the method. It is written to the database using the ExecuteNonQuery method of the SqlCommand object. That's about it. Saving the data is the simple part.

Retrieving the data is only slightly more complicated, because we allow selective retrieval of the data. The parameters passed in are all optional, and if supplied, will tell us how to restrict the data.

```
Public Function GetPerfData( _
    Optional ByVal dtStartDate As Date = #12:00:00 AM#, _
    Optional ByVal dtEndDate As Date = #12:00:00 AM#, _
    Optional ByVal sUser As String = "", _
    Optional ByVal sFunction As String = "") As DataSet

    ' Local data access objects.
    Dim conn As New SqlConnection(CONNSTR)
    Dim ds As New DataSet()
    Dim sSQL As String
    Dim sWhere As String

    ' Set up the SQL.
    sSQL = "SELECT * FROM PerfData "

    ' Set up the lower date range.
    If dtStartDate > #12:00:00 AM# Then
        sWhere = "WHERE RTRIM(CompleteDate) >= '" & dtStartDate & "'"
    End If

    ' Set up the upper date range.
    If dtEndDate > #12:00:00 AM# And dtEndDate > dtStartDate Then
        If Len(sWhere) > 0 Then
            sWhere += " AND RTRIM(CompleteDate) <= '" & _
                    dtEndDate & "'"
        Else
            sWhere = "WHERE RTRIM(CompleteDate) <= '" & _
                    dtEndDate & "'"
        End If
    End If

    ' Set the where clause for the username.
    If Len(sUser) > 0 Then
        If Len(sWhere) > 0 Then
            sWhere += " AND RTRIM(Username) = '" & sUser & "'"
        Else
            sWhere = "WHERE RTRIM(Username) = '" & sUser & "'"
        End If
    End If

    ' Set the where clause for the requested function name.
    If Len(sFunction) > 0 Then
        If Len(sWhere) > 0 Then
```

```
                    sWhere += " AND RTRIM(FunctionName) = '" & sFunction & "'"
                Else
                    sWhere = "WHERE RTRIM(FunctionName) = '" & sFunction & "'"
                End If
            End If


            ' Tack on the where clause.
            sSQL += sWhere


            ' Load the data.
            Try
                Dim da As New SqlDataAdapter(sSQL, CONNSTR)
                conn.Open()
                da.Fill(ds, "perfdata")
                conn.Close()
            Catch ex As SqlException
                conn.Close()
                Throw ex
            End Try


            Return (ds)


        End Function
```

If a beginning date is supplied, we will only retrieve data later than that date. If an end date is supplied, we only retrieve data earlier than that date. If a username is supplied, only records that match that username will be retrieved. The same goes for the FunctionName. The bulk of the GetPerfData method is dedicated to building the WHERE clause based on these parameters.

Once the WHERE clause is constructed, we simply retrieve the data using a DataAdapter. Lastly, we return the DataSet to the caller. Remember that DataSets are derived from MarshalByValueObject, and this can be serialized for Remoting.

The code for the Analysis is more complex but works well. We will be calculating Minimum, Maximum, and Average values for all the data by FunctionName. Therefore, we need to get data back from the database by function name for all the function names. There are two steps in this process. First, we load a list of unique function names that currently reside in the database. Second, this list is used to load performance data for each function name that we just loaded. Take a look at the code, then we'll talk.

```
        Public Function BasicStats() As DataSet

            Dim conn As New SqlConnection(CONNSTR)
            Dim dsFunctions As New DataSet()    ' Holds returned functions
            Dim dsData As New DataSet()         ' Holds all data for a
                                                    function
            Dim dsStats As New DataSet()        ' Our return DataSet
            Dim sSQL As String
```

```
Dim sWhere As String
Dim cmd As New SqlCommand()

' Get the list of functions we need to process.
sSQL = "SELECT DISTINCT FunctionName FROM PerfData"
Dim da As New SqlDataAdapter(sSQL, CONNSTR)
Try
    conn.Open()
    da.Fill(dsFunctions, "functions")
Catch ex As SqlException
    conn.Close()
    Throw ex
End Try

' Get our return DataSet ready to be filled with stats.
Dim dt As New DataTable("stats")
dt.Columns.Add("FunctionName", _
    System.Type.GetType("System.String"))
dt.Columns.Add("Avg", System.Type.GetType("System.Double"))
dt.Columns.Add("Min", System.Type.GetType("System.Double"))
dt.Columns.Add("Max", System.Type.GetType("System.Double"))
dsStats.Tables.Add(dt)

' For each row in the Functions list, load all records
' that match its name. Calculate stats for each name.
Dim FunctionRow As DataRow
Dim aRow As DataRow
Dim avg As Double
Dim min As Double
Dim max As Double
Dim iElapsed As Int32

' Loop through each function, getting all records for that
' function and calculating stats.
Try
    Dim tempRow As DataRow
    For Each FunctionRow In dsFunctions.Tables("functions").Rows
        ' Get the SQL statement ready and load performance data
        ' for the specified function name.
        sSQL = "SELECT * FROM PerfData " & _
                "WHERE RTRIM(FunctionName)='" & _
                "RTrim(FunctionRow("FunctionName")) & "'"
        Try
            da.SelectCommand.CommandText = sSQL
            da.Fill(dsData, "perfdata")
        Catch ex As SqlException
            conn.Close()
            Throw (ex)
        End Try

        ' Clear our statistics accumulators.
```

```
        avg = 0
        min = 999999999999
        max = 0

        ' Go through each row in the dataset and
        ' accumulate statistical information.
        For Each aRow In dsData.Tables("perfdata").Rows
            iElapsed = CInt(aRow("ElapsedMillisecs"))
            avg += CDbl(iElapsed)
            If iElapsed > max Then
                max = iElapsed
            End If
            If iElapsed < min Then
                min = iElapsed
            End If
        Next
        ' Final average calc.
        avg /= dsData.Tables("perfdata").Rows.Count

        ' Load the data for this function into the dataset.
        dsData.Tables(0).Clear()    ' Get ready for the next
        tempRow = dsStats.Tables(0).NewRow
        tempRow("FunctionName") = _
            Trim(FunctionRow("FunctionName"))
        tempRow("Avg") = avg
        tempRow("Min") = min
        tempRow("Max") = max
        dsStats.Tables(0).Rows.Add(tempRow)
    Next
Catch ex As Exception
    conn.Close()
    Throw (ex)
End Try

conn.Close()
Return (dsStats)

    End Function
```

As mentioned, we first need a list of function names from the database. However, we need a unique list with no repeats. The database can take care of this for us, using the DISTINCT clause, as shown:

```
SELECT DISTINCT FunctionName FROM PerfData
```

This will not load the same name twice, so we'll only get a list of unique names. Once the list is loaded, we need to loop through it, processing each name and loading all performance data for each name. We create a DataTable object and then create four new columns for it: FunctionName, Avg, Min, and Max. We will be adding rows of data to it later.

After the performance data for a given name is loaded, we have to deal with it. This means that we have to pack it into a DataSet for return to the caller. We are creating a DataSet manually, setting up a table with columns and stuffing data into it.

The For..Each loop, which iterates through the FunctionNames, starts. We construct a SQL statement based on the current FunctionName and load the data. Once the rows for that function name are loaded, we have to extract the data for each row and process it. We use another For..Each loop to navigate the date and deal with it. This is what we do for the elapsed time (duration) of each row:

- For the Average calculation, we simply accumulate the elapsed time value. When the For..Each loop is complete, we can use it to calculate the average for that FunctionName.

- If the value is lower than our Min value, we assign the new value to the Min variable. Each value is checked so that we find the lowest one and save it.

- If the value is higher than our currently stored Max value, we assign the new value to the Max variable.

The processing and calculating of a given function name is done. Now we have to store the information in our manually created DataSet. The code shows how to do this using a temporary DataRow object. Once that's complete, we're done and ready for the next function name. When all the function names are done, we can return the DataSet to the caller.

If we ever need to modify the code here, or decide to add to its functionality, it will be easy to redeploy because we're hosting it on a single server. Clients need only to call it.

Component Configuration

We need a web.config file in the project directory (not the BIN directory) for the component. Our config file should look like this:

```
<configuration>
  <system.runtime.remoting>
    <application>

      <service>
        <wellknown mode="SingleCall"
          type="prj04remote.prj04svc,prj04remote"
          objectUri="prj04remote.soap" />
      </service>

    </application>
  </system.runtime.remoting>
</configuration>
```

Lastly, we must configure the component in IIS, just like we did for the walkthrough example. Open Internet Services Manager, select the Default Web Site, and select New Virtual Directory from the Actions menu. Name the virtual directory prj04remote, and point it to the directory where the project is, up to but not including the BIN directory. The component is now ready for remote use.

The Client Program

Now that we can store, retrieve, and analyze performance data, we need to do something with it. Presumably we would like to look at it in order to improve the performance of our software. To make this easier, as well as illustrate how to use the remote component, we will create a data viewer that shows the data and the analysis results. We'll even graph it for you.

Start by creating a new WinForms project in Visual Studio. Name it prj04client. Rename the main form to frmMain. Now add a reference to our remote component so that we can use it. Right-click on the References section in the Solution Explorer, and from the context menu, select Add Reference. Browse to the location where you created the remote component and its BIN directory, and add the reference.

Drop a few controls onto the form, specifically those listed in Table 4.2. Once they are in place, we'll start adding some really interesting code.

Start the code by importing the SqlClient and Remoting namespaces, as follows:

```
Imports System.Runtime.Remoting
Imports System.Data.SqlClient
```

The Remoting namespace will give us easy access to the RemoteConfiguration object. We'll also be doing some data work, so the SqlClient namespace is useful.

When the form is loaded, we take care of a couple details. We center the form in the window and set the caption on the DataGrid:

```
Private Sub frmMain_Load(ByVal sender As System.Object, _
    ByVal e As System.EventArgs) Handles MyBase.Load

    dgPerfData.CaptionText = "Click Get Data button..."
    Me.CenterToScreen()

End Sub
```

Table 4.2 The Controls for the Main Form

CONTROL	NAME	PROPERTIES
Label	LblTitle	Text="Performance Data and Statistics", AutoSize=True, Font=Arial 12pt Bold
Button	btnData	Text="Get Data", Anchor=Bottom, Left, FlatStyle=Popup
Button	btnStats	Text="Get Stats", Anchor=Bottom, Left, FlatStyle=Popup
Button	btnDone	Text="Done", Anchor=Bottom, Right, FlatStyle=Popup
DataGrid	dgPerfData	Anchor=Top, Bottom, Left, Right

When the Get Data button is clicked, we want to load all the performance data from the database into the DataGrid. The remote component will take care of retrieving the data and sending it to our client. We'll handle putting it into the grid as follows:

```
Private Sub btnData_Click(ByVal sender As System.Object,
    ByVal e As System.EventArgs) Handles btnData.Click

    Dim rc As New prj04remote.prj04svc()   ' Our remote component
    Dim ds As DataSet

    Try
        ' Get the data
        ds = rc.GetPerfData()
        ' Bind it to the grid
        dgPerfData.SetDataBinding(ds, "perfdata")
        ' Title the grid
        dgPerfData.CaptionText = "Performance Data"
    Catch ex As Exception
        ' Oops...
        MsgBox(ex.Message())
    End Try

End Sub
```

Notice that we create an instance of our remote component just like we would create any other local component. The GetPerfData method in the remote component is called, which returns a DataSet that contains all the raw performance data.

We then bind that DataSet to the DataGrid using a single statement. The DataGrid supplies a method called SetDataBindings that takes a DataSet and the name of a table to use within that DataSet. Once the data is loaded, we change the caption of the DataGrid to indicate what data was being displayed.

Lastly, we show our second form, for statistics display, when the Get Stats button is clicked. The form is loaded and displayed and then it takes over dealing with the statistical display. Figure 4.2 shows what the form looks like when running and loaded with data.

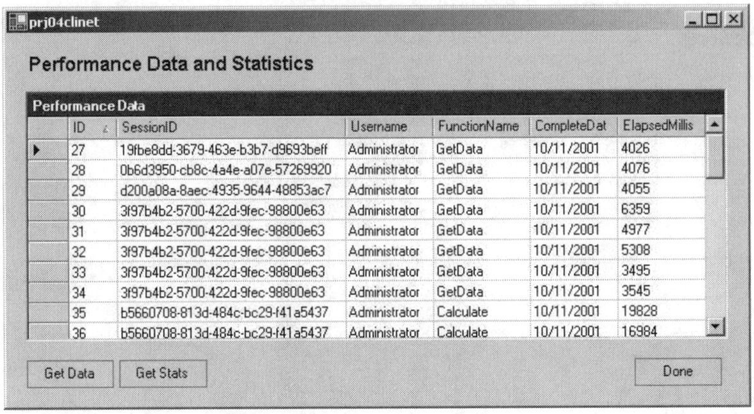

Figure 4.2   The Executing prj04client Program.

The Statistics Form

The real fun in this program is the statistics form. It shows the statistics by function name in text form as well as in a cute little graph that helps you visualize the data at a glance. It does most of its work in the form load event. Start by adding a new form to the project, naming it frmStats, and dropping controls into it as listed in Table 4.3.

You will have to add the chart control to the toolbox by right-clicking on the toolbox and from the context menu, select Customize Toolbox. From the dialog, illustrated in Figure 4.3, and click the browse button. Locate the file mschrt20.ocx, which should be hiding out in your Windows\System32 directory. If the control is already listed in the dialog, just check it on.

Table 4.3   The frmStats Controls

CONTROL	NAME	PROPERTIES
Button	btnDone	Text="Done", Anchor=Bottom, Right
Label	Label1	Text="Performance Chart:"
Label	lblTextTitle	Text="Performance Data:"
Label	lblTitle	Text="Performance Statistics", Font=Arial 12pt Bold
MSChart	chtStats	Anchor=Top, Bottom, Left, Right
RadioButton	rb2D	Text="2D", Anchor=Top, Right
RadioButton	rb3D	Text="3D", Anchor=Top, Right
TextBox	tbStats	Text="", Anchor=Top, Bottom, Left, MultiLine=True, ScrollBars=Vertical

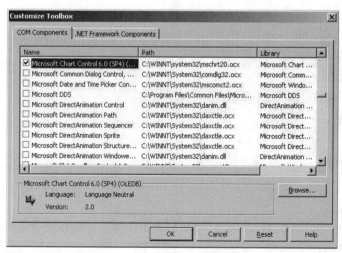

Figure 4.3   The Customize Toolbox Dialog.

Once the form is set up, you can start entering code behind it. Start by doing a little groundwork with namespaces and class variable:

```
Imports System.Data.SqlClient

Public Class frmStats
    Inherits System.Windows.Forms.Form

    Private bLoadDone As Boolean = False
```

The local class variable bLoadDone is used to indicate that all the work in the form load event is done. This is important because if we try to change the chart type before the load is done (which occurs automatically once before the form load event is complete), then we'll get a nice NULL error and a crash.

One of the features that our form supports is the ability to switch between a 2D and a 3D chart. We use radio buttons to do this, and we need events to handle it and make the change. The following code takes care of this.

```
Private Sub rb3D_CheckedChanged(ByVal sender As System.Object, _
    ByVal e As System.EventArgs) Handles rb3D.CheckedChanged

    If bLoadDone Then
        SetChartType()
    End If

End Sub

Private Sub rb2D_CheckedChanged(ByVal sender As System.Object, _
    ByVal e As System.EventArgs) Handles rb2D.CheckedChanged

    If bLoadDone Then
        SetChartType()
    End If

End Sub

Private Sub SetChartType()

    If rb3D.Checked Then
        chtStats.chartType = _
            MSChart20Lib.VtChChartType.VtChChartType3dBar
    Else
        chtStats.chartType = _
            MSChart20Lib.VtChChartType.VtChChartType2dBar
    End If

End Sub
```

The most interesting part of the code is the load event, where all the data retrieval and processing takes place. Here's the code you should add to the load event:

```
Private Sub frmStats_Load(ByVal sender As System.Object, _
    ByVal e As System.EventArgs) Handles MyBase.Load

    Dim ds As DataSet                        ' Hold returned perf
                                             data.
    Dim rc As New prj04remote.prj04svc()     ' Our remote component.
    Dim s As String

    RemotingConfiguration.Configure("prj04client.exe.config")
    Me.CenterToScreen()

    ' Load the statistics from the remote component.
    Try
        ds = rc.BasicStats()
    Catch ex As Exception
        MsgBox(ex.Message())
        Me.Close()
    End Try

    ' Fill in the text data. As long as we're looping through
    ' the data, build the data array for the chart.
    Dim arrChartData(ds.Tables(0).Rows.Count, 5) As String
    Dim i As Int32 = 0
    Dim aRow As DataRow

    ' This loop processes a row of data at a time. Each row
    ' equates to a single function for which performance
    ' statistics are being reported.
    For Each aRow In ds.Tables(0).Rows
        ' Set up the text display string for this function.
        s &= "Function: " & aRow("FunctionName") & vbCrLf
        s &= "  • Average time (ms): " & CStr(aRow("Avg")) & vbCrLf
        s &= "  • Min time (ms): " & CStr(aRow("Min")) & vbCrLf
        s &= "  • Max time (ms): " & CStr(aRow("Max")) & -
            vbCrLf & vbCrLf

        ' Collect chart data for this function.
        arrChartData(i, 0) = aRow("FunctionName")
        arrChartData(i, 1) = CStr(aRow("Min"))
        arrChartData(i, 2) = CStr(aRow("Avg"))
        arrChartData(i, 3) = CStr(aRow("Max"))
        i += 1     ' Next element in chart data array
    Next

    tbStats.Text = s

    ' Set up and fill in the chart.
    chtStats.ChartData = arrChartData
    chtStats.RowCount = ds.Tables(0).Rows.Count
    chtStats.ColumnCount = 3
    chtStats.ShowLegend = True

    ' Set up the column labels for the chart
    For i = 1 To chtStats.ColumnCount
        chtStats.Column = i
```

```
      Select Case i
          Case 1 : chtStats.ColumnLabel = "Min"
          Case 2 : chtStats.ColumnLabel = "Avg"
          Case 3 : chtStats.ColumnLabel = "Max"
      End Select
  Next i

  ' Now that we're done loading the form, it's OK to
  ' change the chart type.
  bLoadDone = True

End Sub
```

The first and all-important step is to set up the Remoting environment. Our call to RemotingConfiguration.Configure passes in the name of our configuration file, which is loaded and used to prepare our program for remote operations.

Then we create an instance of the remote component and call its BasicStats method to get the analyzed data. Once that's done, we need to extract it from the DataSet and do two things with it: Fill it into the text box and stuff it into the chart control. We iterate through each row in the DataSet and format a string that will go into the textbox. We keep adding to that string for each row in the DataSet. Once we have finished moving through the data, we'll pass it off to the control. We also fill the data into a two-dimensional array that we will hand off to the control when we're done.

After the loop is complete, we need to set up the chart control. We hand off the data array that we built to the control's ChartData property. We set the row count and turn on the legend. Lastly, we add some text labels to the chart columns so that they display correctly. Set our done flag and we're finished. Figure 4.4 shows what the form looks like when it is running and loaded with performance data. You can resize this form and enlarge the graph to see it better. Switch it to 2D graph mode for a more analytical view of the data, as shown in Figure 4.5.

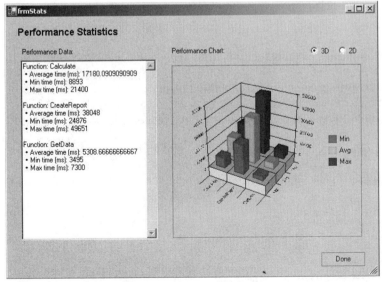

Figure 4.4 The frmStats Form during Execution.

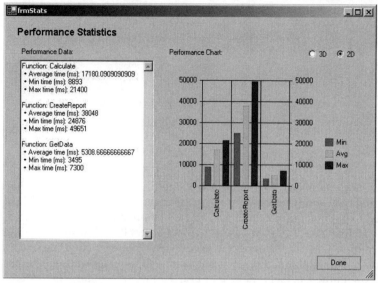

Figure 4.5   The frmStats Form with a 2D Graph.

The Configuration File

The last detail is the configuration file for the client. The following listing for the file prj04client.exe.config shows what it should be for this application. Make sure it goes in the project's BIN subdirectory.

```
<configuration>
  <system.runtime.remoting>
    <application name="prj04client">

      <client url="http://localhost/prj04remote">
        <wellknown type="prj04remote.prj04Svc, prj04remote"
         url="http://localhost/prj04remote/prj04remote.soap" />
      </client>

      <channels>
        <channel
          type="System.Runtime.Remoting.Channels.Http.HttpChannel,
          System.Runtime.Remoting" />
      </channels>

    </application>
  </system.runtime.remoting>
</configuration>
```

The Test Program

Last in our lineup of Remoting-related programs is the test application. It will act as the program being timed, such as your own application. It will also illustrate techniques for doing the timing and using the remote component. In addition, we create a very handy class that does most of the work for you.

The application is a single form that has three main buttons. Clicking one of the buttons will simulate a function being run, each button creating delays of varying lengths. When the function simulation completes, performance data for the function will be sent to the remote component for saving to the database.

Start by creating a new WinForms project, naming it prj04app. Add a reference to our remote component as we did with the client application. Then add controls to the form as detailed in Table 4.4.

The most important part of this program is the internal PerfLogger class. This class can be extracted and used in your own programs. It takes cares of the details of the timing and logging of data. Let's look at the code and then discuss it.

Table 4.4   The Controls on the Test Program Form

CONTROL	NAME	PROPERTIES
Button	btnDone	Text="Done"
Button	btnF1	Text="GetData Function"
Button	btnF2	Text="Calculate Function"
Button	btnF3	Text="CreateReport Function"
Label	Label1	Text=" Generates random short-duration performance data for a function called GetData."
Label	Label2	Text=" Generates random medium-duration performance data for a function called Calculate."
Label	Label3	Text=" Generates random long-duration performance data for a function called CreateReport."
Label	lblTitle	Text="Remoting Test Application", Font=Arial 12pt Bold
Label	lblStatus	Text="Ready.", Font=Bold

```
Private Class PerfLogger

    Private gSessionID As Guid          ' Holds our session ID.
    Private iStart As Int32 = 0         ' Holds the start time.
    Private iEnd As Int32 = 0           ' Holds the end time.
    Private sFuncName As String = ""    ' Name of the timed. function
    Private bLoggingOn As Boolean       ' Should we log or not?

    Public Sub New()

        gSessionID = Guid.NewGuid()
        bLoggingOn = True

    End Sub

    ' Call this function to start a new timing run.
    Public Sub StartTiming(ByVal sFunction As String)

        ' Store the name of the function we're about to
        ' time and create a starting time mark.
        If bLoggingOn Then
            sFuncName = sFunction
            iStart = CInt(Timer() * 1000)
        End If

    End Sub

    ' This property turns loggin on or off. Turn it on
    ' for performance testing and off for release versions
    ' of your application.
    Public Property LoggingOn() As Boolean
        Get
            LoggingOn = bLoggingOn
        End Get
        Set(ByVal Value As Boolean)
            bLoggingOn = Value
        End Set
    End Property

    ' This method stops the timing run, calculates the
    ' elapsed time, and reports the new data to the
    ' remote component for saving to the database.
    Public Function StopTiming() As Int32

        If bLoggingOn Then
            ' Stop the timing by getting the endpoint of
            ' the timing run.
            iEnd = CInt(Timer() * 1000)

            ' Report the data to our remote component.
            Dim rc As New prj04remote.prj04svc()
```

```
            Try
                rc.SavePerfData(Environment.UserName, _
                    sFuncName, Now, iEnd - iStart, _
                    gSessionID.ToString)
            Catch ex As Exception
                Throw ex
            End Try

            ' Send the elapsed time back to the caller, in
            ' case it wants to see it.
            Return iEnd - iStart

            ' Get ready for the next timing run.
            Reset()
        End If

    End Function

    ' This method clears out the data reported to the
    ' remote component so that we can start the next timing
    ' run. We do NOT want to clear the SessionID!
    Public Sub Reset()

        iStart = 0
        iEnd = 0
        sFuncName = ""

    End Sub

End Class
```

We created a few internal class variables, including SessionID, start time, end time, and a function name. These will be set as the class is used. Notice also that we created our own constructor that makes sure logging is turned on and that we have a new session ID.

> **TIP**
> **Need a globally unique identifier in your program? I did, for the session ID, and decided that GUIDs were an excellent solution. I just wasn't sure that GUIDs would be practical because they can sometimes be tedious to generate. It turns out that GUIDs are a snap in VB and .NET. There is a nice class called Guid that will take care of it. It has a method called NewGuid that generates them for you. The following line of code will do the job:**

```
Dim g As Guid = Guid.NewGuid()
```

The two core methods in the class are StartTiming and StopTiming. When you are ready to start execution of your function, call StartTime. This will create a beginning time mark and store it in the class. When the function has finished executing, call the StopTime method. This will create an ending time mark, calculate the elapsed time, and save the data to the database using the remote component. The component's internal data, the time marks, and the function name are then reset to get the class ready for the next run.

That would be enough functionality to make the class useful for us; however I added one more feature that lets you turn the logging on and off. Use the LoggingOn property, setting it to True or False to turn the logging of performance data on or off, respectively. This will allow you to leave your instrumenting code in your program when you release your production versions. Simply turn off logging before you do your final build. Leave logging on when you need performance data.

The main program code starts by creating an instance of the class we just defined called cTimer:

```
Private cTimer As New PerfLogger()
```

Our form load event takes care of centering the form on the screen and turns logging on to make sure it's running. More importantly, this is where the Remoting environment is configured:

```
Private Sub frmMain_Load(ByVal sender As System.Object, _
    ByVal e As System.EventArgs) Handles MyBase.Load

    RemotingConfiguration.Configure("prj04app.exe.config")
    Me.CenterToScreen()
    cTimer.LoggingOn = False

End Sub
```

The handlers for the button controls that kick off simulated functionality are simple, and all call the same function, specifying the function name and the delays to use for the function timing.

```
Private Sub btnF1_Click(ByVal sender As System.Object, _
    ByVal e As System.EventArgs) Handles btnF1.Click

    TimeIt("GetData", 400000, 100000)     ' 100,000 to 500,000

End Sub

Private Sub btnF2_Click(ByVal sender As System.Object, _
    ByVal e As System.EventArgs) Handles btnF2.Click

    TimeIt("Calculate", 1000000, 500000)    ' 500,000 to 1,500,000

End Sub

Private Sub btnF3_Click(ByVal sender As System.Object, _
    ByVal e As System.EventArgs) Handles btnF3.Click

    TimeIt("CreateReport", 2000000, 1500000)  ' 1,500,000 to 3,500,000

End Sub
```

The method TimeIt that all these functions call is where the timing occurs. It simulates the execution of real functionality that takes time to run. Take a look at the code and see how we used our PerfLogger class to handle most of the timing work:

```
Private Sub TimeIt(ByVal sFunc As String, ByVal iRange As Int32,
ByVal iMin As Int32)

    Dim et As Int32

    ' Tell the user to wait.
    lblStatus.Text = "Timing - Please wait..."
    System.Windows.Forms.Application.DoEvents()

    ' Start the timing.
    cTimer.StartTiming(sFunc)

    ' *** Everything from here to the end marker comment that follows ***
    ' *** represents the normal functionality in the        ***
    ' *** program that you want timed.                          ***

    ' Simulates some time passing.
    Dim v As VariantType
    Dim s As String
    For v = 1 To CInt(Rnd(1) * iRange) + iMin    ' 500,000 to 1,500,000
        ' Do anything!
        s = v.ToString()
    Next v

    ' *** End of dummy code. ***

    ' End the timing and save data.
    Try
        et = cTimer.StopTiming()
    Catch ex As Exception
        MsgBox(ex.Message)
    End Try

    MsgBox("Elapsed time (ms): " & et)
    lblStatus.Text = "Ready."

End Sub
```

Pretty simple. We start the timer using our class, run a time delay loop with random timing, and stop the timer using the class. You can use the same technique with any chunk of code in just about any program to record performance data to the millisecond. The overhead of the calls to the class is insignificant. The running program is shown in Figure 4.6.

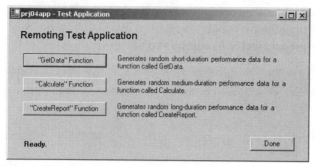

Figure 4.6   The Test Application executing.

The Configuration File

We need a configuration file for this application, as we did for our other client program. This one is called prj04app.exe.config, goes in the project's BIN directory, and looks like this:

```
<configuration>
  <system.runtime.remoting>
    <application name="prj04app">

      <client url="http://localhost/prj04remote">
        <wellknown type="prj04remote.prj04Svc, prj04remote"
        url="http://localhost/prj04remote/prj04remote.soap" />
      </client>

      <channels>
        <channel
        type="System.Runtime.Remoting.Channels.Http.HttpChannel,
        System.Runtime.Remoting" />
      </channels>

    </application>
  </system.runtime.remoting>
</configuration>
```

You now have some tools at your disposal to aid you with performance testing of your applications. The distributed nature of the logging component allows many users to access it easily with good scalability. It is also remotely hosted; therefore, you can make a global change to it easily; all users will get the change simultaneously.

Enhancing the Project

You've been shown the basics of creating remote components and getting them to work, end to end. You can create Remotable objects, configure them in the remote environment, and create clients that successfully call their functionality. You even know some of the technology going on in the background to make it happen.

Remoting, like many topics in .NET, can get far more involved. You can learn more about the topic, including Remoting events, creating your own channels, using the TCP channel instead of the HTTP channel, exploring the binary formatter to send information like images to a remote component, returning complex objects like collections back to the client, and even creating your own channel sinks that let you watch messages on a channel. It's a big topic that could occupy several good workdays when you have nothing else to do.

There are some excellent opportunities for adding functionality to this project. We've created a set of programs here that, useful as they are, could easily benefit from a few upgrades. Try some of these ideas for fun and profit:

More analysis.   I demonstrated techniques for extracting, aggregating, and analyzing performance data in the database. You could easily add more methods to the remote class that performed additional analysis to yield a better view of your performance. For example, if you have a large number of functions, create a method that looks for and reports on the top 10 percent slowest methods in your database.

Use the SessionID.   There was not space to provide serious use of the SessionID in the program. However, it could be extremely useful for grouping data. Any records with the same SessionID must have been run on the same computer with the same equipment. This will make the data relatively more useful because there are no performance variances in the hardware. Add some functionality to report statistics and analysis by SessionID.

Add some reporting.   The more expensive versions of Visual Studio .NET come with Crystal Reports. Although it's nice to see data and graphs on the screen, it would be better to be able to see them in a report that you could print, save, and distribute to other programmers. It would not be difficult, and the Crystal system supports graphs in the reports.

When midnight comes.   This set of programs is very nice, but the timer has one small problem. It will not work correctly if the timing session wraps past midnight. The VB Timer function returns the milliseconds past midnight and will reset if that boundary passes. There is a very simple way to fix this problem. See if you can figure out what it is.

WHAT'S COMING NEXT

Our next project is about deployment using the tools supplied with Visual Studio .NET. If you've used the Package and Deployment Wizard that comes with Visual Studio 6, you'll be pleasantly surprised with what it has been replaced with. You can create real, professional installations with these tools, and I'll show you how to do several different kinds of deployments.

Deployment Packages

If you've ever built an installation package with the tools built into Visual Basic 6.0, you have probably noticed how utterly cheesy and limited the results were. It was only good for the very simplest installation tasks, laying down a program and maybe a few extra files. Any customization to the appearance or functionality required messing with the code that was used to create the installation package, which was a scary prospect. Besides, the UI was awful and looked like my dog created it.

Alternatives were third-party installation tools that required a college degree with a major in installation programs. They are somewhat flexible and capable but need lots of expertise to make them do what they are advertised to do. You had to learn their programming language. They were extensible but only by writing DLLs that had custom interfaces. Invariably you would run into a wall as soon as you tried to do something out of the ordinary. How do we get out of this dilemma? Microsoft has surpassed the installation tools in VB6 by an order of magnitude and provided us with both the Microsoft Installer 1.5 and some very nice tools in Visual Studio to make installation packages a snap. We're going to take a look at these tools in depth and create a few installations of our own.

THE PROBLEM:

We, as engineers, need to easily and quickly create installation packages for our .NET applications and components that are fast, functional, and professional in appearance. We need to be able to do this without spending 6 months learning the tools. And, because we work in such heterogeneous environments with many operating systems, the installation needs to be self-contained and run on any Windows platform.

THE SOLUTION:

The Microsoft Installer and the tools in Visual Studio help you satisfy all the problems we just detailed. It's fairly easy, fast to use, flexible and extensible, and can do a lot of work without programming; if it needs to be extended, this can be done with standard Microsoft programming languages. We will be using these tools to create installation packages, or *deployment packages*, for the WinForms class library we built in Project 1, the bug-tracking system we built in Project 2, and the Web service from Project 3.

You Will Need

✔ **Visual Studio .NET**

✔ **A basic knowledge of Visual Basic .NET**

✔ **Compiled results of Projects 1, 2, and 3**

The Project

We'll be creating several installation deployment packages for our previous projects. Each will illustrate a different aspect or type of deployment. The deployments we'll be building include:

1. **Merge module.**   We will be creating a merge module deployment package for the WinForms class library, a DLL assembly, in Project 1. This will be used as an input to the next project.

2. **Application installation.**   This project will be an installation package for the bug-tracking system that we created in Project 2. We will cover most of the installation tools and details here.

3. **Web setup.**   Our final project will package the bug-tracking Web service from Project 3 into a Web setup package. This will allow us to install the service into Internet Information Server.

Any of these deployments can be modified to suit your own needs. You'll even see how to use the results of your deployment efforts on older Windows platforms.

Technology Overview

You've probably seen the installation tool that was provided with Visual Basic 6.0. Although I wouldn't actually wish this on anyone, it will give you an excellent perspective on how much things have improved. The VB6 installer was created using the infamous Packaging and Deployment Wizard. It was easy to use and would let you include additional files in the installation. Beyond that, there wasn't much you could customize. Even changing the font in the title of the installation screen involved manipulating the code templates that the wizard used to create the final result. Its appearance was sophomoric and unprofessional.

Microsoft addressed a lot of these problems when it created the Microsoft Installer. It is actually a full-blown, professional installation tool that is very flexible and fully programmable, complete with its own programming interfaces. It operates on a completely different principle that only Microsoft could get away with.

Installer Concepts

The Microsoft Installer is actually an engine that is embedded in the operating system. It currently ships as part of Windows ME, Windows 2000, and Windows XP. It operates on Microsoft Installer (MSI) files. When you build an installation package for the Microsoft Installer, the file you create, ending with a .MSI extension, contains almost everything you would expect:

- All the files you want to install on the user's computer
- Instructions for how and where the files should be installed
- Any files to support the installation, such as graphics displayed during the install
- Any custom code you have written to supplement the installation

However, it does *not* contain an executable to run the installation.

When you double-click on an MSI file, it is associated with the Installer engine and is executed by the engine as if it were part of the installation application. There is one exception to this, however. If you need to install your application on a platform that does not have the installer engine built in, you can include the installation engine with your package. It will install the engine on the OS and then use it to run the installation. I'll show you how to do this later on.

Is Uninstall Included?

Windows 2000 and Windows XP use a concept called the Application Database to keep track of what is installed on a particular computer. When a program is installed on these platforms, information is entered into the database to track the files that are installed and where they are, along with other information. It also tracks some installed common files that are shared among applications, much like registered COM components.

The Windows Installer naturally takes advantage of the Application Database. It also provides functionality to uninstall applications, removing all necessary information about the application from the Application Database. It executes when you remove the program through the Add/Remove Programs item in the Control Panel. You don't have to do anything to your install package to provide the uninstall feature. It comes along free. That's the best kind of functionality.

Another feature, related to uninstall and called *Rollback,* is provided with the Windows Installer. When the user aborts an installation before it completes, or if an error occurs during the execution of the installation or in your own supplementary code, files that have been dropped need to be removed. Any settings or other changes that have been made also need to be undone. The Microsoft Installer, under these circumstances, will perform a rollback, undoing anything that has changed since the installation started.

All the Installation Details

There are some other concepts you'll need to have a solid grasp of before you dive into installations of your own with .NET projects. Some of the information coming your way includes:

Namespaces.   These things are big now, especially with .NET components and XML. What's the big deal? We'll tell you.

Assemblies.   You've probably heard of assemblies and have an idea what they are, but maybe the details are elusive. You need to know what they are, as well as why they are important to installations.

Microsoft installer capabilities.   Before you start planning your installation, you need to know exactly what the installer can do.

In this section, I'll cover all these, as well as many other concepts and techniques that will make you into an installation aficionado. Stick with me through the initial stages here, and it will all make sense soon. You'll have the big picture before you know it.

Namespaces

Namespaces are one of those concepts that seem complex because they are not clearly understood. In reality, namespaces are quite simple. A namespace simply wraps a name around a region of code. It is used for organization and scoping and to prevent naming conflicts. A quick example will help make it clear. Consider the following class definitions with namespaces wrapped around them:

```
Namespace Namespace1

    Public Class Class1
        Public Sub MyName()
            MsgBox("Namespace1, Class1")
```

```
                End Sub
        End Class

        Public Class Class2
                Public Sub MyName()
                        MsgBox("Namespace1, Class2")
                End Sub
        End Class

End Namespace

Namespace Namespace2

        Public Class Class1
                Public Sub MyName()
                        MsgBox("Namespace1, Class1")
                End Sub
        End Class

End Namespace
```

All this code is contained in the same class module called *Namespaces* and is compiled as a single component. However, you can declare and create these separate components and even import them separately. Here is some sample usage code that will help illustrate this:

```
Dim c1 As New Namespaces.Namespace1.Class1()
Dim c2 As New Namespaces.Namespace1.Class2()
Dim c3 As New Namespaces.Namespace2.Class1()
c1.MyName()
c2.MyName()
c3.MyName()
```

Each of these object references uses fully qualified names, and there is no ambiguity, even though we have two definitions of Class1 in the same class module. The code in each of these classes will run correctly. However, assume that we add a couple of Imports statements so that we can reference these without the fully qualified names we just used. The statements look like the following code, and we add a couple lines of code to create instances of our classes:

```
Imports Namespaces.Namespace1
Imports Namespaces.Namespace2
...
Dim c1 As New Class1()
```

This will result in a compile-time error because, now that both namespaces are in scope, the name Class1 is ambiguous. Both namespaces have a Class1 defined and require more fully qualified names for proper differentiation. You can instead use an intermediate solution, importing the higher-level namespace and reducing the degree of qualification required to name the classes. An example is:

```
Imports Namespaces
...
Dim c1 As NameSpace1.Class1()
```

You can see how you can use namespaces to control the visibility and scope of classes within your components. How does this relate to installations? Excellent question. Namespaces relate indirectly through the concept of assemblies. An assembly can contain multiple namespaces, each of which can be used to organize objects (classes) in an assembly. In our example, we defined two different implementations of Class1, which can coexist peacefully because they are in different namespaces.

Assemblies

Assemblies are the next level up of organization. An assembly is the basic unit of distribution and deployment in .NET. An assembly equates roughly to an EXE application or a DLL. You can, of course, cram anything you like into these assemblies. A DLL can contain classes, namespaces, forms, resource elements such as image files, or anything else that's legal. An assembly contains a little more than a traditional DLL or EXE, though.

The assembly also contains *type information*. This makes an assembly essentially a combination of functionality and a type library. It is more self-contained and self-describing than DLLs of yore. As you have seen, the assembly and the namespaces within it help define scope. Assemblies are also the level at which security access is assigned, as well as the level at which functionality is versioned.

There are some other nice benefits to this organization. Back when you had to create COM components (seems just like yesterday), it was very difficult to deal with DLL versions. A condition commonly known as DLL-hell would occur. Essentially, it was tricky keeping DLL versions accurate and sequential and keeping components backward compatible with previous versions. Applications could (and often did) install incompatible versions of components on top of one another that would break one of the programs. With assemblies, it is easier to version the components, and different versions of the same assembly can run on the same machine. This is called side-by-side execution. I won't go into detail about that, but it is possible.

Assemblies are also easier to deploy. These components do not have to be registered as did COM components. Have you ever had to clean up a registry because you were developing COM components with wrong versions? It could take hours and still not work correctly when you were done. This problem is all gone with assemblies; there is no registration at all. This alone was enough to make me do back handsprings down the halls at the office.

The Assembly Manifest

The assembly, beyond all the items mentioned already, also contains a *manifest*, which is essentially a listing of everything the assembly contains. It includes the name (a name and a version) of the assembly and a listing of all the files that make up the assembly, including resource files and, more importantly, any external files on which the assembly relies.

The list of external dependencies is called the Assembly Reference. It lists any DLLs you may have created, any third-party components you may have used to create the assembly, and any common components, such as the Visual Basic library. You'll hear about common components later when I discuss the Global Assembly Cache.

You may be seeing why assemblies do not need to be registered to work properly. They carry all the information along with them that any other components or applications might need in order to use their services. Assemblies are easier to deploy and use. As you have seen already, you only need to add a reference to an assembly in your project in order to use it.

Interested in the actual contents of the assembly manifest? You can look at the actual manifest data by using a handy little utility called ILDASM.EXE. This is the Intermediate Language Disassembler. As you know, all .NET languages are compiled to a common intermediate language (IL), which is then executed by the common language runtime. However, ILDASM also shows you what's in the assembly. Simply run the program and select a DLL or EXE file that you want to explore. Figure 5.1 shows the manifest contents as an expanded tree.

Figure 5.1   The ILDASM dump of our example assembly.

ILDASM'S REAL CALLING

In addition to viewing the contents of an assembly, ILDASM will also show a complete listing of the intermediate language code that is executed by the common language runtime. The listing below is only partial, but it gives you an idea of what it looks like. Notice that for this one class there is a constructor (.ctor) and our method, MyName. The MyName code executes a single line of code, a call to MsgBox, but you can see how that expands into several IL statements.

```
.namespace NameSpaces.NameSpace2
{
  .class public auto ansi Class1
        extends [mscorlib]System.Object
  {
    .method public specialname rtspecialname
           instance void  .ctor() cil managed
    {
      // Code size       8 (0x8)
      .maxstack  8
      IL_0000:  ldarg.0
      IL_0001:  call         instance void
[mscorlib]System.Object::.ctor()
      IL_0006:  nop
      IL_0007:  ret
    } // end of method Class1::.ctor

    .method public instance void  MyName() cil managed
    {
      // Code size       16 (0x10)
      .maxstack  8
      IL_0000:  nop
      IL_0001:  ldstr        "NameSpace2.Class1"
      IL_0006:  ldc.i4.0
      IL_0007:  ldnull
      IL_0008:  call         valuetype
[Microsoft.VisualBasic]Microsoft.VisualBasic.MsgBoxResult

[Microsoft.VisualBasic]Microsoft.VisualBasic.Interaction::MsgBox
(object,
          valuetype
[Microsoft.VisualBasic]Microsoft.VisualBasic.MsgBoxStyle,
          object)
      IL_000d:  pop
      IL_000e:  nop
      IL_000f:  ret
    } // end of method Class1::MyName

  } // end of class Class1

} // end of namespace NameSpaces.NameSpace2
```

Locating Assemblies

Way back when we created COM components and they were registered, an executable or component that referenced another could look it up in the registry and find out exactly where the code was located. This made them pretty easy to locate at execution time, despite the many other drawbacks of having to register components. However, .NET assemblies do not require registration and can be located anywhere. So when an assembly is needed, how does it find the code?

The complete assembly location process is a little complicated; however, there are two primary locations for assemblies that make them easy to locate at runtime:

- The application directory
- The Global Assembly Cache

The application directory is pretty obvious. If the assemblies that make up an application are located in the application directory, or in subdirectories of the application, they'll be found at runtime. But what is the Global Assembly Cache? You are probably already familiar with installing components in the Windows\System32 directory. This is the standard location for components that are shared among applications. With .NET, the new place for shared components is the Global Assembly Cache, located in the runtime directory. Components that are created properly can be installed into the Global Assembly Cache and shared among applications. If you are interested in installing components of your own in the Cache, you'll want to look into creating assemblies with Strong Names. For our purposes, putting components in the application directory will do nicely.

The Microsoft Installer

The Microsoft Installer is an extremely capable tool, and when combined with the front end that Visual Studio provides, it makes it easy to put your own deployment packages together. There are few different types of installation packages that it can create.

Application installers.   Everyone knows about these. They allow you to package your application into an installation that will drop files anywhere. It provides you with a standard but professional user interface that can be customized and with capabilities that will accommodate most needs.

Merge Modules.   You can package components that are used by your application into Merge Modules. A module contains a DLL component, along with any supporting files it needs. It helps ensure that a known version of a component is installed with an application. Modules cannot be installed by themselves but are instead embedded in other installations. If you create components for other programmers, you can package them in a Merge Module, and other programmers can include the Merge Module in their own application installations.

CAB File installers.   These installations create CAB files, usually for use when you need to install ActiveX controls on a Web page. They are simple but cannot be created with a wizard.

Web setup installers.   These are pretty nifty and allow you to build installation packages that install components or applications on a Web server. Create the installer, copy it to the server, and run it. It knows all about Web servers and virtual directories.

Components of an Installation

Installations have many parts that you can use to create installers, customize them, and make them do what you want. All of them are accessible through the Visual Studio tools, and we'll get to that shortly. So what are they?

Assemblies and files.   You know what assemblies are, the components of your application. You might also want to add some supporting files, such as graphics or a database file. You can add as many as you need.

Folders.   The installation system allows you to create folders and put files in them as you require. It also includes system variables that you can use to represent standard folders, such as the Program Files folder.

Conditions.   The installer will let you create complex conditions that control the deployment of files or the entire application, or even the launch of the installation. A complete installation syntax, full of operators and system variables, makes the condition a powerful tool.

Custom Actions.   Functionality can be executed at the end of the installation and is called an Action. You can use the standard actions that come with the Installer or create your own using standard programming languages like Visual Basic.

The registry.   Frequently applications make use of the registry, and modification or creation of registry settings during installation is a common task. The Microsoft Installer makes registry manipulation fairly easy with its Registry Editor.

File associations.   Windows associates file types with applications, making it possible to open a document and have the correct application load. The Installer allows you to create your own file associations during the installation.

Shortcuts.   The Installer provides capabilities to create your own shortcuts as part of the installation process. You can create shortcuts both on the desktop and in the Program Files menu.

All these components add up to some pretty nice installation capabilities. However, so far you've only seen the pieces of the complete picture. It's time to examine the tools themselves, assemble the pieces into a coherent vision of the whole process, and start making some installations of our own.

Creating Installations with Visual Studio .NET

You've been very patient so far. The basic knowledge behind the Installer is now yours. Your reward is an immediate overview of the process of making an installation. The following steps, though not the same for every installation task, describe a typical installation scenario that will give you an excellent idea of how to build an installation package. After that, we'll get into the details and options available to you and how to use them.

Installation Process Overview

The following steps illustrate the generic process for building an application installation. Not every option is listed, but the primary items are covered.

1. Start by creating a deployment project in Visual Studio. There are several types available. This wizard allows you to start with a little guidance. Specify the project name and location, as well as any known files you'd like to create.

2. Once the deployment project is created, use the File Editor to add any other files and rearrange them into other folders.

3. Adjust any properties for the files you have added to the deployment project. These include settings such as whether or not the file is read-only, its name once it is installed, and the directory into which it should be installed.

4. Define any conditions you may need, at various levels. You can set conditions for the installation of specific files, the installation itself, and many other activities, such as the creation of registry entries or shortcuts.

5. Set the properties for the deployment solution. You can specify the author, description, keywords, version, and other items.

6. Add any custom user interface elements you might need. The Installer provides a handful of optional dialogs that you can customize to your own needs and changes and customizes the standard user interface dialogs.

7. Set the build target type using the Configuration Manager. You can select either the Debug or Release option, each with its own settings.

8. Add any shortcuts or file associations to the installation that you might need. You can add both desktop and Program Files menu shortcuts.

9. Add the Windows Installer Bootstrap program files to the installation if required.

10. Build the installation project. This will result in an MSI file that you can double-click and run to test it.

This list should help to clarify things a little. This is just an example; there are many more capabilities, installation types, and tools that help us do our job.

Creating Deployment Projects

There are two ways to create a deployment project and add files to it. Each has its benefits. You can either start a new installation and create it from scratch, or you can add a deployment project to your application solution.

Starting a new installation from scratch is a good option if you don't have access to the installation target's source code or if you want to keep the deployment project separate (for example, so that different people can work on the application and the installation). You create a standalone installation project the same way you create any new project: select New Solution from the Visual Studio file menu. The deployment projects are not located in the default group of projects in the New Solution dialog. You have to select the Deployment Projects option first.

You can create several types of installation solutions, as already mentioned. You can also use the wizard in the group; it will walk you through a few of the steps. Either way, you end up with a new installation project that you can do with as you please. It stands alone, and you can add any files you like to it.

The other route allows you to add a deployment project to an existing project, probably the project for the component or application you want to install. This helps to keep the deployment solution associated with the application solution. It is easy to add files from the application solution, called Project Outputs, to the deployment solution.

Once this is done, you can start changing things around and adding to the project. You'll probably want to start with one of the many editors included in the package of installation tools.

The Editors

Editors is a slightly misleading term. You certainly don't use the editors to edit text. However, you can use them to edit, or manipulate, the contents of the deployment package. They are the primary components of the Installer creation system, and you'll be using them to build all of your deployment packages. You are provided with the following editors in the toolset:

- File Editor
- File Types Editor
- Registry Editor
- UI Editor
- The Launch Conditions Editor
- The Custom Actions Editor

Each editor is designed to take care of a different aspect of creating an installation, and although the number of editors may look confusing, it's really not. Once you're familiar with them, you'll know exactly what to do with each one and when to use it.

The File Editor

The File Editor is where you spend most of your time when creating an installation. It is the default editor that is displayed when you create a new deployment project. It allows you to add to the project files that will be installed when your deployment package is executed. You can organize them into folders that will also be created when the installation runs. Take a look at Figure 5.2 to see what it looks like.

Figure 5.2   The Installer File Editor.

On the left side is a tree that represents the file system on the target computer, the machine on which your files will be installed. It has some default folders, including:

Application Folder.   Where most of your normal assemblies and other files are placed. The actual folder can be specified in the Properties window, which we'll cover later.

Global Assembly Cache Folder.   The standard location for common reusable components. Assemblies placed here must follow certain guidelines, but it is the place for components that will be used by multiple applications.

User's Desktop.   Just like it sounds. Usually you will be putting shortcuts here, but you can also put files in this spot if you need to.

User's Programs Menu.   Also for shortcuts, this allows you to add items to the user's start menu.

On the right side is a list of the files that will be installed into the currently selected folder on the left side. In Figure 5.2, you can see that there are two types of files listed there: assemblies and files. Assemblies are the executable components that we've already discussed. You can also add any other files you like. In this case, there is a JPG image file and an MS Access database file. You can also create your own folders. Look at Figure 5.3 and you'll see a folder that was created underneath the Application Folder, as well as a file that was put there. When the program is installed, the folders you create here will be created on the target machine.

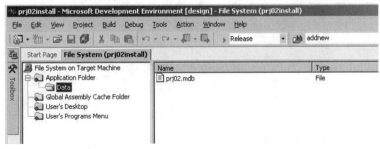

Figure 5.3   Creating a subfolder in File Editor.

Figure 5.4 The properties available for files.

Over in the Properties section of Visual Studio, you can set a number of properties for each file in your installation package. Figure 5.4 shows the Properties window full of file properties. Some of these will be discussed later.

The File Types Editor

Being able to create your own file types is a valuable tool if your program uses its own data file types. For example, perhaps you are creating a program to generate rhyming advertising jingles (if you've been through Project 2 or 3, you will be a little familiar with this concept). You save your jingle files as a binary data file with a .JNG extension. You can create a file type in the File Types Editor that associates the .JNG files with your application. See Figure 5.5 for a glimpse of what the editor looks like.

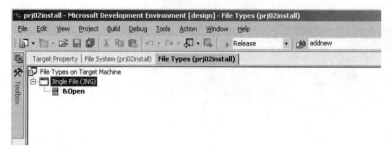

Figure 5.5 The Installer File Types Editor.

The editor allows you to create a named file type, in this case, the Jingle Data File. Figure 5.6 shows the properties associated with this file type, which is where the real meat is. You can specify the following important details about the file type:

Name. The name of the file type, as it will be displayed in Windows Explorer.

Arguments. Any data passed to the application when it is executed.

Condition. A condition that must evaluate to true if the file type is to be installed.

Although this isn't a feature that everyone will need all the time, and you probably won't be creating 15 or 20 file types, the capability is there if you need it. Microsoft didn't create only the absolutely necessary tools; it went the extra mile to provide tools that will help you out on those rare occasions when you need them.

The Registry Editor

As a programmer you are intimately familiar with the Windows Registry Editor. That is not what this is. It does, however, let you tell the Installer what registry edits you would like it to make. Look at Figure 5.7 to see the Installer's version of the Registry Editor.

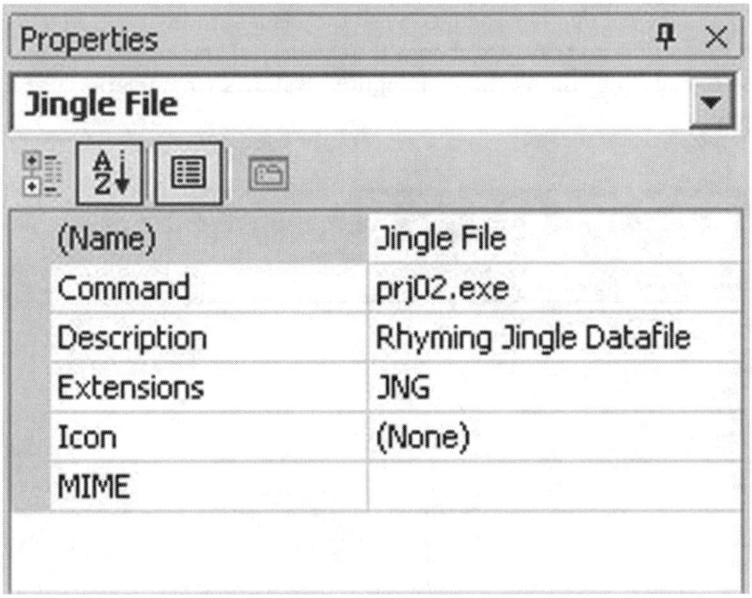

Figure 5.6   The Installer File Type properties window.

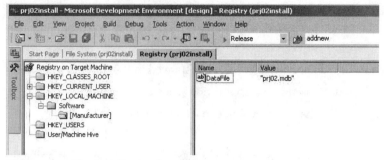

Figure 5.7   The Installer Registry Editor.

You can navigate a replica of the registry hierarchy on the left side of the window. Find the spot where you'd like to add a new registry entry, and you can create it on the left. The value for the new registry key can be entered in the properties window for the new registry entry. When you're done, the Installer will make the registry entries that you just created.

The UI Editor

The Package and Deployment Wizard that came with Visual Basic 6.0 had a pretty awful UI that was almost unmalleable. To change it, you had to get into the code and edit it without messing up anything else. Even small changes took time, and adding a new dialog was a big deal. All that has changed with the Visual Studio .NET Installer tools. Using the UI Editor, it is quite easy to change the existing UI and even to add new dialogs to take care of tasks they didn't think of. Figure 5.8 shows what it looks like.

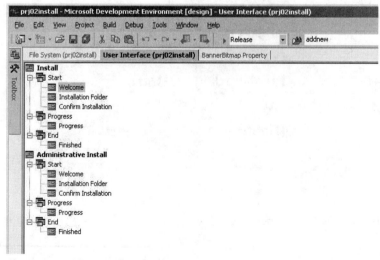

Figure 5.8   The Installer UI Editor.

The tree view shows the dialogs that will be displayed during the course of the installation process in the order in which they will be executed. By selecting one of the items in the tree, you can modify its properties in the Properties window. You can also add your own dialogs and customize them to suit your needs. We'll be covering this in detail in our project. For now it's important to know that you can change the look and text of most of the dialogs, add new dialogs to handle your check box or radio button needs, and remove dialogs that you don't need.

The Launch Conditions Editor

There are often conditions in which you might want to prevent the installation of your application. For example, your application might require Windows 2000 to run properly. Or you might want to make sure that the latest version of your UI library is already installed on the machine. Whatever your qualifications for deployment, you can create Launch Conditions that will be checked before the installation can take place. The Launch Conditions Editor is used for this and can be seen in Figure 5.9.

In the main window, you create the condition object and name it. In the illustration, we have one called CheckPlatform. In the Properties window for the condition, you can actually specify the condition itself. In this case, our condition is:

```
VersionNT >= 500
```

This condition makes the installation check the version of Windows NT or 2000 that is hosting the installation, and if it is over or equal to version 5.00, the installation can proceed. If not, it will abort the installation and display a message that you specify.

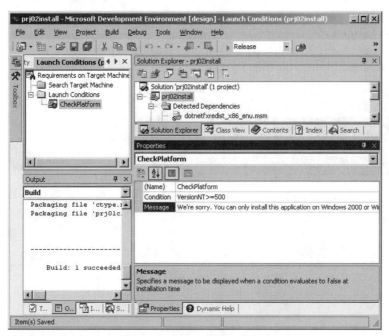

Figure 5.9 The Installer Launch Conditions Editor.

The Custom Actions Editor

Custom Actions are executables that you can run at certain points in your installation, usually at the end. Figure 5.10 shows what the editor looks like.

You might use them to launch a user registration page, display some tips, start the program itself, or create a database. There are several places where you can add an action, shown by the categories in the editor. As Figure 5.10 shows, we have created an action that runs the prj02.exe program. You could place just about anything there, from a simple Web page to a completely different program.

Let's Start the Project

Our project this time is really three smaller, related projects. We'll be creating three deployment packages that will be used together. Each will illustrate a different type of deployment; all deployment types are likely to be of immediate benefit to almost any programmer charged with creating installations. Along the way I'll cover some of the additional details and capabilities that you have at your disposal with the Visual Studio Installer tools. Here is a short overview of the installation projects we will be building:

Project 5a: Merge Module.   We will be creating a merge module deployment package for the WinForms class library, a DLL assembly, in Project 1. This will be used as an input to the next project.

Project 5b: Application Installation.   This project will be an installation package for the bug-tracking system that we created in Project 2. We will cover most of the installation tools and details here.

Project 5c: Web Setup.   Our final project will package the bug-tracking Web service from Project 3 into a Web Setup package. This will allow us to install the service into Internet Information Server.

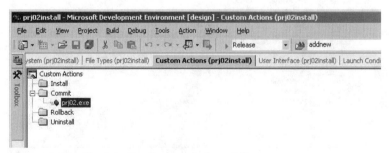

Figure 5.10   The Installer Custom Actions Editor.

If you can't wait to see what it looks like and how it works, you can run the installations from the CD-ROM. They are located in the prj05 project directory. Look for prj02install.exe to fire up the application installer. Otherwise, keep reading.

Note that while all the install projects are located on the accompanying CD-ROM, they depend on specific locations to find the files you are installing. Therefore, it may be easier to create the projects yourself. Otherwise, you'll have to re-create the original directory structure.

Project 5a: Merge Module

A Merge Module is an installation with no UI that is intended to install components used by other applications. It cannot run by itself; it can only execute as part of another installation. Our WinForms class library from Project 1 is a perfect fit because the bug-tracking system makes use of it.

Start by creating a new project in Visual Studio. On the left side of the New Project dialog, select the *Setup and Deployment Projects* option. This will change the contents of the right side of the dialog so that it contains all the deployment projects available. For now, select the Setup Wizard option. Enter a name for our project, in this case, *prj01merge*. Figure 5.11 shows what all this looks like. Click OK to continue.

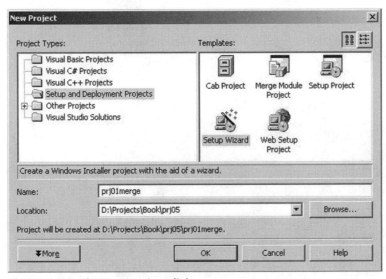

Figure 5.11   The New Project dialog.

Ignore the first panel of the Setup Wizard and move on to the second, which looks just like Figure 5.12. This is where you choose the type of installation package you will be creating. You can see options for the types of installation projects we have described in this chapter. Select the Merge Module option and click Next.

The third panel, shown in Figure 5.13, allows you to select files that you would like to include in your project. Click the Browse button to locate and select them, and they will be added to the list. For our project, we simply add the prj01classes.dll assembly, the only component we're actually installing.

Note that any files you select here will be added to the Application Folder group in the File Editor. You can always move them later, as well as add any other files you like later on. This wizard panel is a convenience that allows you to pick files at an early stage.

The final panel is simply a summary of your selections, there for you to review before you commit the options to a new project. Make sure it resembles Figure 5.14 and click the Finish button. You will be placed in the File Editor for this project, which will contain the files you selected in the wizard.

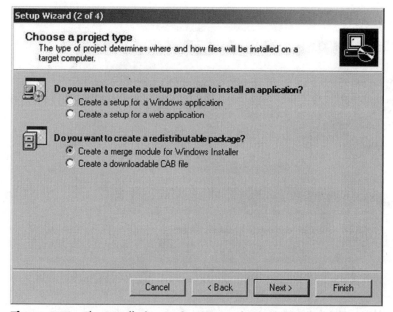

Figure 5.12   The Installation Project Type selection wizard panel.

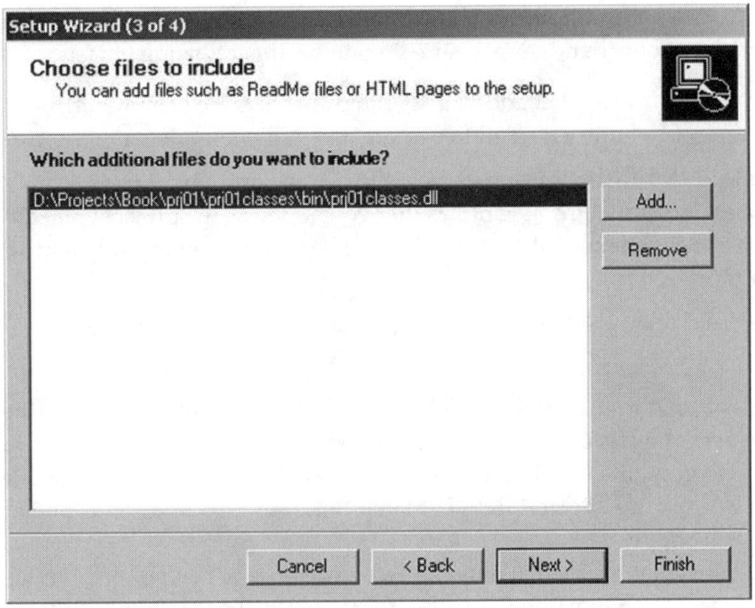

Figure 5.13   The File Inclusion wizard panel.

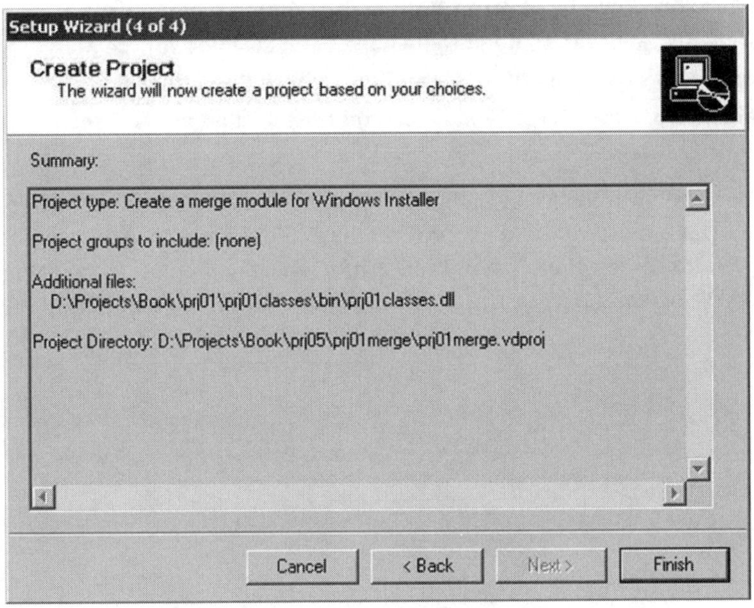

Figure 5.14   The options summary wizard panel.

Take a minute to look around. See how many interesting things you can find. See if you can find more than your friends. Make sure you notice the following items:

- In addition to prj0classes.dll; it added mscorlib.dll. This is the Common Language Runtime class library needed to execute any .NET components.

- The same file, mscorlib.dll, is listed in the Solution Explorer under Detected Dependencies. It scanned the assemblies that you added to the project yourself and found any dependencies that they rely on. The system conveniently added them to your project.

- It also found and added dotnetfxredist_x86_enu.msm, part of the installation runtime.

The last thing you might want to do is add some descriptive information to the project itself. This will allow programmers who are looking at the file's properties in Windows Explorer to get some useful information about it. Figure 5.15 shows the settings that we filled in for our Merge Module. Match these settings or fill in different values that make you happy.

That's almost all the setup we need. It only remains to determine the type of build we want: debug or release. Usually you will want a release build. To specify which type, use the Visual Studio toolbar. There is a list box there for the build type. Select Release.

> **TIP**　**Normally you would be able to select all the editors from the View / Editor menu. However, some of them have been disabled for the Merge Module project type. The UI Editor and the Launch Conditions Editors are not available because the Merge Module cannot be launched on its own.**

Now build the project from the Build menu. The program will be compiled into an MSM module. You can browse to the disk location that you specified for the project and check in the *Release* folder. Pretty cool, huh? Unfortunately, there isn't anything you can do with it. We will add it as a component in the next installation project.

Figure 5.15 The Merge Module project properties.

Project 5b: The Application Installation

You will most likely be deploying standard applications most of the time. Therefore, the meat of this project is an application installation. We are deploying the bug-tracking application from Project 2, which includes one external file, the database. We will be using some of the more interesting features of the installation tools, including changing the look of the UI, adding a dialog to the UI, creating a deployment (launch) condition, and using the results from our customized dialog.

Creating the Project

Begin by creating a new project in Visual Studio. Select the Setup Wizard project type. Name the project prj02install, and put it wherever you like. Figure 5.16 shows the correct option settings for the new project dialog.

The setup project wizard will start up; you can skip over the welcome panel and move to the project type selection panel, shown in Figure 5.17. In this case, select the Windows Application setup option and click the Next button.

The next panel allows you to add files to the project. For now, select only the program's EXE by browsing for it. We'll add the database file later when we look at the file editor. Figure 5.18 shows the file selection panel of the Setup Wizard.

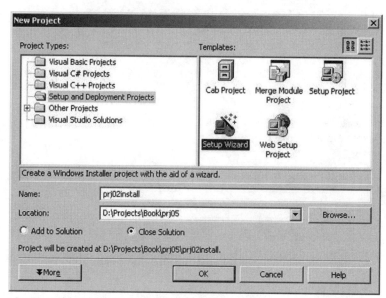

Figure 5.16   The prj02install New Project dialog.

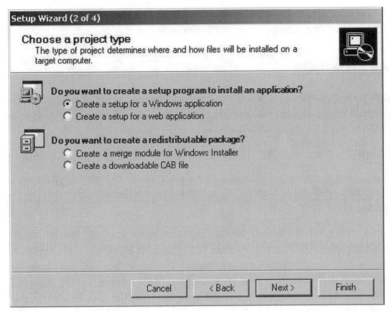

Figure 5.17   The prj02install Project Type panel.

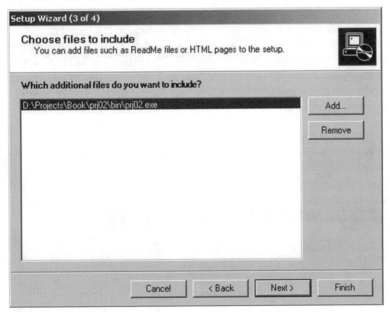

Figure 5.18   The prj02install File Selection panel.

The final panel shows a summary of our options. Click the Finish button to create the project. Once complete, you will be dumped into the Setup File Editor.

Add Files to Be Installed

We have a couple of files that we want to add to the installation. Make sure the Application Folder is selected and right-click in the file area of the File Editor. Select Add File from the context menu and add the following files to our project:

Prj02.mdb. This is the Microsoft Access database file that contains the bug data.

Prj05banner.jpg. This is a graphic that will replace the standard banner graphic at the top of all the installation dialogs. It can be found on the accompanying CD-ROM in the prj05 directory.

Figure 5.19 shows all these files added to the File Editor. As you can see, all these files will be installed into the Application Folder. The question is, what is the application folder? What physical directory does it represent? The short answer is, whatever directory you want. The long answer is that you need to specify the directory yourself in the properties for the Application Folder. Highlight the Application Folder in the File Editor and examine the Properties window, shown in Figure 5.20. The Default-Location property is the one we're looking for.

The DefaultLocation property contains the physical directory represented by the Application Folder. The system provides you with a handful of predefined variables that you can use to represent directories on the target machine. For example, the variable ProgramFilesFolder represents the Program Files directory on the target machine, whatever it is actually called and on whichever drive it resides. The other two we are using, Manufacturer and ProductName, are properties of the project. Select the project in the Solution Explorer and in the Properties window and fill in values for the Manufacturer and ProductName. We used *Vulture Corp* and *Bug Tracking System*, respectively. Our final DefaultLocation, where the program will be installed, will end being something like this:

```
C:\Program Files\Vulture Corp\Bug Tracking System
```

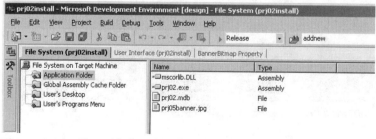

Figure 5.19   Files added to the File Editor.

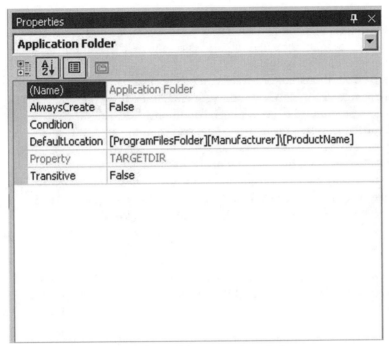

Figure 5.20   The Application Folder Properties window.

Adding in the Merge Module

Our first deployment project created a merge module that contains the WinForms classes from Project 1. We will be installing this merge module as part of the application installation because our application makes use of it. This is fairly simple to do, but we do not add it as another file to the File Editor. We add it to the project itself.

Select the project in the Solution Explorer and right-click on it. From the context menu, select the Add Merge Module item. When the file selection dialog appears, locate and add the prj01merge.msm file we built earlier. The contents of the merge module will now be installed as part of the application installation. You can repeat this process for any number of controlled components that you need to drop on the target machine, each with its own destination and special requirements defined in its own deployment project.

Adding a Launch Condition

There are plenty of reasons that you might want to prevent the installation of your project. You might require specific version of the operating system, or perhaps that another product is already installed on the system (for an upgrade?). The Visual Studio

Installer tools let you create all kinds of conditions, called Launch Conditions, that must be met before the Installer engine will deploy your project. In this project, we will add a launch condition to make sure that the user is running either Windows 2000 or Windows XP before the install takes place.

Open the Launch Conditions Editor by selecting its toolbar icon over the Solution Explorer or by choosing it from the View/Editors menu. You will be presented with a window that allows you to manage your launch conditions. Add a new one by right-clicking on the Launch Conditions item in the tree, and from the context menu, select Add Launch Condition. It will create a blank item for you, which you can name Check-Platform. Figure 5.21 show what the resulting item looks like.

Now select the new launch condition and look at its properties in the property window. The particular property we need to modify is the Condition property. Add a condition that will check the version of the operating system, as follows:

```
VersionNT >= 500
```

This will force a check to make sure that the version of Windows NT running is higher than 5.00. This implicitly excludes all Windows 9x variants and Windows ME. That's all there is to that.

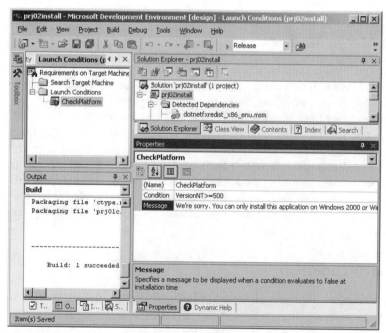

Figure 5.21   The Launch Conditions Editor.

CONDITIONS

You can create many types of conditions in a deployment project: launch conditions, conditions that must be met before a particular file is installed, or conditions under which a custom action will be executed. All of these conditions use the same syntax, and it is beneficial to be familiar with their syntax and capabilities.

The basic syntax follows logical conditional expression syntax with which you are familiar from programming languages: two operands joined in the middle by an operator. These can be combined like other expressions using parentheses and other operators. There are some rules and operators to be aware of that are very useful; they are listed here for your reference. Note that when I refer to operands, this could also mean a complete logical expression.

GENERAL RULES:

- ◆ Text strings must be enclosed in double quotes.

- ◆ You can reference property values in your expressions.

- ◆ If a property value does not exist, it equates to a null string.

- ◆ Any names of symbols and values are case sensitive.

- ◆ Operators are *not* case sensitive.

- ◆ Environment variable names are *not* case sensitive.

- ◆ Perform a case-insensitive string comparison using the ~ prefix.

- ◆ Operator precedence works just as it does in BASIC.

- ◆ *Floating point numbers are not allowed—don't forget this one!*

- ◆ Arithmetic operators are not allowed, only logical ones.

ACCESS PREFIXES:

These tell the condition evaluator what type of operand you are providing it. The only important one for now is the % sign. This indicates that the variable is an environment variable. Installer properties do not require any prefix.

LOGICAL OPERATORS:

These work between operands with logical values or between complete logical expressions.

> And: True if both operands are true
>
> Or: True if either operand is true or if both are true
>
> Xor: True only if one of the operands is true
>
> Imp: True if left operand is false or right operand is true
>
> Eqv: True if both operands have the same logical value
>
> Not: Returns the negative state of the following operand

Continues

CONDITIONS (CONTINUED)

COMPARISON OPERATORS:

These only work with actual values, not expressions.

    =

    >

    <

    <>

    >=

    <=

STRING OPERATORS:

>> : True if the end of left string is the same as the right string

<< : True if the beginning of left string is the same as the right string

>< : True if the right string is found in the left string

Customizing UI Appearance

The VB6 Package and Deployment Wizard was very difficult to change, and as a result, it was obvious when an installation was made with it. It was an indicator of an amateur attempt at installation and did not look professional. The Visual Studio .NET Installer tools not only create installations that look more professional out of the box, they also let you easily customize the UI to suit your specific needs. We will be changing some of the displayed text as well as the banner graphic that is shown at the top of each dialog, a graphic that matches our sample company, the Vulture Corp.

Open the UI Editor by clicking its icon in the toolbar over the Solution Explorer or by selecting it from the View/Editors menu. The editor looks like Figure 5.22.

First, let's change the text on the first panel of the Installation Wizard. It contains a basic welcome message, as well as a warning about illegal copying of software. Select the Welcome dialog under the Start item in the UI dialog tree. In the properties window, look for the CopyrightWarning and WelcomeText properties and change them to something else. We made them a little less harsh and a little more informative, respectively. See Figure 5.23 for examples.

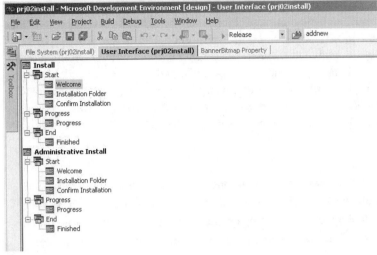

Figure 5.22 The UI Editor.

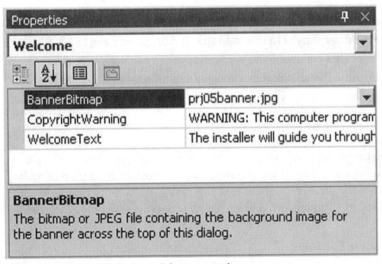

Figure 5.23 The Welcome Dialog properties.

Next we will change the banner graphic at the top of the installation dialogs. The graphic we used, prj05banner.jpg, is located on the CD-ROM. When we set up the files to be deployed in the project, we added it to the list in the File Editor. You must do this for the graphic to be accessible to the installer when it executes. To use it as a replacement for the standard banner graphic, select the dialog whose banner needs changing in the UI tree on the left and examine its properties in the Properties window. The BannerBitmap property is the one we want, so open the dropdown list and select the new banner graphic we added to the project. It will be changed when you execute the installer.

When creating new graphics for dialog banners, note that the graphic size is 500 by 70 pixels. Also, up to the first (left-most) 420 pixels may be overlaid by text, depending on the length of the dialog titles. You can create bitmap or JPG files for banner graphics, but JPGs are much smaller.

TIP

The only drawback to this technique is that you now have to do it for every dialog in the list. The good part is that you can actually create different banner graphics for each dialog, setting them appropriately. Personally, I have better things to do than creating five different graphics for an installation. I'll leave that to the marketing department.

When making changes to the UI in the UI editor, you need to make sure that you make the same changes to the dialogs in the Administrative Installation section. You can also make different changes, such as the welcome text, for the admin install, to inform an administrator of additional installation information.

TIP

There are other properties you can change about the UI, depending on the dialog selected. For example, you can turn the progress bar on or off for the Progress dialog. You can also change the order of execution of the dialogs by simply dragging them around the tree. You can even remove dialogs that you don't need from the execution.

Adding Your Own Dialogs

The dialogs in the UI Editor are great, but fairly limited. They let you inquire about the installation folder, but that's about it. Typically, you will need to add your own dialogs that ask your own questions. The Installer tools let you do this. We will be adding a dialog that asks users if they want to install the database file or not. If the installation is a reinstall, we don't want to overwrite their data unless they want us to.

We will be providing a dialog with a check box on it, providing the option to install the database or not. Right-click on the Start dialog group in the UI Editor and select Add Dialog from the context menu. The Add Dialog window appears; it is where you can select one of the customizable optional dialogs. Select the item labeled *Checkboxes (B)* and click OK. This will add the dialog item to the UI Editor. If the dialog is not positioned after the Welcome dialog, drag it around so that it is.

Right now, we have a dialog with nothing on it. To make it look like we want it to, select the new Checkboxes (B) dialog in the editor and then examine the properties window for it, shown in Figure 5.24. Notice that there are four properties for each of four checkboxes on the dialog. Their purposes are described in Table 5.1.

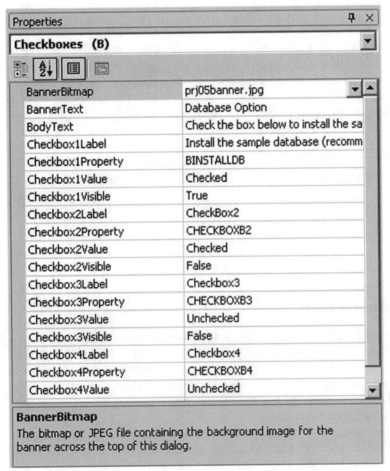

Figure 5.24 Properties window for the Checkboxes (B) dialog.

Table 5.1 The Checkbox Dialog Properties

PROPERTY	PURPOSE
CheckboxNLabel	The text displayed next to the check box, describing the option you are providing.
CheckboxNProperty	A name for the property that represents that value stored in the check box. This name will be referenced by the Installer elsewhere and must be all uppercase.
CheckboxNValue	The initial value of the check box, Checked or Unchecked.
CheckboxNVisible	Indicates whether or not the control is visible on the form.

We are using only a single check box in our case, so make sure you set the Visible property of all but the first check box to false. The rest of the settings in the Properties window should be adjusted as shown in Figure 5.24. Note the name we have supplied in the Checkbox1Property field, *BINSTALLDB*. We will use this name later to refer to the check box, allowing us to reference the value the user selected.

That takes care of setting up and defining our dialog. Now we have to make use of the check box we provided to the user. We will set a File Condition that will only install the database file if the check box is on. Return to the File Editor and select the prj02.mdb file. Enter the following condition into the Condition field of the Properties window:

```
BINSTALLDB = 1
```

If this condition equates to true, meaning that the check box we created is, in fact, checked, the file will be installed. Otherwise, it will be ignored.

Adding a Custom Action

The Windows Installer gives you the opportunity to execute any code of your own when an installation task (deployment, rollback, uninstall, etc.) has completed. You can either use a canned action that comes with the installation tools or write custom code of your own. To illustrate the process, we are going to create a simple custom process that displays a Thank You message box to users, stating that we appreciate that they have installed our bug-tracking product.

You can create any sort of executable that you like and run it when the installation is over. I'm going to show you how to build a basic executable shell that you can use to launch other processes. Using this simple shell, you could write all sorts of utilities that would be useful for an installation.

Let's build the custom action quickly using a step-by-step process. We'll start by building the program we want to run during the custom action, and then we'll add it to the deployment project. The instructions follow:

1. Create a new project in Visual Studio. It should be of the Class Library type, and you should name it ThankYou.

2. In the Solution Explorer, delete the item called Class1.vb.

3. Right-click on the project name in the Solution Explorer, and from the context menu, select Add Module. When the dialog appears, name it ThankYouModule and click OK. This creates an empty namespace for us to work in,

4. Add the code we want to execute. It looks just like this:

```
Public Sub Main()
    MsgBox("We at Vulture Corporation wanted to say a " & _
           "special thanks for taking the time to install " & _
           "our bug-tracking system." & vbCrLf & vbCrLf & _
           "Feel free to contact our customer support line " & _
           "at (123) 555-1234 should you have any questions." & _
           vbCrLf & vbCrLf & _
           "Good luck and good code!" MsgBoxStyle.Information, _
           "Thanks!")
End Sub
```

The Public Sub Main is our standard entry point.

5. In the Solution Explorer, select the project, right-click on it, and select Properties from the context menu. Set the Output Type to *Windows Application*, and the Startup Object to *Sub Main*.

6. Save the project and build it. We have created a simple Windows EXE program that displays a message box and has no other UI. You can use the same technique, replacing our message box code with any code you like.

7. Test the application by locating ThankYou.exe in Windows Explorer and executing it. It should display our message box and then go away.

8. Close the ThankYou project and Load the deployment project. In the File Editor, select the Add Assembly option and add our ThankYou.exe program to the file list.

9. In the Custom Actions Editor, select the Commit item from the event tree and right-click on it. Select the Add Custom Action option. In the selection dialog, open the Application Folder and choose the ThankYou.exe program that we just added using the File Editor. Click OK, and the new action should appear in the tree underneath the Commit event.

10. Make sure the new action, ThankYou.exe, is selected and examine the properties window for that item. Change the value of the property called InstallerClass to false.

11. Save the deployment project and build it.

You have now added a custom action to your deployment. When you execute the installation, the custom action will run at approximately the end of the installation operation.

Building and Running the Installation

There is one last setting to make. On the toolbar, select Release mode. And now that everything is configured, you can build the installation.

Select Build from the Build menu. The tools build your installation package, detailing the files it is adding in the Output window. Take a look at this to see some of the items in the runtime that are being added for you.

When the installation build is complete, execute it by browsing to the Release directory under the project directory and double-click the MSI file. This file type is associated with the Microsoft Installer Engine and will run without a specific EXE. This can be a useful deployment feature. For one thing, the installation package is a little smaller because the engine is not part of the deal. Additionally, some Web site administrators will not allow EXE files to be placed on their servers as available downloads for security purposes. MSI files, lacking the EXE extension, can be placed there without fear.

Run the execution and take a look at it. The welcome screen makes a nice first impression, especially with our new banner graphic. Figure 5.25 shows the new welcome screen with the new banner and our text updates.

The next dialog is our custom options dialog, where you can see the check box that provides the database installation option. Figure 5.26 shows what it looks like. Leave the box checked and click Next.

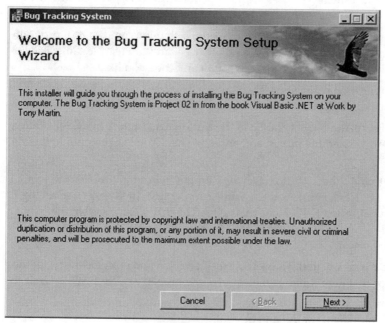

Figure 5.25   The new installation welcome dialog.

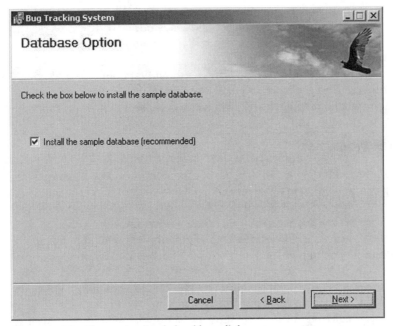

Figure 5.26 The customized checkbox dialog.

The installation dialog box is next, and it looks pretty normal. One interesting feature of this dialog is the Disk Cost button, which is provided free. A click of this button will display a dialog for the user that details how much disk space the installation will take. It is illustrated in Figure 5.27.

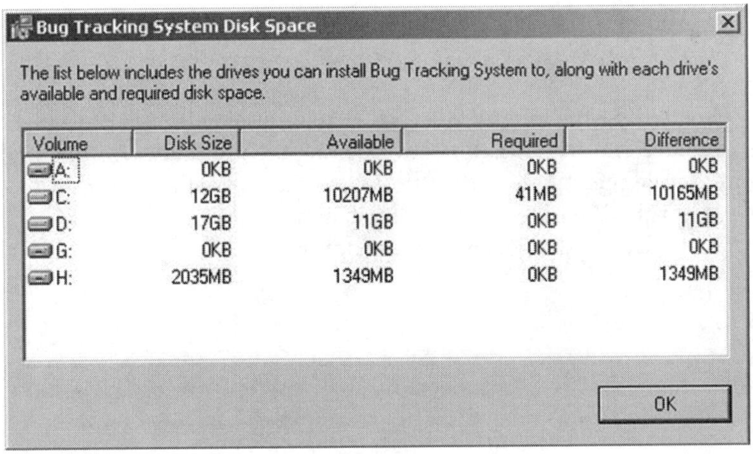

Figure 5.27 The Disk Cost dialog.

Finish everything else up and the installation begins to run. When it's all over, the custom action we created launches the browser and loads our advertising page. The application is completely installed, including uninstall information in the Add/Remove Programs control panel.

If we were to run our installation package again, without first uninstalling it, the UI we see would be different. We get a wizard panel that asks us if we want to uninstall or repair the existing installation, which it will do for us if selected.

Installing on Windows 9x

The Windows Installer engine is included as part of the Windows 2000, Windows XP, and Windows ME operating systems. However, if you need to deploy your application on Windows 95 or Windows 98, you would need an actual executable program to run the installation. Microsoft has taken care of this need by providing you with an option to include the *Windows Installation Bootstrap* along with your deployment package.

This option adds a few extra files into your release or debug deployment directory when the package is built. Instead of running the MSI file, you run the Setup.exe program. This is a runtime version of the installation engine that you can use on Windows platforms that do not have the engine built in. When you create your deployment media, or move your deployment files to a network, simply include these few extra files and anyone will be able to install your program.

Note that, although Windows ME includes the installation engine, it may not include the same version, 1.5, that comes with Visual Studio .NET. If it does not, clients without it will have to use the setup.exe program instead.

Project 5c: Web Setup

Web Setup projects allow you to deploy projects to an IIS Web server. I will be illustrating a slightly different method of creating a deployment project: using Project Outputs, which allows you to add a deployment project to your main project. This not only keeps the two projects together, but it makes it easier to add the correct files to the installation project.

We will be deploying the bug-tracking Web service that we built in Project 3 to a Web server (make sure you have one around). Begin by opening the project file for prj03 in Visual Studio. From the file menu, add a new project to the current solution. In the New Project dialog select the Web setup project type, and name it prj03setup. Click Next, and in the content selection dialog, check these options:

- Primary output
- Debug symbols
- Content files

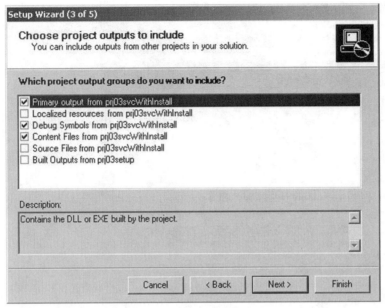

Figure 5.28 The Web setup content options dialog.

Figure 5.28 shows these selections checked. This dialog lists all the outputs from the primary project in the solution, in this case, the Web service. Click Next to move on, and click Next again to clear the Additional Files dialog. Click Finish to create the project.

The deployment project has been added to our solution, alongside our primary project. When you build the solution (go ahead, try it now), it will build your primary project first and then the deployment project using the outputs from the primary project.

All that remains is to run the installation for the Web service. Run through the installation, which should deploy the Web service to your instance of IIS. You can test it out by pointing to the Web site it created, like this (assuming you installed it to your local machine):

```
http://localhost/prj03setup/ProblemLogger.asmx
```

The successful execution will look like Figure 5.29. If it does not run properly, you may need to adjust the properties of the Web site in the IIS Admin tool. Change the execute permissions on the prj03setup to Scripts and Executables, as shown in Figure 5.30.

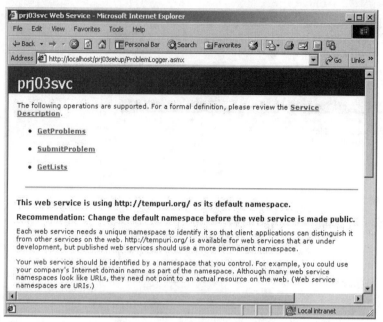

Figure 5.29   Successful execution of the deployed Web service.

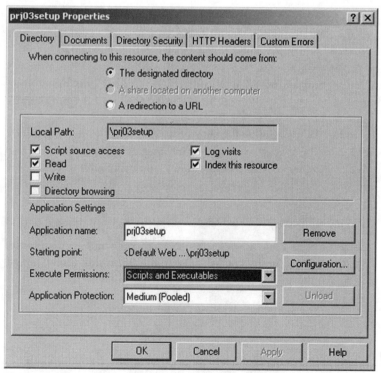

Figure 5.30   Adjusting the Web service execution permissions.

That's it for a Web setup deployment. Very simple, especially for setting up a Web service. We don't have to understand much about the deployment of a Web application or the intricacies of IIS. The setup tools know it all.

Enhancing the Project

You've seen a lot of deployment capabilities and options in this project, but there are many more. Buried in the Installer tools documentation are features such as the ability to create CAB file projects for the deployment of ActiveX controls; adding splash screens, user registration, read me, or other dialogs; registry manipulations; and tons of low-level details that make fine-tuning your control over your deployment a breeze. Although the installation tools won't handle every situation you can throw at it, it's orders of magnitude better than the tools that previously came with Visual Studio.

There is a lot to cover in the topic of deployment and plenty of opportunities to use some of the capabilities we didn't get to, including:

Write another custom action.   For the Web service deployment, create a custom action to actually create the database it needs in SQL Server. A little code and a couple of SQL scripts would take care of it.

Make the Merge Module global.   With a little work, you can rebuild the prj01classes component as a strongly named component. This would allow you to install it in the Global Assembly Cache, available for use by other applications.

Add some splash.   Create a splash screen and add it to your installation project. You could do the same thing with a read me file, or even add another check box that would ask users if they want to see the read me.

Register a user.   Add functionality to handle user registration to the project. You can add custom dialogs to the project that make a great starting point for letting users register your product.

WHAT'S COMING NEXT

Enter the world of ASP.NET development when we build a customizable Web portal. It will be an action-packed tour through ASP.NET, including Web development, a new ADO.NET trick or two, and how to tune the project to suit your own needs.

Web Portal with ASP.NET

Active Server Pages have become a widely used solution for the development of Web applications. The ease of use has opened up the use of Web servers from a small group of Unix programmers who could implement CGI in PERL or straight C to millions of developers worldwide who know Visual Basic. Serverside VBScript, combined with the intrinsic objects exposed by the ASP runtime (Request, Response, Server, Application, and Session) vastly reduced the learning curve required to move from static HTML to processes that executed on the Web server, incorporating relational data and other business logic into the HTML output sent to the Web browsing clients.

This ease of use has not come without a downside. VBScript is an interpreted language, requiring the Web server to parse and compile ASP pages on the server as requests for them come in. ASP script is inserted inline into the HTML output of a page, rapidly creating a spaghetti mess of code that is difficult to maintain and enhance. WYSIWYG editors frequently squashed this server side code that it could not understand. The popular Session object provided state maintenance in an intrinsically stateless environment, but the solution would not work in a Web farm environment. No good infrastructure for server side caching of output existed. We came close before the release of Windows 2000, with the IMDB, but this subsystem mysteriously vanished when the OS was released. Although business objects implemented in a COM-compliant language and hosted in MTS provided fine separation of the user interface from business logic, deploying and versioning these COM DLLs was a nightmare, especially on Web sites where high availability was a must, because the Web server must be stopped to update the DLLs. Poor coding practices made it exceedingly easy to bring a Web site to its knees as the number of users increased (ever try storing a COM object instance in the Session object?).

Microsoft is well aware of all of these problems and has created the ASP.NET Framework from the ground up to address them.

In this project we'll be examining this new Framework in detail. At first glance, ASP.NET can have a strong resemblance to traditional Active Server Pages. Microsoft says you can simply change the extension of an ASP page to ASPX and it will work in the new Framework. But as you dig deeper into the richness of the Framework, you begin to see that the Framework is a total overhaul of ASP, and fully utilized, an ASP.NET solution begins to look more like a VB6 solution than the mire of script code we've become accustomed to.

We are going to create a Web portal solution. This is a site that demonstrates functionality that (depending on content) could be deployed on a company intranet or as a public Internet site, aggregating custom content for our visitors. We will see how to use the new Framework to build custom content for different users, authenticate our visitors, drive content with relational data and XML, and build rich user interfaces for modification of our backend data stores. All this will be done with standard, cross-browser compatible, W3C-compliant, HTML.

THE PROBLEM:

We want to deliver public and corporate information to our employees in a secure environment. We want this information to be tailored to different employees and different departments. It needs to be easily extensible so that we can add functionality as our business needs change.

THE SOLUTION:

We will deliver this solution using a custom portal for the users of our company's intranet. This will be a secure site that renders content based on the user visiting the pages. We'll provide user interfaces so that users can select which content appears in specific areas based on their preferences. We'll also provide interfaces for managers to provide news to the people in their departments and an interface for an administrator to create and maintain a list of authorized users of the application.

The Project

Our project will build a Web page that our employees will use as their homepage in their browsers. The content rendered will be specific both to the department they work in and selections they've made on an individual basis. As well as rendering content for our users, we will build areas for department heads and administrators to configure and customize the application. The main navigation for the application will be controlled by an XML file, so it will be easily extensible.

1. **Separate and implement the functionality.**   We'll start by building the different areas of functionality as separate ASP.NET pages.

2. **Convert pages to User Controls.**   After getting the different functional areas implemented, we'll convert them to User Controls so that we can use them together on the same page. User Controls are an excellent vehicle for reuse of code that is new to ASP.Net.

3. **Create the portal page.**   Once we get the pages converted, we'll create the portal page itself by dynamically loading User Controls on the page in response to the menu choices our users make.

 ## You Will Need

✔ **Visual Basic .NET**

✔ **A basic knowledge of Visual Basic .NET and Active Server Pages**

✔ **SQL Server**

✔ **Functional IIS installation**

What Is ASP.NET?

ASP.NET is an entirely new framework for the development of scalable Web applications. IIS can be configured to delegate requests for different types of files to different subsystems installed on the server. With Active Server Pages, requests for files with an .asp extension are delegated to ASP.DLL. This is the ASP runtime, which parses the script code embedded within the HTML in the file, and because it does so dynamically, it generates the HTML output of the page. The ASP.NET Framework is an entirely new runtime geared toward the generation of HTML. Requests for files with an .aspx extension are delegated to aspnet_isapi.dll. This is a managed component that creates instances of .NET classes in the service of the request.

The ASP.NET Framework is a subset of the .NET system classes. Included are myriad classes to dynamically create HTML for you, including a dozen types of lists, HTML tables and forms, and validation logic; classes to manage state and caching and to configure and secure your application; and a set of classes to provide backward compatibility to traditional ASP. When you create an ASPX page, you are actually creating a class that inherits from and extends the System.Web.Page class. The runtime creates an instance of this class when your page is requested, and its job is to return the HTML that services the request. Because the class inherits from the Page object, there are standard methods that the runtime knows to call to execute your page's logic. Using Visual Studio .NET, this infrastructure is provided for you, so the code you create can look very much like a traditional Active Server Page. However, as you learn the services and infrastructure of the Framework, your code will more likely resemble a Visual Basic form, with a file for the user interface elements and a separate file for your code.

Because of the .NET architecture, the code that you write is very object oriented. Need to set the current item of an HTML select list? Set the SelectedIndex property of an HTMLSelect object. Need to generate an HTML table based on a SELECT statement? Set the DataSource property of a DataGrid object and call DataBind on that object. The work of HTML generation is done for you, under the hood, by these objects.

Does this all sound like a strange new environment? As we start to examine some code and create our own ASP.NET pages, you'll see that it's not really that difficult at all. And once you get used to the changes in the new Framework, you'll find that your work is much easier than with traditional ASP. Let's start by comparing the new Framework to what we're used to.

How Is ASP.NET Different from Traditional ASP?

There are a number of striking differences between ASP.NET and ASP. For some of these differences, the benefits will be immediately obvious. For others, we'll have to get used to new ways of thinking about dynamic Web pages. Among the changes are:

ASP.NET pages are compiled, not interpreted.   A binary executable is compiled upon the first request to the page. This image is stored in an in-memory cache on the Web server, and subsequent requests to this page use this executable to service the request.

Because we no longer need a script interpreter, we have full access to the language features of Visual Basic .NET.   We'll actually be writing programs that interact with objects instead of writing script to output HTML. Consider the generation of an HTML SELECT list to use as a combo box on a data entry form to populate a foreign key value. With ASP your code would generate an OPTION tag for each row in the recordset used to populate the list. Each OPTION tag generated would need to check that value against the foreign key value, and if a match were found, it would output the SELECTED attribute on the option tag. With ASP.NET, you use an instance of the DropDownList Server Control. This object exposes an item collection. To create the SELECT list, you simply add a ListItem object to this collection for each row in your resultset. To set the selected row, you set the SelectedIndex property. The data binding services exposed by this object actually reduce this task to four lines of code. If it sounds more like VB than ASP, it is.

The Framework provides a very clean separation of code from content.   With ASP, because the HTML is generated as the page is interpreted, your page logic must be embedded into the page at the location where you want the HTML generated by this logic to be output. With ASP.NET, no HTML is generated until all of the code in your page has finished executing. The entire task of HTML generation is done in the page's *rendering* step, which uses the properties of the objects you've created to generate HTML for you. This is great news for all of us who consider script writing and HTML generation a poor substitute to sitting down and writing real code.

Of all the differences, this one is the biggest. In ASP your task was to add script code to the body of an HTML page. The job of this script was to generate HTML. With ASP.NET you create and interact with objects, setting properties like Visible, calling methods, and using data binding services. After all of your code has executed, the HTML for the page is rendered, and the output is sent to the client. This leaves you with pages that have a clearer separation of content from code and are easier to maintain; your code looks more like traditional code than script that generates HTML. This is accomplished by the abstraction layer created between you and the HTML you're generating by the ASP.NET Framework.

ASP.NET Framework maintains state for you.   Do you ever have to post to the server to apply validation logic to a data entry HTML form? When there's a problem, you must write code to repopulate every input on your HTML form. You must also execute script inline to add validation messages next to the fields that have errors. The resulting code is often a tangled mess. If the business logic changes, that's a tough page to maintain. With the ASP.NET Framework, this state maintenance is done for you. The fields maintain their value without a single line of code written by you. This applies not only to simple text inputs but also to SELECT lists, check boxes, radio buttons, and any other input types on your form. Built-in validation controls allow you to enforce your business logic by adding a single tag to your page and simply checking the Page.IsValid property when it posts to the server.

ASP.NET runs events on the server.   In ASP, because of the amount of script that must be mixed with the HTML, it's common to split a single functional area across several pages. One page may collect data from a user, whereas another accepts the HTTP post and updates your relational data, telling your user the result of the operation. Although it's possible to put this functionality into a single ASP page, you do so at the risk of needing to maintain a garbled mess of code over the long haul. Breaking these functions into separate pages causes the number of files in your Web site to balloon. With ASP.NET, you can set up *server side event traps*. This is similar to Remote Scripting, but it works with standard HTML. You can add an HTML button to a page and have its click event trapped on the server, where a method of your page class applies validation, updates persistence, and informs the user of the result. With this single event sink, the operation is easily done without adding a smidgeon of code to the body of the HTML page. All of the work is done in your method by interacting with the objects exposed by the page.

ASP.NET provides a consistent event model. With ASP, script is executed on the page in a top-down manner. Although it's possible to put your script within functions that you call from the page body, there's no event model that fires at specific points in the lifecycle of your page. With ASP.NET, this event model has been added. Most importantly, there's an event fired whenever your page begins to load. This is very much like the Form_Load event in VB. The page load event can be trapped in a script tag or from your code behind the page. This gives you a consistent model for setting up your output. This is where you do things like initialize database data you're going to output on the page, pre-populate form values, and apply custom attributes. We'll take a look at the page load event in detail in a bit because you will probably be using it from most of the ASP.NET pages you create.

Before we jump into the project, you'll need to be familiar with a few of the important parts of the ASP.NET Framework. Let's take a look at them now.

Abstraction Layer between Code and HTML

The abstraction layer is created with a new suite of server-side objects. These objects have the sole task of generating HTML. Exactly what HTML is generated is determined by the properties and methods you call on these objects before the page is rendered. Instances of these objects can be created declaratively in code, or you can use special tags in the body of your HTML document. By declaring them on your page, you're telling the Framework in advance where the HTML generated by the object should reside within the final output.

The first set of objects we'll look at are the HTML controls. This is a set of objects that generate a single HTML element for you, elements like anchor tags, image tags, and form inputs of different types. You create an instance of an object by adding two attributes to your HTML tag:

```
<a href='' runat=server id=objAnchor>Link Text</a>
```

Adding the attributes runat and id to the tag causes an instance of HTMLAnchor object to be created when your page is requested. This object exposes properties and methods that are specific to an HTML anchor tag. The HTMLAnchor object is part of the System.Web.UI.HTMLControls namespace. Let's take a look at a simple use of the object from the Page_Load event of our page. You can find the complete listing for this page in HTMLControl.aspx in the demo folder.

What we're doing here is controlling what the hyperlink does and where it goes by the season in which our user visits our page. Let's start at the top. The footprint for the page_load event looks like this:

```
Private Sub Page_Load _
  (ByVal sender As System.Object, ByVal e As System.EventArgs)
```

This footprint is very common in ASP.NET and is used by most event traps in the Framework. The first parameter is always of type System.Object. This is actually an instance of the object that has raised the event. So for example, when you're trapping the On_Click event for a button, the first parameter will contain a reference to an instance of that button object. The second parameter varies in type depending on the event but is always a class that inherits from System.EventArgs. These parameters are used less in the Page_Load event than in other, more specific types of event traps. The next block of code sets up the dynamic output of the page:

```
Select Case aMonth
   Case Is <= 3
    sSeason = "Winter"
    sURL = "http://www.lenvillanophotography.com/generic.html?pid=1"
   Case Is <= 6
    sSeason = "Spring"
    sURL =
"http://members4.clubphoto.com/james190173/277323/guest.phtml"
   Case Is <= 9
    sSeason = "Summer"
    sURL =
"http://www.myneighborsgarden.com/summerpages/summerthumbnails.htm"
   Case Is <= 12
    sSeason = "Fall"
    sURL = "http://www.kidsdomain.com/holiday/fall/clip.html"
  End Select
```

We are set up two string variables with values that depend on the current month. These values could easily be retrieved from the query string and post information included with the request, an XML file, or a database. In this simple example it's these values that are used to set up the two properties of the anchor tag:

```
objAnchor.InnerText = "Images of " & sSeason
objAnchor.HRef = sURL
```

The first is the innerText property. You may recognize this from working with DHTML on the client. This is the text that appears between the begin and end tags of any element on our page. This is a property that is exposed by all of the HTML server controls. It will cause the displayed text of the anchor tag to be equal to the value of the sSeason string. The second property is specific to the HTML anchor control. This is the target URL of the anchor, the page that the browser will navigate to when a user clicks on the anchor's text. After the function executes, the page enters its rendering stage, and the HTML for the document is generated. Notice that we have not written any code to generate HTML. The anchor object does this for us based on the properties we have set from the code. If we choose View Source from the browser, here is how the anchor tag gets rendered (in September):

```
<a id="objAnchor"
href="http://www.myneighborsgarden.com/summerpages/summerthumbnails.htm"
>Images of Summer</a>
```

Notice that the original text of the anchor tag and the runat=server attribute are not part of the HTML that gets sent to the client. The runat=server attribute is always removed when the element is rendered, and the original text of the anchor tag (Link Text) was replaced when we set the InnerHTML property of the object. Notice also that, although we had to declare our string variables, there is no declaration for the objAnchor class instance. This is done for us under the hood by the Framework, driven by the runat=server attribute on the declaration of the anchor tag.

We can add a runat=server attribute to any element on our page. The attributes of these elements are then exposed as properties of the corresponding object that gets instantiated. In this way we can keep all server-side script tags we would have used in traditional ASP out of the body of our document, relying instead on the properties exposed on the object. Some other HTML elements exposed as objects in the System.Web.UI.HTMLControls namespace are listed in Table 6.1.

Even tags not listed in the table can be created as server-side objects. If a specific class doesn't exist for a tag you want programmatic access to on the server (for example, the BODY tag), you can still add a runat=server attribute to the tag declaration. The type of object that gets created will be an HTMLGenericControl. This object exposes properties that are common attributes of HTML elements. Absent are specific properties for more specialized tags. All of the HTML control classes inherit from the HTMLContainerControl class.

An ASP.NET page request follows this lifecycle:

- Request ASPX page.
- Compile image or retrieve from cache.
- Execute Page_Load event.
- Execute events included with request.
- Execute data binding called by event traps.
- Execute Page_Unload event.
- Enter render stage.
- Use in-memory state of all server-side objects and VIEWSTATE to render HTML.
- Return HTML to client.

Server Controls

In addition to the HTML controls, the Framework ships with dozens of what are called server controls. These controls also require the runat=server attribute, and many are very similar in other ways to the HTML controls. The syntax for a server control tag declaration is:

```
<asp:ControlName runat=server Id=ControlID />
```

When you declare a server control on your page, you can use the control from your code by using the ID as a variable name, as you can with HTML controls. However,

Table 6.1 Controls in the HTMLControls Namespace

HTML ELEMENT	OBJECT IN HTMLCONTROLS
<a>	HTMLAnchor
<button>	HTMLButton
<img>	HTMLImage
<input type='Type'>	HTMLInput *Type*
<select>	HTMLSelect
<table>	HTMLTable
<tr>	HTMLTableRow
<td>	HTMLTableCell
<textarea>	HTMLTextArea
All Other Tags	HTMLGenericControl

instead of having properties that map directly to HTML attributes, the server controls more closely resemble VB6 controls. For example, instead of exposing a VALUE property for controls that render as an INPUT type, the server controls expose a TEXT property, like a VB text box does. Many of the server controls render as a single HTML tag. Table 6.2 lists of some of these server controls.

Table 6.2 Simple Server Controls

SERVER CONTROL	HTML ELEMENT
<asp:Button>	<input type='submit *or* type='button'>
<asp:Textbox>	<input type='text'> or <textarea>
<asp:Panel>	<div>
<asp:Label>	<span>
<asp:DropDownList>	<select>
<asp:ListBox>	<select size='...'>
<asp:RadioButton>	<input type='radio'>
<asp:CheckBox>	<input type='checkbox'>
<asp:HyperLink>	<a>
<asp:Image>	<img>
<asp:AdRotator>	Advanced HTML Code Generator
<asp:Calendar>	Advanced HTML Code Generator

A few of the controls have more advanced capabilities. The ASP:Calendar control renders a complete client-side calendar in standard HTML. The control supports day and week selection and has a look and feel that can easily be customized. The ASP:Datagrid control exists solely to render an HTML table. Remember the days of opening a recordset, setting up a WHILE loop, and iterating the rows in the resultset to generate a TD cell for each column of data in your recordset? Well, those days are over. Now you simply bind a data grid to a resultset and call the data binding engine. The data grid does the rest for you. We'll be taking a closer look at this a bit later.

Support for Scalability

Access to the full language features of Visual Basic .NET is not only a great benefit to us during development, but it also enhances the scalability of our application. The aspx pages are actually compiled into binary images and cached by the Web server as executables. They run under the common language runtime, like any other managed component. These aspx pages are going to perform much better than our traditional ASP pages, which were always interpreted at runtime by the script parser.

Some changes have also been made to the Framework to support scalability in a Web farm environment. With Active Server Pages, the Session object was a great place to store user-specific information as users used the application. There was a problem with this architecture in a Web farm environment, however, because the session information was stored in the memory space of the Web server and therefore could not be shared across the different servers in a Web farm. With ASP.NET, there are two new options for where session information is stored. The Framework ships with an NT service that will store session state. This allows us to dedicate a single machine as our session server; it can be a dedicated machine or one of the Web servers in the Web farm. All information stored in the Session object is automatically shipped off to the state server, so it becomes a single resource shared by all of the Web servers. If any of the servers goes down, the session information will be maintained on this dedicated box, and the user can continue unaffected by the outage.

Our third option is to store session information in SQL Server. The Framework creates a set of tables for doing this and automatically connects to the SQL Server and stores information put into the Session object there. This configuration can be done at a machine level, or for specific applications on your server. The code we write in the page is totally unaffected. This means that you can use the Session object and configure your server to store this information in-process with the Web server. As your application use grows and you need to throw a couple more servers up to manage the load, you can change one simple entry in the configuration file, and your application will continue to work without a single code change. Your session information will automatically move to the session server to be shared by the new machines.

An excellent set of objects is also available for caching output on the Web server. Page output can be cached on the server. This caching can depend on the page or vary depending on query string values in the URL. Once a page is in the cache, the next time this URL is requested, instead of executing your program logic again, the server will retrieve this page from an in-memory cache. Page fragments can also be cached, allowing several pages to share cached resources that are retrieved from memory. The cache can be invalidated after a time out, when a file changes (great for caching parsed XML docs), or programmatically. This allows you to store information that's expensive to retrieve or calculate in memory, where it's instantly available until some dependency changes and the information needs to be retrieved or calculated again.

Configuration and Deployment

Configuration has been vastly simplified. All configuration information for the Framework is stored in XML format. There is a machine-specific file named machine.config, and each Web application has its own configuration file, called Web.config. The information in these files is applied at the machine level first and then with application entries, overriding the machine configuration, much like CSS.

Options for configuration include authorization and authentication; debugging, tracing, and error handling; what programs deal with which file types; where session state is stored; and settings global to the application, like a connection string.

Deployment is also much easier. Ever hear of XCOPY? Go ahead and use it to move all of your application's files onto the Web server, even if your site currently has thousands of visitors. The Web server will finish up all currently running requests with the old components, automatically load the new ones, and pick up from there. No downtime, no locked files, no registry entries. Just copy them over.

Support for Extensibility

There are many more options for reuse than ASP includes. Although the include syntax is still supported for backward compatibility, you'll throw this right out when you see the new options available. One of the best vehicles for reuse is called User Controls. User Controls are like a mix between ASP include files and ActiveX controls. They allow you to take an arbitrary chunk of HTML and code and package it as its own control. When the control is placed on the page, whatever content it contains is rendered in that location. This is very much like an include. However, with an ASP include, the file can only be placed on the page once. You would never package the code to output a text-type input with a specific look and feel in an ASP include because you couldn't change the caption on the control and text box contents if you included it more than once. With User Controls, you can expose properties and methods on the control, and each time the control is declared, an instance of an object is created. Using the ID of your declaration, you have a unique reference to each instance and can therefore reuse the control as many times as you'd like per page. You can also create User Controls programmatically, radically altering the content on any portion of your page. We'll be looking at User Controls in detail when implementing our chapter project.

With the services of the Common Language Runtime, you can also implement your own server controls. Want to create a list box that always gets its selected items via a many-to-many relationship in your database? You can simply inherit from and extend the ASP:ListBox control, adding your own properties, methods, and behaviors, while inheriting all of the existing functionality the control intrinsically supports.

Example

Let's take a look at a simple demonstration of some of the controls and features of the framework we've been talking about. Figure 6.1 (PostBackIE.aspx in the Demo folder) starts out as a standard HTML form. No code is executed on the server to generate this page; it could be static HTML.

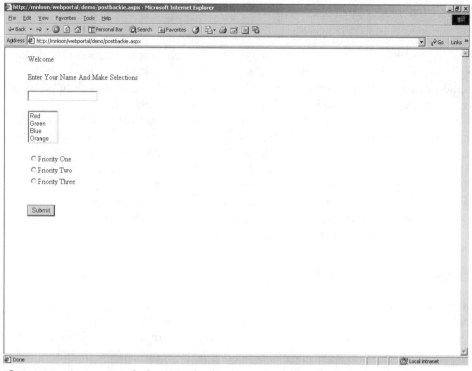

Figure 6.1   Demo page before post back.

After our users enter their name and make selections from the lists present, the page is posted back to the server in response to the server-side event trap we've set up on the button control at the bottom of the form, as shown in Figure 6.2.

Let's start with the body of the page, where we declare our server-side controls:

```
<body runat=server id=objBody style='margin-left:50px'>
   <form id="Form1" method="post" runat="server">
           <asp:Image Runat=server id=imgSelected />
           <asp:Label Runat=server ID=lblWelcome text='Welcome' />
           <br><br>
           Enter Your Name And Make Selections<br><br>
           <asp:TextBox Runat=server ID=txtName />
           <br><br>
           <asp:ListBox runat=server ID=lstColor />
           <br><br>
           <asp:RadioButtonList Runat=server ID=chkImage />
           <br><br>
           <asp:Button Runat=server ID=btnPost OnClick='ProcessChoices'
                   Text=Submit />
   </form>
</body>
```

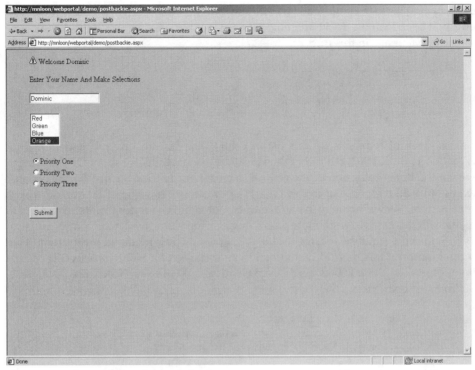

Figure 6.2 Demo page after post back.

The code is very straightforward. For each runat=server attribute we've declared, there will be a corresponding object created for us behind the scenes to use from code when our page is requested. The declarations here are of the simplest form, using only the runat and id attributes. We'll set these controls up from the page load event in code. The only additional thing we set up here is the event trap on the server for our button control. We declare that using the OnClick attribute of the control. This will cause the Framework to render HTML that will post to the server when the button is clicked. Once posted, the Framework will look for a method that we've implemented named ProcessChoices. We'll examine our implementation of this trap in a minute. First, let's take a look at our implementation of the Page_Load event. This is where we populate our lists and prepare the form. Let's start by looking at the event footprint:

```
Sub Page_Load(ByVal sender As System.Object, _
   ByVal e As System.EventArgs)
End Sub
```

The footprint for this event trap is the same as our last example. This is a common footprint for event traps and is worth memorizing. The If statement checks the IsPost-Back property, making sure this is the first time the page is rendered. The page load function fires every time the page is requested. When our user clicks the button and causes a post back, the page load will still fire. We will almost always do different stuff on a post back than we do on an initial rendering of the page, so this If block is a common check to make in this trap.

```
lstColor.Items.Add("Red")
lstColor.Items.Add("Green")
lstColor.Items.Add("Blue")
lstColor.Items.Add("Orange")
```

This block of code sets up our list of colors. The ListBox control renders it into HTML as a SELECT list, but rather than creating or even thinking about OPTION tags, we use the Items collection of the control to create our entries. As in VB6, collections expose an Add method. But in the .NET Framework, we have function overrides and constructors, so we actually have a number of options for footprints of the Add method. In this case we're going to pass a single string value, which the control will use as both the value and the text for the OPTION tag that gets rendered for the item. The second footprint for the Add method takes an instance of a ListItem object. The List-Item object is shared between DropDownLists, ListBoxes, CheckBoxLists, and RadioButtonLists. Here's the code:

```
chkImage.Items.Add(New ListItem("Priority One", _
                                "../images/priority1.gif"))
   chkImage.Items.Add(New ListItem("Priority Two", _
                                "../images/priority2.gif"))
   chkImage.Items.Add(New ListItem("Priority Three", _
                                "../images/priority3.gif"))
```

Rather than creating an instance of a ListItem object, we create one inline for the parameter value. By using the New ListItem declaration, we get access to all of the constructors for the ListItem object. The footprint we'll use accepts two string values, name and value. The name is what's displayed to the user, and the value controls the value of the control as the selection changes. We're going to use this value to display an image when the page gets posted back, so the string we pass is a complete relative reference to the selected image.

```
imgSelected.Visible = False
```

Because we're not displaying an image until after the user submits his or her choices on the form, we hide the image for the initial rendering of the page. This is a good example of the power exposed by this programming model. Not only is there no logic embedded in the body of our page, but this single line of code causes our Image control to render no content at all. On the post back we'll set the Visible property back to true, and the control will render its HTML output. This model is so much simpler than doing the same thing with ASP that once you start using the new Framework, you'll never want to go back.

After this function executes, our page enters the rendering stage and the output goes to our client. When the user clicks the submit button, all the values and state information for the page are posted back to the server, the binary image of our page executable is retrieved from the Web server's cache, our objects are re-created and their properties set according to the state information on the page (i.e., the txtName control has its text property set equal to whatever our user type in on the HTML text box), and our page load event is fired. Because the post back occurred when the user clicked the submit button, the ProcessChoices method is also fired. Let's take a look at that code:

```
Sub ProcessChoices(ByVal o As Object, ByVal e As EventArgs)
  lblWelcome.Text = "Welcome " & txtName.Text
  objBody.Attributes("bgcolor") = lstColor.SelectedItem.Value
  imgSelected.Visible = True
  imgSelected.ImageUrl = chkImage.SelectedItem.Value
End Sub
```

Notice the footprint of the trap. It's the same again. The first line of code changes our Welcome message to incorporate the user's name. We do this by setting the Text property of our label control. We use the Text property of the text box to build this output.

We set the background color of the page using the objBody HTMLGenericControl. This control exposes an attributes collection, which we can use to set any HTML attribute we'd like to use. In this case we're going to set the BGCOLOR attribute equal to whatever our user has chosen from the ListBox control. We get this from the Value property of the SelectedItem of ListBox. Keep in mind that no HTML is generated as this code executes; we're simply setting the properties and methods of those objects that were exposed for us to work with. HTML generation does not occur until our code has finished executing and we enter the rendering stage of the page.

The last couple lines set up our image control. This will display a small image in front of our welcome message. We set its visibility to false in the initial load of our page, so we toggle it back here. We then set the ImageURL equal to the value that's been selected from the RadioButtonList. Because we set these values up to be relative references to image files on our site, the <img> tag rendered by our image control will display the corresponding file.

Notice also that when the page content is rendered, TextBbox, ListBox, and RadioButtonList all still have the values that they did when the page was posted. Because of the stateless nature of the HTTP protocol, we are completely regenerating this page before it goes back to the client. This state maintenance does not occur automatically. In traditional ASP this would actually require quite a bit of code, but it's part of the built-in state maintenance features of the ASP.NET Framework.

Let's Start the Project

The project we're going to create is a Web portal of the type that would be used on a corporate intranet. Our portal will have four main functional areas. We will display current items that are specific to the department our user is in, and we will display stock prices for tickers of our user's choosing. We will also have a main navigation area on the left-hand side of our site. This will provide links to all of the functional areas that are exposed by our portal. In this case the functional areas revolve mainly around configuration and preference settings for our Web portal, but they will illustrate the exposure of functionality that in an Enterprise environment would be solutions to specific business problems. The portal is shown in Figure 6.3.

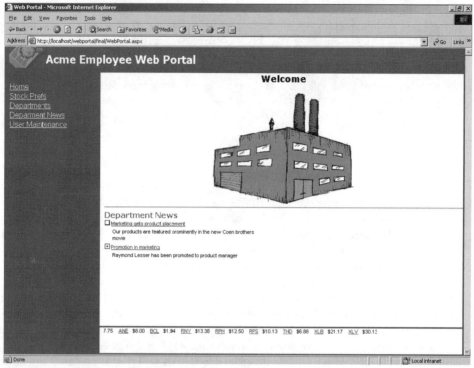

Figure 6.3 The main page of the Web portal.

On the site, the left, and bottom areas will remain constant, and the middle one will be our area for current content. Clicking on the menu items on the left will cause the content pane to be updated with the user's selection. The department news items and the factory image are displayed by default and considered the home page of the site. Configuration of the other areas is controlled by the different choices on the menu, and the site will update to reflect those choices. When users use the main content area to choose a different stock, the marquee at the bottom of the page will update with prices for the stocks they have chosen.

To work with the examples in this chapter, you will want to start by creating a new Web application with Visual Studio .NET. Name it WebPortal and create it using your local Web server. Once the project has been created, use the Solution Explorer to add the three directories from the WebPortal directory of the companion CD-ROM to your new Web application project. You can do this by dragging the three folders from Windows Explorer and dropping them on the Web portal project in the Solution Explorer window. You will also need to execute the AtWorkWebPortal.sql file using the Query Analyzer. This script will create the database and all the tables and other objects you need and populate the database. For this script to work, you will need to be connected to your database as an administrator.

The Portal Framework

The main structure of the page will be controlled with an HTML table. Using combinations of rowspan and colspan, this is an amazingly flexible way to create frameset-like functionality. You can see the raw declarations of this table with no content in Figure 6.4, which shows the WebPortalTemplate.htm. This is the static HTML page that we'll use as the starting point for later portal implementation.

Note that the source for this page is pure HTML. We will develop each functional area on its own so that we can test each piece separately to make sure that they all work before putting them together. After each area is developed, we'll convert them to ASP.NET User Controls. This will allow us to add them to our Web portal template by simply replacing the static descriptions there now with our own server-side elements that will create our User Controls. This strategy is very flexible and also very easy to implement, as you'll see. The main content area will then be invoked programmatically, creating different User Controls and adding them to the content frame as our user makes different selections. This functional division is a good design architecturally because each User Control is responsible for its own functionality, whereas the Framework uses any attributes exposed on the controls to modify its behavior in the larger context. It's a lot like a COM interface-based design in that any context-specific behavior is exposed as properties of the control, whereas the implementation details are hidden within the individual controls. If the behavior of a given area needs to change (i.e., business rules change), the only thing that needs to change is the implementation of the control. The control will continue to function in the context of the Framework, or in whatever other functional areas in which we're using it, as long as the interface behavior does not change. This is a lot cleaner in the .NET Framework than in the world of COM because we don't have class IDs, interfaces IDs, and AppIDs in the registry ready to inflict pain upon us if we change the interface. Because of their self-descriptive, reflective architecture, the managed components will adjust in real time after a simple file copy.

The Database

The simple database that we'll be using is geared around the storage of user preferences. This puts our UserPreferences table at the logical center of the schema. In this table we're storing users ID, their e-mail address, and the department in which they work, as shown in Figure 6.5.

The other tables include:

Department.   Stores department descriptions. DepartmentID is carried as a foreign key in the UserPreferences table, so each user belongs in a single department.

DepartmentItem.   Stores interest items that are specific to a department. The columns here are set up to provide some descriptive text and a URL to a resource that has more information about the item. The priority of the item is used to control which bullet image to use when displaying the item. Users will see all department items for their department, filtered to those items where the current date is between the begin and end date of the item.

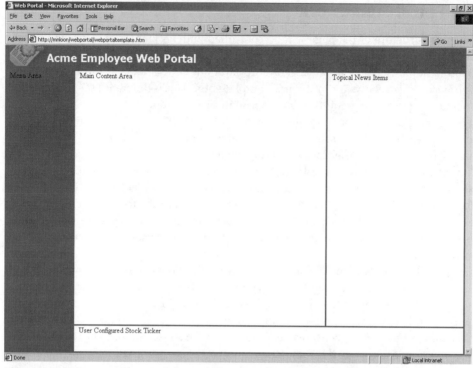

Figure 6.4 The portal framework.

TickerPrice.   This is a table that stores stock tickers and their current prices. It would normally be populated by a feed from an online stock price service. For our purposes, these values will be static, but this table could easily be updated periodically with current information.

UserTicker.   This table provides a many-to-many reconciliation between User-Preferences and TickerPrice so that a single user can see many stocks, and a single stock can be seen by many users.

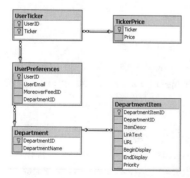

Figure 6.5 The portal database.

Portal Pieces and Parts

The portal functionality consists of a number of pairs. Each pair has a component that displays the customized information and another component that allows configuration of these customizations. Let's examine each of these:

Department news.   This area consists of a user control that uses the DepartmentID of the current user and the current date to retrieve a list of department news items to display. It then uses a DataList control to display these items. There are two areas of configuration for this content area. The first simply allows a user to enter a department. This area will be used infrequently, mainly on initial setup and then if the company structure ever changes. The second area provides an interface for department heads to enter news items and URLs that contain the full story of the items.

Stock ticker.   This is a simple content area that relies on the specific Marquee tag. Here we're using the UserTicker table to get a list of stocks for display in the pane. We get the prices for each of the stocks our user has expressed an interest in from the TickerPrice table. To allow our user to choose stocks, we render a check box list with an item for each row in the TickerPrice table. Any stocks our user selects cause this component to create a corresponding row in the UserTicker table. Our users get to this area by clicking on the Stock Prefs menu choice in the left-hand pane.

User maintenance.   This is an area for an administrator to use to add and remove users. This is the information that will be used when we're identifying and authorizing our users and then again when we're rendering their custom content. This is user-specific information that is controlled by an administrator instead of a user, such as what department users are in and their e-mail address.

We will build the application as separate parts and then assemble them as a whole using the WebPortalTemplate document. We will start with the content display areas and then move on to the configuration areas. This will allow us to first build static content areas based on different types of data stores (XML and database data) and then move on to building interfaces that update our database data. After we have the different display and configuration areas built, we'll move on to making User Controls out of them and wiring them into our framework. Let's take a look at a high-level plan.

The Project Plan

We'll decide which pages to do first and which to save for last based on the techniques we'll use in each to code the page. We'll start with the simple ones first and build on what we have learned when we go on to the next page. We'll do our implementation in the order shown in Table 6.3.

After completing our implementation, we'll take a look at some of the ways we could extend the application and some improvements we could make, and go over the techniques we've used at a high level. In the meantime, let's get started.

Table 6.3 Project Plan for the Web Portal Implementation

FILE NAME	FUNCTIONAL DESCRIPTION	TOPICS, TECHNIQUES
WPMenu.aspx	Renders the list of Menu Items for the Web portal. This list is driven by an internal XML document for easy extensibility.	Data binding a data grid to an XML document.
DepartmentItem. aspx	Displays a list of current items of interest from the current user's department.	Binding relational data to a DataList control using a DataReader.
Ticker.aspx	Displays a list of stock prices for user-selected stocks of interest.	Using the header and footer of the DataList control. Incorporating client-side script into an ASP.NET page.
UserMaint.aspx	Displays list of users. Users may be selected for editing or deleted, or a new user may be added.	Using HTML form to update relational data. Using panels for different content views. Using ItemCommand columns from a data grid.
UserTickers.aspx	Displays a list of all stocks for selection. Preselects user's current choices.	Use of a CheckListBox for editing a many-to-many database table.
Departments. aspx	Allows creation of new departments and editing of existing departments.	Using a data grid for editing database content.
DepartmentNews .aspx	Allows the creation of news items for a specific department.	Using a DataList control for editing database content.
WebPortal.aspx	Main landing page of application. Displays all content for current selections.	Conversion of pages to User Controls and wiring the Web portal framework.
Web.Config and Login.aspx	Allows unrecognized users to login to the Web site by providing credentials.	Security configuration in the ASP.NET Framework.

Portal Content

In developing our portal we will first create standalone aspx pages that we will later convert into User Controls to more easily incorporate them into the portal template. This is a good design technique because it ensures that our controls have no artificial dependencies on other portions of the portal page. Our best design is going to be one that decouples each unit of functionality from the bigger picture so that controls can be reused in other solutions if a business need arises. It is also very easy to convert an aspx page into a User Control using only a couple of simple copy and paste operations. Let's start by creating the Web project we will use to do our development. Start Visual Studio .NET and choose to create a new project. Choose Visual Basic Project from the tree on the left, and select ASP.NET Web Application from the choices that appear in the right-hand pane. The dialog shown in Figure 6.6 will appear.

We will name our project WebPortal. Notice that after typing the name, the label under the project name has been updated with the URL of our Web application. You can do development on a local machine or on another machine that has the ASP.NET Framework installed. Put the machine name into the Location text box, and click OK. Visual Studio .NET will now create a new virtual root on the Web server we have chosen and will create some template files and add them to the new IIS application. Configuration of the application is done for you by the IDE. The IDE even creates a starter ASP.NET page named WebForm1.aspx. After the project has been successfully created, the IDE will look something like Figure 6.7 (depending on your own toolbar visibility and placement).

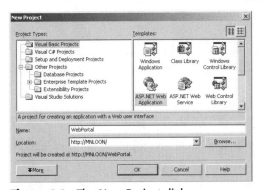

Figure 6.6   The New Project dialog.

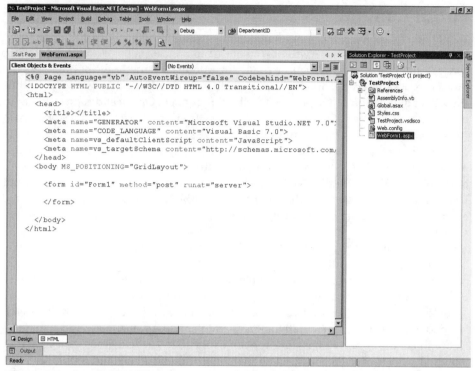

Figure 6.7   A new ASP.NET project.

The Solution Explorer is an indispensable window during development. I like to unpin it (by clicking the pushpin in the upper right-hand corner of the toolbox) so that it slides out of the way when not in use. If you hover over its docked icon, the window will slide back out. I also like to keep the Server Explorer and toolbox handy in this way. Let's take a look at the template page the IDE has created for us by default:

```
<%@ Page Language="vb" AutoEventWireup="false"
Codebehind="WebForm1.aspx.vb" Inherits="WebPortal.WebForm1"%>
<!DOCTYPE HTML PUBLIC "-//W3C//DTD HTML 4.0 Transitional//EN">
<html>
  <head>
    <title></title>
    <meta name="GENERATOR" content="Microsoft Visual Studio.NET 7.0">
    <meta name="CODE_LANGUAGE" content="Visual Basic 7.0">
    <meta name=vs_defaultClientScript content="JavaScript">
    <meta name=vs_targetSchema
content="http://schemas.microsoft.com/intellisense/ie5">
  </head>
  <body MS_POSITIONING="GridLayout">

    <form id="Form1" method="post" runat="server">

    </form>

  </body>
</html>
```

The body of the document has only a FORM tag with a runat=server attribute. Post backs are accomplished with an HTML post, so this form is needed for any page that is doing post backs. The meta tags and the attribute on the body tag are useless, and I usually delete them right away. The PAGE directive is by far the most interesting thing on the page. You may recognize this type of tag from ASP. Each page can have only one PAGE directive. The language attribute tells the runtime which language to expect on the page. The other attributes actually wire our page to the code-behind-page module. This is a class that we will create that inherits from the System.Web.UI.Page class, which our ASPX page in turn inherits from when the page is compiled.

The Page object exposes all of the functionality and services of the Framework to us during development. It's the class that manages the objects we create in our page on the server side: the data binding, validation, and eventual rendering of the HTML output from our page. All of the intrinsic objects from traditional ASP that we know and love are properties of the page object (Response, Request, Server, Session, and Application). Also present are the Cache object, where we can programmatically store result-sets or other objects in the Web server's memory; the Trace object, which we can use for debugging and instrumentation; the IsPostPack property, which we use to determine if our page is requested by a post back or for the first time; and other properties and methods. By inheriting from the page object, we get all of these services and default behavior free and can add our own logic and objects. Press F7 from your page and you'll see the code behind our page, shown in Figure 6.8.

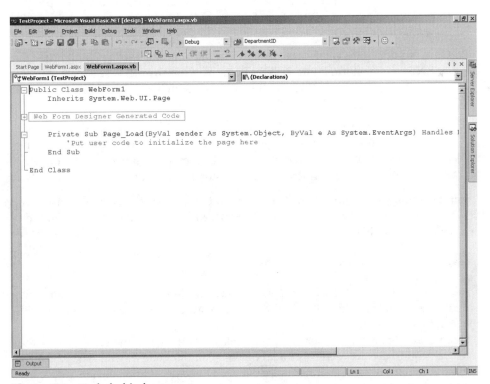

Figure 6.8   Code behind page.

Here the IDE also generates a default template for us. Hidden in a region is the code that the IDE generates as you use the design pane. The stubbed out function is an event trap for the Page_Load event, where we can add our own page initialization logic. When we're using data binding on the page, this is where we'll read our persistent data and bind it to the controls on our page. The page object exposes the IsPostBack function, which we can use to tell if the page is being requested for the first time or is being requested by a post back from a control on our page.

We'll look at how the code behind the page and our ASPX files get compiled in a bit. For now let's get started with our solution by implementing the portal menu.

The Portal Menu Page

Right-click on the project in the Solution Explorer and choose Add | Add Web Form. Name the form WPMenu and click Open. The ASPX template appears in the code editor. On this page we are interested in displaying all of the items in an XML file as HTML anchor tags on our page. All of our links will be WebPortal.aspx, the main page hosting all of our content. We'll tell our host page what to put into the main content area by passing a query string value with the request. We'll be building this host page later; for now let's focus on rendering our XML document as a list of hyperlinks. To transform our XML file into a list of hyperlinks we'll be using a few key ASP.NET techniques:

1. First we'll read our XML file into a data set object. Because the data set represents data internally as XML, it can load an XML document as easily as it can a relational data source.

2. Once our data set is created, we can use the data binding services built into ASP.NET to transform it into HTML. Because of the abstraction the data set introduces between our XML and how we deal with it, this will work very much the same way as it would for relational data.

3. The DataGrid object is the ASP.NET Web control we'll use to display our links. This control has one purpose: to generate an HTML table. By default it will render an HTML table with a column for each column present in our data source. We'll use its templating functionality to customize this output.

Start by adding a data grid to the FORM present on our page. As we saw earlier, all Web controls use the syntax <asp:*ControlName Attributes...*>. The default declaration for a data grid looks like this:

```
<asp:datagrid runat=server Id=dgMenu />
```

Add this tag to your HTML form. The DataGrid always renders its contents by using the data binding engine. This will be done in our code behind the page. Press F7 to switch to the code pane.

Because our ASPX page inherits from the class we define in the code behind the page, we need to declare each control on our page in our code as well. The ASP.NET runtime automatically sets up inheritance between these declarations when the page is compiled on the first request for it. Whatever value we use for the ID attribute is the name we need to use for the variable declaration. Because we gave our DataGrid an ID value of dgMenu, we need to declare a corresponding instance of the DataGrid in our code with the same name. Add this declaration at the top of the class definition. After doing this the code behind page will look like this:

```
Public Class WPMenu
    Inherits System.Web.UI.Page
    Protected WithEvents dgMenu As DataGrid

+ " Web Form Designer Generated Code "

        Private Sub Page_Load(ByVal sender As System.Object, _
        ByVal e As System.EventArgs) Handles MyBase.Load


    End Sub
End Class
```

The DataGrid declaration exposes all of the properties and methods of the control to us in our class. We will use this from the page load event to bind the data grid to the XML document via the services of a data set object. Add the following implementation to the Page_Load stub:

```
        Dim ds As New DataSet("MenuItems")

        ds.ReadXml(Server.MapPath("Menu.xml"))
        dgMenu.DataSource = ds
        dgMenu.DataBind()

        ds = Nothing
```

The first thing we do is to create a new instance of a data set object, using the constructor to name it MenuItems. When reading XML documents, we don't need the services of a data adapter as we would when reading from a database. We simply use the ReadXML method to load our document directly from the file system. The parameter ReadXML accepts is just the filename. Here you may recognize some ASP functionality where we're using the Server object's MapPath method. This returns the physical directory from which our page is executing. We pass menu.xml to the MapPath function to create a well-formed complete path to our XML document on the local file system of the Web server. Let's take a look at this XML document:

```
<?xml version="1.0" encoding="utf-8" ?>
<MenuItems>
    <MenuItem descr='Home' command='Home' />
    <MenuItem descr='Stock Prefs' command='EditUserTicker' />
    <MenuItem descr='Departments' command='EditDepartments' />
    <MenuItem descr='Deparment News' command='EditDepartmentItems' />
    <MenuItem descr='User Maintenance' command='EditUsers' />
</MenuItems>
```

Our document contains a MenuItem element for each hyperlink we want displayed in the menu. The table objects created by the data set to model this data depend entirely on the structure of the document. If we had a more complex document with nested elements and hierarchies, we would get more than one corresponding table object to model the document in relational form. For this simple document the data set will decide to create only one table. It will have a column for each attribute on the MenuItem elements. A DataRow object will be created in the table's row collection for each MenuItem element present. Once it is loaded into the data set, we can think of our document as a database table with two columns, one named descr and one named command. Binding this data to the grid is pretty tough. It requires two whole lines of code:

```
dgMenu.DataSource = ds .Tables(0).DefaultView
dgMenu.DataBind()
```

The first line assigns the DataSource of the data grid to the table in our data set. The DefaultView property of our DataTable is an instance of a DataView object that exposes all of the columns of the table. You can programmatically create other DataView objects to bind objects to a subset of the columns in your DataTables. The DataView object is one of scores of objects that are supported by the data binding engine. Actually, any object that implements the ICollection interface, of which there are quite a few, can be used in data binding.

Once the DataSource has been assigned, nothing actually happens until we call DataBind. This invokes the data binding engine, which will generate the data grid's HTML table. The last line of code is just cleanup, where we set the data set to nothing. Compile your project choosing Build | Build and request the page from the Web browser. The output is shown in Figure 6.9.

This is the default behavior of the DataGrid control. We get an HTML table with a border of 1 pixel and a column for each column in our data source. The first row contains column names. We get a row in the HTML table for each row in our data source. Notice that we generated this output with about four lines of code. Consider for a second how much code we would have to write for the same functionality with ASP or XSLT.

But this output is not what we need, nor are there often times when it will be needed. To generate our hyperlinks, we will need to tailor our output using the templating functionality of the data grid. Let's first consider exactly what kind of output we desire. For each row in our data source we need an HTML anchor tag that uses our descr column for display, and the command column needs to be built into the URL as a query string value. For the third row in our table the desired HTML would be:

```
<a href='WebPortal.aspx?Command=EditUserTicker'>Stock Prefs</a>
```

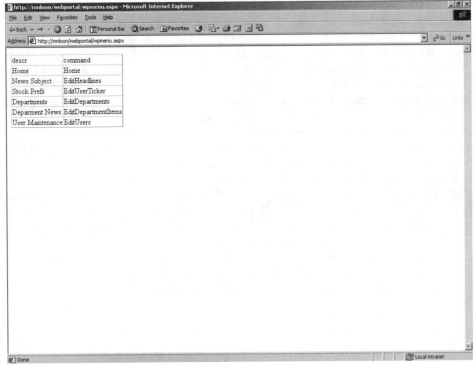

Figure 6.9   Default output of a DataGrid.

Most of this is static output. Only the value of our Command parameter and the text of the anchor tag are dynamic. Modify the declaration of the DataGrid to create this template:

```
<asp:DataGrid Runat=server ID=dgMenu
                    BorderWidth=0
                    AutoGenerateColumns=False
                    Font-Name='arial'>
  <Columns>
   <asp:TemplateColumn>
    <ItemTemplate>
     <a href='WebPortal.aspx?Command=<%# Container.DataItem("command") %>
'>
<%# Container.DataItem("descr") %></a>
       </ItemTemplate>
   </asp:TemplateColumn>
  </Columns>
</asp:DataGrid>
```

Let's start by looking at the attributes we've added to the DataGrid declaration. The first is the BorderWidth attribute. This will render as a Border attribute on the HTML table. The next attribute, AutoGenerateColumns, causes the DataGrid to not render a column for each column in our data source because it will be relying instead on the template we are providing. The third is one of dozens of attributes exposed by the DataGrid to control the style of the output. This family of attributes exposes CSS functionality to our control, allowing us to render inline style attributes to control the look and feel of our output. There is also a CSSClass attribute that we can use to rely on a traditional CSS stylesheet to control the look of our table instead.

The first child element of the DataGrid declaration is the Columns tag. This is always the first and only child of the DataGrid declaration. Under this element we can declare any number of columns that we want to output on the table. In this case we only want one column, which we define with the TemplateColumn element. We can create a number of different column types on the DataGrid. TemplateColumn is the most flexible because it allows us to use free-form HTML to define our output. The valid children of the Columns element are summarized in Table 6.4.

We will be covering these types on other pages in our solution. Of these column types, we could use either a template column or a hyperlink column to render the output that we want in this case. Let's take a look at the solution using a template column:

```
<ItemTemplate>
<a href='WebPortal.aspx?Command=<%# Container.DataItem("command") %> '>
<%# Container.DataItem("descr") %></a>
</ItemTemplate>
```

Table 6.4 Valid Children of Columns Element

TAG	FUNCTION
<asp:BoundColumn>	Displays the value of a specific column in our data source as the contents of a table data cell. CSS attributes are exposed per column, allowing us to change the look and feel of our output from cell to cell.
<asp:ButtonColumn>	Renders an HTML input of type button or a hyperlink. Can be used to implement a post back, where our server-side event trap gets passed information specifically about the row that was clicked.
<asp:EditCommandColumn>	Renders a button or hyperlink that, when clicked, raises the EditCommand on the server for our DataGrid.
<asp:HyperlinkColumn>	Exposes attributes to aid us in rendering an anchor tag from our source data.
<asp:TemplateColumn>	Allows for free-form creation of HTML output. Uses a tag-based syntax for replacing portions of our template with values from our data source.

All of the text between the begin and end tags of the ItemTemplate element is our HTML output. In the HREF attribute of the anchor tag we are creating, we use the ASP.NET data binding tag <%# *Expression* %> to pull in values from our data source. This tag looks a bit like the ASP shortcut <% = *Output* %>, but the # sign lets the data binding engine know that it's specific to a data binding operation. In this tag we call Container.DataItem and pass the name of the column from the data source that we want to substitute into that part of the template. With the two data binding tags that we're using on the template, we're inserting the command value from each row of our data source into the query string and inserting the descr value into the text of each our anchor tags. The resulting output is shown in Figure 6.10.

For now these hyperlinks will return a 404:File Not Found because we have not created the WebPortal.aspx yet, but later we'll convert this page to a User Control and use it on the WebPortal.aspx page.

Linking to Internal Content

When our portal first renders, the main content area will display links to news items of interest to the department of the visiting employee. To do this we'll use the DepartmentID of the visiting user to look up all current items in the DepartmentItem table. This will be our first example of binding relational data to Web controls. In the previous page we used an XML document. Because of the abstraction layer created by the data components in the .NET Framework, you will see that there is very little difference in how we set up the Web control itself; the only changes are in how we retrieve the information.

Figure 6.10   Template output of a DataGrid.

We'll also be using a DataList instead of a DataGrid. These controls are very similar in functionality, with a couple of important differences. The DataGrid is designed to generate an HTML table. We do this by defining each column that we want output when the grid renders. Sometimes an HTML table is not how we want each row of our data output. We may want a complete HTML table for each row in our data set, or perhaps we want each row rendered as its own HTML paragraph tag. The DataList control is designed to support more flexible types of output like this. Instead of defining how we want each column from our data source rendered, we define a template for the entire row of output. This greatly increases the flexibility that we have in how the output appears. When we want columnar output, the DataGrid is very good for quickly defining this. When we want something more flexible, the DataList is the control for the job.

Start by adding a Web Form to your project named DepartmentItem.aspx. Let's take a look at the output we get from this page, shown in Figure 6.11.

Each row of our data source creates a distinct block of HTML. Because each of these blocks does not occupy a single row of an HTML table, the DataList control is better suited for generating this output. There are no visible static portions of the output, but there is some underlying HTML that will be constant from row to row. The text of the hyperlink is driven by the LinkText column of the DepartmentItem table. The HREF of the anchor tag is driven by the URL column. The more verbose description beneath each hyperlink is pulled from the ItemDescr column. The image displayed to the left of the hyperlink is dynamic as well. This is driven by the Priority column of the database, and we have a corresponding image for each priority level that we can expect.

Let's take a look at the declaration for the DataList:

```
<asp:DataList Runat=server ID=dlDepartmentItem
              ItemStyle-Font-Name=arial
              ItemStyle-Font-Size=8pt>
  <ItemTemplate>
    <img src='images/Priority<%# Container.DataItem("Priority") %>.gif'>
    <asp:HyperLink Target=_blank Runat=server ID=hlDI
                   NavigateUrl='<%# Container.DataItem("URL") %>'
                   text='<%# Container.DataItem("LinkText") %>' />
    <table style='padding-left:15px' width=160px>
            <tr><td style='font-family:arial;font-size:8pt'>
                <%# Container.DataItem("ItemDescr") %>
            </td></tr>
    </table>
  </ItemTemplate>
</asp:DataList>
```

This is very similar to how we would declare a DataGrid, but gone is the Columns element. Because a DataList is not a column-based output format, we use a single ItemTemplate for the output of an entire row from our data source. Everything between the beginning and ending ItemTemplate tags will be output for each row of our data source.

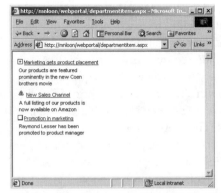

Figure 6.11 DepartmentItem output using a DataList.

The first thing on our template is an HTML image tag. The valid values for the priority column are 1, 2, and 3. We have corresponding images named Priority1.gif, Priority2.gif, and Priority3.gif. Here we're using a data binding tag to dynamically build the source attribute of our image tag, causing the correct priority image to display for the different department items.

Next we're using a Hyperlink Web server control to build our anchor tag. The Hyperlink control is driven by two attributes, NavigateURL and Text. NavigateURL renders as the HREF attribute of the resultant anchor tag. We're using data binding syntax to substitute the value from the URL column for each row of output. We're driving the text attribute with the LinkText column.

The last thing we output for each row of our data source is the ItemDescr column. Here we wrap the output in an HTML table to which we apply CSS attributes to get a line break and to indent the description by 160 pixels.

Now that our DataList is set up, we need only to add the code to our Page_Load event to bind the control to the rows from DepartmentItem in which we're interested. Press F7 to move to the code window. First we'll import the System.Data.SQLClient because we'll be using objects from this namespace to read our relational data. Then we'll declare a DataList control with the same name as the ID that we used in our ASPX page (dlDepartmentItem):

```
Imports System.Data.SqlClient

Public Class DepartmentItem
    Inherits System.Web.UI.Page

    Protected WithEvents dlDepartmentItem As DataList

+ Web Form Designer Generated Code

    Private Sub Page_Load(ByVal sender As System.Object, _
                    ByVal e As System.EventArgs) Handles MyBase.Load

    End Sub

End Class
```

To retrieve our relational data and bind the data list, we'll be using the SQL-DataReader. The DataReader control is quite a bit different from a DataSet.

Instead of retrieving all of the data from the database up front and storing it all in the memory allocated for the object, a DataReader retrieves rows only as they are requested and discards them from memory when the next row is requested. This allows us to move through very large resultsets with a much lower memory footprint on the Web server. The downside to this is that we do not have random access to our resultset. We cannot modify it, search it, or sort it. These operations are all well suited to a DataSet. Many times when creating HTML, however, the only operation that we want to do is to move through the resultset once in a forward-only manner and generate some HTML for each row in the set. A data reader is ideal for this job, and by using a DataReader instead of a DataSet for these types of tasks, we will greatly enhance the performance and scalability of our Web applications. The lower-memory footprint of the data reader will use much less of our Web server's resources, meaning that it can service more concurrent requests, and the reduced allocation of memory means we move the result faster than we would with a DataSet.

For problems requiring modifying, sorting, or querying a resultset after it's been retrieved from the database, use the DataSet. But when a fast, forward-only, read-only resultset will do the job, use a data reader. Each managed provider has a DataReader object. For OLEDB, it's OLEDBDataRead. For SQLClient it's SQLDataReader.

As I mentioned, a data reader can only be used once. When we use a data reader in a data binding operation, it's the data binding engine that needs this single use. So the only thing we'll be doing with the reader is defining the query that we want to use to populate the DataList, assigning it as the DataSource of our DataList and calling Data-Bind on the DataList. Here's the implementation of our Page_Load event:

```
Dim cn As New _
SqlConnection("server=(local);database=AtWorkWebPortal;uid=sa")
Dim sql As String = _
"SELECT DepartmentItem.ItemDescr, DepartmentItem.LinkText, " _
& "DepartmentItem.URL, DepartmentItem.Priority " _
& "FROM DepartmentItem INNER JOIN UserPreferences ON " _
& "DepartmentItem.DepartmentID = UserPreferences.DepartmentID " _
& "WHERE (DepartmentItem.BeginDisplay <= @CurrentDate) " _
& "AND (DepartmentItem.EndDisplay > @CurrentDate) " _
& "AND (UserPreferences.UserID = @UserID)"

    Dim cm As New SqlCommand(sql, cn)
    Dim pm As SqlParameter
    Dim dr As SqlDataReader

    Session("UserID") = 1

    pm = cm.Parameters.Add( _
    New SqlParameter("@CurrentDate", SqlDbType.DateTime))
    pm.Value = Now
```

```
pm = cm.Parameters.Add(
New SqlParameter("@UserID", SqlDbType.Int))
pm.Value = Session("UserID")

cn.Open()
dr = cm.ExecuteReader
dlDepartmentItem.DataSource = dr
dlDepartmentItem.DataBind()

cn.Close()
dr = Nothing
cm = Nothing
cn = Nothing
```

We're hard-coding the Session variable that we're using to determine who is currently using our application. Later we'll populate this when our users log in, so this line of code is temporary for now:

```
Session("UserID") = 1
```

The command object that we use is the same type of object that we'd use when creating a data set, and it's the same object we use as the SELECTCommand property of the SQLDataAdapter. The data adapter actually uses a data reader under the hood to get the data from the database. It then creates the in-memory representation of the data exposed by the data set; you use this when the Fill operation is complete.

To use a command object directly, you use one of the execute methods it exposes. When you want a data reader, you use the ExecuteReader method of the command object. We'll look at the other execute methods, ExecuteNonQuery and ExecuteScalar, later on in the project. The ExecuteReader method returns a reference to a data reader object, so we capture that instance with our own instance of a data reader. The parameterized query and creation of the parameter objects should be familiar from the chapter on ADO.NET. It's worth noting that once our connection and command are set up, the code that actually gets the data and transforms it into the output that we defined with a DataList runs in just three lines:

```
dr = cm.ExecuteReader
dlDepartmentItem.DataSource = dr
dlDepartmentItem.DataBind()
```

These lines execute the statement against the database, associate the result with the DataList, and invoke the data binding engine to do the transformation.

Creating the Stock Ticker

The radical transformation of the type of coding that is done on the server in the new Framework can create the impression that the benefits gained from this model are there at the expense of client-side functionality. Although no one seems to enjoy the effort involved in creating cross-browser applications with rich client-side functionality, there are still many times where an application's target audience is captive and has a specific browser mandated. This is often true in an intranet environment. This page will illustrate that there really is nothing lost as far as functionality on the client-side goes. This page uses the IE-specific Marquee tag and client-side event traps implemented in VBScript. Not only is all of the client-side functionality provided by scripting languages and DHTML still available to us, but we can still implement ActiveX controls and include them in our pages. In fact, because the ASP.NET Framework is very focused on server-side processing, it has virtually no impact at all on what can or cannot be done on the client-side. The Web controls exposed to us on the server are flexible enough that they can often aid us in our generation of client-side functionality. Although the output from this page will be constantly on the move, a static shot of it appears in Figure 6.12.

Start by creating a page named Ticker.aspx. This page will display a horizontally scrolling list of stock prices. The stocks displayed will be driven by the UserTicker table, and later we will build an interface to this table so that our users can choose which prices they want to see. Additionally, our marquee will have hyperlinks embedded into it so that our users can click on a price and see the current quote for that stock on Nasdaq.com.

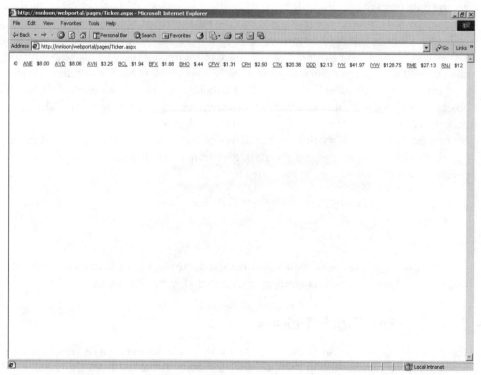

Figure 6.12   Stock prices displayed with the Marquee tag.

Let's start by looking at the DataList we'll add to the HTML form on our page:

```
<asp:DataList Runat=server ID=dlTicker
        RepeatLayout=Flow
        RepeatDirection=Horizontal>
  <HeaderTemplate>
   <marquee id=TickList>
  </HeaderTemplate>
  <ItemTemplate>
    <a href='http://quotes.nasdaq.com/Quote.dll?mode=stock&symbol=
<%# Container.DataItem("Ticker") %>&quick.x=4&quick.y=14'>
    <%# Container.DataItem("Ticker") %></a>
     
    <%# Format(Container.DataItem("Price"),"$#.00") %>
      
  </ItemTemplate>
  <FooterTemplate>
   </marquee>
  </FooterTemplate>
</asp:DataList>
```

Now let's take a look at the attributes we're setting on the DataList before digging into the templates.

In our previous use of the DataList, examine the HTML generated as output and notice that each row of our output is cradled by an HTML table that is generated by the control. Although this may seem to contradict the difference I stated between the Data-Grid and the DataList, the table generated by the DataList is for formatting each row of output instead of formatting the individual columns of our output. Each entire row of output gets its own cell of the table instead of being broken up into different cells per row of output. This provides breaks between our data items in the output. In this case, however, we don't want these breaks. We want everything to be display contiguously on a single line of output that will scroll across the screen in the marquee. To tell the DataList that we no longer want it to generate a table row for each line of output, we use the RepeatLayour property to Flow and the RepeatDirection property to Horizontal.

You will also notice two new template tags. We've used the ItemTemplate tag, which is the template used for repeating rows of data in our data source. We can use the header and footer templates to define the output we want to appear once at the top and bottom of our data rows. We'll use these in this case to wrap the output generated by our data items in a Marquee tag.

The anchor tag is built in a manner similar to what we used for the menu. We have a mostly static URL whose only dynamic portion is a value for the symbol query string value. The other difference in this case is that this is an external link and will take users directly to Nasdaq's site and display information for the symbol that they have clicked on.

When we output the price as of our data rows, you will notice that we're not just using the Container.DataItem, as we have done so far. We are also calling an intrinsic VB.NET function: Format. We are in turn passing a value from our data item as a parameter to the format function. This function will be called by the data binding engine for each row that is generated during binding. It's important to realize that not only can we call intrinsic functions from data binding operations, but we can also call functions that we have defined ourselves. We can even create a public instance of a business object in our class file and call methods on it from our data binding expressions, passing values from our data items as parameters. We'll cover some of this flexibility of the data binding engine when we implement the DepartmentNews page.

Having defined the template for our output, we have only to tie it to our data source and call the data binding engine. Let's start by adding our Import and Datalist declaration to the code behind the page:

```
Imports System.Data.SqlClient

Public Class Ticker
    Inherits System.Web.UI.Page
    Protected WithEvents dlTicker As DataList

+ Web Form Designer Generated Code

    Private Sub Page_Load(ByVal sender As System.Object, _
      ByVal e As System.EventArgs) Handles MyBase.Load


    End Sub

End Class
```

Remember that the name of the Datalist declared in our page needs to match that of the ID attribute of the DataList tag on our ASPX page. Because we'll be using the SQL Managed Provider for our data access, we'll also again import the SQLClient namespace. The implementation of the Page_Load event will query both the TickerPrice and UserTicker table for prices of symbols that users have indicated they are interested in. We will parameterize the UserID value of our where clause, helping the database server optimize its execution plans as multiple users get into the office in the morning and request their portals for the first time:

```
        Dim cn As New SqlConnection _
        ("server=(local);database=AtWorkWebPortal;uid=sa")
        Dim sql As String = "SELECT TickerPrice.Ticker, " _
  & "TickerPrice.Price " _
                        & "FROM UserTicker INNER JOIN " _
                        & "TickerPrice ON " _
  & "UserTicker.Ticker = TickerPrice.Ticker" _
                        & " WHERE (UserTicker.UserID = @UserID) " _
                        & "ORDER BY TickerPrice.Ticker"
        Dim cm As New SqlCommand(sql, cn)
        Dim pm As SqlParameter
        Dim dr As SqlDataReader

        Session("UserID") = 1

        pm = cm.Parameters.Add( _
```

```
New SqlParameter("@UserID", SqlDbType.Int))
      pm.Value = Session("UserID")

      cn.Open()
      dr = cm.ExecuteReader()

      dlTicker.DataSource = dr
      dlTicker.DataBind()

      cn.Close()
      dr = Nothing
      cm = Nothing
      cn = Nothing
```

Our Session variable is hard-coded again. We'll strip this once we get security implemented and have a login page populate this variable for us when the user first logs in.

The last thing we'll look at on this page is some client-side event trapping that we'll add to make our users' experience a little less aggravating. Let's say they come in some morning and see that a stock they own is way down. They want to click on the symbol to go out to Nasdaq's site to see what is going on, but our little marquee is scrolling so fast that they can't track that symbol down with the mouse to actually get a click in. This is easily remedied with a couple of simple client-side functions added to the <HEAD> of our page:

```
<script language=vbscript>
      sub TickList_onMouseOver()
            TickList.scrolldelay = 2000
      end sub

      sub TickList_onMouseOut()
            TickList.scrolldelay = 85
      end sub
</script>
```

This sets up traps for two events that are raised by the Marquee element once the page deploys to the client. Notice that in our HeaderTemplate of the DataList, we gave the marquee an ID of TickList. All of the rich DHTML functionality exposed to us by IE is still available, even though we're generating the page with the ASP.NET Framework on the server. The client cares not a bit how the page was generated on the server; once it gets to the client, the script engine built into the browser will continue to function just as it always has.

User Maintenance

We've implemented quite a few pages that gather information from various sources and display it to the user. We've used internal and external XML documents to generate HTML and used relational data to generate HTML linking to both internal and external content. The amount of code required has been staggeringly small. Has it seemed more like VB code than ASP? That's because it is.

Most of us involved in Web application development know that the display of the data is only half of the job. Very few business problems are solved exclusively by the display of data. Eventually we have to gather data from our users and use that data to update the data stores in our enterprise. Even if it's only to ask visitors for their e-mail so we can barrage them with our eloquent spam, this round-tripping of information is imperative.

The user maintenance page will introduce this concept and several new techniques available to us in the Framework. Some of the things we'll demonstrate with this piece of the solution follow:

- Post back events
- Building a user interface to gather data from our user that we'll use to update and create relational data
- Building multiple functions into a single ASPX page
- Different ways of trapping events

The user maintenance page, on its first request, renders a data grid that displays the details of all of the users in the UserPreferences table. We'll also use a ButtonColumn to sink a post back event that we can use to move users to an HTML form so that we can edit these details about our users.

Although this page has many times the amount of code as the previous pages we've looked at have had, bear in mind as we move through the solution how much code would be required to implement the same solution with traditional ASP or other frameworks. Even as we move on to the complex functionality of summarizing, creating, and updating data, you can notice how compact and logically isolated the individual code elements remain. And everything we're doing here is still going to be cross-browser compatible.

So let's begin by creating a new page named UserMaint.aspx. This page will provide two major functions: displaying a list of all users and creating an interface for editing and updating users. We will do this with the Panel Web control. This control renders as an HTML div tag, which makes it very simple to logically segment the functionality of our page on the server by interacting with the Panel control. This is set up simply by setting the visible attribute of the panel tag:

```
<%@ Page Language="vb" AutoEventWireup="false"
Codebehind="UserMaint.aspx.vb" Inherits="WebPortal.UserMaint"%>
<!DOCTYPE HTML PUBLIC "-//W3C//DTD HTML 4.0 Transitional//EN">
<html>
  <head>
    <title></title>
  </head>
  <body>

    <form id="Form1" method="post" runat="server">
          <asp:Panel ID=pnGrid Runat=server>

          </asp:Panel>
```

```
                  <asp:Panel ID=pnDetail Runat=server Visible=False>

                  </asp:Panel>

         </form>

      </body>
   </html>
```

This creates two logical areas of the page that we can use to isolate specific functionality. On post back events we can toggle the visibility of these panels programmatically, moving between functional areas that we would typically isolate on different pages. There's no reason to limit this segmentation to two panels; I've made pages that hold many atomic functions in a single page with the same technique.

The first panel accepts the default value for its visibility, which is true. The second panel, where we'll implement the HTML form for editing user data explicitly, sets its visibility to false. Let's take a look at the declaration for our data grid, which we'll add to the first panel:

```
<asp:Label Runat=server ID=lblTitle text='Users' />
<asp:Button Runat=server ID=btnAdd Text='Add User'
style='margin-left:40px' OnClick='AddUser' /><br><br>
<asp:DataGrid Runat=server ID=dgUsers
                AutoGenerateColumns=False>
  <Columns>
    <asp:BoundColumn DataField='UserID'
    HeaderText='ID' ItemStyle-Width=15px />
    <asp:ButtonColumn ButtonType=LinkButton
    CommandName='EditUser' Text='Edit' />
    <asp:BoundColumn DataField='FirstName' HeaderText='First'
    ItemStyle-Width=175px />
    <asp:BoundColumn DataField='LastName' HeaderText='Last'
    ItemStyle-Width=175px />
    <asp:BoundColumn DataField='UserEmail' HeaderText='E-mail'
    ItemStyle-Width=175px />
    <asp:BoundColumn DataField='DepartmentName' HeaderText='Dept'
    ItemStyle-Width=175px />
    <asp:BoundColumn DataField='DepartmentID' Visible=False />
  </Columns>
</asp:DataGrid>
```

Here, by setting the AutoGenerateColumns property of the data grid to false, we're able to declare the exact output that we expect from the data grid. Using the Bound-Column property type, we're basically getting columns that we would under the default behavior. There are a couple of important differences between the default behavior and what we want that require this degree of specificity. These can be seen in the second and seventh children of the Column element. Let's take a look at the output of this grid, shown in Figure 6.13.

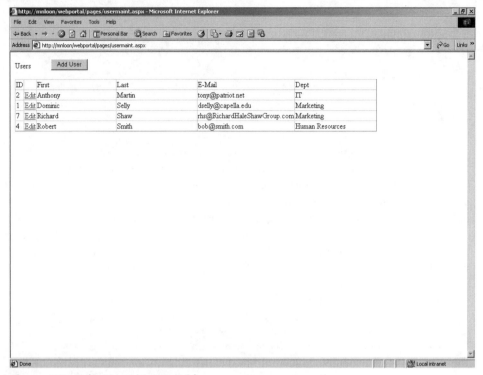

Figure 6.13   The User List DataGrid.

You can see that the second table data cell of each row of the grid displays a hyper-link with the text "Edit." This is rendered by the ButtonColumn declaration on the data grid:

```
<asp:ButtonColumn ButtonType=LinkButton CommandName='EditUser'
Text='Edit' />
```

The hyperlink is rendered in this column because we've set the ButtonType equal to LinkButton. The other valid value for this attribute is PushButton, which would render an HTML input of type button. There's no functional difference between these; it's a purely cosmetic choice. In either case the presence of this column type fires the Edit-Command event on the server when a user clicks on this column. We'll take a look at the trap for this event when we get into the code for the page. For now, suffice it to say that this is where we'll swap the visibility of our panels and get the HTML form on the second panel ready for editing that the user displayed on the clicked row.

The seventh column is a BoundColumn with its visibility set to false:

```
<asp:BoundColumn DataField='DepartmentID' Visible=False />
```

This is important because it exposes the DepartmentID value to us in the server-side event trap, while leaving the display of the department up to the sixth column, which is bound to DepartmentName. This type of hidden misdirection between a name and a value is common and necessary almost anytime you're carrying an arbitrary ID value as a foreign key in one table that is meaningful to your users only in a more descriptive column from the source key's target table. In this case we're carrying the department ID value in our user preferences table but need to display the DepartmentName field from our Department table to our users. This is even more important when rendering an HTML select list of these values for our users. Although we want to display the DepartmentName value to our users, we want the bound value of the control to carry the department ID. The data binding engine supports this with two lines of code, which we'll see when we get into the editing form.

The other items of note on this panel are the two control declarations that precede the data grid:

```
<asp:Label Runat=server ID=lblTitle text='Users' />
<asp:Button Runat=server ID=btnAdd Text='Add User'
style='margin-left:40px' OnClick='AddUser' />
```

The first control is the label Web control. This control renders as an HTML span tag, but by using this object on the server, you have dozens of CSS attributes that can be set declaratively or programmatically, as well as the ability to change what is displayed by simply setting the text property of the control.

The second is a button Web server control. This cool little guy is the simplest and quickest means by which we can set up a server-side event trap. The OnClick attribute of this control names a function on the server that should be called via a post back whenever this button is clicked. This one will fire the AddUser function, which we'll take a look at in a moment. We're using an inline CSS declaration on this guy to set it off from our title label. This is no different from a regular HTML inline style attribute declaration. All of the Web server controls provide excellent support for this attribute in their rendering behavior.

Let's take our first look at the code behind this page:

```
Imports System.Data.SqlClient

Public Class UserMaint
    Inherits System.Web.UI.Page
    Protected WithEvents dgUsers As System.Web.UI.WebControls.DataGrid
    Protected WithEvents pnGrid As System.Web.UI.WebControls.Panel
    Protected WithEvents txtUserID As System.Web.UI.WebControls.TextBox
    Protected WithEvents txtFirstName As
System.Web.UI.WebControls.TextBox
    Protected WithEvents txtLastName As
System.Web.UI.WebControls.TextBox
    Protected WithEvents txtUserEmail As
System.Web.UI.WebControls.TextBox
    Protected WithEvents dlDepartment As
System.Web.UI.WebControls.DropDownList
```

```
        Protected WithEvents pnDetail As System.Web.UI.WebControls.Panel

+ Web Form Designer Generated Code

    Private Sub Page_Load(ByVal sender As System.Object, _
 ByVal e As System.EventArgs) _
 Handles MyBase.Load
    End Sub
```

Here we have our standard import declaration and *a lot* of control declarations. Let me show you a trick. Move back to the UserMaint.aspx page. At the bottom of the window you'll see buttons for Design and HTML. Click on Design. Let it churn until it displays some content. Click on HTML. Notice how squashed your code is? This is why I don't use the designer. Hit control-z and these changes will be rolled back at once. Now press F7. Any server-side control on the page is now declared in your code behind the page. This is the one use of the design pane I have found valuable.

Let's take a look first at the implementation of the Page_Load event, a single line of code:

```
If Not Page.IsPostBack Then BindGrid()
```

We've moved the code out into a private method of the class. We're also only calling it if we're *not* doing a post back because this is the first page that we've implemented that's using post backs. These things become very important when your page starts submitting to itself. We'll be doing a post back every time users switch their view between the grid and the detail panes. This will include requests to add users, update them, and cancel changes. Every time we move our view from the detail pane to the grid pane, we need to bind the grid again. This is why we need to break the logic for binding the grid out into its own subroutine so that we can call it from other event traps besides the page load.

Speaking of binding this grid, let's take a look at the BindGrid routine:

```
Dim cn As New SqlConnection _
("server=(local);database=AtWorkWebPortal;uid=sa")
        Dim sql As String = "SELECT UserPreferences.UserID, " _
        & "UserPreferences.FirstName, " _
        & "UserPreferences.LastName, " _
        & "UserPreferences.UserEmail, " _
        & "UserPreferences.DepartmentID, " _
        & "Department.DepartmentName " _
        & "FROM UserPreferences " _
        & "INNER JOIN Department ON " _
        & "UserPreferences.DepartmentID= Department.DepartmentID " _
        & "ORDER BY UserPreferences.LastName"
    Dim cm As New SqlCommand(sql, cn)
    Dim dr As SqlDataReader

    Session("UserID") = 1
```

```
cn.Open()
dr = cm.ExecuteReader()

dgUsers.DataSource = dr
dgUsers.DataBind()

cn.Close()
dr = Nothing
cm = Nothing
cn = Nothing
```

The functionality here should look very familiar by now. We create our DataReader using a Command object, bind the grid to the reader, and DataBind on the grid. Our template then combines the data from our UserPreferences table with the Edit command column, and we're ready to go. At this point there are two actions users can take. They can click the Add New button to create a new user, or they can click one of the links rendered in our edit command column on the grid. Let's first examine the code that gets fired when a user clicks the edit command column. Figure 6.14 is a peek at the page rendered after this button is clicked, so you can see where we're going.

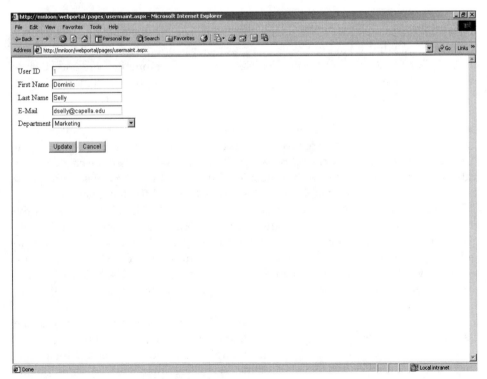

Figure 6.14   The User Details HTML form.

And here's the event trap for the ButtonColumn that gets us there:

```
Private Sub dgUsers_ItemCommand(ByVal source As Object, _
    ByVal e As System.Web.UI.WebControls.DataGridCommandEventArgs) _
    Handles dgUsers.ItemCommand

      If e.CommandName = "EditUser" Then
        Dim li As ListItem

        pnGrid.Visible = False
        pnDetail.Visible = True
        txtUserID.Text = e.Item.Cells(0).Text
        txtFirstName.Text = e.Item.Cells(2).Text
        txtLastName.Text = e.Item.Cells(3).Text
        txtUserEmail.Text = e.Item.Cells(4).Text
        BindDepartmentList()
        For Each li In dlDepartment.Items
            If li.Value = e.Item.Cells(6).Text Then
                li.Selected = True
                Exit For
            End If
        Next
      End If


    End Sub
```

Let's first pick apart the method footprint. This is similar to the event trap footprint we've worked with so far, but the second parameter is not of type EventArgs. In this case, it's DataGridCommandEventArgs. This is a class that inherits from and extends EventArgs. The inheritance provides type and functional support for all the portions of the Framework that deal with post backs generically. The extension allows the data grid to add some additional information to the type that is specific to the event it is raising. This is like COM object, which supports more than one interface, but it's even better than that because this extended type has the same interface as the original Event-Args class and all of the functionality as well. This means that when the creator of the data grid control needed the built-in functionality of the EventArgs class, they got it free and had only to add a couple properties to create the additional functionality.

The other difference in the footprint is the addition of the Handles keyword at the end. This is one way to set up an event trap in the .NET Framework. When the data grid control raises this event via a post back, the Framework knows automatically to call this routine to handle the event because, quite simply, we've told the Framework as much by saying it handles the ItemCommand event of the dgUsers DataGrid control. We'll take a look at the other way to set up event traps when we talk about the Add New button.

The implementation of this trap first checks the CommandName property of the DataGridCommandEventArgs parameter that's been passed in by the Framework. This is one of the ways the data grid control implementation has extended the Event-Args class; this property is not part of the EventArgs interface. The value of this property ties directly back to the CommandName attribute in the data grid template:

```
<asp:ButtonColumn ButtonType=LinkButton CommandName='EditUser'
Text='Edit' />
```

This allows us to have more than one ButtonColumn declared on our template and have different functionality execute in our event trap, depending on the value of the CommandName attribute. We could, for example, add another ButtonColumn and set its CommandName and Text attributes to Delete. We could then modify this event trap to respond differently to each of these commands:

```
If e.CommandName = "EditUser" then
' ' Edit logic here
ElseIf e.CommandName = "Delete" then
' ' Delete logic here
End If
```

In our example we have only one ButtonColumn, but we're checking the CommandName anyway to minimize the impact to the code if we later add delete functionality.

The first line contained in this branch of logic declares a ListItem object:

```
Dim li As ListItem
```

Although it may be a common coding practice to put all of your declarations at the top of a routine, there's a good reason to do this here. Visual Basic .NET introduces a new level of scope that's specific to conditional branches in our code. What this means is that if this branch of code doesn't get executed at runtime, this object will never get instantiated. No memory will be allocated for it. It also means that the li variable is usable only within this conditional branch of our logic. This is a very cool optimization that becomes especially important when you think about using constructors in your code. Let's say, for example, you have a routine that checks to see if some information is present in memory. If it is, it retrieves the information from there. Otherwise, it creates a connection and command object and retrieves the information from a relational database. By declaring these objects from within the conditional branch of our code, we skip the overhead of instantiating these objects and setting all of these properties we've set in the constructors. This is a significant optimization!

I really like the next two lines of code in this routine:

```
pnGrid.Visible = False
pnDetail.Visible = True
```

These lines are basically what make it possible for us to include two complete functional areas on this one page of code. The data grid, label, and button controls on the first pane will now not render, and the HTML form that we've prepared on the second pane will. All of this occurs without using any server-side tags, <% %>, in the body of our HTML and with using no code at all in the ASPX portion of our page. The next four lines are where we begin to set up the inputs on our HTML controls, via the services of the TextBox controls we're using:

```
txtUserID.Text = e.Item.Cells(0).Text
txtFirstName.Text = e.Item.Cells(2).Text
txtLastName.Text = e.Item.Cells(3).Text
txtUserEmail.Text = e.Item.Cells(4).Text
```

The text property of each of these controls is what renders as the value attribute in the corresponding HTML. We're retrieving these values from the second parameter that is passed to the event, using its cells collection. The cells collection is populated with information about each column in the data grid, specific to the row that raised the event. That means when users click on a row where the UserID is 172, the first cell in the data row will have a text value of 172. Like all arrays in the .NET Framework, the cell's collection is a zero-based array, so here we're getting the values of columns 1, 3, 4, and 5 and mapping them to the corresponding TextBox controls. Keep in mind that in a real implementation we would probably want to use the ID value to pull the user information out of the database, in case it had changed since a user requested it. I've used this example to illustrate another use of the DataGridCommandEventArgs object.

The only control that remains to be set up on this page is the department drop down list. You've probably implemented many of these types of lists, where we display some descriptive text to the user but want to carry an ID value behind the scenes. It's needed almost everytime you're building an interface to a table that has a foreign key value in one of its columns. We'll need to display all of the departments in this list, and then we'll need to select the appropriate row from that list for the user we're currently editing. We bind the list in a separate routine, named BindDepartmentList. Here's the code:

```
Private Sub BindDepartmentList()
        If dlDepartment.Items.Count = 0 Then
            Dim cn As New
SqlConnection("server=(local);database=AtWorkWebPortal;uid=sa")
            Dim sql As String = "select * from department order by
departmentname"
            Dim cm As New SqlCommand(sql, cn)
            Dim dr As SqlDataReader

            cn.Open()
            dr = cm.ExecuteReader()

            dlDepartment.DataSource = dr
            dlDepartment.DataTextField = "DepartmentName"
            dlDepartment.DataValueField = "DepartmentID"
            dlDepartment.DataBind()

            cn.Close()
            dr = Nothing
            cm = Nothing
            cn = Nothing
        End If
    End Sub
```

The first thing we do is check to see if the list currently has any items. This control will maintain its state across post backs, so if we've already set up this control, we'll avoid doing it again. Be careful when using this technique. It's not suited for data that changes frequently because our list could get out of sync with the database. Next, we create the DataReader that we will use to bind the list. Notice that we have twice as much code to accomplish this binding as we do for the data grid.

The DropDownList control supports two additional properties that are specific to data binding operations, DataTextField and DataValueField. The first is the value that will be displayed for each item in our list, and the second is the value that the control will carry when the corresponding text is selected. The DropDownList, ListBox, RadioButtonList, and CheckBoxList controls all support these data binding properties.

Back to the ButtonColumn's event trap:

```
For Each li In dlDepartment.Items
   If li.Value = e.Item.Cells(6).Text Then
        li.Selected = True
        Exit For
   End If
Next
```

Now that our list is bound, the DropDownList has a collection of Item objects of type ListItem, one for each row in our list. Here's another nice feature of the ASP.NET Framework's rendering model: We now have a chance to change these objects between the time they're created and the time the HTML for the page is rendered. This would be impossible with traditional ASP.

As our loop iterates, we're checking the value of each list item against the DepartmentId value of the selected user. This is the seventh column in our template, the one whose visibility we set to false. We're displaying the name of the department in the sixth column, but we added the seventh column to the grid specifically so that we could interrogate its value right here while building our department list. When we find a ListItem in the Items collection whose value matches the selected user's Department-ID, we set that ListItem's Selected property to true and terminate our loop. The appropriate HTML is automatically generated when our page is rendered.

Once our event trap terminates, the HTML for the page is rendered and returned to our clients. See Figure 6.13 for a reminder of what exactly it looks like. We've disable the ID text box because that's our primary key value, it's an identity in the database, and we have no real interest in letting our users change it. There's one other way for our users to get to the detail panel of our page, by clicking the "add User' button. Let's take a quick look at the declaration of that button and the corresponding event trap before looking at the update functions called by post backs from our detail form.

Here's the control declaration:

```
<asp:Button Runat=server ID=btnAdd
Text='Add User'
style='margin-left:40px'
OnClick='AddUser' />
```

And here's the event trap:

```
Public Sub AddUser(ByVal o As Object, ByVal e As EventArgs)
        pnGrid.Visible = False
        pnDetail.Visible = True
        txtUserID.Text = ""
        txtFirstName.Text = ""
        txtLastName.Text = ""
        txtUserEmail.Text = ""
        BindDepartmentList()
        dlDepartment.SelectedIndex = -1
End Sub
```

This is the second way to set up a server-side event trap. Rather than using the handles keyword on a function footprint, we simply name the function with the onClick attribute of our button declaration. The footprint of the corresponding function that we added to the code behind the page is the same as for other events. Notice that its declaration must be public in order for the Framework to successfully wire the trap. If you add an onClick attribute and don't provide a corresponding function declaration with this footprint, a compile error will occur when your page is requested.

The implementation of the trap again swaps the visibility of the panels and then clears out the values of our controls, readying the form for data entry by a new user. Without this, we risk displaying information about a user that was previously edited with the page; this is because these input controls maintain their state even when the panel is not displayed. Setting the SelectedIndex property of the DropDownList clears any previous selection from the list.

We've gone through setting up a summary screen that our end users can use to select a user for editing and have trapped a couple of different post back events to set up an HTML form to use to edit the user data. The only thing that remains for our implementation is to move that data back to the server and update our database.

To allow users to commit or cancel their changes, we've provided a couple of Button controls at the bottom of the second panel:

```
<asp:Button Runat=server ID=btnUpdate Text=Update OnClick='UpdateUser'
/>
<asp:Button Runat=server ID=btnCancel Text=Cancel onclick='CancelUpdate'
/>
```

Again, we're using the onClick attribute of our Button tags to name the server-side function to call when the buttons get clicked. Let's take a look at the Update button's event trap:

```
Public Sub UpdateUser(ByVal o As Object, ByVal e As EventArgs)
        Dim cn As New
SqlConnection("server=(local);database=AtWorkWebPortal;uid=sa")
        Dim cm As New SqlCommand("", cn)
        Dim pm As SqlParameter
        Dim sql As String

        If Len(txtUserID.Text) = 0 Then
            sql = "INSERT INTO UserPreferences " _
```

```
                    & "(FirstName, LastName, UserEmail, DepartmentID) " _
                    & "VALUES (@FirstName, @LastName, @UserEmail,
    @DepartmentID)"
        Else
            sql = "UPDATE UserPreferences SET " _
                    & "FirstName = @FirstName, " _
                    & "LastName = @LastName, " _
                    & "UserEmail = @UserEmail, " _
                    & "DepartmentID = @DepartmentID " _
                    & "WHERE (UserID = @UserID)"
            pm = cm.Parameters.Add(New SqlParameter("@UserID",
    SqlDbType.Int))
                pm.Value = txtUserID.Text
        End If

        pm = cm.Parameters.Add(New SqlParameter("@FirstName",
    SqlDbType.VarChar, 30))
            pm.Value = txtFirstName.Text
        pm = cm.Parameters.Add(New SqlParameter("@LastName",
    SqlDbType.VarChar, 50))
            pm.Value = txtLastName.Text
        pm = cm.Parameters.Add(New SqlParameter("@UserEmail",
    SqlDbType.VarChar, 50))
            pm.Value = txtUserEmail.Text
        pm = cm.Parameters.Add(New SqlParameter("@DepartmentID",
    SqlDbType.Int))
            pm.Value = dlDepartment.SelectedItem.Value

        cm.CommandText = sql
        cn.Open()
        cm.ExecuteNonQuery()
        cn.Close()

        pnDetail.Visible = False
        pnGrid.Visible = True
        BindGrid()

        cm = Nothing
        cn = Nothing

    End Sub
```

Our declarations are familiar. Notice, however, that we are not providing the SQL statement in the contructor of our Command object, passing "" (an empty string) instead. This is because we don't know in advance what our SQL statement should be; we have to programmatically figure that out by deciding if we're updating an existing user or creating a new user. It's still worth using the contructor, though, because it saves us the additional line of setting the Connection property of our Command object.

We will use the ID text box to determine which function we're performing. Because we clear out all of the controls when we're creating a user, and because the ID text box is not enabled, we can check its length to see what's going on. If the length is zero, we're creating a new user. If it's not, we're updating an existing user. The following block of code sets up our SQL statement accordingly:

```
If Len(txtUserID.Text) = 0 Then
        sql = "INSERT INTO UserPreferences " _
            & "(FirstName, LastName, UserEmail, DepartmentID) " _
            & "VALUES (@FirstName, @LastName, @UserEmail,
@DepartmentID)"
        Else
        sql = "UPDATE UserPreferences SET " _
            & "FirstName = @FirstName, " _
            & "LastName = @LastName, " _
            & "UserEmail = @UserEmail, " _
            & "DepartmentID = @DepartmentID " _
            & "WHERE (UserID = @UserID)"
        pm = cm.Parameters.Add(New SqlParameter("@UserID",
SqlDbType.Int))
        pm.Value = txtUserID.Text
        End If
```

Notice that the two SQL statements have four parameters in common: FirstName, LastName, UserEmail, and DepartmentID. Because the UPDATE statement requires a fifth parameter, UserID, that we use in the WHERE clause of the statement, we create it in the branch that only executed when we are updating an existing user. The other parameters we create are the same for both operations in the lines that follow our statement definition:

```
pm = cm.Parameters.Add(New SqlParameter("@FirstName", SqlDbType.VarChar,
30))
        pm.Value = txtFirstName.Text
        pm = cm.Parameters.Add(New SqlParameter("@LastName",
SqlDbType.VarChar, 50))
        pm.Value = txtLastName.Text
        pm = cm.Parameters.Add(New SqlParameter("@UserEmail",
SqlDbType.VarChar, 50))
        pm.Value = txtUserEmail.Text
        pm = cm.Parameters.Add(New SqlParameter("@DepartmentID",
SqlDbType.Int))
        pm.Value = dlDepartment.SelectedItem.Value
```

Here we're using the object factory services of the Add method of the command's parameter collection to define the four parameters that our statements have in common. We hold a reference to each of these parameters only long enough to set its value equal to whatever data our user has filled in on our form. Notice the last value assignment:

```
dlDepartment.SelectedItem.Value
```

This statement uses the SelectedItem property of our DropDownList control, which will return a reference to the ListItem object of whatever item is selected in the list. The

ListItem object exposes a Value property. Because of the way we set up the data binding for this control, this property will hold the DepartmentID of whichever department our user picked from the list.

The next block of code is where we do all the hard work of establishing a network connection to the database server from the Web server to which our page was posted, authenticating our process against the database, sending the appropriate statement to update or insert the user, making sure nothing goes wrong, and releasing the resources we've consumed in the process:

```
cm.CommandText = sql
cn.Open()
cm.ExecuteNonQuery()
cn.Close()
```

The execute method that we're using in this case is what we use when we are not expecting a resultset back from the server. This would be true for INSERT, UPDATE, and DELETE statements, as well as for stored procedures that return their values using output parameters or return values. ExecuteNonQuery does return an integer value that indicates how many rows were affected by the operation. We could grab and use that value here to check for errors or send information back to our users:

```
cm.CommandText = sql
cn.Open()
dim ra as integer = cm.ExecuteNonQuery()
cn.Close()
if ra <> 1 then
     'Let the user know we failed
end if
```

The last function is the one called when the user clicks the Cancel button. Here we simply swap the visibility of the panels again, and rebind the grid:

```
Public Sub CancelUpdate(ByVal o As Object, ByVal e As EventArgs)
        pnDetail.Visible = False
        pnGrid.Visible = True
        BindGrid()
End Sub
```

And there you have it. Complete Web-based functionality to update or create a single row in a single table in a database. This is the simplest of all database operations; however, in the next section we'll take a look at creating and modifying several rows in a table as we provide an interface to our users to let us know specifically which stocks in the database they're interested in having displayed on their stock marquee.

User Tickers

Next we'll provide an interface for our users to edit which stocks appear on their stock ticker. This is fundamentally a table that reconciles a many-to-many relation between the UserPreferences table and the TickerPrice table. The UserTicker table simply carries a primary key value from each of these two tables. This allows users to view many stocks on their marquee and one stock to be viewed by many users on their marquee. To provide an interface to the users for editing this information, we'll use the CheckBoxList Web control. This control is one of the more advanced Web server controls. It generates a check box and a label for the check box for each item in whatever data source you bind it to. Because it's a list control, setting up and interacting with the control is very much like using a list box or drop down list. The control has an Items collection, which will have a ListItem object for every check box in the list. The ListItem object is the same object that is used by the other list controls. The CheckBoxList also supports the same data binding properties.

Because a check box list supports multiple selections (for single selection use a RadioButtonList), we will interact with the control a bit differently when a post back occurs. With a drop down list we referenced the control SelectItem property to retrieve the value of the user's selection, whereas with the check box list we will iterate through all of the items in the list and check their Selected property. For each item in the control that's selected, we will create a row in the UserTicker table. Let's look at the output for this page, shown in Figure 6.15.

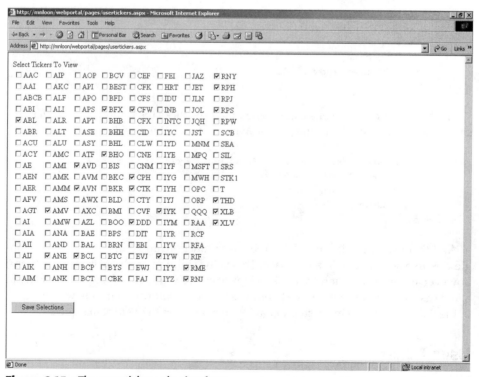

Figure 6.15 The user ticker selection form.

Notice the items in the list are displayed in multiple columns, with the items displayed horizontally. The check box list is very flexible in this regard, easily exposing a number of different outputs by specifying column counts and directional flow. Let's first take a look at the code we have on the ASPX page:

```
<%@ Page Language="vb" AutoEventWireup="false"
Codebehind="UserTickers.aspx.vb" Inherits="WebPortal.UserTickers"%>
<!DOCTYPE HTML PUBLIC "-//W3C//DTD HTML 4.0 Transitional//EN">
<html>
  <head>
    <title></title>
  </head>
  <body>

    <form id="Form1" method="post" runat="server">
            <asp:Label Runat=server CssClass=Heading text='Select
Tickers To View' />
            <asp:CheckBoxList Runat=server RepeatColumns=3
ID=chkUserTicker />
            <br><br>
            <asp:Button Runat=server ID=btnUpdate
                                Text='Save Selections'
                                OnClick='UpdateUserTickers' />
    </form>

  </body>
</html>
```

Not a lot to it, is there? We have only three controls on this form, a label to display instructions to the user, the check box list itself, and the button to kick off our post back. The interesting attribute on the check box list is named RepeatColumns. We can use this in combination with the RepeatDirection and RepeatLayout attributes to tightly control the arrangement of the check boxes' output. The Page_Load event is fairly simple as well and its pattern will be mostly familiar by now:

```
If Not Page.IsPostBack Then
            Dim cn As New
SqlConnection("server=(local);database=AtWorkWebPortal;uid=sa")
            Dim sql As String = "select Ticker FROM TickerPrice ORDER BY
Ticker " _
                              & "select Ticker FROM UserTicker WHERE
UserID = @UserID"
            Dim cm As New SqlCommand(sql, cn)
            Dim pm As SqlParameter
            Dim dr As SqlDataReader
            Dim li As ListItem

            Session("UserID") = 1
```

```
        pm = cm.Parameters.Add(New SqlParameter("@UserID",
SqlDbType.Int))
        pm.Value = Session("UserID")

        cn.Open()
        dr = cm.ExecuteReader

        chkUserTicker.DataSource = dr
        chkUserTicker.DataValueField = "Ticker"
        chkUserTicker.DataTextField = "Ticker"
        chkUserTicker.DataBind()

        dr.NextResult()

        While dr.Read
            For Each li In chkUserTicker.Items
                If dr("Ticker") = li.Value Then
                    li.Selected = True
                    Exit For
                End If
            Next
        End While

        cn.Close()
        dr = Nothing
        cm = Nothing
        cn = Nothing
    End If
```

So once again, we use a parameterized query to retrieve our desired resultset from the database and set up our data reader to return the results to us. Notice that there are two statements defined in the SQL string. We'll talk about that shortly. The binding we're doing with the CheckBoxList will use only the first statement. We then set up data binding on the CheckBoxList by setting the four data binding attributes. For this control, DataTextField will be displayed as text next to the check box. You can use the TextAlign attribute of the control to have the label appear on the left- or right-hand side of the check box. The default for this attribute is *left*. In this case we are using the same value for the display as we are for the value of the control. The DataValueField is used to populate the values of the list items. Calling the DataBind method on the Check-BoxList uses the one forward-only read through the resultset that the data reader provides, and after execution returns to our next line of code we could not get to the resultset if we wanted to. Random access to data must be done with a data set. However, because we sent two SQL statements as part of the command text, we can move on to another resultset using the NextResult method. This is a convenient shortcut that allows us to queue up several statements and move through them very quickly. You can pass any number of statements to a data reader in this way, separating each statement only with some white space. The managed provider is smart enough to parse out one statement from the next. As you use the results, you can queue up the next set using the NextResult method of the data reader.

We're going to use the second set to check all of the boxes on our Web control that the user already has selected. It's important to note that the control must be bound before we can do this. This same method could also be used for a ListBox that is supporting multiple selections. The syntax would be identical because both controls carry a collection of ListItem objects. The only difference between the controls is the HTML they generate when the page is rendered. The loop that we use to do this is going to iterate through all of the rows in our second resultset. Although ADO exposes the MoveNext and EOF methods to move through the rows in a RecordSet, the data reader greatly simplifies this by exposing the Read method. The Read method retrieves a row from the database and returns true. When there are no more rows to retrieve, the Read method returns false. In this way our simple While loop will execute once for each row in the resultset. Because we're querying the UserTickers table for those rows with a user ID that matches our current user, we'll get a row in our resultset for each ticker that the user has already chosen to see. For each of those rows we'll need to find the corresponding item in the check box list's collection of ListItems and set its selected property to true. Once we've found the corresponding check box, there's no reason to continue checking the remaining ListItems, so we exit the For loop. This vastly increases the efficiency of these nested loops. Without the exit from our loop, we would iterate NumberOfStocks times NumberOfSelectedStocks times. With the exit, the loop iterates exactly as many times as it needs to.

After the loops, we clean up and our page renders. Our users will see all of the stocks that are available for their marquee, with checks next to the ones they already have selected. They can make any number of changes, either clicking on new stocks or deselecting the ones they're no longer interested in. When they've made their choices, they click the button and our UpdateUserTickers post back event fires. Let's take a look at that routine:

```
Public Sub UpdateUserTickers(ByVal o As Object, ByVal e As EventArgs)
        Session("UserID") = 1

        Dim ID As Integer = Session("UserID")
        Dim cn As New
SqlConnection("server=(local);database=AtWorkWebPortal;uid=sa")
        Dim sql As String = "DELETE FROM UserTicker WHERE UserID = " & ID
        Dim cm As New SqlCommand(sql, cn)
        Dim li As ListItem

        For Each li In chkUserTicker.Items
            If li.Selected Then
                sql &= " INSERT INTO UserTicker (UserID, Ticker) " _
                    & "VALUES (" & ID & ", '" & li.Value & "')"
            End If
        Next
```

```
cm.CommandText = sql
cn.Open()
cm.ExecuteNonQuery()
cn.Close()

Response.Redirect("WebPortal.aspx")

End Sub
```

Once again we'll be using the support that the managed provider gives us for batching up SQL statements to be sent in one round trip to the database. The first thing we'll do is to delete all existing stock selections for our current user. This is much simpler than trying to figure out which ones need to be deleted, which ones need updating, and which ones need to be created anew. Having deleted them all, we once again iterate though all ListItems in our check box list, seeking out those with the Selected attribute set to true. For each selected item we find, we tack on an insert statement to our SQL string, using the user ID (which is constant), and the value from the selected list item we found. After all this nifty setup is complete, we open a connection to the database and send the whole lot off at once, allowing the managed provider to sort it out and pass our commands along to the database. After closing our connection, we redirect users to the Web portal page. This will cause their stock banner at the bottom to be refreshed, and they'll instantly see the prices of their newly selected stocks rolling by.

Department Maintenance

The next page we'll implement will allow for maintenance of the Department table, which is a very simple table, having only two columns: DepartmentID and DepartmentName. The DepartmentID column is an identity column, so management of those values is delegated entirely to SQL Server. The only thing we really need to expose for maintenance is the DepartmentName column.

We'll use the data-editing capabilities of the DataGrid control to do this. We saw the DataGrid in action when we used it to create HTML tables to display information to our users. We've also seen how to set up event traps on the server for events that are occurring on specific rows of the grid. On the User Maintenance page we used a ButtonColumn to post to the server and display an HTML form for editing the information on the row that had been clicked.

In this case our editing requirements are simple enough that we'll use the built-in editing functionality of the DataGrid itself. This saves us from generating an entire HTML form for editing departments and makes implementation much simpler. Although the DataGrid is good at exposing UPDATE functionality to our users, there's no built-in facility for adding data to our table. Therefore, we'll provide an additional control that will allow our users to add a department to the table. Upon its first rendering the Departments.aspx page will appear as shown in Figure 6.16.

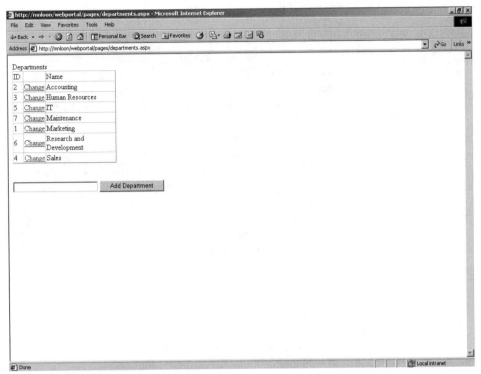

Figure 6.16 Department maintenance.

Our grid has three columns. Two of them display the two values from our table. The third displays a hyperlink that causes a post back to occur and gives us a chance to set up that row of the grid for editing. We use an EditCommandColumn for this, which was mentioned earlier. Here we'll dig into the details of how it works. Let's take a look at the control declarations on our ASPX page:

```
<%@ Page Language="vb" AutoEventWireup="false"
Codebehind="Departments.aspx.vb" Inherits="WebPortal.Departments"%>
<!DOCTYPE HTML PUBLIC "-//W3C//DTD HTML 4.0 Transitional//EN">
<html>
  <head>
    <title></title>
  </head>
  <body>
    <form id="Form1" method="post" runat="server">
```

```
                    <asp:Label Runat=server ID=lblDep
                         CssClass='Heading'
                         text='Departments' />
                    <asp:DataGrid Runat=server ID=dgDepartments
                         AutoGenerateColumns=False>
                         <Columns>
                              <asp:BoundColumn DataField='DepartmentID'
                                   ReadOnly=True
                                   HeaderText='ID'
                                   ItemStyle-Width='20' />
                              <asp:EditCommandColumn ButtonType=LinkButton
                                   EditText='Change'
                                   UpdateText='Update'
                                   CancelText='Undo' />
                              <asp:BoundColumn DataField='DepartmentName'
                                   HeaderText='Name'
                                   ItemStyle-Width='150' />

                         </Columns>
                    </asp:DataGrid>
                    <br><br>
                    <asp:TextBox Runat=server ID=txtName
                         MaxLength=100
                         Columns=25 />
                    <asp:Button Runat=server ID=btnAdd
                         Text='Add Department'
                         OnClick='CreateDepartment' />
               </form>

          </body>
     </html>
```

On our DataGrid declaration the only attribute we need to set turns off the automatic generation of columns that would be rendered by the control by default. When using a DataGrid for editing, the default behavior is to generate an HTML text box for every column in our data source. Because we don't want to expose the DepartmentID field to our users for updates (because the SQL Server manages this value for us), the default behavior of the grid will not work for us in this case. Instead we use two BoundColumn declarations. For the first one, whose DataField is DepartmentID, we've set the ReadOnly attribute to true. This will prevent the DataGrid from rendering an HTML input for the column when we put the grid into edit mode. For the second bound column, bound to DepartmentName, we've accepted the default ReadOnly value of false.

The EditCommandColumn has four important attributes. The first is ButtonType. This accepts values of either LinkButton or PushButton. When the grid renders,

LinkButton generates an HTML anchor tag, and PushButton generates an HTML button. EditText is the text of the anchor tag or the caption of the button when the grid first renders. UpdateText and CancelText are what appear when we put a row into edit mode. All three of these links cause a specific server-side event to occur, which is where we implement the editing functionality. Before we jump into that, let's look for a minute at the Page_Load event:

```
Private Sub Page_Load(ByVal sender As System.Object, ByVal e As
System.EventArgs) Handles MyBase.Load

        If Not Page.IsPostBack Then BindGrid()

    End Sub
```

This will look familiar because you've seen it on the User Maintenance page. We must again break out the grid binding code into its own routine because there will be several post back events that occur on the page, and we'll need to bind the grid again on each one. The BindGrid routine looks like this:

```
Private Sub BindGrid()
        Dim cn As New
SqlConnection("server=(local);database=AtWorkWebPortal;uid=sa")
        Dim sql As String = "select DepartmentID, DepartmentName From
Department ORDER BY DepartmentName"
        Dim cm As New SqlCommand(sql, cn)
        Dim dr As SqlDataReader

        cn.Open()
        dr = cm.ExecuteReader
        dgDepartments.DataSource = dr
        dgDepartments.DataBind()

        cn.Close()
        cm = Nothing
        cn = Nothing
    End Sub
```

This code is old hat by now. It's nice to realize that, although this code might have seemed a little strange the first time you laid eyes on it, this simple pattern can be used for a vast array of functionality in the Framework. We've been looking at list controls for the last pages, so notice here that we're back to two lines of data binding syntax because we do not need the DataTextField or DataValueField for DataGrid or DataList binding.

Now we've looked at everything that gives us the page displayed in Figure 6.16. Let's take a look at the page when our user clicks on one of the links in the EditCommandColumn, shown in Figure 6.17.

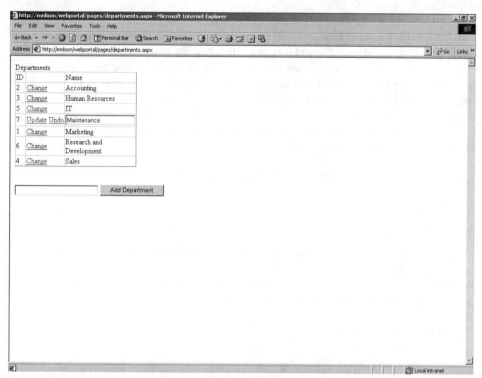

Figure 6.17   The DataGrid Control in edit mode.

What do we have here? Everything is the same with the exception of the row where we clicked the Change link. This caused a post back event to occur, where we were able to set the grid into edit mode and call BindGrid again to render the HTML anew. The Change link has been replaced with Update and Undo links. This text is driven by the UpdateText and CancelText attributes on the EditCommandColumn tag of the Data-Grid. The ID column is still displayed as simple table data text because we set the ReadOnly attribute of that BoundColumn tag to true. And finally, we have a text box that displays the department name field. This is the default behavior for the grid when you set it into edit mode; we did nothing special on the corresponding BoundColumn tag to accomplish this. We also had to write one line of code in the event trap that fires when the Change link is clicked. Here's that trap:

```
Private Sub dgDepartments_EditCommand _
    (ByVal source As Object, _
    ByVal e As System.Web.UI.WebControls.DataGridCommandEventArgs) _
    Handles dgDepartments.EditCommand
        dgDepartments.EditItemIndex = e.Item.ItemIndex
        BindGrid()
    End Sub
```

The footprint of this trap is similar to others we have seen so far. The second parameter is an object of type DataGridCommandEventArgs, which is a class that inherits from EventArgs, the type that we're accustomed to seeing for that second parameter. The DataGrid extends the EventArgs class to provide us with some additional information about the event. It does this with an object of DataGridItem, to which the Item property of the parameter contains a reference. One of the properties of the Data-GridItem is an integer named ItemIndex. This carries the index of the row that raised the event. The DataGrid control exposes an EditItemIndex property. When you set this property and bind the grid, the corresponding row of output will be rendered in edit mode instead of the default output. So with a single line of code post back, we can bind the grid and have the row our user clicked on rendered in edit mode:

```
dgDepartments.EditItemIndex = e.Item.ItemIndex
```

I've mentioned that the default rendering of this edit mode is to display each bound column as an HTML text-type input instead of as static text. Although this is fine for our simple requirements, it's more likely that you'll want to provide some fanciness to your user when they're editing. I'm talking about drop down lists, check boxes, calendar controls, and so on. The data grid is capable of producing these rich UIs for you, but it requires a bit more work. To do this you use a TemplateColumn and specifiy an EditItemTemplate. We've seen the template column in action using just the ItemTemplate, so you know that you have very good control over the exact HTML that gets generated using it. In addition, the EditItemTemplate can be defined to the ItemTemplate, and the grid will use the ItemTemplate by default and will use the EditItemTemplate for whichever row its EditItemIndex is set to. In the next page we implement we'll use the DataList's EditItemTemplate to produce a much richer UI for editing. But first, let's take a look at the rest of this solution.

From here our users will start their editing, furiously making modifications to the name of the department. When they're satisfied that the department is now named appropriately, they'll click on the Update link. This will fire the DataGrid's Update-Command event, which we will trap and implement. Let's have a look:

```
Private Sub dgDepartments_UpdateCommand _
        (ByVal source As Object, _
        ByVal e As System.Web.UI.WebControls.DataGridCommandEventArgs) _
        Handles dgDepartments.UpdateCommand

        Dim cn As New
SqlConnection("server=(local);database=AtWorkWebPortal;uid=sa")
        Dim sql As String = "UPDATE Department SET DepartmentName =
@DepartmentName WHERE DepartmentID = @DepartmentID"
        Dim cm As New SqlCommand(sql, cn)
        Dim pm As SqlParameter

        pm = cm.Parameters.Add(New SqlParameter("@DepartmentID",
SqlDbType.Int))
        pm.Value = e.Item.Cells(0).Text
        pm = cm.Parameters.Add(New SqlParameter("@DepartmentName",
```

```
SqlDbType.VarChar, 100))
        pm.Value = CType(e.Item.Cells(2).Controls(0), TextBox).Text
        cn.Open()
        cm.ExecuteNonQuery()
        cn.Close()

        cm = Nothing
        cn = Nothing
        dgDepartments.EditItemIndex = -1
        BindGrid()

    End Sub
```

The trap has the same footprint as the EditCommand event. Again we'll have the DataGridItem exposed to us as the Item property of the second parameter. For this event we'll be digging further into that item and using more of the goodies exposed there.

Our strategy here is to use a parameterized SQL statement to retrieve the new name from the DataGridItem and issue an UPDATE statement against the database. To do this we'll also need the department ID for our WHERE clause. Both of these values are present in the DataListItem, squirreled away in a property of that object: the Cells collection. The Cells collection is a zero-based set of TableCell objects, one for each column in the grid. For this grid we'll have three objects in the collection, numbered 0, 1, and 2. Cell 0 is our department ID. The Text property of the TableCell is just like the innerText property in DHTML. It returns all the text contained between the begin and end tags of the table data cell. Because our first column contains only the text value of the department ID, we can retrieve it with the Text property of the TableCell object at position 0 in the Cells collection. We use this to set our @DepartmentID parameter value:

```
pm = cm.Parameters.Add(New SqlParameter("@DepartmentID", SqlDbType.Int))
pm.Value = e.Item.Cells(0).Text
```

The DepartmentName column is a different matter entirely. Let's take a look at the HTML that is generated by the grid for the table data cell holding the HTML text type input we've used to edit this value:

```
<td style="width:150px;">
<input name="dgDepartments:ctrl4:ctrl2" type="text" value="IT" />
</td>
```

You can see here that the Text property of this cell will not give us what we need. Because the Text property contains only character data of a given tag, the Text property of this TableCell will be an empty string. This tag contains no text content whatsoever; it has one child element of type input. What we're really interested in is the value attribute of that input.

To expose this value to us the TableCell object exposes a Controls collection. The Controls collection is actually defined in the Control object, from which virtually every object we've been using inherits. The Controls collection is used to keep track of all child controls that any given object has. In HTML terms, there will be an object in the

Controls collection for every child tag of the corresponding HTML tag. For those of you familiar with XML, it's much like the DOM. For those of you familiar with DHTML, it's much like the object model exposed there. In the case of this TableCell, we have one child control, the input of type text. This is exposed in the Controls collection as an instance of a TextBox server control. We can retrieve this object from the Table-Cell's Controls collection, cast into an object of type TextBox, and use the Text property exposed by the TextBox to finally get to the value with which our user has christened this department:

```
pm = cm.Parameters.Add(New SqlParameter("@DepartmentName",
SqlDbType.VarChar, 100))
pm.Value = CType(e.Item.Cells(2).Controls(0), TextBox).Text
```

Having defined our parameters and their values, we fire the statement off to the database and the corresponding row in the Department table is updated. We then reset the EditItemIndex of the data grid to –1. This effectively takes the grid out of edit mode. We then must rebind the grid. This will cause the grid to go back to the database, read the data fresh, and then regenerate its underlying HTML before our page ships it back to the client. This will display the grid back in static mode with the changes our user has just made and also with any changes that have been made by other users since the grid was last rendered.

So what else are our users going to do on this page? They might click the Undo link instead of the Update link, but that is not a problem:

```
Private Sub dgDepartments_CancelCommand _
      ByVal source As Object, _
      ByVal e As System.Web.UI.WebControls.DataGridCommandEventArgs) _
      Handles dgDepartments.CancelCommand

      dgDepartments.EditItemIndex = -1
      BindGrid()
End Sub
```

We just saw this code at the end of the Update routine. Instead of moving any changes to the database, we simply take the grid out of edit mode and rebind it. Notice that we're handling the CancelCommand here. The events fired by the three links that make up an EditCommandColumn are wired automatically for us by the DataGrid control when it renders and sets up its post backs. It's a built-in function of the Edit-CommandColumn.

The last thing our user could do on this form is type in the name of a new department and click the Add Department button. This button raises a post back that is handled by the CreateDepartment routine. This routine will retrieve the text from the TextBox control, build an INSERT statement with it, and create a new row in the Department table. This is all functionality that we've seen before:

```
Public Sub CreateDepartment(ByVal o As Object, ByVal e As EventArgs)
      Dim cn As New
SqlConnection("server=(local);database=AtWorkWebPortal;uid=sa")
      Dim sql As String = "INSERT INTO Department (DepartmentName)
VALUES (@DepartmentName)"
```

```
            Dim cm As New SqlCommand(sql, cn)
            Dim pm As SqlParameter

            pm = cm.Parameters.Add(New SqlParameter("@DepartmentName",
   SqlDbType.VarChar, 100))
            pm.Value = txtName.Text

            cn.Open()
            cm.ExecuteNonQuery()
            cn.Close()

            txtName.Text = ""
            BindGrid()

     End Sub
```

Notice that we're also resetting the value of the txtName control to an empty string. This is needed because of the inherent state maintenance behavior of the Framework. If we did not do this, the user would click on the Add Department, the department would appear in the grid, and the name would still be displayed in the text box. Most users would probably click the button a few more times before realizing that they had created a department each time they clicked, and because we have not implemented delete functionality, they'd probably be getting on the phone to complain.

The DataGrid control really exposes a wealth of functionality to us. In this solution we've seen the editing capabilities that we get right out of the gate. The data binding infrastructure does not intrinsically support updates to the database as some of the older VB data binding frameworks do, but that model is really a throwback to client-server architectures and would not work well in a distributed environment. Therefore, in the new Framework we have to write some code to make changes to our persistent data. This is as it should be. In the next example we'll take a look at using the Edit-ItemTemplate of the DataList control to render a rich editing interface, and we'll also use SQL Server-stored procedures to push our changes back into the database.

Maintaining Department News

We've covered a lot of ground so far. We have all but one of the pieces we'll need to construct our Enterprise Web portal. In the following section we'll start converting the pages we've made into User Controls and plugging them into our portal page. But first, we need to provide a way to create and update department news items. This will serve as the interface for customizing the output that appears on the DepartmentItem page that we created earlier.

The data that we'll be editing is stored in the DepartmentItem table. We'll be using a DataList control to expose editing capabilities against this data. We'll actually be reusing the template that we created for the DepartmentItem page's DataList control. This will allow the creators of these news items to see what the output they're creating will look like when it goes live on the Web site. We'll be extending this template to provide the editing capabilities. When the page first renders, it will appear as it does in Figure 6.18.

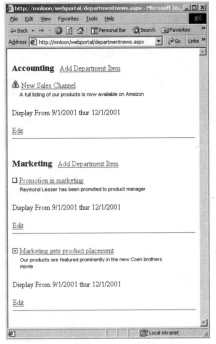

Figure 6.18   The DepartmentNews page.

The pieces we'll add to the template display things that don't appear for individual users at runtime. These include the name of the department the news belongs to, the day the item will first appear, and the day the item will last appear. These values are used on the DepartmentItem page when we're querying the news items for the relevant ones to display. We've also added an Edit link. We'll use the built-in editing capabilities of the DataList control to allow our users to maintain this data, as we did with the DataGrid on the Department page in the previous section. This edit template will be much more complex than what we used on the DataGrid. When we put the Data-List into edit mode (for the second item in this case), the page will look like Figure 6.19.

At the top of the screen we can see the regular item template rendering of the first item in the list. The second item is in edit mode, and you can see we've created an entire form for modifying this information. On the DataGrid in the previous section we had a single text box. Here we have a number of new features:

- A text area to allow enough space for what could be a large description for the news item

- Text boxes to edit the URL and link text of the news item's hyperlink

- Calendar controls to accept the begin and end dates for the news item

- Drop down lists for editing the Priority and Department fields for the news items

- Links to raise our Update and Cancel post back events

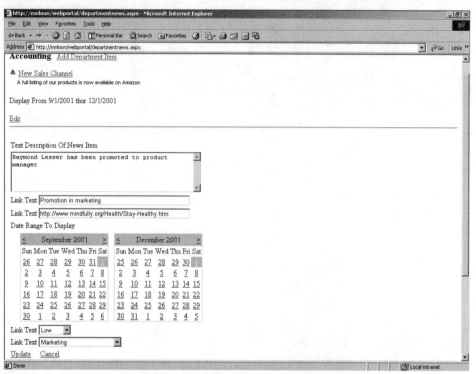

Figure 6.19   The DepartmentNews page in Edit mode.

Setting up and assigning values to these controls does not come without cost. The code behind this page runs almost 200 lines, which is much more than any page we've done so far. The techniques we'll use here are also more advanced than what we've looked at so far. At the end of the effort, you may decide you'd rather implement another page or another panel on this page and render this HTML form without the built-in editing capabilities of the DataList. I would not discourage this technique. We'll be using the editing capabilities of the DataList in this case to showcase the extent of what *can* be done with the services and events exposed by server controls. This does not mean it is always the way it *should* be done. The techniques here are intended to demonstrate the flexibility of the data binding engine and the DataList control. The concepts we learn here will apply to the DataGrid control as well. Demonstrating some of the depth of the Framework will help you to solve your own business problems when your requirements and designs don't fit neatly into the default functionality exposed by these controls. Some of the features of this page that require some extra effort to implement are:

- The section header we have for the department name that appears only when the department changes

- Using the OnItemCommand event to trap events for four different commands (Edit, Update, Add, and Cancel)

- Creating bound ListItems on a drop down list that lives on a DataList or Data-Grid template

- Setting the value of the drop down list that lives on a DataList or DataGrid template

- Overcoming the lack of ability to add a new row using the DataList editing functionality (you can only edit existing items)

- Maintaining state with hidden controls and private class variables

So let's get started by looking at the declaration of the DataList:

```
<asp:DataList Runat=server ID=dlNewsItems OnItemCommand='ListCommand'>
</asp:DataList>
```

Only one additional attribute is here in addition to the default declaration. Setting the OnItemCommand attribute allows us to name the routine by which the events that we'll fire from ListButtons on the DataList will be handled. The footprint for this trap in the code behind our page will look like this:

```
Public Sub ListCommand(ByVal o As Object, _
ByVal e As DataListCommandEventArgs)
End Sub
```

This is the standard event trap footprint, with the DataListCommandEventArgs inheriting from and extending the EventArgs object. Some of the attributes added include the following:

CommandName. The value of the CommandName attribute set on the object that raised the event.

CommandArgument. The value of the CommandArgument attribute set on the object that raised the event.

Item. An instance of the DataListItem object, containing all information and data specific to the row on the DataList where the event was raised.

This simple wiring will allow us to raise all four of the events that we need from the DataList. These will include events for putting the DataList into edit mode, updating changes, canceling changes, and adding a new row to the DepartmentItem table.

Let's examine the ItemTemplate element of the DataList. This element is a child of the DataList declaration. We will also have an EditItemTemplate element as a child of the DataList element. We'll take a look at that later. Here's the ItemTemplate:

```
<ItemTemplate>
    <div runat=server id=divDepartmentHeader
            style='padding-bottom:15px;padding-top:15px'>
        <span runat=server id=lblDepartmentName
                style='font-weight:bold;font-size:14pt' >
            <%# Container.DataItem("DepartmentName") %>
        </span>
          
        <asp:LinkButton Runat=server ID=lbAddItem
                CommandName='AddItem'
                text='Add Department Item' />
```

```
        </div>
        <img src='images/Priority<%# Container.DataItem("Priority") %>.gif'>
        <asp:HyperLink Target=_blank
                                        Runat=server
                                        ID=hlDI
                                        NavigateUrl='<%#
Container.DataItem("URL") %>'
                                        text='<%#
Container.DataItem("LinkText") %>' />
        <table width=360px>
            <tr>
                    <td style='padding-left:15px;font-family:arial;font-
size:8pt'>
                    <%# Container.DataItem("ItemDescr") %>
                    </td>
            </tr>
        </table>
        <p>Display From <%#
FormatDateTime(Container.DataItem("BeginDisplay"),DateFormat.ShortDate) %>
            thru <%#
FormatDateTime(Container.DataItem("EndDisplay"),DateFormat.ShortDate)
%>></p>
        <asp:LinkButton Runat=server ID=lbEdit
            CommandName='Edit'
            text='Edit' />
        <asp:TextBox Runat=server ID="txtDepartmentItemID"
            Visible=False
            Text=<%# Container.DataItem("DepartmentItemID") %> />
        <asp:TextBox Runat=server ID=txtDepartmentID
            Visible=False
            Text=<%# Container.DataItem("DepartmentID") %> />
        <asp:TextBox Runat=server ID="txtPriority"
            Visible=False
            Text=<%# Container.DataItem("Priority") %> />
        <hr>
</ItemTemplate>
```

Let's break it down. We'll start with the first section of the template. This is a div tag that we'll use to display the department header:

```
<div runat=server id=divDepartmentHeader
    style='padding-bottom:15px;padding-top:15px'>
    <span runat=server id=lblDepartmentName
            style='font-weight:bold;font-size:14pt' >
        <%# Container.DataItem("DepartmentName") %>
    </span>
      
    <asp:LinkButton Runat=server ID=lbAddItem
        CommandName='AddItem'
        text='Add Department Item' />
</div>
```

From events we trap as the data binding is occurring, we'll programmatically hide or display this section every time the department changes. This event, which we'll examine in detail in a bit, is fired *after* every item from our data source is evaluated and bound. It's a hook that allows us to change what was done during the binding process for each row in our data source. You can use this event to do things like color code numbers based on ranges of values (i.e., displaying negative numbers in red). One of the things we'll be doing from this event is hiding this div by setting its visibility to false for all but the first row from each department from our data source. On the SPAN tag we're outputting the department name using the following syntax:

```
<%# Container.DataItem("SourceColumnName")  %>
```

We're placing this output on the span that has the runat=server attribute declared on it so that we'll have programmatic access to this value from the ItemDataBound event trap.

The last tag in this portion of the template declares a link button that will render as an HTML anchor tag. We specify AddItem as the value for the CommandName attribute. Remember that this will be passed to our ListCommand routine, which is trapping the ItemCommand event of the DataList. We will look at this value in the implementation of this trap to know which actions to take when the post back occurs.

The next few tags on the template are copied from the DataList on the Department-Item page. They do the work of displaying the news item. We will not go over these again here. After those tags, the rest of the tags on the template display the date range from which this item will appear and the link to throw the DataList into edit mode:

```
<p>Display From <%#
FormatDateTime(Container.DataItem("BeginDisplay"),DateFormat.ShortDate) %>
            thru <%#
FormatDateTime(Container.DataItem("EndDisplay"),DateFormat.ShortDate)
%></p>
<asp:LinkButton Runat=server ID=lbEdit
     CommandName='Edit'
     text='Edit' />
<asp:TextBox Runat=server ID="txtDepartmentItemID"
     Visible=False
     Text=<%# Container.DataItem("DepartmentItemID") %> />
<asp:TextBox Runat=server ID=txtDepartmentID
     Visible=False
     Text=<%# Container.DataItem("DepartmentID") %> />
<asp:TextBox Runat=server ID="txtPriority"
     Visible=False
     Text=<%# Container.DataItem("Priority") %> />
<hr>
```

Let's examine the first couple of data binding expressions. Again we are calling an intrinsic VB function, as we did when we implemented the Stock Ticker. This time we're using the FormatDateTime function, passing first the value that the data binding engine returns when we call Container.DataItem, and passing second a value from the

DateFormat enumeration. Enumerations are ubiquitous in the .NET Framework. Intellisense for these works very well from the HTML editor and the code editor, making them very easy to work with. The output we're generating on this first paragraph tag renders as the description of the news items date range:

```
Display From 9/11/2001 thru 10/7/2001
```

The last output we're doing renders our Edit link. This will fire the ListCommand routine, where we will check for the Edit command name that we have set here.

Following our LinkButton are three TextBox controls. Although these do not appear on our output, we need them here so that they are available to us when the post backs for our different events occur. The DepartmentItemID is the primary key to the DepartmentItem table. Our users do not care about this value, so we are not displaying it to them. When we throw the DataList into edit mode, this value is extremely important to us. By placing it on a hidden TextBox, it is exposed to us programmatically but remains hidden from the user. You may have used this technique with HTML inputs of type hidden. This method is even better because users will not see this value even if they view the HTML source from the browser. The other two values will be used from our server-side event traps as well. We'll discuss these more later.

Let's move to the code and examine some of the routines that deal with the item template. First, of course, is the Page_Load event, where we again call a routine to bind the DataList on the first rendering of the page:

```
Private Sub Page_Load(ByVal sender As System.Object, _
          ByVal e As System.EventArgs) _
          Handles MyBase.Load

    If Not Page.IsPostBack Then BindDataList()

End Sub
```

These lines of code are probably very familiar by now. Let's look at the BindDataList routine:

```
Private Sub BindDataList()
    Dim cn As New SqlConnection _
                ("server=(local);database=AtWorkWebPortal;uid=sa")
Dim sql As String = "SELECT DepartmentItem.ItemDescr, " _
    & "DepartmentItem.LinkText, " _
        & "DepartmentItem.URL, " _
        & "DepartmentItem.BeginDisplay, DepartmentItem.EndDisplay, " _
        & "DepartmentItem.Priority, Department.DepartmentName, " _
        & "Department.DepartmentID, DepartmentItem.DepartmentItemID " _
        & "FROM DepartmentItem INNER JOIN Department " _
        & "ON DepartmentItem.DepartmentID = Department.DepartmentID " _
        & "ORDER BY CommitSave, DepartmentName, BeginDisplay"
    Dim cm As New SqlCommand(sql, cn)
    Dim dr As SqlDataReader
```

```
        cn.Open()
        dr = cm.ExecuteReader
        dlNewsItems.DataSource = dr
        dlNewsItems.DataBind()
        cn.Close()
    End Sub
```

Again, this is a very familiar pattern. The SQL statement is a little more verbose because we're retrieving a lot of data and we're joining to the Department table to get the DepartmentName for display to the user, while tracking the DepartmentID in a hidden TextBox. The ORDER BY clause is very important. We are using it to ensure that all of our departments appear together so that we may display the department name a single time as a header field instead of repeating it with each news item. Within departments we are sorting by the date that they will first be displayed. The first column in the sort is a boolean that we will use when adding a row to the DepartmentItem table. We will discuss this further soon. For now realize that rows in the DepartmentItem table will usually have a CommitSave value of true, so this column will not affect the sort.

This is the first time that a DataList or DataGrid control's template and a call to its DataBind method do not deliver all of the functionality that we need. Let's take a look at the output rendered by the code that we have looked at so far, shown in Figure 6.20.

Figure 6.20 An incorrect rendering of the DataList.

Close, but no cigar. The DataList has rendered exactly as we told it to. The problem is, we want the department name to appear once as a header over all of the news items for that department. This works well for the accounting department, because there's only one news item for that department in the database. The marketing department has two news items displayed here, and we basically just want the second Marketing label and its accompanying link to go away.

To do this we will need to implement the OnItemDataBound event trap. This is an event that fires *after* each row in our data source has been processed by the data binding engine. As I mentioned earlier, it gives us a chance to refine the work that the engine has done. Let's take a look at the footprint for this event trap:

```
Private Sub dlNewsItems_ItemDataBound _
    (ByVal sender As Object, _
     ByVal e As System.Web.UI.WebControls.DataListItemEventArgs) _
     Handles dlNewsItems.ItemDataBound
End Sub
```

Exposed by the DataListItemEventArgs is the old familiar Item object. This is another instance of the DataListItem object. Using this object, we can modify, replace, or remove the entire output generated by the data binding engine.

An important property of the DataListItem object is the ItemType property. This property carries one of the values defined by the ListItemType enum. The ListItemType has the following domain of values:

- AlternatingItem
- EditItem
- Footer
- Header
- Item
- Pager
- SelectedItem
- Separator

Each of these values corresponds to a template that can be defined for the DataList control. In this page, we're using the ItemTemplate and EditItemTemplate, which constrain the range of values that ItemType can contain in our event to Item or EditItem. We will be using this event trap for EditItem types, but for now let's look at just the code that deals with our Item types:

```
Dim div As HtmlGenericControl = _
    CType(e.Item.FindControl("divDepartmentHeader"), HtmlGenericControl)
If e.Item.DataItem("DepartmentName") <> DepartmentName Then
    DepartmentName = e.Item.DataItem("DepartmentName")
    div.Visible = True
Else
    div.Visible = False
End If
```

The first thing we do is pull a reference to the HTML div that is wrapping the department name. Once that has been obtained, we use the DataItem collection of the DataListItem to check the value of the row that has just been rendered. The DataItem exposes to us all of values from the row of the data source that has just been bound. This is a critical collection in this event trap because it will usually be some value in our data that drives our desire to change the binding engine's output. The Department-Name is a string variable that we have declared with class-level scope. This means that it will retain its value between calls to this event trap. This is because this event will fire once for each row in our data source before the content of our page actually renders and gets returned to the client. We'll use this state to compare the value of the current department name to the value of the department name on the previous firing of the event. Whenever there's a difference, we know that our data source has moved through all the items in one department and is beginning the next department. In this case we set the visibility of the div to true and change the value of the Department-Name local variable to match that of the new department. This means that this branch of code will not execute again until we have moved through all of the items for the new department. On the binding of the first row in our data source, DepartmentName will be an empty string, our header will be displayed, and we will update our local variable value to match the first department. Note that the ORDER BY clause used in our data source is needed for this strategy to work.

When our page is first requested, the code that we have looked at here will render the template we have examined. At this point our users have the option of choosing the Edit link on the individual row items or the Add Department Item link next to the department name headers (see Figure 6.18).

Let's walk through what will happen when the user clicks on the Edit link. All the link buttons are trapped by the ListCommand routine because we named that routine with the OnItemCommand attribute in our DataList declaration. We have already examined the footprint of this routine. Let's add the code that will execute when the Edit link is selected:

```
Public Sub ListCommand(ByVal o As Object, ByVal e As
DataListCommandEventArgs)
    If e.CommandName = "Edit" Then
        dlNewsItems.EditItemIndex = e.Item.ItemIndex
        DepartmentID = CType(e.Item.FindControl("txtDepartmentID"),
TextBox).Text
        Priority = CInt(CType(e.Item.FindControl("txtPriority"),
TextBox).Text)
        BindDataList()
ElseIf ... 'Code For Other Commands
```

The first thing that we need to do is to check the value of the CommandName property of the event argument. Remember, this corresponds to the CommandName attribute on our link button declarations. The first line of code, as we saw on the Department page with the DataGrid, sets the EditItemIndex of the DataList equal to the index of the row where the Edit link was clicked. DepartmentID and Priority are private variables with class-level scope. We will use these from the ItemDataBound event that we'll examine after looking at the EditItemTemplate. The final line of code rebinds the DataList control, the difference being this time that we have set the Edit-ItemIndex; therefore, that row will render using the EditItemTemplate instead of the ItemTemplate of the DataList.

Refer to Figure 6.19 to see the output that the template generates as we discuss it. The EditItemTemplate formats its output using an HTML table:

```
<EditItemTemplate>
     <table>
     </table>
</EditItemTemplate>
```

Let's start with the first two rows of the table as defined by the template:

```
<tr>
     <td colspan=3>
            <asp:Label Runat=server ID=lblItemDescr
                   text="Text Description Of News Item" />
     </td>
</tr>
<tr>
     <td colspan=3>
            <asp:TextBox Runat=server ID=txtItemDescr
                 TextMode=MultiLine
                 Rows=5
                 Columns=50
                 MaxLength=250
                 text='<%# Container.DataItem("ItemDescr") %>' />
     </td>
</tr>
```

The label control provides a caption for the text area that follows. An HTML text area can be rendered by ASP.NET using the TextBox server control. We've used this control extensively to generate HTML inputs of type text, but we can also render a text area by setting the TextMode attribute of the control equal to MultiLine. We can control the size of the text area with the Rows and Columns attributes. The length of the database column that stores the description is 250, so we set the MaxLength of the text area to match. Notice also that rows times columns is also equal to the maximum length that we can accept. The text of the area is bound to our data source with the data binding expression used on the final attribute of the declaration.

The next two rows of the table label and bind a couple of simple text box controls:

```
<tr>
     <td>
            <asp:Label Runat=server ID="lblLinkText"
                   text="Link Text" />
     </td>
     <td colspan=2>
            <asp:TextBox Runat=server ID=txtLinkText
                   Columns=50
                   MaxLength=50
```

```
            text='<%# Container.DataItem("LinkText") %>' />
        </td>
    </tr>
    <tr>
        <td>
            <asp:Label Runat=server ID="lblURL"
                text="Link Text" />
        </td>
        <td colspan=2>
            <asp:TextBox Runat=server ID="txtURL"
                Columns=50
                MaxLength=150
                text='<%# Container.DataItem("URL") %>' />
        </td>
    </tr>
```

Again, we use MaxLength to enforce the maximum size of the data type defined in the table. We're using the Columns attribute to make the inputs render at the same physical size. The browser will support scrolling of the text when the value exceeds the displayed area.

The next two rows defined in the template are where we render the Calendar controls to gather the date range when the news item should be displayed:

```
    <tr>
        <td colspan=3>
            <asp:Label Runat=server ID="lblBeginDate"
                text="Date Range To Display" />
        </td>
    </tr>
    <tr>
        <td colspan=3 align=center>
            <table>
            <tr>
            <td>
            <asp:Calendar Runat=server id=calBeginDate
              SelectedDate='<%# Container.DataItem("BeginDisplay") %>'
              VisibleDate='<%# Container.DataItem("BeginDisplay") %>' />
            </td>
            <td style='padding-left:10px'>
            <asp:Calendar Runat=server id="calEndDate"
              SelectedDate='<%# Container.DataItem("EndDisplay") %>'
              VisibleDate='<%# Container.DataItem("EndDisplay") %>' />
            </td>
            </tr>
            </table>
        </td>
    </tr>
```

The first row labels the calendars. The second row is where we declare our calendars. Notice that we use two data binding expressions for each declaration. The first sets the date *value* of the control, and the second tells the calendar to render its first display on the month and year of the selected date. Why you would want to render a control with a selected date on a month or year that is not displayed is beyond me, but unless you set both of these attributes, the VisibleDate will default to the current system date on the Web server. This will be true in any use of the calendar control even when it's not on a DataList or DataGrid template.

```
<tr>
    <td>
            <asp:Label Runat=server ID="lblPriority"
                    text="Priority" />
    </td>
    <td colspan=2>
            <asp:DropDownList Runat=server ID=ddlPriority
                    DataSource=<%# BindPriority() %>
                    DataTextField='PriorityName'
                    DataValueField='PriorityID' />
    </td>
</tr>
<tr>
    <td>
            <asp:Label Runat=server ID="lblDepartment"
                    text="Department" />
    </td>
    <td colspan=2>
            <asp:DropDownList Runat=server ID="ddlDepartment"
                    DataSource=<%# BindDepartment() %>
                    DataTextField='DepartmentName'
                    DataValueField='DepartmentID' />
    </td>
</tr>
```

This code is quite a bit different from anything we have looked at up until now. Although we have bound data lists and have bound drop down lists before, we've never tried to bind a drop down list that lives on the template of a data list. Usually we set the attributes we see on our DropDownLists from code. Setting them from our control declarations is not a problem for the DataTextField and DataValueField, because these properties accept string values. The DataSource property, however, accepts an instance of an object that supports the data binding engine. In our examples this has been an instance of a DataTable or a SQLDataReader. We have no way to instantiate these objects from our template in a manner that the data binding engine will be able to reconcile; therefore, we need to use a data binding expression that calls a public method that we define in the class that lives in our code behind the page. This is not much different from when we earlier called the Format and FormatDateTime functions from data binding expressions. The difference here is that we are calling functions that we have defined ourselves. These functions return instances of objects that the data binding engine will use to generate the ListItems for our DropDownLists. The data binding engine will automatically call DataBind on these drop down lists for us as part of the binding process. Let's look at the BindPriority implementation. The priority drop down list will be bound to an XML file:

```
Public Function BindPriority() As DataView
    Dim ds As New DataSet("Priorities")

    ds.ReadXml(Server.MapPath("Priority.xml"))
    Return ds.Tables(0).DefaultView

End Function
```

We've seen this pattern before when binding the DataGrid that displays the menu items. The priority.xml file has three elements that map the three values (1, 2, 3) to three descriptions (low, medium, high):

```
<Priorities>
    <Priority PriorityName='High' PriorityID='1' />
    <Priority PriorityName='Medium' PriorityID='2' />
    <Priority PriorityName='Low' PriorityID='3' />
</Priorities>
```

The Department DropDownList needs to be bound to the Deparment table in our database. To accomplish this we will have the BindDepartment method return an instance of a SQLDataReader:

```
Public Function BindDepartment() As SqlDataReader
    Dim cn As New
SqlConnection("server=(local);database=AtWorkWebPortal;uid=sa")
    Dim cm As New SqlCommand _
    ("select DepartmentID, DepartmentName From Department ORDER BY
DepartmentName", cn)
    Dim dr As SqlDataReader

    cn.Open()
    dr = cm.ExecuteReader
    Return dr

End Function
```

Again, this is a very simple implementation. In this case we're returning a SQL-DataReader instead of a DataView. The data binding engine does not care as long as the object we return supports the ICollection interface. So what's missing from this solution? Although we've successfully created the ListItems for our DropDownLists, we're editing an existing row of data and need these lists to have the corresponding ListItem selected. Although this is easy to do with a TextBox, where all we have to do is set the Text attribute, a DropDownList needs to have the Selected property of a corresponding list item set to true. There is no attribute exposed on the DropDownList that lets us do this with a data binding expression; therefore, it's back to the ItemData-Bound event for us:

```
If e.Item.ItemType = ListItemType.EditItem Then
    Dim li As ListItem
    Dim ddl As DropDownList = CType(e.Item.FindControl("ddlPriority"),
DropDownList)

    For Each li In ddl.Items
        If li.Value = e.Item.DataItem("Priority") Then
            li.Selected = True
            Exit For
        End If
    Next

    ddl = CType(e.Item.FindControl("ddlDepartment"), DropDownList)
    For Each li In ddl.Items
        If li.Value = e.Item.DataItem("DepartmentID") Then
            li.Selected = True
            Exit For
        End If
    Next
Else 'Code For Item type ListItems
```

This pattern is familiar; its location is what's new. This is the same general type of loop that we have set up every time we've wanted to set the selected item of a list control (DropDownList, ListBox, CheckBoxList, or RadioButtonList). Because we're executing only when the ListItemType is EditItem, we know that the DropDownLists will have been rendered and bound by the data binding engine just before this event fired. Before executing our loop, we dig a reference to the DropDownList out of the Controls collection of the DataListItem. Then we iterate through the items in the list, checking the value of the ListItem against the value in the DataItem collection. Here again we're using the DataItem collection to get to the values of our source data for the row that has just been bound.

Our output now matches that of Figure 6.19. Our user has seven controls with which to edit the data for this news item. Note that whenever the user interacts with the Calendar control, a post back will occur. The state maintenance of the Framework means that no action is required on our part when this occurs. The one precaution that we've taken is in the Page_Load event that executes on every post back. Because we take no action when IsPostBack is true, this event trap does nothing, and we leave the calendar control to go about its business. After users make their changes, they can click on the Update or Cancel links. Let's take a look at what happens when they choose the Update link:

```
Dim cn As New
SqlConnection("server=(local);database=AtWorkWebPortal;uid=sa")
Dim cm As New SqlCommand("usp_UpdateDepartmentItem", cn)
Dim pm As SqlParameter

pm = cm.Parameters.Add(New SqlParameter("@DepartmentItemID",
SqlDbType.Int))
```

```
pm.Value = CType(e.Item.FindControl("txtEditDepartmentItemID"),
TextBox).Text

pm = cm.Parameters.Add(New SqlParameter("@DepartmentID", SqlDbType.Int))
pm.Value = CType(e.Item.FindControl("ddlDepartment"),
DropDownList).SelectedItem.Value

pm = cm.Parameters.Add(New SqlParameter("@ItemDescr", SqlDbType.VarChar,
250))
pm.Value = CType(e.Item.FindControl("txtItemDescr"), TextBox).Text

pm = cm.Parameters.Add(New SqlParameter("@LinkText", SqlDbType.VarChar,
50))
pm.Value = CType(e.Item.FindControl("txtLinkText"), TextBox).Text

pm = cm.Parameters.Add(New SqlParameter("@URL", SqlDbType.VarChar, 150))
pm.Value = CType(e.Item.FindControl("txtURL"), TextBox).Text

pm = cm.Parameters.Add(New SqlParameter("@BeginDisplay",
SqlDbType.DateTime))
pm.Value = CType(e.Item.FindControl("calBeginDate"),
Calendar).SelectedDate

pm = cm.Parameters.Add(New SqlParameter("@EndDisplay",
SqlDbType.DateTime))
pm.Value = CType(e.Item.FindControl("calEndDate"),
Calendar).SelectedDate

pm = cm.Parameters.Add(New SqlParameter("@Priority", SqlDbType.Int))
pm.Value = CType(e.Item.FindControl("ddlPriority"),
DropDownList).SelectedItem.Value

cm.CommandType = CommandType.StoredProcedure
cn.Open()
cm.ExecuteNonQuery()
cn.Close()

cm = Nothing
cn = Nothing

dlNewsItems.EditItemIndex = -1
BindDataList()
```

Here is our first use of a SQL Server-stored procedure. It's very similar to using a parameterized SQL statement. We must set the CommandType of our SQLCommand object to StoredProcedure. We also set the CommandText to the name of the stored procedure that we're executing. Aside from these changes, our requirements are very similar. We must create a SQLParameter for each parameter that the stored procedure expects. To set the value of these parameters we again use the Controls collection of the DataListItem, pulling out references to controls that we know exist on the Edit-ItemTemplate of our DataList. Using CType to cast the return values of the Find-Control method to the corresponding control type, we then use the appropriate property of that control to retrieve the value that our user has given us. The property that we use depends entirely on the control to which we're retrieving a reference. For TextBoxes we use the Text property. For the Calendar control we use the SelectedDate property. For DropDownLists we use the Value of the SelectedItem property.

Let's take a look at what happens when our user wants to create a new news item. The DataList doesn't support this functionality. It can only render a template for a row that exists in the resultset to which it's bound. To work around this, we will create a stub row in the DepartmentItem table. The Add links are rendered next to the depart-ment name headers. Because we can tell what department a user wants to add a news item to, we will populate the DepartmentID in our stub row. So that the Calendar con-trol has a date to work with, we will also populate the BeginDate and EndDate columns with today's date. This is also where we'll use the CommitSave boolean. We took a look at this boolean in the ORDER BY clause of the SQL statement that we use to bind the DataList. For committed news items, this value is always true. For our stub row we will set this value to false. This will cause our stub row to float to the top of our sort order and will also give us some concrete criteria to get rid of the stub if the user should cancel the creation of the row.

Here's the code from the ListCommand routine that will execute when the Com-mandName equals AddItem:

```
Dim cn As New
SqlConnection("server=(local);database=AtWorkWebPortal;uid=sa")
Dim cm As New SqlCommand("usp_CreateDepartmentItemStub", cn)
Dim pm As SqlParameter

pm = cm.Parameters.Add(New SqlParameter("@DepartmentID", SqlDbType.Int))
pm.Value = CType(e.Item.FindControl("txtDepartmentID"), TextBox).Text

pm = cm.Parameters.Add(New SqlParameter("RETVAL", SqlDbType.Int))
pm.Direction = ParameterDirection.ReturnValue

cm.CommandType = CommandType.StoredProcedure
cn.Open()
cm.ExecuteNonQuery()
cn.Close()

dlNewsItems.EditItemIndex = 0
BindDataList()
```

Here's something new and different. We're using a stored procedure to create the stub. This stored procedure has a return value. Let's take a look at the TransactSQL code for this procedure:

```
ALTER PROCEDURE dbo.usp_CreateDepartmentItemStub
@DepartmentID int
AS
      INSERT INTO DepartmentItem
      (DepartmentID, CommitSave, BeginDisplay, EndDisplay)
      VALUES
      (@DepartmentID, 0, GetDate(), GetDate())
      RETURN scope_identity()
```

You can see that in this procedure we create a row in the DepartmentItem table and use the TransactSQL function scope_identity to return the DepartmentItemID that was used by SQL Server to create this row. We retrieve this value with our command object by adding a return value parameter to the command's parameter collection:

```
pm = cm.Parameters.Add(New SqlParameter("RETVAL", SqlDbType.Int))
pm.Direction = ParameterDirection.ReturnValue
```

After execution of the stored procedure, we could retrieve the return value of the procedure with the following code:

```
NewID = cm.Parameters("RETVAL").Value
```

We don't need this value here. I've included this syntax only for your reference because it is very handy, and you will probably find many instances where you do need to use it.

At this point, having created the stub row in the DepartmentItem table, we have only to set the EditItemIndex of the DataList equal to zero. This is the first row in our list, which guarantees that our stub row will be rendered with the EditItemTemplate. This is because it is now the only row in our table with a CommitSave value of zero and will therefore be the first row returned in our resultset.

The beauty of this solution is that there's nothing else we need to do for new rows. We've created a row in the database, and from here on out we will rely on the update functionality that we have already implemented because in essence, that's what we are now doing, updating an existing table row.

There is one more place we have to deal with our stub, and that's in the code that executes when our user clicks the Cancel link. Normally we would just set the Edit-ItemIndex of the DataList back to –1 and rebind the grid. For this page we will also delete any rows in the DepartmentItem table where CommitSave is equal to zero:

```
Dim cn As New
SqlConnection("server=(local);database=AtWorkWebPortal;uid=sa")
Dim cm As New SqlCommand("delete from departmentitem where
CommitSave=0", cn)

cn.open()
cm.executenonquery()
cn.close()

dlNewsItems.EditItemIndex = -1
BindDataList()
```

Well, there's a whole boatload of functionality. We've now created all of our content output and all of our content management functionality. We have a number of disparate pages, each providing a piece of the total functionality for our portal. Next we'll take these pages and transform them into atomic, reusable components and wire them into our portal page. Anyone who has ever used ASP includes as a code reuse mechanism should get ready for liberation. The ASP.NET Framework exposes an entirely new reuse regime, and once you get a taste of it, you'll never want to go back.

Wiring the Web Portal

It's time to take our body of work and build it into a coherent interface. This will involve a few steps. We need to take our individual pages and plug them into our portal interface. To do this we will need to convert them to User Controls so that they can be aggregated on a single page. We also need to add a security layer to the application so that only authorized users can gain access to our application and so that we can identify our users and provide them with content tailored to their role and choices. The steps we will take involve the following:

1. Conversion of the ASPX pages into ASP.NET User Controls.

2. Implementing WebPortal.aspx to display the pieces of our portal in the right time and place.

3. Identifying our user.

Once we do these steps, we'll have a fully functional Web portal. We'll also have all the tools in place that we need to easily extend our applications. Adding functionality to the portal will consist of implementing a User Control, providing the functionality, and modifying the Menu.XML file to add it to the portal interface.

After we move through the preceding four steps, our Web portal will appear as it does in Figure 6.3, and there'll be only one thing left to do. Ship it!

Converting Pages to User Controls

You may be groaning because of the title of this step. Why have we set up our project so that we have to do a conversion to complete it? Aren't conversions something you do only when you have to? There are a couple of reasons why we've implemented the pieces and parts of our application as ASPX, knowing that we'll later have to convert them to User Controls:

- Implementing them as pages first makes it much easier to test and debug the pages as we're doing development. They're able to stand on their own, and we are saved the trouble of creating a host page to test them.

- There's no support for Intellisense in Visual Studio .NET when coding User Controls.

- Conversion to User Controls is extremely simple.

Conversion so simple that I'll outline the steps here and bet that you could skip the rest of this section and start the implementation of the portal:

1. Add a User Control to your project with the same name as your ASPX page.

2. Rename the class inheriting from UserContol from *ClassName* to *ClassNameControl*.

3. Copy the contents of your HTML form from your ASPX page to the ASCX. Include everything *between* <FORM runat=server id=form1> and </FORM> but not the form tags themselves.

4. Copy all of your code from the class inheriting from Web.UI.Page in *PageName*.aspx.vb to the class inheriting from Web.UI.UserControl in *PageName*.ascx.vb. Exclude the "Web Form Designer Generated Code" region. Copy any IMPORTS statements preceding your class delcaration as well.

5. Compile. That's it. You now have a User Control.

A User Control is a reusable unit of code in the ASP.NET Framework. It's like a cross between an ASP include file and an ActiveX control (this is an analogy; there's not actually any COM involved here). It's like an ASP include in that the HTML rendered by the User Control is inserted inline into the HTML rendered by the page. But a User Control is much more useful for a number of reasons. Instead of using a special tag syntax as you would with an ASP include, a User Control is declared with an element, much the same way server controls are. You actually determine the prefix and name of the tag when you include a User Control on the page. So, if you have a user control-named address that provides all the normal inputs to gather address information, the element on the page to insert the User Control could look like this:

```
<myControls:Address runat=server Id=ucAddress />
```

It looks just like any other server control, doesn't it? This is where we depart from the functionality of ASP includes. Having declared the control on the page, we now have an instance of the class object that we've defined available to us in the code behind the page. We can add properties to the User Control and set them programmatically or with attributes on the tag that declares the control. If we need to gather more than one address, we can declare multiple instances of User Controls on the page and interact with them separately using the different ID attributes that we assign to them. We'll get into the details of using the controls when we implement the Web portal page. For now just understand some of the benefits that the User Controls provide.

Let's go through the conversion steps for a specific control. The User Controls are in the Final subdirectory of the project. We'll be copying code from the corresponding pages in the Pages directory. (See Figure 6.21.) When we put in the name of an existing ASPX page, like Departments, and click OK, because of a naming conflict Visual Studio .NET displays the error dialog shown in Figure 6.22.

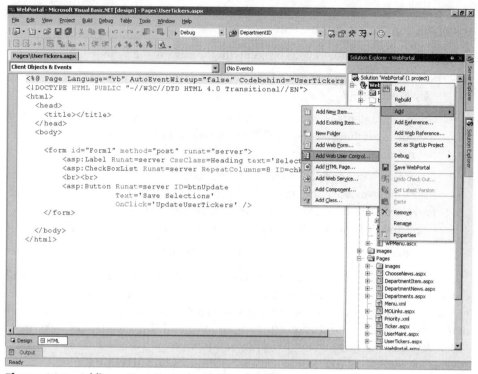

Figure 6.21 Adding a User Control with Visual Studio .NET.

Clear the error and the add User Control dialogs, and you will return to the code editor and the code stub for the User Control that we just created. Because we've given the User Control the same name as our page, there's a conflict in the public class name that we define in our code behind the page. The code editor underlines this conflict for you in the code pane:

```
Public MustInherit Class Departments
    Inherits System.Web.UI.UserControl
+ Web Form Designer Generated Code

    Private Sub Page_Load(ByVal sender As System.Object, ByVal e As
System.EventArgs) Handles MyBase.Load
        'Put user code to initialize the page here
    End Sub


End Class
```

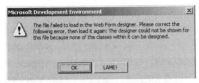

Figure 6.22 Visual Studio .NET error dialog.

To get around this, we can simply rename the class from Departments to Departments Control. Now we can use the Solution Explorer to open the ASCX file, which could not previously be displayed. The only code generated for us with a User Control is the Control page directive, which looks like this:

```
<%@ Control Language="vb" AutoEventWireup="false"
Codebehind="Departments.ascx.vb" Inherits="Webportal.Departments" %>
```

Notice the class named by the Inherits attribute. We need to change this class name as well, to match the name we gave the class in our code behind the page:

```
Inherits="Webportal.DepartmentsControl"
```

Now we're ready to port the ASPX to the User Control. Open Departments.aspx, copy all of the tags from within the form tag, and paste them onto the body of the ASCX file. Your page will look like this:

```
<%@ Control Language="vb" AutoEventWireup="false"
Codebehind="Departments.ascx.vb" Inherits="WebPortal.DepartmentsControl"
%>
<asp:Label Runat=server ID=lblDep CssClass='Heading' text='Departments' />
<asp:DataGrid Runat=server ID=dgDepartments AutoGenerateColumns=False>
     <Columns>
            <asp:BoundColumn DataField='DepartmentID' ReadOnly=True
HeaderText='ID' ItemStyle-Width='20' />
            <asp:EditCommandColumn ButtonType=LinkButton
EditText='Change' UpdateText='Update' CancelText='Undo' />
            <asp:BoundColumn DataField='DepartmentName'
HeaderText='Name' ItemStyle-Width='150' />
     </Columns>
</asp:DataGrid>
<br><br>
<asp:TextBox Runat=server ID=txtName MaxLength=100 Columns=25 />
<asp:Button Runat=server ID=btnAdd Text='Add Department'
OnClick='CreateDepartment' />
```

Now switch to the code behind the control by pressing F7. The template for a User Control is the same as a template for an ASPX page, except that the class we define here inherits from the UserControl class instead of the Page class. All of the code from our ASPX page will work the same way in the User Control. Copy the Imports statement from Departments.aspx.vb and paste it above the class declaration in Departments.ascx.vb. Copy the control declaration from between the class declaration and the Web Form designer region and paste it into the user control code. Then copy the rest of the code below the declarations region and replace the template code below the region with it. Your conversion is now complete. Build the project to catch any errors or omissions. Repeat the process for the other ASPX pages. We now have the User Controls that we will need to wire the Web portal page.

Creating the Web Portal Page

Now all of the atomic pieces of functionality that we need for our portal are defined as User Controls. To create the Web portal we have only to plug those pieces into a single

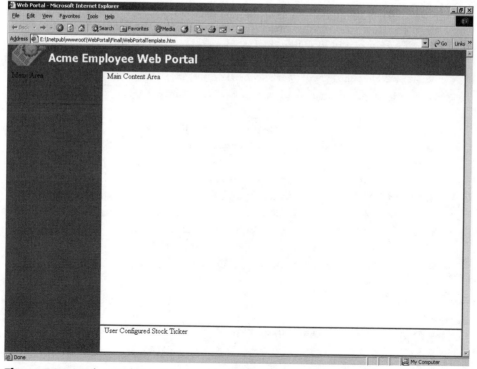

Figure 6.23   Web portal template.

page, displaying them where and when we want them. The structure of our portal page is shown in Figure 6.23. This file is named WebPortalTemplate.htm and is in the Final directory of the solution files.

We'll start by adding a page named WebPortal1.aspx to the solution (WebPortal. aspx, the completed solution, is already present in the Final directory). Copy everything between the HTML tags on WebPortalTemplate into this new file. Everything except the Main Content Area on our portal will remain constant. The different functionality of the portal will be exposed in the content area.

Let's start by wiring the menu into the left-hand side of the portal page. Adding a User Control to an ASPX page requires two steps. We must first register the control with the page by adding a register directive to the top of the page. Add the following line of code under the Page directive line.

```
<%@ Register TagPrefix="WP" TagName="WPMenu" Src="WPMenu.ascx" %>
```

This is much like adding a reference to a COM DLL in VB6. It exposes the control for use by our page. The Src attribute of the register directive needs to point to the ascx file that contains the definition of our User Control. This can be a relative path within your Web application, but it must be within the IIS application of the hosting page. Having added this directive, we can now use a tag named WP:WPMenu anywhere on our ASPX. The left-hand side of the tag name is determined by the TagPrefix attribute of our Register directive. The right-hand side of the tag name corresponds to the TagName attribute. This leaves the form of the tag name up to the page hosting the control instead of being up to the control itself. This introduces the possibility of using different tag names for the same control hosted on different pages.

Find the table data cell where the text Menu Area is currently displayed. Replace the text content of the cell with the following element declaration of our User Control:

```
<WP:WPMenu id=ucWPMenu runat="server" />
```

The tag name is determined entirely by our Register directive, as already described. The ID is arbitrary, as it is with all server controls, but it becomes the variable name that we would use to interact with our control from the code in our page. The runat=server tag is still required, although it does seem a bit redundant in this context.

Build the project and request the WebPortal1.aspx page from your browser. It will appear as shown in Figure 6.24.

Let's add the User Control for the content frame next. When the page is first requested, we will display a company image and the department news items by default. Soon we'll be adding the functionality to dynamically swap the content frame out with other User Controls as menu items are selected. The DepartmentItem User Control will be the first whose services we'll call on. Add another register directive under the WPMenu declaration:

```
<%@ Register TagPrefix="WP" TagName="DepartmentItem"
Src="DepartmentItem.ascx" %>
```

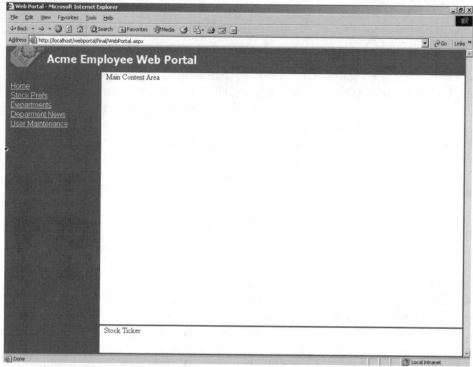

Figure 6.24   Web portal menu wired.

The tag name for this control will now be WP:DepartmentItem in the body of our page. Replace the Main Content Area text of the table data cell with the following code:

```
<center>
<p><asp:Label Runat=server ID=lblWelcome
        text='Welcome'
        Font-Names='verdana'
        Font-Bold=True
        Font-Size=14pt /></p>
<img align=middle src='images/factoryc.gif'>
</center>
<hr>
<WP:DepartmentItem id=ucDepartmentItem runat="server" />
```

Build the project again and refresh the view of WebPortal1.aspx in your browser. We now have the correct output for the default content area. Notice how the User Control output is inserted inline in the rendered HTML wherever we declare the control. This is a very flexible architecture that allows us a fine degree of control over the placement of our content, while contributing to maintainability and reuse by allowing us to easily isolate distinct pieces of functionality.

The external stock banner is just as easy to add. Add Register directives for each of these controls to the top of the page:

```
<%@ Register TagPrefix="WP" TagName="Ticker" Src="Ticker.ascx" %>
```

And replace the User Configured Stock Ticker text with a declaration of the Ticker User Control:

```
<WP:Ticker id=ucTicker runat="server" />
```

The portal page is now completely wired for its initial rendering. Build the project again and refresh the browser view. Your output should appear as it does in Figure 6.3.

The next step is to teach the portal to respond to the user selecting different menu items. Let's first review the functionality that we built into this menu. It uses the Menu.xml document to render a list of HTML anchor tags using a DataGrid control. The XML document contains attributes that describe the link text and a query string parameter to pass to the link. On the template of the DataGrid we built all of our links to post back to the WebPortal.aspx page. The only difference in these URLs is the query string value, which is driven by the XML file. So, for example, the element in the Menu.xml file that look like this:

```
<MenuItem descr='Departments' command='EditDepartments' />
```

renders as an HTML anchor tag that looks like this:

```
<a href='WebPortal.aspx?Command=EditDepartments'>Departments</a>
```

We now know what the default rendering of the portal displays for us. If you click on any of the menu links in the current WebPortal1.aspx page, the page will be requested again, and because we're not responding to the Command query string parameter, the page will render again with its default output. So the only thing we need to do is teach the page to respond to this query string parameter.

And how do we want the page to respond? Each of the values for the Command parameter map to one of our User Controls. If the query string parameter is present, we need to replace the output of the main content area with the output from the desired user control. Table 6.5 lists the mapping of commands to User Controls.

Table 6.5   Command Name to User Control Mapping

COMMAND	USER CONTROL
Home	Default rendering
EditUserTicker	UserTickers.ascx
EditDepartments	Departments.ascx
EditDepartmentItems	DepartmentNews.ascx
EditUsers	UserMaint.ascx

To dynamically load these controls, we will need to use the LoadControl method of the page object. This is a convenient method that is provided specifically for the dynamic loading of User Controls at runtime. This method accepts the name of a User Control file as a parameter and will return a reference to a UserControl object. Because the UserControl class inherits from the Control class, we can use it generically like any other instance of a server control or HTML control.

To place the object on the page, we will use the Add method of the Controls collection. We have used the Controls collection a few times to retrieve references to our controls from the templates of DataGrids and DataLists. In this case we will replace the contents of the table data cell that defines the main content area of the page with the output of our User Control. We will do this by first clearing out the contents of the cell and then adding the reference to our User Control to the Controls collection of the table data cell.

To gain programmatic access to our table data cell from code, we will need to give it an ID and add the runat=server attribute to its element declaration. The declaration of this table data cell currently looks like this:

```
<td class='ContentFrame' valign=top rowspan=2 width='15%'
BGCOLOR="#336666">
```

Modify this declaration by adding the ID and runat attributes:

```
<td runat=server id=ContentCell class='ContentFrame' valign=top
height='90%' width='55%'>
```

We must also add a corresponding declaration of the table data cell to our code behind the page. Press F7 to move to the WebPortal1.aspx.vb page and add the following declaration just under the class declaration:

```
Protected WithEvents ContentCell As HtmlTableCell
```

Now we have full programmatic access to this cell from the code behind our page. We will do the checking for the query string parameter from the page load event. Add the following implementation to this event:

```
Dim sCommand As String = Request.Params("Command")
Dim sControlName As String

If Len(sCommand) > 0 Then
    Select Case sCommand
        Case "EditUserTicker"
            sControlName = "UserTickers"
        Case "EditDepartments"
            sControlName = "Departments"
        Case "EditUsers"
            sControlName = "UserMaint"
        Case "EditDepartmentItems"
            sControlName = "DepartmentNews"
    End Select
```

```
End If

If Len(sControlName) > 0 Then
Dim uc As UserControl = Page.LoadControl(sControlName & ".ascx")
ContentCell.InnerHtml = ""
ContentCell.Controls.Add(uc)
End If
```

The first thing we do here is to retrieve the query string parameter into a string variable named sCommand. To do this we use the Params collection of the Request object. The Params collection is new to ASP.NET, and it holds the contents of what would be in both the QueryString and Form collections from traditional ASP. This is a convenience mechanism that allows us to use a single syntax for HTTP POSTs or GETs. We could use Request.QueryString here but will use the Params collection in case some functionality in the future requests content using an HTTP POST instead of building the value into the URL.

We then find the value of the sCommand string and assign a control name. This mapping corresponds directly to what we defined in the preceding table. If we have found a match for the value of sCommand, we declare a UserControl named uc and initialize it using the LoadControl method of the Page object. We then use the ContentCell variable to clear out the default output of the content pane and replace it with the output of the selected User Control.

If we don't find a value in the query string, or don't find a valid mapping for that value, our routine does not really do any work, and the default rendering of the Web portal will ensue. This will happen on the first rendering of our page (no value in the query string) and when our user clicks on the Home link on the page (no mapping for that command's query string value).

Build your project and try it out. You now have a fully functional Web portal.

Identifying Our Users

We are using a Session variable to identify our users and look up their preferences. This Session variable has a hard-coded value in the current solution. To correctly populate this variable, we would need some means of identifying our users. We have a number of options for doing this. Although ASP.NET security is covered in detail in Project 8, we will go over the options here as they relate to our portal.

Our first choice is to use Forms-based security within our ASP.NET application. This would involve creating a login form and modifying our Web.config file to redirect unauthorized requests to this login page. The block of code within this page that executes when our user successfully logs in is where we would opportunistically give this session variable a value.

The second, and probably more desirable, option in our case is to rely on IIS integrated security. This would involve turning off anonymous access for our Web application in the MMC IIS configuration snap-in and restricting access to only those users who have been authenticated on the local area domain. We could then populate the UserID column of our UserPreferences table with their NT login, retrieve this login from IIS, and use this value to populate the session variable. Project 8 covers this in more detail.

Enhancing the Project

You can see from the infrastructure with which we've created our project how easily it can be extended. Whatever functionality we want to add, we can do so in three simple steps. Implement a User Control with the functionality, add an element to the Menu.xml document, and add the mapping to the menu's event trap to load the User Control. Here are some more ideas for you to try on your own:

Security.   After reading Project 8, come back and add a security layer to the portal application. You can also add logic to the menu to render specific menu items for people in specific roles. This could be done by adding a security-level attribute to each menu item and adding the same attribute to the users' table. The menu could then only render menu items that were at or less than the security level of the current user. This would be very easy to filter out of the data set used to read the XML doc by using the Select method of the DataTable object.

Code free extensibility.   Many of you have probably picked this one out already. Why have a mapping of command names on the menu to User Control names? Why not just use the User Control name as the command name in the first place? Great idea. Go for it. Doing this would enable us to extend the application without modifying any of our code. The implementation used in the project was for clarity in the use of the LoadControl method. You could actually leave the mapping in place and add a Case Else command that loads a User Control named by the command name. When you extend the functionality, just name your commands in Menu.xml after the physical names of the User Controls, and you can extend the application without modifying the code.

Menu editing.   Build an interface to make changes to the Menu.xml file. You can do this with the DataSet object or with any number of objects from the System.XML namespace.

Extend the portal for your business.   Take an existing Active Server Page from your intranet and convert it to an ASP.Net user control. Modify Menu.xml to load this User Control in the content pane.

Explore the bonus material.   The companion CD-ROM contains a project06b directory that has another solution for the Web portal. New functionality has been added to the right-hand side of the portal in this solution; it contains lists to links of external news stories. The DataGrid uses external XML documents as a data source to render this list of links. There's also an interface for the users to choose what news topic they're interested in, driving the XML document used to render the links. You can find this version of the portal in the Project06b directory.

WHAT'S COMING NEXT

The next project is focused on XML. We'll take a look at the structure of XML documents, XML schemas, and some of the XML-specific functionality that is built into Visual Studio .NET.

XML seems to be everywhere today, and even if you haven't had a chance to work with it directly, it's always right around the corner or just under the surface when you are working with the .NET Framework. The next project will spell out some of the real reasons behind the XML hype and show you how to put it to work in your own solutions.

Schema Generator with XML

Have you been able to spend a single day at the office without hearing the term *XML* at least once? I have not. In fact, I have heard about XML in one form or another for 438 workdays straight. At first I tried to ignore it, thinking that another acronym had entered the programming world and would soon be departing. Little did I know how persistent it would be. Eventually I decided to look into what all the noise was about and was quite surprised. Everyone had been saying how great XML was, and the fact that they were right really burned my toast.

XML is amazing not because it's a huge technical achievement, it's vastly complicated, or it took a long time to invent. It's amazing for the opposite reasons. It is a simple standard based on text, it is not particularly complicated, and it did not take long to conceive. More importantly, it easily and simply solves a problem that has existed in the computing industry for decades: the sharing of data between disparate systems and over long remote connections. It also does other things as well, which we'll also explore a little.

THE PROBLEM:

For years companies have struggled, for many different reasons and in many different circumstances, with exchanging data between programs, systems, and other companies. There were too many databases, each with its own proprietary format. Sure, you could export the data to a few inadequate formats, like CSV, but that told the receiving program nothing about the data. So how do we help these companies solve this problem?

THE SOLUTION:

I'll show you how XML can be used to pass data between companies and programs, and also how to validate it against a schema. Our project has two separate companion programs, one for the supplier of data and one for the consumer. These programs, written to accommodate a fictitious toy distributor, can easily be modified to suit your own needs.

The Project

During the course of the project, I'll show you several techniques that VB.NET gives you to make using and interacting with XML easy. I'll also show you one way in which XML can solve data interaction problems. The following activities will be part of the project:

1. **Defining databases.**   We'll define and create databases for both the supplier of data and the consumer.

2. **Create WinForms data generator.**   The first program is the one used by the supplier of data. It will allow users to extract data from their database and generate an XML version of that data. It will also create a schema that can be used to validate the data. I'll show you the schema and the XML.

3. **Create WinForms data reader.**   The second program is a reader utility that the consumer of the data would use to load the XML data.

4. **Validate the data.**   The loaded XML data will be validated against the schema created by the data supplier. Once the data is validated, it can optionally be written to the consumer's own database.

You'll know all you need by the time we get to the actual project because I'm going to give it all to you: XML, XSD, namespaces, and validation; you'll know what they all are and how to use them to make your dreams come true.

You Will Need

✔ **Visual Studio .NET**

✔ **SQL Server (or other database)**

✔ **Only the very basics of XML**

XML Technology

There are many things that XML can be used for and that it does well. It enables you to exchange data between data systems fairly easily, it allows you to transfer complex data sets across HTTP wires from servers to Web sites, and it is a standard that is easy to conform to and actually helps the computing industry. That it came about quickly and is so useful makes it hard to believe that the fiercely competitive business of computing ever came up with it.

XML is a vast topic, with many details and technologies related to it. We will be focusing on using XML to help disparate data systems exchange information, although we will cover some of its other uses and benefits.

Quick Introduction

XML is shorthand for Extended Markup Language. Its full name certainly doesn't give you much of a clue about what it really is and what it is capable of. It is a derivative of HTML and uses a similar syntax, with opening and closing tags. Although HTML is the king when it comes to displaying text and organizing documents, XML is the czar of data transport and description. It not only contains data from databases and other sources, but it can also define what that data should look like.

Databases themselves do not typically interoperate well. They all have their own internal binary formats that are ideally suited to their own needs. Exchanging information between databases is possible, but not easy or fast. It usually requires custom programming or some form of import/export process. XML solved these problems by adopting the following characteristics:

Text-based. XML is all text and does not store its information in a binary format. Any program or database that can read text can read XML. It has to be parsed, but that has already been solved.

Universal. XML has caught on. It is widely used and accepted as an industry standard. Without this, XML would be just another mildly interesting programming experiment. However, the industry saw the benefits and decided that XML had lots of potential. It is in use all over the place, from Web sites to Visual Studio .NET (as we'll see later).

Works over HTTP. It has always been difficult to get data to Web sites. Typically, data would remain on the server, where the processing would take place with the data, and the results would be dynamically filled into a Web page and sent back to the client. This requires costly server round trips. It is now possible to get data over the HTTP wire, in several XML forms, and process it on the client using client code. For example, you can data bind XML information to an HTML table.

Plenty of parsers. XML, being text-based, has to be parsed to get the data out of it. There is a small sect of programmers who like to write parsers, but personally, I prefer to get actual work done. So, thanks to that small group of industrious tool-writers, there are plenty of parsers already available to read and deal with your XML data in code. Microsoft's is called MSXML, and we'll learn more about that later.

XML for Everything (Not Quite)

XML does many things well and solves a wide set of problems. However, don't be tempted to use it for absolutely every data problem that arises. Databases still have their places, and XML can't do everything. For example, the following situations would probably not lend themselves well to XML:

Speed.   If you need maximum data processing speed, XML is probably not for you. XML, being text-based, typically requires more processing power and time to deal with data than do internal binary database formats.

Size.   XML can be somewhat wordy. Because of the way it is constructed, the metadata information is repeated for every record. This can result in a larger amount of raw data needed to represent your specific data.

Both of these items are related to performance, whether processing speed or throughput. Clearly if these are the most important aspect of your data requirements, a normal database format is a better choice. However, if an open format and inter-changeability are important, or you will be using your data in Web applications, XML is an outstanding option. But data exchange is not the only thing you can do with XML.

XML for Everything Else

You've already been told that XML can be used for data exchange (I'll show you why over the course of this project). However, there are all sorts of opportunities to use XML. You just have to be creative about it. Because XML is just text, you can write and read data with it for just about any reason. Visual Studio uses it all over the place. For example, all the WinForms you create with Visual Studio are stored as XML. Here are a couple interesting ways to use XML that aren't immediately obvious:

Messaging.   Need to make special functionality requests across an HTTP wire? With the latest technology, you could use SOAP to do this. However, SOAP, despite the meaning of the S, simple, in its name, can be a little complicated. You could create your own simple protocol for functionality requests from a Web client to a server. You only need a component to receive and interpret the requests on the server.

Object serialization and transmission.   Suppose you have an object on your server that's sitting in memory doing something useful. That object, that specific instance of that object and all its data, is needed on the Web client. So, the client writes out its state, including its data and any state information it may possess. That XML can be sent to the client across the HTTP line. Once there, the object can be reconstituted from the XML information sent to it.

Customized UI information.   You're building a Web application with controls on it. However, it is important for your application to allow the user to customize the layout of the UI. Once the user changes the layout, information about that layout can be stored in XML, including control types and positions, and sent back to the server. When the same user calls up the page again later, the XML can be sent back down to the client, which uses the information to create the customized UI dynamically.

There are lots of other good reasons and situations to use XML. It can be read and understood by people, which cannot be done with other database formats. It is based on Unicode, which makes it easier to internationalize. Plus, you don't have to worry about doing parsing yourself. High-level functionality is available that allows you to access XML data, already parsed, like a RecordSet or DataSet.

Basic XML Syntax

Now we will look at some actual XML. Like HTML, from which it hails, XML is made up of tags and information within those tags. Tags can have various attributes as well. The brief example below illustrates some information about some pets available at a local animal shelter. The shelter might provide this information in XML format for use on its own Web site to help animals find homes, in addition to sending the XML to other resources like adoption agencies. Take a look at it and then I'll dissect it and talk about some other XML syntax details.

```xml
<?xml version="1.0" encoding="utf-8" ?>
<XMLSchema1>
    <PetsAvailable xmlns="http://tempuri.org/XMLSchema1.xsd">
        <PetType>dog</PetType>
        <PetGender>f</PetGender>
        <PetName>Tirith</PetName>
        <PetAge>12</PetAge>
        <PetAcquired>2001-10-01T00:00:00.0000000-04:00</PetAcquired>
    </PetsAvailable>
    <PetsAvailable>
        <PetType>dog</PetType>
        <PetGender>f</PetGender>
        <PetName>Bear</PetName>
        <PetAge>8</PetAge>
        <PetAcquired>2001-09-15T00:00:00.0000000-04:00</PetAcquired>
    </PetsAvailable>
    <PetsAvailable>
        <PetType>cat</PetType>
        <PetGender>m</PetGender>
        <PetName>Tigger</PetName>
        <PetAge>16</PetAge>
        <PetAcquired>2001-07-12T00:00:00.0000000-04:00</PetAcquired>
    </PetsAvailable>
    <PetsAvailable>
        <PetType>cat</PetType>
        <PetGender>m</PetGender>
        <PetName>Barney</PetName>
        <PetAge>7</PetAge>
        <PetAcquired>2001-10-08T00:00:00.0000000-04:00</PetAcquired>
    </PetsAvailable>
</XMLSchema1>
```

The first line is a standard XML header that tells the parser or reader what version of the XML specification this data complies with, as well as some Unicode information.

The second line starts a section of data based on a schema called XMLSchema1. You'll see more about schemas later. The real substance begins with the <PetsAvailable> tag. This tag, and its closing </PetsAvailable> tag, enclose the equivalent of a record or database row. This chunk of XML has four records. Within these tags are other tags that represent fields or columns, including PetType, PetGender, PetName, and others. Each has a matching closing tag. Tags that enclose data fields are called *elements*. In this way, we define a female dog named Tirith that is 12 years old and was acquired by the shelter on October 1, 2001.

As in HTML, you cannot use the < and > elements as part of your data. They are reserved characters for tag delimiters. In HTML, you can use alternatives inside your content for these characters: *&gt* and *&lt*. Neither can you use the ampersand as part of your content because this character precedes special character code, just like the &gt. The ampersand alternative is *&amp*.

It is important to search through your data, replacing <, >, and & with the alternative character codes before the XML is generated. You can do this between the time the data is retrieved from the database and the time that XML is generated from it. If you don't, your XML will not function properly (all processing stops when a single error is found), and the problem will be difficult to track down unless you know what you are looking for.

This XML is very simple, about as easy as it gets. Notice that the field metadata, specifically the name of the fields and the name of the records, is repeated every time. This is what is meant by XML being a little verbose.

XML syntax is very important. Unlike HTML parsers, which are pretty flexible, XML parsers are unforgiving. A single typo will screw up the entire data set, causing processing to stop. If you are working with XML manually, check it thoroughly to make sure all your tags are closed and everything is spelled consistently. The most important thing about syntax in XML, however, is that it is *case sensitive*. An open tag named <PetType> will not match a closing tag called </Pettype>. This is taken care of for you if your XML is generated by a program or database, but pay careful attention to it if you edit the data manually.

Attributes

You are probably familiar with attributes in HTML tags. For example, the Anchor tag, <A> in HTML, has several attributes specific to it, the most prominent of which is the HREF attribute. Attributes are typically name-value pairs, as in:

```
HREF="http://www.wiley.com/compbooks"
```

In HTML, you can get away with all kinds of laziness. The attribute value can be quoted or unquoted (even though they should all be quoted), and attributes can come in any order. The case of the name is not important. Much of this changes in XML.

You can add attributes to XML tags as well. Typically you are adding information about the field or tag that is not necessarily part of the data but perhaps describes the data. For example, take one of our pet records from above. Suppose we wanted to know what the unit of measure was in the PetAge field. We could add our own attribute to indicate this:

```
<PetsAvailable>
        <PetType>cat</PetType>
        <PetGender>m</PetGender>
        <PetName>Tigger</PetName>
        <PetAge units="years">16</PetAge>
        <PetAcquired>2001-07-12T00:00:00.0000000-04:00</PetAcquired>
</PetsAvailable>
```

Of course, you'd have to write your own code to deal with this information, but the parser will provide the information for you. There are many reasons to use attributes, and their utility is limited only by your creativity. However, they are not as forgiving as HTML attributes. There are a couple rules you must follow when creating your own attributes:

- Quotations around attribute values are not optional. You must provide them, although you can use single or double quotes. However, you should pick one style and be consistent.

- Attributes are name-value pairs. You are not allowed to have a name that has no value. Make sure that every name is matched with a properly quoted value.

- Attribute values can only contain text. They cannot contain additional markup tags.

- Attribute names are case sensitive like other parts of XML.

- Attributes within an element must have unique names. Duplicate names are not permitted.

- Attribute names must begin with an underscore or a letter. After that, the names may contain letters, digits, periods, underscores, or dashes.

XML Schemas

Sending text-based data around the world in such a generic format seems very powerful, and it is. However, it is a little unsettling knowing that the format is so completely *open*, that data in the XML file you just received could be anything and could be full of errors. In short, you have no guarantee of the quality or consistency of the data. This is a serious problem.

The designers of XML thought of this. They wanted to provide developers with a way to verify that the XML obtained from outside sources is correct. They invented the

XML schema to do this for us. An XML schema defines the structures, types, and relationships that XML data must conform to in order to be considered correct and well formed. A schema definition is also in text format and follows syntax that is much like XML data.

If you've ever worked with COM components, you know that the COM interface is the most important part. It defines exactly what functionality the component makes available to users of the component. The XML schema is very similar in purpose. It defines a contract, almost like an interface, that data must adhere to in order to be correct.

The XML schema has two primary purposes. First, it is used to advertise, like the COM interface, how data must be formed in order to be correct and consistent. For example, if you have a large database to which many different companies or programs contribute data using XML, you can give them the XML schema so that they know what data to provide and in what format. Secondly, the actual schema definition can be used to validate data that is supposed to conform to a particular schema. In the same example, you could use the schema definition to validate the data provided by outside sources, making sure they have created their data correctly.

XML Schema Syntax

XML schemas are defined using a syntax that is similar to XML data. It has a few differences specific to schemas, so yet another acronym has been created for it: XSD, for XML Schema Definition language. Schema files end with an XSD extension. The definition language uses tags just like XML but has other additions to suit its own needs. Let's take a look at a simple XML schema and then talk about it. The schema below defines the products a kitchenware distributor might have in its inventory:

```
<?xml version="1.0" encoding="utf-8" ?>
<xsd:schema id="KitchenProducts"
targetNamespace="http://www.kitchenproducts.com">
    <xsd:complexType>
        <xsd:sequence>
            <xsd:element name="ID" type="xsd:unsignedInt" />
            <xsd:element name="Description" type="xsd:string" />
            <xsd:element name="Category" type="xsd:string" />
            <xsd:element name="Price" type="xsd:decimal" />
            <xsd:element name="Manufacturer" type="xsd:string" />
            <xsd:element name="QuantityAvailable" type="xsd:integer" />
        </xsd:sequence>
    </xsd:complexType>
</xsd:schema>
```

Let's start with the first line. We've seen something like this before, in XML data:

```
<?xml version="1.0" encoding="utf-8" ?>
```

This tells us, just like XML data, the version of the XML specification to which the schema conforms. It also provides information on the Unicode encoding used. The second line is far more interesting:

```
<xsd:schema id="KitchenProducts"
targetNamespace="http://www.kitchenproducts.com">
```

This line starts the XSD schema definition. First, we see that we are working with an XSD schema. The *xsd:* prefix goes in front of any XSD element to distinguish it as part of XSD and not some other user-defined information. The schema has an ID that we provided for it, *KitchenProducts*. The *targetNamespace* attribute allows you to match the schema with namespaces in your data. This helps with validation, and you'll see a little more about namespaces later.

The bulk of the definition is next. We define a complex type, which is similar to a user-defined type in Visual Basic:

```
<xsd:complexType>
    <xsd:sequence>
        <xsd:element name="ID" type="xsd:unsignedInt" />
        <xsd:element name="Description" type="xsd:string" />
        <xsd:element name="Category" type="xsd:string" />
        <xsd:element name="Price" type="xsd:decimal" />
        <xsd:element name="Manufacturer" type="xsd:string" />
        <xsd:element name="QuantityAvailable" type="xsd:integer" />
    </xsd:sequence>
</xsd:complexType>
```

We start the complex type definition. Then we define an element for each field we want to represent the product. Each element has a name, which we use to refer to it, and a data type. There are a few different types shown here, but there are many more. See the sidebar about XML data types for more information. The final line in this schema closes out the schema definition.

XML DATA TYPES

There are many data types supported by XSD and XML, most of which can be equated with standard data types with which you are already familiar. The following table lists those data types and the equivalent type in the .NET framework.

XML DATA TYPE	.NET DATA TYPE
Boolean	bool
Byte	sbyte
date	DateTime
dateTime	DateTime
decimal	decimal
double	double
duration	Timespan

Continues

XML DATA TYPE	.NET DATA TYPE
float	single
gDay	DateTime
gMonth	DateTime
gMonthDay	DateTime
gYear	DateTime
gYearMonth	DateTime
ID	string
int	Int32
integer	Int64
long	Int64
Name	string
negativeInteger	Int64
nonNegativeInteger	UInt64
nonPositiveInteger	Int64
normalizedString	string
positiveInteger	UInt64
short	Int16
string	string
time	DateTime
unsignedByte	Byte
unsignedLong	UInt64
unsignedShort	UInt16
UnsignedInt	UInt32

Elements, Attributes, and Facets

You've seen the basic layout of XML schemas. There are a few more options available to you, details about the items you can create in your schema. The primary pieces used to build schemas are elements, attributes, and facets.

Elements

An XML element is code that describes data. You've seen this before in our examples. An element looks like this:

```
<xsd:element name="ID" type="xsd:unsignedInt" />
```

This is the basic form of the element. It has a name and a data type. As you can see, elements are very flexible. They can be intrinsic simple types, your own simple types, or complex types. You can also add attributes to elements, or you can add other elements to elements.

The other interesting thing about elements is that they define the order in which data must appear. For example, in the previous complex type, we created six elements that make up the type. When you create matching data in an XML file, it must appear in the same order as it does in the schema. In our case, that would be ID, Description, Category, and so on.

Attributes

An attribute is much like an element, with a few differences:

- An attribute is a simple type that must be declared at the end of complex type.
- It cannot contain other elements or attributes.
- Attributes, unlike elements, can appear in any order.
- The most interesting part of attributes is that they can have default values and are optional.

Considering our earlier example that defined kitchenware products, suppose we want to add an optional attribute of that record that indicated the amount of any current rebate, if it exists. Here is the modified definition with the attribute added to the schema:

```
<xsd:complexType name="Product">
    <xsd:sequence>
        <xsd:element name="ID" type="xsd:unsignedInt" />
        <xsd:element name="Description" type="xsd:string" />
        <xsd:element name="Category" type="xsd:string" />
        <xsd:element name="Price" type="xsd:decimal" />
        <xsd:element name="Manufacturer" type="xsd:string" />
        <xsd:element name="QuantityAvailable" type="xsd:integer" />
    </xsd:sequence>
    <xsd:attribute name="Rebate" type="xsd:decimal">
</xsd:complexType>
```

This additional attribute is perfect for a rebate because there may or may not be one available, and the attribute is optional data.

Facets

A facet is part of an element that is used to help define constraints on the data types that you create in your schemas. In fact, there are a number of predefined facets that you can use. Here are a few examples:

enumeration.   This facet allows you to restrict the allowable values of your data type to a set of specific values that you supply.

maxExclusive.   This is a facet that restricts values of the data type to those less than a maximum limit that you supply as part of the facet.

minLength.   This requires the value of the type to be greater than or equal to the minimum length you specify when defining the facet.

pattern.   This facet allows you to specify a pattern that the data that the data type contains must match to be valid. The pattern is supplied as a regular expression, so you have lots of options.

Facets are used primarily when you define simple data types in XML. And because we have yet to cover simple data types, let's take a look at that right now, along with some other common data types and structures you'll want to know about.

Common Data Structures

XML schemas allow you to define types, data relationships and structures in your XML data. Typically, you will create a schema to match your database structure or some subset of it. To help you do this, the XSD language provides facilities to help you define the structures you need.

Simple Types

Simple data types have single values. XSD has a number of them predefined, which we listed in a sidebar earlier. Integer, short, and string are examples. XSD allows you to build on these simple types to create your own simple types by adding facets to them. For example, you could start with an Integer and create from it a type that represents a number limited to the values between 0 and 100. The definition of the type looks like this:

```
<xsd:simpleType name="HundredOrLess">
    <xsd:restriction base="integer">
        <xsd:minInclusive value="0" fixed="true">
        <xsd:maxInclusive value="100" fixed="true">
    </xsd:restriction>
</xsd:simpleType>
```

We have given a name to our type, *HundredOrLess*, and based it on the intrinsic data type Integer. Then we placed two facets on the type, to limit its minimum value to 0 and its maximum value to 100. The *fixed* part of the definition will prevent the type from being modified by someone else. We can now use this type in any other complex type we want to define.

Complex Types

We saw an example of the complex type when we defined out Kitchenware product
data type. Complex types, as mentioned, are very much like enumerated types. However, they are more closely related to, and directly represent, tables in a database. The
following example shows our Kitchenware product example using our simple data
type in one of the elements:

```
<xsd:complexType name="Product">
    <xsd:sequence>
        <xsd:element name="ID" type="xsd:unsignedInt" />
        <xsd:element name="Description" type="xsd:string" />
        <xsd:element name="Category" type="xsd:string" />
        <xsd:element name="Price" type="xsd:decimal" />
        <xsd:element name="Manufacturer" type="xsd:string" />
        <xsd:element name="QuantityAvailable"
            type="xsd:HundredOrLess" />
    </xsd:sequence>
    <xsd:attribute name="Rebate" type="xsd:decimal">
</xsd:complexType>
```

We can create complex types to suite almost any table we want. The really interesting part is that these complex types can be used like any other type. Consider the following schema definition that makes use of the complex type we just defined, inside
another type:

```
<?xml version="1.0" encoding="utf-8" ?>
<xsd:schema id="KitchenProducts"
targetNamespace="http://www.kitchenproducts.com">
    <xsd:complexType name="Product">
        <xsd:sequence>
            <xsd:element name="ID" type="xsd:unsignedInt" />
            <xsd:element name="Description" type="xsd:string" />
            <xsd:element name="Category" type="xsd:string" />
            <xsd:element name="Price" type="xsd:decimal" />
            <xsd:element name="Manufacturer" type="xsd:string" />
            <xsd:element name="QuantityAvailable"
                type="xsd:HundredOrLess" />
        </xsd:sequence>
        <xsd:attribute name="Rebate" type="xsd:decimal">
    </xsd:complexType>
    <xsd:complexType name="KitchenBundle">
        <xsd:sequence>
            <xsd:element name="ID" type="xsd:unsignedInt" />
            <xsd:element name="Product1" type="Product" />
            <xsd:element name="Product2" type="Product" />
            <xsd:element name="Product3" type="Product" />
            <xsd:element name="PriceTotal" type="xsd:decimal" />
        </xsd:sequence>
    </xsd:complexType>
</xsd:schema>
```

We have used our Kitchenware complex type inside of another complex type called KitchenBundle, which contains three products.

All the types we created here are *named types*. Each one has a name in the complex-Type tag. Naming a type makes it abstract, meaning that you can only use it as a type in another element definition, as in:

```
<xsd:element name="Product1" type="Product" />
```

The Product type is used to define another element called Product1. If you want to create a complex type that allows you to actually create data, you use an *unnamed type*. These look just like named types but don't have the name portion. The schema implementation of the Product that we first saw in the Schemas section was an unnamed type:

```
<xsd:complexType>
    <xsd:sequence>
        <xsd:element name="ID" type="xsd:unsignedInt" />
        <xsd:element name="Description" type="xsd:string" />
        <xsd:element name="Category" type="xsd:string" />
        <xsd:element name="Price" type="xsd:decimal" />
        <xsd:element name="Manufacturer" type="xsd:string" />
        <xsd:element name="QuantityAvailable" type="xsd:integer" />
    </xsd:sequence>
</xsd:complexType>
```

When you enter data in an XML file, it will be matched directly against this com-plexType element. That's another important point to note. Although a named type is actually referred to as a Complex Type when creating it, an unnamed type is just another element, albeit a complexType element.

Constraints

You can create basic keys and constraints in your XSD schema. This is a valuable tool for anyone working with schemas and data. The following code creates a primary key on our bundle ID field, preventing nulls and requiring unique values:

```
<xsd:complexType name="KitchenBundle">
    <xsd:sequence>
        <xsd:element name="ID" type="xsd:unsignedInt">
            <xsd:key name="ProductKey" msdata:PrimaryKey="true">
                <xsd:selector xpath="." />
                <xsd:field xpath="ID">
            </xsd:key>
        </xsd:element>
        <xsd:element name="Product1" type="Product" />
        <xsd:element name="Product2" type="Product" />
        <xsd:element name="Product3" type="Product" />
        <xsd:element name="PriceTotal" type="xsd:decimal" />
    </xsd:sequence>
</xsd:complexType>
```

There are plenty of other things you can do with XSD, including creating relationships between tables and enforcing referential integrity.

XML Namespaces

Namespaces are part of XML and, for some reason, are shunned by most programmers, mostly because they're not sure what a namespace is. Granted, it sounds very abstract and hard to understand, much like Windows Security. However, namespaces are pretty simple and have a concrete, clear purpose. Put as simply as possible, an XML namespace is a region of XML that has a unique name. Boy, that was hard! Glad it's over? Now you can say you know what namespaces are. There are some more details, but that's the idea.

The main reason to name a region of XML is to keep your XML and its definitions separate from those of anyone else who might use the same element names. For example, assume that our simple Pet example is just one part of data that is used by a larger application. This application might also use data from pet food providers that have an element in their data called PetType, indicating what type of animal their food is meant for. A combined XML record could not use them together without a clash of names. The following is what we want, but it is not correct or legal:

```
<PetsAvailable>
        <PetType>cat</PetType>
        <PetGender>m</PetGender>
        <PetName>Tigger</PetName>
        <PetAge units="years">16</PetAge>
        <PetAcquired>2001-07-12T00:00:00.0000000-04:00</PetAcquired>
        <PetFood>Dead Fish</PetFood>
        <PetType>Feline</PetType>
</PetsAvailable>
```

We can't have two elements with the same name. Therefore, we need to qualify them as belonging to different sources of data. We can do this with a namespace. The simple way to qualify each is to prefix each field with a namespace. The namespace is just a name, a unique string that will keep one pile of data separate from another pile. Take a look at this:

```
<shelter:PetsAvailable>
        <shelter:PetType>cat</shelter:PetType>
        <shelter:PetGender>m</shelter:PetGender>
        <shelter:PetName>Tigger</shelter:PetName>
        <shelter:PetAge units="years">16</PetAge>
        <shelter:PetAcquired>
        2001-07-12T00:00:00.0000000-04:00</shelter:PetAcquired>
        <pewreenuh_foods:PetFood>Dead Fish</pewreenuh_foods:PetFood>
        <pewreenuh_foods:PetType>Feline</pewreenuh_foods:PetType>
</shelter:PetsAvailable>
```

Most of the fields are provided by the animal shelter and are qualified using the *shelter* namespace. Remember, we just made up the shelter part. The last two fields are from a fictitious pet food company called Pewreenuh Foods. We indicate their fields using the *pewreenuh_foods* namespace. So now the fully qualified field names of the Pet-Type fields are:

```
shelter:PetType
pewreenuh_foods:PetType
```

Making it Easier

Now we can combine data from both sources without them getting mixed up. But do you really want to type all those namespace qualifiers all the time? I don't. Instead, we can define a namespace that is used by default when no qualifier is specified. With that in place, our XML looks like this:

```
<PetsAvailable xmlns="shelter">
        <PetType>cat</PetType>
        <PetGender>m</PetGender>
        <PetName>Tigger</PetName>
        <PetAge units="years">16</PetAge>
        <PetAcquired>2001-07-12T00:00:00.0000000-04:00</PetAcquired>
        <pewreenuh_foods:PetFood>Dead Fish</pewreenuh_foods:PetFood>
        <pewreenuh_foods:PetType>Feline</pewreenuh_foods:PetType>
</PetsAvailable>
```

The namespace used by default has the *xmlns* attribute and a unique string for a value. You can also define other namespaces up front, creating a shorthand notation for them. Consider the following example, which defines a shorter name we can use for the pet food company:

```
<PetsAvailable xmlns="shelter" xmlns:pf="pewreenuh_foods">
        <PetType>cat</PetType>
        <PetGender>m</PetGender>
        <PetName>Tigger</PetName>
        <PetAge units="years">16</PetAge>
        <PetAcquired>2001-07-12T00:00:00.0000000-04:00</PetAcquired>
        <pf:PetFood>Dead Fish</pf:PetFood>
        <pf:PetType>Feline</pf:PetType>
</PetsAvailable>
```

Once the namespace shorthand has been defined, we can use the abbreviation *pf* instead of the long name.

Keep Your Namespace to Yourself

The namespaces we've defined are okay for local operation but are not terribly unique. Granted the pet food company namespace is not likely to be used by anyone else, but the shelter namespace is too generic. If your data ever gets out in the open, perhaps in a lager nationwide shelter project run by the Humane Society, you will need to keep your data namespace more unique. This is generally true whenever you are creating public namespaces.

When you look at a namespace, you have probably seen an xmlns attribute that contains a URL. This is a little misleading because the URL really means nothing. The organization that created the namespace just picked its Web site address as a relatively unique string. You could just as easily use the name of your dog (low likelihood of being unique) or a GUID (very good likelihood of being unique). The following are all valid namespaces:

```
xmlns="Tirith"
xmlns="Your_Mother_Wears_Army_Shoes"
xmlns="D45FD31B-5C6E-11D1-9EC1-00C04FD7081F"
```

Using Namespaces with a Schema

Namespaces help you associate schemas with your XML. You can link them using the targetNamespace attribute of the XSD file and the active namespace in the XML file. The following example XML fragment illustrates how to attach our Kitchenware schema to a sample XML file:

```
<?xml version="1.0" encoding="utf-8" ?>
<root xmlns="http://www.kitchenproducts.com">
```

The namespace that we specified in the schema was http://www.kitchenproducts. com (remember, the Web address is irrelevant; it's just a unique string). Matching the same targetNamespace in the XML file links them together.

Associating the XML with the desired schema will allow easy validation of the data against the schema. You can use this association with parsers and other code to handle validation pretty much automatically. And now that you know how to create all this XML and XSD stuff manually, I'll show you how to do it the easy way, using the XML Designer in Visual Studio .NET.

The XML Designer

It is rare that you would create XML or XSD schemas manually, by simply typing, in any large quantity. You might do so to create examples or test code or for very small projects. Ideally, for large XML files or large schemas, you'd want to generate them. We'll see how to do this in our project. However, there is an excellent intermediate solution that provides you with enhanced editing capabilities that are similar to designing a database: the XML Designer in Visual Studio .NET.

The XML Designer, or the Designer, helps you out with all sorts of XML and XSD-related tasks, including:

- Editing XML data
- Editing XSD schemas
- Defining simple and complex types
- Creating keys and constraints
- Creating data sets and tables
- Creating relationships between tables

I'll take you on a tour of the Designer by walking through a few of the tasks that you can accomplish with relative ease using it.

Creating a Schema

Assuming that you are not generating your schema from an existing database, you can use the Designer to make it much easier to build a schema. We're going to use the Designer to build a simple schema that represents the computers that a PC manufacturer is building for customers. We will:

- Create a named complex type for use in unnamed complex types (elements)
- Create the complex type that represents the computer being built
- Create a second complex type that represents the technician who is building the computer
- Create a one-to-many relationship between the technician type and the computer type

You can add XML to just about any type of project you like. We'll be working with a regular WinForms project, so create one and name it whatever you want. We'll start by creating a named type in the Designer.

Create the Named Type

Step 1 is really to first add a schema to our project. Right-click on the Solution Explorer, and from the context menu, select Add New Item. In the Add New Item dialog, shown in Figure 7.1, select XML Schema from the dialog and give our new schema a name. I used prj07schema, but pick something with a little more zing. Double-click the schema to open it.

The toolbox in Visual Studio .NET now has a tab labeled *XML Schema*. This toolbox tab has all kinds of XML goodies that you can add to your schema. The work area of the Designer should be essentially an empty space to which you can drag and drop items from the toolbox. Once you create and edit items in the Designer, you can switch to the XML view, using the XML/Design tabs at the bottom of the Designer window.

Start by dragging a complexType item from the toolbox and drop it on the workspace. You will see a small, empty grid with one row and two columns. This is where you enter the various element names and types for the complexType. Figure 7.2 shows what the complexType looks like when all our elements are filled in.

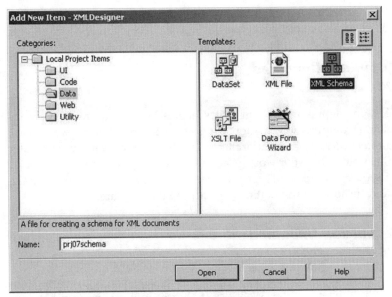

Figure 7.1   Adding an XML Schema to a project.

Notice a couple things about the Designer's view of the type. First, in the upper-left corner of the type window is a little CT. This means you're looking at a complexType (as opposed to an element or other XML building block). Second, you can enter the name of the type in the top-most row right next to the CT. We called ours Component-Type. All the rows beneath the name of the type contain the various elements of the type. Enter elements that match those in Figure 7.2. The first small column on the left is where you select the type of item you're adding to the complexType, such as an element or attribute. The uppercase E indicates an element.

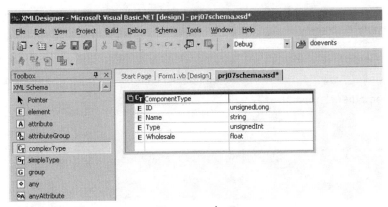

Figure 7.2   The ComponentType complexType.

This type that we have created will represent a component in a computer system. We'll use it next in an unnamed complexType.

Create the Computer Unnamed Complex Type

Unnamed complexTypes represent tables in XML schemas. We need to create a primary table that will hold our computer information. Drag a new element onto the workspace. Name the element *Computer* and enter information into the grid to create our computer data. Figure 7.3 illustrates what your workspace should resemble when you're done.

Note that we used our ComponentType for three of the items in our computer. The Designer automatically adds representations for these in the diagram.

Create the Technician Unnamed Complex Type

To make things a little more interesting, let's create another table that represents a technician who is building the computer. We'll use it shortly in a relationship between tables. To support this relationship, make sure the technician complexType has an element called TechID. Also add this field to the Computer type. Figure 7.4 shows our workspace with the Technician table added.

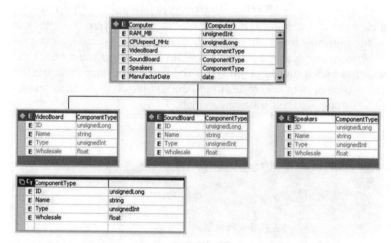

Figure 7.3   The Computer element.

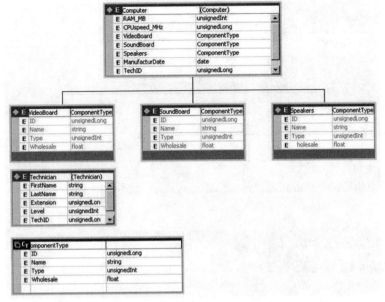

Figure 7.4   The Technician added to the workspace.

Create the One-To-Many Relationship

The same technician may build any number of computers. Therefore, we will create a one-to-many relationship from the technician to the computer table. Before we can do this, however, we need to add a couple keys to the tables. We need to put a key on the TechID field in the Technician table and one on the ComputerID field in the Computer table.

Right-click on the TechID element in the Technician table. From the context menu, select Add/New Key. You'll be faced with the Edit Key dialog. Fill it in as shown in Figure 7.5. Make sure you check the data set primary key option to define this field as the primary key. Do the same thing for the ComputerID field in the Computer table. Once the keys are defined, we can create the relationship between the tables.

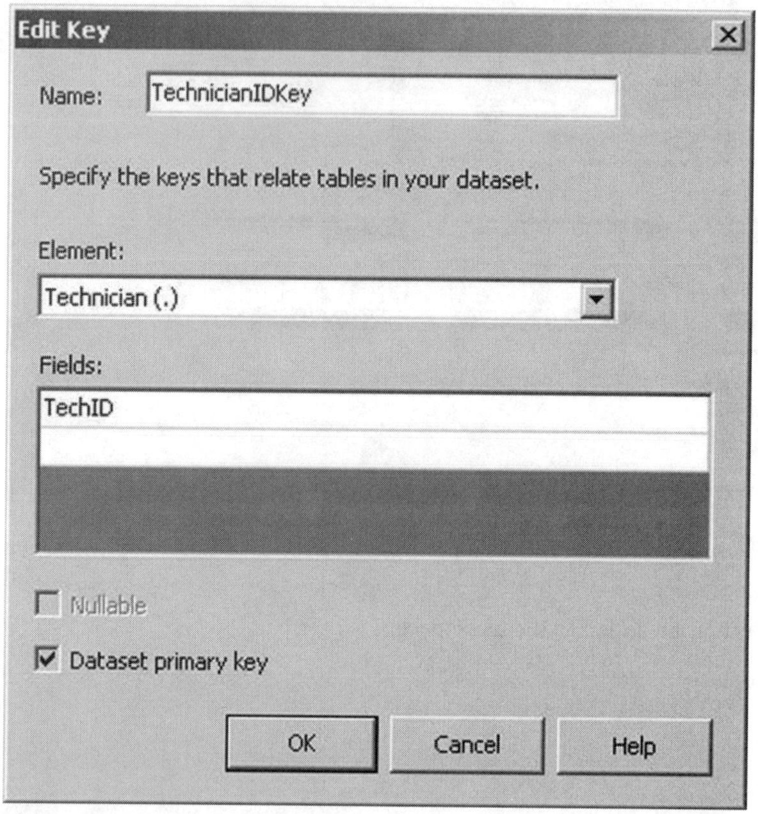

Figure 7.5   The Technician key.

Drag a Relation object from the toolbox onto the Computer table. You have to drop the relation onto the many side of the relationship. The Edit Relation dialog will show up, as illustrated in Figure 7.6, allowing you to set up the relationship between the two tables.

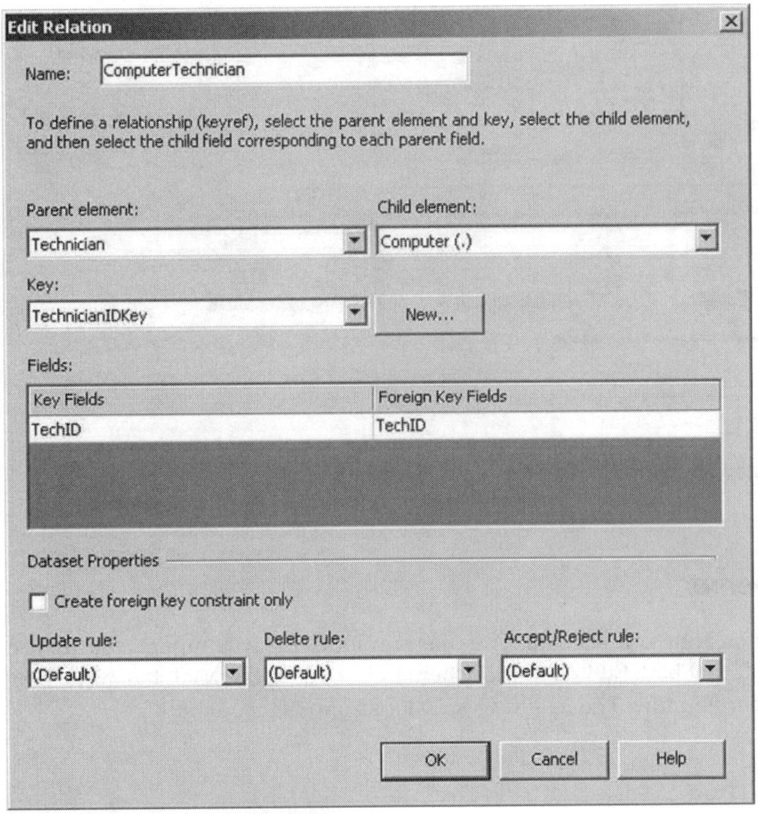

Figure 7.6   The Edit Relation dialog.

The Parent element is the one side of the relationship, and the Child is the many side of it. Set the Parent and Child elements in the dialog like this. Set the key fields both to TechID. The defaults will be fine for the rest of it. Once you click the OK button, the diagram will be updated to reflect the new relationship, as shown in Figure 7.7.

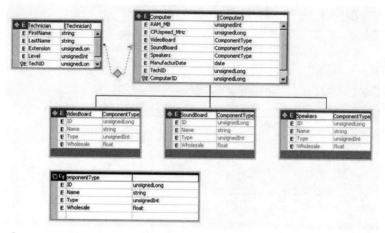

Figure 7.7 The diagram with the relationship added.

The Final Schema

We have finished creating our schema. The diagram looks fairly complicated, but the actual schema isn't that bad. Switch to the schema view using the XML tab at the bottom of the Designer window. The resulting XSD looks like this:

```xml
<?xml version="1.0" encoding="utf-8" ?>
<xsd:schema id="prj07schema"
targetNamespace="http://tempuri.org/prj07schema.xsd"
elementFormDefault="qualified"
xmlns="http://tempuri.org/prj07schema.xsd"
xmlns:xsd="http://www.w3.org/2001/XMLSchema"
xmlns:msdata="urn:schemas-microsoft-com:xml-msdata">
    <xsd:complexType name="ComponentType">
        <xsd:sequence>
            <xsd:element name="ID" type="xsd:unsignedLong" />
            <xsd:element name="Name" type="xsd:string" />
            <xsd:element name="Type" type="xsd:unsignedInt" />
            <xsd:element name="Wholesale" type="xsd:float" />
        </xsd:sequence>
    </xsd:complexType>
    <xsd:element name="Computer">
        <xsd:complexType>
            <xsd:sequence>
                <xsd:element name="RAM_MB" type="xsd:unsignedInt" />
                <xsd:element name="CPUspeed_MHz"
                    type="xsd:unsignedLong" />
                <xsd:element name="VideoBoard" type="ComponentType" />
                <xsd:element name="SoundBoard" type="ComponentType" />
                <xsd:element name="Speakers" type="ComponentType" />
```

```
                    <xsd:element name="ManufacturDate" type="xsd:date" />
                    <xsd:element name="TechID" type="xsd:unsignedLong" />
                    <xsd:element name="ComputerID" type="xsd:unsignedLong" />
                </xsd:sequence>
            </xsd:complexType>
            <xsd:key name="ComputerIDKey" msdata:PrimaryKey="true">
                <xsd:selector xpath="." />
                <xsd:field xpath="ComputerID" />
            </xsd:key>
            <xsd:keyref name="ComputerTechnician" refer="TechnicianIDKey">
                <xsd:selector xpath="." />
                <xsd:field xpath="TechID" />
            </xsd:keyref>
        </xsd:element>
        <xsd:element name="Technician">
            <xsd:complexType>
                <xsd:sequence>
                    <xsd:element name="FirstName" type="xsd:string" />
                    <xsd:element name="LastName" type="xsd:string" />
                    <xsd:element name="Extension" type="xsd:unsignedLong" />
                    <xsd:element name="Level" type="xsd:unsignedInt" />
                    <xsd:element name="TechID" type="xsd:unsignedLong" />
                </xsd:sequence>
            </xsd:complexType>
            <xsd:key name="TechnicianIDKey" msdata:PrimaryKey="true">
                <xsd:selector xpath="." />
                <xsd:field xpath="TechID" />
            </xsd:key>
        </xsd:element>
    </xsd:schema>
```

It's pretty easy to pick out the named Component complexType, the Computer element complexType, and the Technician element. You can also see the keys created for each table and the relationship we added to the Computer table. Now that we've got it, what can we do with it?

Using the Schema

Besides creating schemas, you can also use the Designer to create and edit XML data. You can do this using a standard text editor or a more tablelike interface. The nice thing is that once you attach a schema to the XML file, everything becomes context sensitive. As you enter XML, the editor understands the schema and helps you out with the editing.

Add a new XML file to the project using the Solution Explorer. Once it has been added, open it up and examine its properties. There is one property that you should set called *targetNamespace*. Fill in the targetNamespace from our schema, which should be:

```
http://tempuri.org/prj07schema.xsd
```

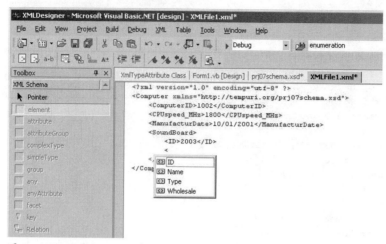

Figure 7.8   Editing XML data.

This will associate the schema with the new XML file. Once this is done, you can edit the XML with knowledge of the data layout. Switch to the XML view if you're not there already, and start typing in some XML. The editor will give you Intellisense help as you type, as shown in Figure 7.8.

Enter a record and then switch to Data view. This grid view of your data makes editing the XML much easier, and even handles child rows, as shown in Figure 7.9. This is pretty slick!

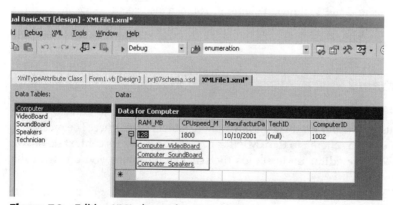

Figure 7.9   Editing XML data using Data view.

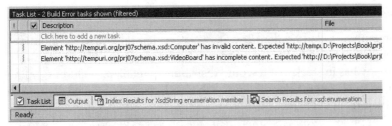

Figure 7.10   Validation errors in XML data.

The last thing we'll cover about the Designer is the validation. The big point of the schema is to be able to validate your data against it to make sure that it is correct. Switch to the XML view of your data. Change something to introduce an error, such as using an incorrect data type or placing elements in the wrong order. Then, from the XML menu, select Validate XML Data. The XML data will be validated against the schema, and any errors will be displayed at the bottom of the screen in the output section. This is shown in Figure 7.10.

The culmination of all this is being able to use XML and XSD in your own Visual Basic programs. The best way to illustrate this is to actually do it, so we'll move on to our project. There you will see how to incorporate XML into your own programs and to read and use it to actually store and validate data. We'll also see how to create schemas and XML the easy way, by generating them from a database.

Let's Start the Project

Our project is actually a pair of programs. They are based on a fictitious toy distributor but can be easily adapted to work for any application domain. The first program was designed for use by the distributor of data, and the second, by the consumer of the data. In summary, the programs do the following:

The Generator.   This program will generate an XSD schema to match an existing database that can be distributed to users of the data to make sure that the data is correct. It will also communicate the data interface so that consumers of the data will know what to expect when using it in their own programs. The Generator program will also create an XML file that can be distributed to data consumers.

The Reader.   This program reads in the XML and XSD files created by the Generator. It will validate the XML against the schema, reporting all errors that it encounters. It will also display the data for the user in a grid once it is loaded, and it provides the option to write the data from the XML file to a local database.

The Data Generator

Our example company is called Xcellent Toy Distributors. It sells toys to retail outlets, which in turn sell them to people like you and me. I created some sample data about the toys the company has in stock that it would distribute to retailers, including online retailers, in XML form. Those retailers could use the XML data to populate their databases or to feed their retail Web sites.

As with our other projects, you can either create the project as we go according to the instructions, or you can load it from the accompanying CD-ROM and just read along.

The Database

The Data Generator is used by the distributor to create XSD schemas and XML data files from its database for distribution to the retailers. The retailers, all of whom have different databases, can use the data as they see fit. We'll start by looking at a fragment of the database layout used by the distributor. Figure 7.11 illustrates the database organization. It's pretty simple for demonstration purposes but could be as complex as you like.

Note that the sample data is included on the accompanying CD-ROM as a Microsoft Access database. You can import that data directly into SQL Server or change the connection string in the program to use the Access database directly.

The Main Form

The main (and only) form in the generator application provides options for the user to:

- Generate all data into an XML file
- Generate a schema that matches the data
- Generate XML and XSD schema to match any valid SQL SELECT statement

The form is illustrated in Figure 7.12. It contains numerous controls, each of which along with its important properties, is listed in Table 7.1. Set up your form the same way.

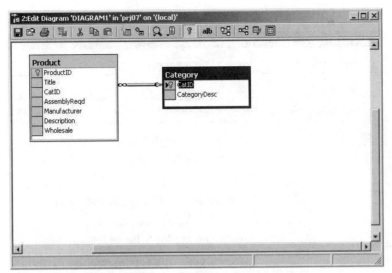

Figure 7.11   The distributor's database layout.

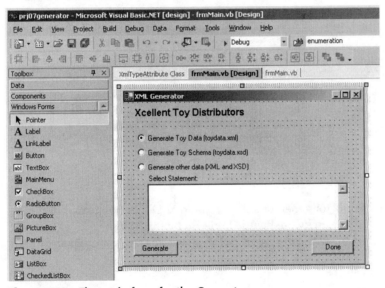

Figure 7.12   The main form for the Generator.

Table 7.1 The Main Form Controls

CONTROL	NAME	PROPERTIES
Form	frmMain	Text="XML Generator"
Button	btnDone	Text="Done"
Button	btnGenerate	Text="Generate"
Label1	Label	Text="Select Statement:"
Label2	Label	Text="Xcellent Toy Distributors", Font=Arial 12pt. Bold
Radio Button	rb1	Text="Generate Toy Data (toydata.xml)", Checked=True
Radio Button	rb2	Text="Generate Toy Schema (toydata.xsd)"
Radio Button	rb3	Text="Generate Other Data (XML and XSD)"
TextBox	tbSQL	Text="", Enabled=False, Multiline=True, Scrollbars=Vertical

The first two options on the form, Generate Toy Data and Generate Toy Schema, are used to generate XML and XSD files that follow a specific SQL select statement. The last option, Generate Other Data, allows the user to enter any SQL SELECT statement based on the toy data in the database to generate both XML and XSD files. This last option is obviously the most flexible and can be used as the basis for a more generic utility.

The Code

The code for this form and for generating the XML and XSD files is remarkably simple. Most of the bits that seem tricky are handled for you by the XML objects in the .NET framework. Let's start by clearing up some of the bookkeeping code. The following listing takes care of setting up the class:

```
Imports System.Data.SqlClient

Public Class frmMain
    Inherits System.Windows.Forms.Form

#Region " Class Data and Types "

    ' Database connection string. We're using SQL Server. Change this if
    ' you want to use something else, like the Access db included with
    ' the book.
```

```
Private Const CONNSTR As String = "PERSIST SECURITY INFO=False; " & _
    "DATA SOURCE=tony; INITIAL CATALOG=prj07; UID=sa; PWD=;"

#End Region
```

The Imports statement makes it easier to deal with the data access objects. Our connection string is set up to talk to the toy database in SQL Server. You will need to edit this connection string to match your own database and server.

The next listing shows our simple event handlers and supporting code for changes in the radio buttons:

```
' Handle a change in the radio buttons on the UI
Private Sub rb1_CheckedChanged(ByVal sender As System.Object, _
    ByVal e As System.EventArgs) Handles rb1.CheckedChanged
    EnableSQL()
End Sub

' Handle a change in the radio buttons on the UI
Private Sub rb2_CheckedChanged(ByVal sender As System.Object, _
    ByVal e As System.EventArgs) Handles rb2.CheckedChanged
    EnableSQL()
End Sub

' Handle a change in the radio buttons on the UI
Private Sub rb3_CheckedChanged(ByVal sender As System.Object, _
    ByVal e As System.EventArgs) Handles rb3.CheckedChanged
    EnableSQL()
End Sub

' This code enables or disables the SQL edit area based on which
' radio button is checked.
Private Sub EnableSQL()

    If rb3.Checked Then
        tbSQL.Enabled = True
        Label1.Enabled = True
    Else
        tbSQL.Enabled = False
        Label1.Enabled = False
    End If

End Sub
```

All the event handlers for the radio buttons do the same thing: call the EnableSQL method. This code turns the SQL statement edit box on and off depending on the settings of the radio buttons. It is only enabled if the third radio button is selected. Otherwise, it is disabled. Enabling or disabling the associated label for the control helps to make it clearer to the user that the textbox is disabled or enabled.

The last method in the code is where all the work is done. Take a look at it and then I'll go over it in more detail:

```
' This method handles the Generate button click. It takes care
' of loading data from the database and then writes out XML or XSD,
' as requested.
Private Sub btnGenerate_Click(ByVal sender As System.Object, _
    ByVal e As System.EventArgs) Handles btnGenerate.Click

    Dim cn As New SqlConnection(CONNSTR)
    Dim ds As New DataSet()
    Dim sSQL As String

    ' If either of the first two radio buttons are selected, then
    ' the SQL is canned and stored here in the code. If the third
    ' radio button is selected, use the SQL that the user has
    ' entered.
    If rb3.Checked Then
        sSQL = tbSQL.Text
    Else
        sSQL = "SELECT Product.Title AS Expr1, " & _
               "Product.AssemblyReqd, Product.Description, " & _
               "Product.Wholesale, Product.Manufacturer, " & _
               "Category.CategoryDesc " & _
               "FROM Product INNER JOIN " & _
               "Category ON Product.CatID = Category.CatID " & _
               "WHERE (Category.CatID = Product.CatID)"
    End If

    ' Set up the DataAdapter to read our data.
    Dim da As New SqlDataAdapter(sSQL, CONNSTR)

    ' Configure the DataSet with the properties necessary to create
    ' valid XML and XSD information.
    ds.Namespace = "http://www.tempuri.org/toyData.xsd"
    ds.DataSetName = "toydata"

    ' Attempt to load the data and then write the XML/XSD.
    Try
        ' Load data.
        cn.Open()
        da.Fill(ds, "toydata")
        cn.Close()

        ' Write out the XML or XSD or both.
        If rb1.Checked Or rb3.Checked Then
            ds.WriteXml("toydata.xml")
        End If
        If rb2.Checked Or rb3.Checked Then
            ds.WriteXmlSchema("toydata.xsd")
```

```
      End If

      ' Let the user know that everything went well.
      MsgBox("Generation complete.", _
          MsgBoxStyle.Information Or MsgBoxStyle.OKOnly, "A-OK")
  Catch ex As SqlException
      ' Whoops - tell the user something went wrong, and what.
      MsgBox(ex.Message, _
          MsgBoxStyle.Critical Or MsgBoxStyle.OKOnly, "Error")
  End Try

End Sub
```

This method is an event handler that is tied to the Generate button on the UI. Its job is to create the XML and/or the XSD based on the radio button setting. The code gets going by setting up some data access objects, including a Connection and a DataSet. If the third radio button is selected, we will be using the user's SQL SELECT statement. Otherwise, we will be using our own. Our SQL statement joins with the associated Category table to pull in the actual names of the toy categories, rather than the IDs.

Next we create a DataAdapter object, passing it our SQL statement and connection string. We'll use the DataAdapter to fill the DataSet with the data that we want in the XML file. Before we do this, we need to set a couple of properties on the DataSet:

```
  ds.Namespace = "http://www.tempuri.org/toyData.xsd"
  ds.DataSetName = "toydata"
```

These properties will make the generated XML or XSD complete. The namespace allows the XML and schema to match up and provides the other benefits of namespaces. The DataSetName translates to the ID of the schema when it is generated, as well as to the name of the records in the XML. You'll see this when we get to the generation results.

The rest of the code is handled inside a Try..Catch construct to handle any errors that might occur during the data generation process. First, we retrieve the data we need to put into XML (or base the XSD schema on) by filling the DataSet. Then, based on the radio button settings, we generate XML data and/or XML schema. This is handled by a couple of very handy methods in the DataSet class, WriteXML and WriteXMLSchema:

```
  If rb1.Checked Or rb3.Checked Then
      ds.WriteXml("toydata.xml")
  End If
  If rb2.Checked Or rb3.Checked Then
      ds.WriteXmlSchema("toydata.xsd")
  End If
```

We pass the methods the name of the file that should contain the data or schema information. These statements take care of generating everything we need. If everything went well, tell the user with a MsgBox. If there was an error, we display a MsgBox with the text of the error message. Figure 7.13 shows the program running.

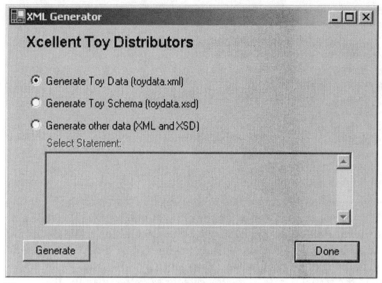

Figure 7.13 The executing Data Generator.

Select the Generate Toy Data option and click the Generate button. The following XML is generated (the listing is somewhat abridged; you only need a few examples to make the point):

```xml
<?xml version="1.0" standalone="yes"?>
<toydata xmlns="http://www.tempuri.org/toyData.xsd">
  <toydata>
    <Expr1>Deputy Droopy</Expr1>
    <AssemblyReqd>0</AssemblyReqd>
    <Description>Soft, plush doll of Deputy Droopy. He was the main
        character in the funniest cartoon ever produced.</Description>
    <Wholesale>9.99</Wholesale>
    <Manufacturer>HB Toys</Manufacturer>
    <CategoryDesc>Dolls</CategoryDesc>
  </toydata>
  <toydata>
    <Expr1>Not-So-Easy Bake Oven</Expr1>
    <AssemblyReqd>1</AssemblyReqd>
    <Description>Use a light bulb in this oven to attempt making a
        cheese souffle, Beef Wellington, and Risotto with Sea
        Bass.</Description>
    <Wholesale>29.99</Wholesale>
    <Manufacturer>Frustration Playthings</Manufacturer>
    <CategoryDesc>Misc</CategoryDesc>
  </toydata>
  <toydata>
    <Expr1>Seargent Schultz</Expr1>
```

```
    <AssemblyReqd>0</AssemblyReqd>
    <Description>Sergeant Schultz is #2 in the Hogan's Heroes action
        figure line. Comes with rifle and apple strudel.</Description>
    <Wholesale>12.99</Wholesale>
    <Manufacturer>Old TV Toys</Manufacturer>
    <CategoryDesc>Action Figures</CategoryDesc>
  </toydata>
</toydata>
```

Select the second radio button to create a schema that matches the data we've just seen. Click the generate button and you'll get the following schema:

```
<?xml version="1.0" standalone="yes"?>
<xsd:schema id="toydata"
targetNamespace="http://www.tempuri.org/toyData.xsd"
xmlns="http://www.tempuri.org/toyData.xsd"
xmlns:xsd="http://www.w3.org/2001/XMLSchema" xmlns:msdata="urn:schemas-
microsoft-com:xml-msdata" attributeFormDefault="qualified"
elementFormDefault="qualified">
  <xsd:element name="toydata" msdata:IsDataSet="true">
    <xsd:complexType>
      <xsd:choice maxOccurs="unbounded">
        <xsd:element name="toydata">
          <xsd:complexType>
            <xsd:sequence>
              <xsd:element name="Expr1" type="xsd:string" minOccurs="0" />
              <xsd:element name="AssemblyReqd" type="xsd:int"
                  minOccurs="0" />
              <xsd:element name="Description" type="xsd:string"
                  minOccurs="0" />
              <xsd:element name="Wholesale" type="xsd:decimal"
                  minOccurs="0" />
              <xsd:element name="Manufacturer" type="xsd:string"
                  minOccurs="0" />
              <xsd:element name="CategoryDesc" type="xsd:string"
                  minOccurs="0" />
            </xsd:sequence>
          </xsd:complexType>
        </xsd:element>
      </xsd:choice>
    </xsd:complexType>
  </xsd:element>
</xsd:schema>
```

Notice that the namespace (xmlns:) of the XML data and the targetNamespace of the schema match. This was defined when we set up the targetNamespace of the DataSet that generated the XML and XSD. However, this canned query, while handling most of the toy distributor's needs, can't handle all situations. Therefore, we have provided the capability for users to enter their own SQL and generate XML and XSD information.

Run the program and select the third radio button. This will enable the textbox in which you can enter your own SELECT statement. Figure 7.14 shows the program running with a sample SELECT statement entered in the textbox.

Click the generate button once this statement has been entered. Both XML and XSD will be generated to reflect the SELECTed data. The following shows both the schema and the XML data (abridged) that was generated:

```
<?xml version="1.0" standalone="yes"?>
<xsd:schema id="toydata"
targetNamespace="http://www.tempuri.org/toyData.xsd"
xmlns="http://www.tempuri.org/toyData.xsd"
xmlns:xsd="http://www.w3.org/2001/XMLSchema"
xmlns:msdata="urn:schemas-microsoft-com:xml-msdata"
attributeFormDefault="qualified" elementFormDefault="qualified">
  <xsd:element name="toydata" msdata:IsDataSet="true">
    <xsd:complexType>
      <xsd:choice maxOccurs="unbounded">
        <xsd:element name="toydata">
          <xsd:complexType>
            <xsd:sequence>
              <xsd:element name="Title" type="xsd:string" minOccurs="0" />
              <xsd:element name="Manufacturer" type="xsd:string"
                  minOccurs="0" />
            </xsd:sequence>
          </xsd:complexType>
        </xsd:element>
      </xsd:choice>
    </xsd:complexType>
  </xsd:element>
</xsd:schema>

<?xml version="1.0" standalone="yes"?>
<toydata xmlns="http://www.tempuri.org/toyData.xsd">
  <toydata>
    <Title>Eiffel Tower Toothpick Kit</Title>
    <Manufacturer>Frustration Playthings</Manufacturer>
  </toydata>
  <toydata>
    <Title>74-speed Mountain Bike</Title>
    <Manufacturer>Ultimate Recreation</Manufacturer>
  </toydata>
  <toydata>
    <Title>Home D-Structo Kit</Title>
    <Manufacturer>Bad Boy Toys</Manufacturer>
  </toydata>
</toydata>
```

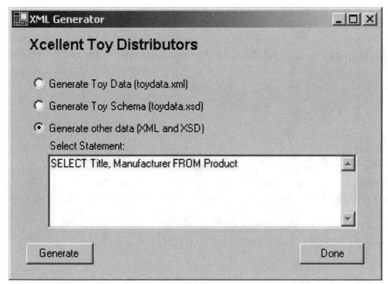

Figure 7.14   Entering your own SELECT statement.

Now that the XML and associated schema have been generated, they are ready to be handed off to the consumers of the data, in our case, retail toy outlets. They could use it to populate their inventory database or feed a Web site with available products. For example, it would be easy to modify the generator database to include a date that indicates when the product was added to the distributor's inventory. Then a user could enter a custom SQL statement to select all products that were added in the last month. Generate a schema and XML data file, and you've got all the new products that you can make available to retailers. They could then use the data to advertise new products to customers. However, the retailers would need to make sure that the data is correct, as well as know what the schema was to incorporate it into their system. The next program handles things from the data consumer's side of the equation.

The Data Reader

The consumers of the XML and XSD data will need to do something with the data and schema when they get them. Validating, reviewing, and incorporating the data into their own systems are key to making the data useful. The Data Reader utility will allow them to do all these things.

The Database

The database for retailers is a little different and a bit simpler. There is one table, and the layout matches the organization of the data that they receive in the XML file. The table is illustrated in Figure 7.15. Note that there is an additional database on the accompanying CD-ROM called prj07target.mdb that you can use to import into SQL Server.

The Main Form

The interface for the Data Reader is simple. The reading of the data file is done when the form loads. Therefore, our UI has only a grid and two buttons (plus a label or two). The main UI component is the data grid. This is where the data is displayed for review once it is loaded. There is also a button that allows the user to write the data, once validated and reviewed, to the database. The form is illustrated in Figure 7.16, and the controls on the form are detailed in Table 7.2.

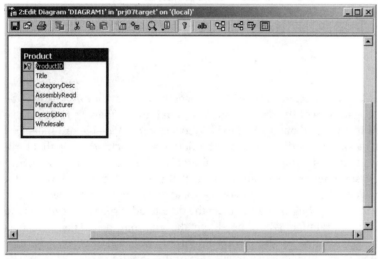

Figure 7.15   The target database.

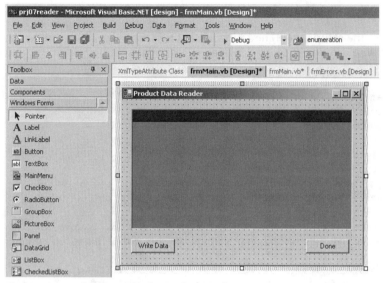

Figure 7.16   The Data Reader main form.

Table 7.2   The Data Reader Controls

CONTROL	NAME	PROPERTIES
Form	frmMain	Text="Product Data Reader"
Button	btnDone	Text="Done", Anchor=Bottom, Right
Button	btnWrite	Text="Write Data", Anchor=Bottom, Left
DataGrid	DataGrid1	Anchor=Top, Bottom, Left, Right
Label	lblStatus	Text="", Anchor=Bottom, Left, Autosize=True

The Code

First, let's clear up the setup code. The following listing takes care of importing the namespaces that we need access to and defines our database connection string and some class data:

```
Imports System.Data.SqlClient
Imports System.Xml
Imports System.Xml.Schema

Public Class frmMain
    Inherits System.Windows.Forms.Form

#Region " Class Data and Types "

    ' Database connection string. We're using SQL Server. Change this if
    ' you want to use something else, like the Access db included with
    ' the book.
    Private Const CONNSTR As String = "PERSIST SECURITY INFO=False; " & _
        "DATA SOURCE=tony; INITIAL CATALOG=prj07target; UID=sa; PWD=;"

    Private sValidateErrs As String
    Private ds As New DataSet("toydata")

#End Region
```

The string sValidateErrs is global to the class because we need it in several places where it is difficult to pass around. Besides, it is used only within this small class, so why pass it around? The DataSet is global for similar reasons. We also have a simple event handler to close the application when the user is done:

```
    ' Shut down the app when the done button is clicked.
    Private Sub btnDone_Click(ByVal sender As System.Object, _
        ByVal e As System.EventArgs) Handles btnDone.Click
        Me.Close()
    End Sub
```

When the form loads, we take the opportunity to load and validate the XML against the XSD schema. If the validation passes, we load the data into the grid and tell the user that everything went well. If the validation fails, we display validation errors for the user. Take a look at the code:

```
    ' During the form load event, we load the XML and validate it
    ' against the supplied schema file.
    Private Sub frmMain_Load(ByVal sender As System.Object, _
        ByVal e As System.EventArgs) Handles MyBase.Load

        Dim doc As New XmlDocument()
        Dim tr As New XmlTextReader("toydata.xml")
        Dim vr As New XmlValidatingReader(tr)
```

```
    Dim x As New XmlSchemaCollection()
    Dim fErr As frmErrors

    ' Tell the user what's going on.
    lblStatus.Text = "Validating XML against schema..."
    System.Windows.Forms.Application.DoEvents()

    ' First, load the schema file and the XML and validate the data
    ' against the schema we have.
    Try
        ' Add the schema to a schema collection
        x.Add("http://www.tempuri.org/toyData.xsd", "toydata.xsd")
        vr.Schemas.Add(x)

        ' Set up an event handler to deal with validation errors as
        ' they occur.
        AddHandler vr.ValidationEventHandler, _
            AddressOf ValidationCallBack
        vr.ValidationType = ValidationType.Schema

        ' Load the data in order to perform the validation.
        doc.Load(vr)
    Catch ex As Exception
        ' Anything wrong? Tell the user and get out.
        MsgBox(ex.message())
        Exit Sub
    End Try

    ' Load the data into the grid for display.
    Try
        ds.ReadXml("toydata.xml")
        DataGrid1.SetDataBinding(ds, "toydata")
        DataGrid1.CaptionText = "Toy Data"
        lblStatus.Text = "Validation passed. Ready."
    Catch ex As Exception
        MsgBox(ex.Message())
    End Try

    ' If there were validation errors, then load the error
    ' display form and pass the collected errors to it.
    If Len(sValidateErrs) > 0 Then
        lblStatus.Text = "There were schema validation errors."
        fErr = New frmErrors()
        fErr.Errors = sValidateErrs
        fErr.ShowDialog()
        btnWrite.Enabled = False
    End If

End Sub
```

The first thing we do is to create a bunch of XML-related objects that you haven't seen yet. Those objects are the keys to using and manipulating XML in your code. They are:

XmlDocument.   This class implements the W3C document object model. It contains and represents your XML data as a parsed XML document. You can use it for all kinds of low-level XML functionality, and it is useful if you need to work with the data in its XML format. You can navigate the data, read from and write to it, and load and save XML to and from files and strings. If you need to perform low-level XML manipulations, this is the place to start. Note that the XmlDocument class stores everything in memory, so it may not be appropriate for very large sets of data.

XmlTextReader.   The XmlTextReader is perfect for those occasions when you only want to read through the XML data once and then be done with it. It provides fast, forward-only reading capabilities, much like an ADO forward-only cursor. It does not store the XML document in memory, so it can handle large sets of data. It also ensures that the data is correctly formed and that there are no syntax mistakes. It does not, however, perform any data validation.

XmlValidatingReader.   The validating reader takes in an actual reader, such as the XmlTextReader, to do the reading work. It adds validation functionality, checking the data against any number of supplied schemas. It reports any errors through a callback function that you provide. This is the object that will make easy work of our data validation.

XmlSchemaCollection.   This collection contains, as its name suggests, one or more XML schemas. It is used by the XMLValidatingReader to hold the schemas against which XML is validated.

We also create an instance of the Errors form for this application, which I'll cover later. Next, we tell the user what we're doing and start the validation process.

In our first Try..Catch structure we begin the process of validation against the schema. We need to load the schema, add it to the schema collection, and then add the collection to the validating reader, like this:

```
x.Add("http://www.tempuri.org/toyData.xsd", "toydata.xsd")
vr.Schemas.Add(x)
```

The item x is our schema collection, which will load the schema information from the specified file. We can then add the schemas in the collection to the internal schema collection in the validating reader. It seems a little roundabout, especially when you only have one schema to deal with. It can be useful, however, when there is more than one schema involved in the validation process.

Next we have to set up the validation so that it runs properly. The following code takes care of this:

```
AddHandler vr.ValidationEventHandler, _
    AddressOf ValidationCallBack
vr.ValidationType = ValidationType.Schema
```

The most important part here is setting up the error handler. When the validating reader processes XML data, it can handle errors in one of two ways. If no handler is provided, it will raise a standard exception that can be caught in a Try..Catch structure. All processing stops at that point, when the first error is encountered, and the reader cannot be restarted. The second and more useful method allows you to provide a callback function that the reader calls whenever an error occurs. Using this method, validation processing will continue until the XML has all been validated or until processing cannot continue due to excessive errors. This is clearly the preferred method because all errors will be reported at once. However, you have to collect and process the errors yourself using a callback function. The preceding code, using the AddHandler method, attaches a method to the validating reader's ValidationEventHandler. Give it the address of your method and it will be called when an error occurs. The AddressOf function will do this for you. Our function, simply called ValidationCallBack, follows:

```
' This method is called by the ValidatingReader if an error occurs
' during validation. Info about the error is sent in the args
' parameter.
Public Sub ValidationCallBack(ByVal sender As Object, _
    ByVal args As ValidationEventArgs)
    ' Add the text of the error message to our running total of
    ' error messages.
    sValidateErrs += args.Message() & vbCrLf
End Sub
```

This method takes the text of the error message, passed in through the *args* parameter, and tacks it onto a string that we maintain during validation. This string will then contain all the errors found during validation in a user-readable format. We will display them later in the Errors form.

Now that we're all set up, we can load the data and validate it. The validating reader, its internal text reader, and the XmlDocument's Load method handle this in one step, as follows:

```
' Load the data in order to perform the validation.
doc.Load(vr)
```

The text reader knows what file to load. We told it that by passing the filename to the reader's constructor when we created the object. If something goes wrong with the basic reading of the document, our Catch clause will display an error for the user and exit the method. This does not account for validation errors.

Once the data is loaded, whether or not we encountered validation errors, it is loaded into the grid on the UI. Our next Try..Catch structure handles this task. The following code takes care of reading the XML data and binding it to the grid:

```
ds.ReadXml("toydata.xml")
DataGrid1.SetDataBinding(ds, "toydata")
DataGrid1.CaptionText = "Toy Data"
lblStatus.Text = "Validation passed. Ready."
```

The DataSet uses its *ReadXml* method to load the data from the specified XML file. The SetDataBindings method of the DataGrid control binds the now-populated DataSet to the grid. Specifying toydata in the method call tells the DataGrid which table in the DataSet to bind to. The rest of the code tells the user what's been going on. Our final bit of code checks to see if there were validation errors. If so, the code creates an instance of our Errors form, passes the errors to it, and displays the form, like this:

```
If Len(sValidateErrs) > 0 Then
    lblStatus.Text = "There were schema validation errors."
    fErr = New frmErrors()
    fErr.Errors = sValidateErrs
    fErr.ShowDialog()
    btnWrite.Enabled = False
End If
```

We also disable the button that allows the user to write the data to the database if there were errors. The last thing we want is bad data going to our production database. Here the method ends and users may review the data. If validation errors occurred, users can look for them in the data. If everything is valid, they could write the data to their database using the functionality we have provided. It is tied to the click event handler for the Write Data button. The code follows:

```
' When the Write button is clicked, we need to write the XML data
' to our SQL Server database.
Private Sub btnWrite_Click(ByVal sender As System.Object, _
    ByVal e As System.EventArgs) Handles btnWrite.Click

    Dim conn As New SqlConnection(CONNSTR)
    Dim sSQL As String
    Dim cmd As New SqlCommand()
    Dim ta As SqlTransaction

    Dim sTitle As String
    Dim sCategoryDesc As String
    Dim sManufacturer As String
    Dim sDescription As String

    ' Tell the user we're getting going.
    lblStatus.Text = "Saving toy data..."
    System.Windows.Forms.Application.DoEvents()

    ' Set up the db connection and a transaction. If any part of the
    ' data writing fails, we can use the transaction to back it
    ' all out.
    cmd.Connection = conn
    conn.Open()
    ta = conn.BeginTransaction("SaveToys")
    cmd.Transaction = ta
```

```
' For each row in the DataSet that was populated from the XML,
' format the data and write it to the database.
Dim aRow As DataRow
For Each aRow In ds.Tables(0).Rows

    ' For the string data, make sure to replace all single
    ' quotes with two in a row. This will prevent premature
    ' string termination errors when writing the data.
    sTitle = Trim(aRow("Expr1"))
    sTitle = sTitle.Replace("'", "''")
    sCategoryDesc = Trim(aRow("CategoryDesc"))
    sCategoryDesc = sCategoryDesc.Replace("'", "''")
    sManufacturer = Trim(aRow("Manufacturer"))
    sManufacturer = sManufacturer.Replace("'", "''")
    sDescription = Trim(aRow("Description"))
    sDescription = sDescription.Replace("'", "''")

    ' Set up the SQL to write this row to the database.
    sSQL = "INSERT INTO Product (Title, CategoryDesc, " & _
        "AssemblyReqd, Manufacturer, Description, Wholesale) " & _
        "VALUES ('" & sTitle & "', '" & sCategoryDesc & "', " & _
        "aRow("AssemblyReqd") & _
        ", '" & sManufacturer & "', '" & sDescription & "', " & _
        "aRow("Wholesale") & ")"
    cmd.CommandText = sSQL

    ' Write the row.
    Try
        cmd.ExecuteNonQuery()
    Catch ex As SqlException
        ' If the row insert fails, tell the user, roll back
        ' the entire transaction, and get outta here.
        MsgBox(ex.Message())
        ta.Rollback("SaveToys")
        conn.Close()
        lblStatus.Text = "There were errors attempting " & _
            "to save the data."
        Exit Sub
    End Try
Next

' If we got this far, all the inserts worked fine. Commit the
' transaction and tell the user we're done.
ta.Commit()
conn.Close()
lblStatus.Text = "Data save completed."

End Sub
```

We set up our data access objects, as we've seen before with other projects that write data to the database. We added another interesting aspect to this project: We're writing the data using a database transaction. This will prevent incomplete data from being written in the event of an error during the writing or a catastrophic error, such as a database server shutdown.

TIP **There are times when processing that follows the update of the UI will prevent those UI updates from being seen in a timely fashion. At the beginning of the method, we inform the user that we are updating the toy data by setting the text method of our status label control. Without doing anything else, the processing that follows does not yield control of the operating system soon enough for the user to see it. The functionality will complete and the message will never be seen. This problem was solved in past versions of Visual Basic using the DoEvents method. It could be called to yield control of the operating system briefly while repainting operations could complete. Oddly enough, we still need this capability in Visual Basic .NET. However, the DoEvents method has changed locations. If you find that you need to call DoEvents for any reason, you'll find it here:**

```
System.Windows.Forms.Application.DoEvents()
```

Next we define a few local variables to be used in this method and tell the user we're starting the data writing process. Then the database setup takes place. We set up the database command and connection and open it, as usual. In addition, we create the transaction and assign it to the command object, like this:

```
ta = conn.BeginTransaction("SaveToys")
cmd.Transaction = ta
```

We give the name *SaveToys* to the transaction so that we can refer to it later. The connection object is used to begin and create the transaction. The command holds on to it for the duration of the transaction.

Now it's time to process the data. We iterate through each row of the table in the DataSet, making adjustments to it and writing it to the database. The four string values that we read in need to have any single quotes (apostrophes) replaced with two apostrophes so that the database will not interpret the single quote as the end of the string. We also strip off any leading or trailing spaces. One example follows:

```
sCategoryDesc = Trim(aRow("CategoryDesc"))
sCategoryDesc = sCategoryDesc.Replace("'", "''")
```

The next step is to build our SQL INSERT statement. Once that's done, we execute the nonquery using the command object inside a Try..Catch structure. If errors occur, we tell the user, roll back the transaction, and leave the method, like this:

```
MsgBox(ex.Message())
ta.Rollback("SaveToys")
conn.Close()
lblStatus.Text = "There were errors attempting " & _
    "to save the data."
Exit Sub
```

If everything went well, we commit the transaction to finalize writing to the database, close down the connection, and tell the user everything is done:

```
ta.Commit()
conn.Close()
lblStatus.Text = "Data save completed."
```

That's it for building the reader. Figure 7.17 shows the reader executing. It shows that there were errors during validation, and the Write Data button has been disabled.

The Errors Form

We need to be able to display any validation errors to the user. The Errors form is a simple form that takes care of the problem. Figure 7.18 shows the form, and Table 7.3 details the controls on the form and their settings.

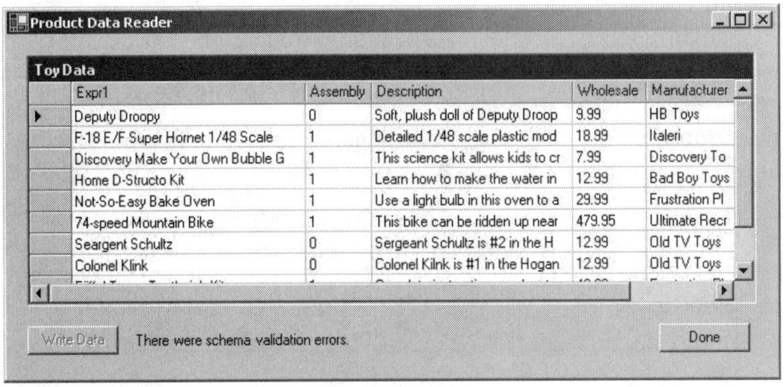

Figure 7.17   The Data Reader with validation errors.

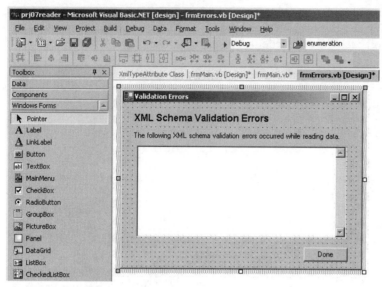

Figure 7.18   The Validation Errors form.

Table 7.3   The Validation Errors Form Controls

CONTROL	NAME	PROPERTIES
Form	frmErrors	Text="Validation Errors"
Button	btnDone	Text="Done", Anchor=Bottom, Right
Label	Label1	Text="XML Schema Validation Errors", Font=Arial 12pt Bold
Label	Label2	Text="The following XML schema validation errors occurred while reading data."
TextBox	tbErrs	Text="", Anchor=Top, Bottom, Left, Right, Multiline=True, Scrollbars=Vertical

The Errors Code

The are only two methods used for error codes, and both are very simple:

```
Private Sub btnDone_Click(ByVal sender As System.Object, _
    ByVal e As System.EventArgs) Handles btnDone.Click
    Me.Close()
End Sub

Public WriteOnly Property Errors() As String
    Set(ByVal Value As String)
        tbErrs.Text = Value
    End Set
End Property
```

This code shuts down the window when the Done button is clicked, and it provides a property that allows the caller to pass in the errors string. The form is created and called by the main form, using the following code:

```
fErr = New frmErrors()
fErr.Errors = sValidateErrs
fErr.ShowDialog()
```

Figure 7.19 shows the form during execution, filled with sample error data.

That completes all the code and discussion for our XML and XSD exchange project. You should be able to easily adapt the tool and techniques used here to suit your own needs.

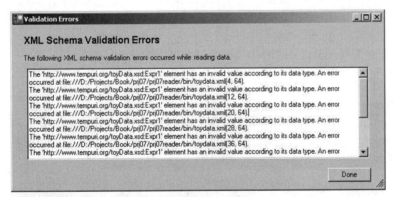

Figure 7.19 The Errors form during execution.

Enhancing the Project

This project taught you about basic XML structure, XML schemas, and how to use the XML functionality in Visual Basic and the .NET framework to make the exchange of data between disparate systems easier. It also took you on a nice tour of the XML Designer, an outstanding tool for internal XML data and schema creation and prototyping.

There are still plenty of areas of XML and related functionality in .NET and Visual Basic to explore. A good place to dig in would be the XmlDocument object in the .NET framework. This object will provide you with some excellent methods for dealing directly with XML data. I also did not discuss XSL (XML Stylesheet Language) or XSLT (XSL Transformations) at all. You can use them to format and manipulate XML data for display in many different forms. There is enough in the topic of XML and related technologies to cover 10 complete books with ease.

There are plenty of opportunities for adding functionality to this project. We've started something here that could be truly useful, given a little time and work. Try some of these ideas for fun:

Where did that file go?   Both of the utilities that we created simply write out or read their XML and XSD data files from the same location that the program runs from. Add a Common Open dialog that will allow the user to specify where files are located (for reading) or where they should go (for writing).

Better data review.   When the data reader displays data in the grid, the user has the opportunity to review it for accuracy and appropriateness. However, you may not want to write all the records to the database. Add the capability for users to select the specific records from the grid that they want to write to the database. This will make the review process far more useful.

Better data matching.   Perhaps users of the reader have changed their database organization and it is not currently caught up to the schema published by the data provider. In this case, users may only want to write specific columns to the database. Update the reader to allow users to select columns, and write only those columns to the database.

Database selection.   Add a dialog to the reader that allows users to select the database to which the data will be written. This would let the user target a test database or a production database, as required.

WHAT'S COMING NEXT

The next project is about security. Most programmers would rather ignore security. It can be tedious, complicated, and downright boring. Our project will focus on ASP.NET security and using security to restrict those who have access to your Web sites and applications.

Whether or not you like security, the next project should clear it up enough to make it more approachable and a little less dry.

User Authentication Login Screen

In any environment security is a big topic that most programmers would rather ignore altogether, yet it is also a very important topic to understand. There is a huge pile of terminology to learn, it's difficult to know which parts apply to what you want to do, and it usually requires lots of configuration and cooperation from system administrators. There is rarely a single, coherent picture of what security is about, how it all works together, and what parts are relevant. Fortunately, you can dispense with the bits you don't need to know.

A complete treatment of security could fill an entire book. This project will provide you with an overview of security in .NET, with a primary focus on ASP.NET security.

THE PROBLEM:

Web sites often have sections of content (or indeed, the entire site) that need securing from unauthorized users. However, wading through the complexities of security and determining what you need to implement can be a daunting task. We need a solution that takes care of the basics of security, one that can be reused and then customized to suit our specific needs.

THE SOLUTION:

Providing secured access is a common task that every Web application programmer should be able to do, and our project helps out there. We will create a basic set of login forms that can be used on almost any Web site and implement password access to content. I'll also show you how to open up parts of the Web site or Web application and how to secure other parts.

The Project

Our project is a pair of ASP.NET forms, one that allows users to log in and another to let them add a new account. The following activities will be part of the project:

1. **Database setup.**   I'll show you the database we'll be using for this project and how to set it up. Our database will hold user names and passwords that will be used for validation when the user logs in.

2. **Security configuration.**   Our application will need to know what users to let in, as well as what to do if an unknown user tries to access the site. We will create a configuration file that will take care of these issues.

3. **Login form.**   We will create the main ASP.NET form that handles user login. It will also provide a link that allows unknown users to create a new account.

4. **New account form.**   If a user in unknown to the system, he or she will be able to add a new account using this ASP.NET form.

You Will Need

✔ **Visual Studio .NET**

✔ **A basic knowledge of Visual Basic .NET**

✔ **Internet Information Server**

✔ **SQL Server (or other database)**

✔ **A basic knowledge of ASP.NET**

Background on Security

The biggest problem with understanding security is the lack of a coherent explanation of the big picture. Starting at the 10,000-foot view, security can be summarized like this: You have something users want, and you have to decide whether or not to give it to them. They come to a Web site or need access to another resource, like a disk directory or file, and you might not want to let them in for one reason or another. The following are all things that are part of the job of security.

- Sensitive information needs to be secured from those who should not have access to it. This includes everything from employee salaries to national secrets.

- Web sites and the resources on which they reside and use need to be protected from malicious attacks. Granted, we want to believe we live in a happy, peaceful world, and this is true much of the time. However, we also know that viruses, hackers, and DoS (Denial of Service) attacks are realities that we need to protect against.

- It is often important to know exactly who is accessing your Web site or Web application before you allow access. Recording that information and validating it against a known list of users is a common task.

As programmers, we need mechanisms that allow us to make sure that users are who they say they are and to match them up with the tasks that they are allowed to do. The security mechanisms available to us do just that, although you typically have to use a combination of techniques and tools to make your scenario work. For example, if you only want to allows users into your Web site who are registered Windows users in your domain, you have to use Windows security to set up accounts, tell IIS that you're using Windows security, and create the right configuration files that tell your Web application what security settings to use.

To understand the details of security and what it will take to allow you as a programmer to implement security, we need to cover a few concepts. At first they will seem disjointed, and it will not be readily apparent how they all coordinate to get the job done. Read through them with the understanding that I'll bring them all together later, and they will fall together into a coherent picture. We'll especially see how enough of it fits together to get the job done in our project.

Security Concepts

Security involves several different tasks and concepts, each of which plays a role in the security system. I'll take a moment to introduce you to them to make it easier to differentiate between them.

User Access

First, there is the concept of identifying users as those allowed into a system or allowed access to resources (meaning Web pages, data, disk files, etc.). This is called *authentication*. It involves accepting some credentials supplied by users, typically an ID and a password combination, and verifying that they are allowed in at all. There are several authentication mechanisms available, and selecting one depends on your needs and your application.

Second, it is important to be able to limit the rights of individuals once they have been authenticated. It would be nice if we only had to worry about authentication, but access to system resources is not a binary state. Once users are in, that doesn't mean that they have access to everything. Different individuals will need different levels of access. Providing users with their specific access rights is called *authorization*. If a user who has already been authenticated makes a request for a resource, say a specific part of a Web application, the system must check to see if that user is authorized to have that access. The authorization mechanisms will be covered later.

Third, you have the option of bypassing your responsibilities with regard to authentication and authorization by using *impersonation*. This allows the application to operate as the user on the server, impersonating him or her for the purpose of security. In this case, IIS takes care of authentication. The application executes on the server as if it were the client, with the same rights and access (or lack thereof) as the impersonated user.

Web Security

You've seen Web security all over the place. Any Web site that asks you to log in uses Web security of one sort or another. The .NET platform and ASP.NET give you a few options and let you build security into your Web sites and Web applications just like those you've seen before. In fact, that's what we'll be doing in our project. You can even secure different parts of a Web site or application with different levels of security. For example, you might provide the entire public (anonymous users) with access to advertising and product information on your site. However, only employees who log in and have proper access will be allowed to see the sales information.

The primary focus of Web security is to redirect users to a login page when they try to access a part of the site that is restricted. The system will handle this for you automatically once you define and configure the access rights to the site. I will be covering this in detail later.

What about Code?

Although we are focusing on Web security, you can also secure code components. The .NET Framework provides a mechanism called *code access security* that allows us to specify the rights of code modules, as well as users.

Based on several criteria, including where the code originated and what sort of guarantees are provided with it, you can decide how much code can be trusted. You can actually specify what sorts of operations and access to resources that code modules have, very much like users. This can reduce the likelihood of malicious code even being allowed to execute on your system. You can get some of these benefits merely by programming in an approved .NET-managed code programming language. However, programming will be required on your part to take full advantage of it.

The code access security system works something like this. You create code components that have specific access needs. For example, your code module might need to read and write to the server registry. This would typically require a high level of security. When a caller makes a request to use your functionality, your code can require that the caller have the same security rights that your module does. In fact, the security system will walk the entire call stack to make sure that every caller in the call chain has proper clearance. If any one of the callers does not meet your security requirements, you can deny access to your services. In this way, code that you write can be built with the correct code access security levels to use the registry module, but malicious code that finds its way into your system and tries to execute whatever it finds would be denied access to your code.

Using the .NET code access programming mechanisms, you can help your code satisfy security requirements and also require that any modules you call have specific permissions. Code access security is a valuable tool for distributed applications, making them more secure at the module and method levels. However, it is not something you can design and build in a couple hours. It will require systemwide planning to decide what resources are available to components at various levels and what modules should be trusted and how much, and a comprehensive security policy will have to be worked out with your system administrator.

Role-Based Security

Often it is not practical to assign specific rights to every user. You can, instead, assign rights to roles and place users in these roles. A role is simply a named set of rights. Users in that role all have the same rights. For example, you would give the Accountant role access to the company's financial database but not to the Human Resources information. The CEO role might, depending on your company, be locked out of most everything or given access to everything.

The .NET security functionality allows you to use role-based security. It's not simple, but it does provide a useful mechanism for implementing security. It involves creating Identity and Principal objects and using them with the PrincipalPermission object to perform security checks. The Identity object contains information about the user involved, and the Principal represents the security context, including the role under which the user is operating. You can use those objects with the PrincipalPermission object to make requests about specific permissions that the user and role are allowed to perform.

Although we will not be covering role-based security in this project, it is important to know what your options are. Consider looking into this mechanism further if it sounds like it might meet your needs. For example, if you have a large number of internal users, role-based security might be appropriate.

Authentication and Authorization

The process of authentication is the biggest task in security. There are several mechanisms available to handle authentication, each of which has its own pros and cons, depending on the situation and the application.

We know that authentication is the process of identifying users. However, typically you have to know something about the users to begin with. On a basic Web site, where you might be simply collecting a list of users for auditing or advertising purposes, you might only ask them for some information on a form and accept it as truth. At the other end of the spectrum, you might only allow known employees to access your site or application. In that case, you would have to have a predefined list of users and a mechanism for maintaining that list. The various authentication mechanisms each have their own ways of providing a list of users.

The authentication mechanisms available with .NET, IIS, and Windows are as follows:

Forms authentication.   This mechanism allows you to handle most of the authentication yourself, but still provides you with redirection mechanisms and the maintenance of security during a session and beyond a session. It is used primarily for Web sites and Web applications.

Windows authentication.   In this authentication scenario, IIS and Windows work in concert to handle authentication. This is one of the easiest mechanisms to use, requiring little work on the part of the programmer. However, it will only allow into your site or application users who are registered with the Windows domain. For internal applications, this is fine. However, a Web site that allows anonymous users or new users to create accounts should not use it.

Passport authentication.   Passport is an authentication service that Microsoft created and runs. Users create a Passport account through Microsoft, which provides them with varying levels of information such as a name, address, password, phone number, and even credit card information. You can use this service to validate user-supplied credentials against information stored in the Passport database. Using Passport authentication is a little involved, but if you'd like to learn more about it, you can do so at http://www.passport.com. Developer links are on the site.

Authorization with Web Forms is the process of allowing authenticated (or otherwise) users access to specific resources. We can define what those access levels are by user, role, or in general. These settings are defined for portions of a Web application or site using the configuration file, which I'll cover in detail later.

Forms Authentication and Authorization

Forms authentication and authorization are ideal for Web sites and Web applications that are open to the public or that provide varied levels of access to different parts of the site. Programmers have the most control over these mechanisms. They provide a redirection mechanism that presents your own login page if the user requests a restricted resource and has not yet been authenticated. The basic process looks like this:

1. The user requests a secured resource on the Web server, a Web page to which you have restricted access. At this point, the user has not been authenticated, so the server automatically redirects the request to your specific login page.

2. The user enters login information, usually a user name or ID and a password. These are sent to the server when the user submits the form using a button or other mechanism.

3. The login credentials are validated on the server. This is done by your code. There are plenty of mechanisms available to you to do this, from the simple to the complex. In the end, however, you decide if the user should be allowed to access the requested resource.

4. If users pass your inspection, you can send them to their originally requested page. You don't have to know what the page was; the FormsAuthentication system knows it. They are now authenticated on the system, and the authentication information will automatically be passed around from page to page during the current session or between sessions.

5. At this point, the authorization is checked. If the authorizations prohibit users from viewing the requested resource, even though they are authenticated on the site, they will not be allowed access to the page and will be informed of this. If they are authorized, the redirection will continue and the page will be displayed for them.

6. If users do not pass authentication, you can leave them on the current URL and display a nice login error message for them. They are not authenticated on the

system. If they try to access the page again, or other restricted pages, they will be sent right back to the login page.

The forms security concepts and execution flow are now established. So how do we make it happen as programmers? There are two basic steps: securing the parts of the Web site that we want to protect and implementing the code to make it work.

Configuration Files

Securing portions (or all) of a Web site or application is controlled, with Web Forms, using configuration files. The files, named *Web.config*, are placed in directories of the Web server to tell IIS how to secure the resources in those directories. This is where you define the authentications and authorizations for the files in the particular directories. The file is an XML file that you can edit manually. Here's an example:

```
<configuration>
    <system.web>
        <authentication mode="forms">
            <forms loginURL="myLogin.aspx" name=".ASPXAUTH"/>
        </authentication>
        <authorization>
            <deny users="?"/>
        </authorization>
    </system.web>
</configuration>
```

This configuration file defines both authentication and authorization. The authentication mode has been set to forms mode. Other authentication mode options include Windows, Passport, and None. It then defines the login page that users should be redirected to if they request a secured page and have not yet been authenticated. The simple authorization section tells IIS to deny access to all anonymous users. There are many more options for authorization. A few examples are shown in Table 8.1.

Table 8.1 Examples of the Authorization Clauses

AUTHORIZATION CLAUSE	DESCRIPTION
<allow users="*">	Allow anyone into the resources in this directory
<allow users="homer, tony">	Allow only these two users access to the directory
<allow roles="HR">	Allow only those users in the HR roles group access to this director
<deny users="*">	Don't allow anyone in here, except those defined in an "allow" clause

The last clause given in the table is important. It shows that these clauses can be combined. Consider the following:

```
<deny users="*">
<allow users="homer, tony">
```

This pair of clauses keeps everyone out except the users Homer and Tony. Use the combinations, but test them out once they are in place to make sure they do what you expect them to. It's fairly easy to mess these up, so use caution.

> **TIP** **When you create a Web forms project with Visual Studio .NET, it creates a Web.config file for you at the root level. You can open and edit this file like any other file in your project. It defaults your application to Windows authentication mode, and if you want to use forms mode, you can just change it in the authentication section of the file.**
>
> **You can also create new directories for your Web application in the Solution Explorer. Do this to organize the sections of your application by the access you'd like to provide, and then create additional Web.config files to restrict or grant access to these directories as needed.**

The configuration file is placed in a specific directory on the Web server. For example, if you had an application that is completely restricted, it will go in the root directory of the Web application, like this:

```
C:\Inetpub\wwwroot\RestrictedApp\web.config
```

You can use a single configuration file to restrict access to a specific directory and all subdirectories below it. You can then override those settings in subdirectories by placing additional web.config files in those directories. For example, if we allow everyone into the main Web application, we can place a web.config file in the Web application root directory with the following authorization:

```
<allow users="*"/>
```

However, we want to restrict a portion of the Web site that displays usage statistics to only selected, specific users. We would organize our Web site into directories that reflect our authorization needs, and the usage statistics content would be located in its own directory, restricted by its own web.config file. The file would be located in a subdirectory called Usage that contained our usage statistics content. That web.config file would look like this:

```
<configuration>
    <system.web>
        <authorization>
            <deny users="*"/>
            <allows users="statadmin"/>
```

```
            </authorization>
        </system.web>
</configuration>
```

Only the user called statadmin would be allowed access to the resources in the directory that contains this web.config file. Note that we only need the authorization information for this configuration file. Authentication is provided in the web.config file at the application root.

Authentication and Authorization in Code

We've seen configuration files and we've talked about security concepts and setup. However, we need to tie them together in the final step: code. We'll take an amazingly simple example wherein we only allow a few specific people into a Web site. We'll provide a very basic login page, a placeholder page for the requested resource, and a configuration file to set things up. To begin with, here's a configuration file that will let all anonymous users at least attempt to log in to the page:

```
<configuration>
    <system.web>
        <authentication mode="forms">
            <forms loginURL="myLogin.aspx" name=".ASPXFORMSAUTH"/>
        </authentication>
        <authorization>
            <allow users="*"/>
        </authorization>
    </system.web>
</configuration>
```

Now we can create a simple Web page that has the necessary login fields. You can do this manually or using Visual Studio. The login form looks like Figure 8.1. The simple default form, the one that we're going to restrict access to, looks like Figure 8.2.

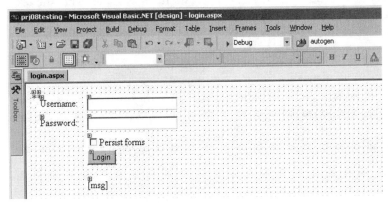

Figure 8.1 The myLogin.aspx form.

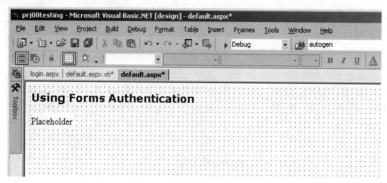

Figure 8.2 The default.aspx form.

When users try to access the default.aspx file through their Web browser, the configuration file tells IIS to redirect their request to the file myLogin.aspx. When this file is displayed, users enter a user ID and password and then click the Login button. At this point, the button event code fires; the code looks like this:

```
Private Sub btnLogin_ServerClick(ByVal sender As System.Object, _
    ByVal e As System.EventArgs) Handles btnLogin.ServerClick

    If ((tbName.Text = "tony") And (tbPwd.Text = "doggie")) Then
        FormsAuthentication.RedirectFromLoginPage( _
            tbName.Text, False)
    Else
        msg.Text = "Invalid login information. Please try again."
    End If

End Sub
```

This code is very simple, and the only validation we do is to match what the user entered against a specific ID and password. You could replace this with any sort of validation code you like, and as you'll see in our project, I replaced it with something much more useful.

If the user ID and password match the ones we're allowing, we make use of the FormsAuthentication object that's part of the System.Web.Security namespace. The method we're using, RedirectFromLoginPage, actually handles the redirection to the originally requested page. So we don't have to remember it or even know it in the first place.

If the user ID and password don't match, we tell the user and stay on the page. The redirection from the requested page is handled by IIS for us, and for any other pages that are restricted.

Let's Start the Project

If your business creates lots of Web sites or Web applications, you will probably want a standard login page that you can use to gain access to any of them. Our project is a set of pages that you can use as a front end to any of your sites. With a little modification to the appearance to match your company's look, this project could find a nice home in front of all your Web sites that need security.

The project is similar to the samples you've seen so far. We need two configuration files to define the authentication method and the authorizations. We will have a login page and a placeholder for our application. We went a step further with the password checking, however. All our users and their respective passwords are located in a SQL Server database. This makes them a little more secure, more expandable, and easier to edit and maintain. We've even added a form that will let users add an account for themselves and then login.

Setting Up

We need to create the project, get the database set up, and create a new directory for the unsecured part of the site. Once that's done, we can create the pages and the code behind it.

The Database

You saw simple password and user ID verification in a prior example, where we compared the user's credentials to hard-coded values. In this application, we're going to store all the users in a SQL Server database. The database design we need for this application is simple. It has only one table. The columns are defined as shown in Figure 8.3.

As for previous projects, a Microsoft Access version of this database is on the accompanying CD-ROM; you can import into SQL Server. It includes a few sample user accounts that you can try out. The connection string that we use for it is defined in the code-behind module for the two ASP pages that we created.

The Site Organization

This project has three pages: the login page, the New Account page, and default.aspx, which represents the main page of your application or site. The default.aspx page is the one that needs to be secured; the New Account page needs to be accessible to everyone with no restrictions. To make that happen, we are putting the New Account page in a subdirectory of its own where we can control its more open access with another web.config file.

When we create the project, we'll add a folder to the project called NewAccount where we'll create the new account form. We'll also add a web.config file there that we will type in manually.

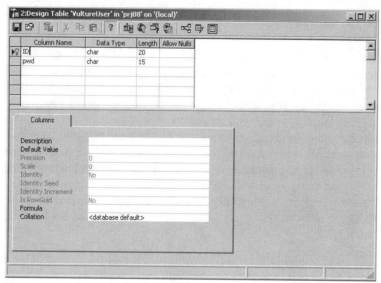

Figure 8.3   The security project database.

Create the Project

Start everything by creating a new Web Forms project in Visual Studio. I called mine prj08, but you can name yours whatever you like. It should include the first empty Web Form, as well as a web.config file in the project root.

As long as we're here, and because we need it for the next section, create the subdirectory for the new account form. Right-click on the solution name in the Solution Explorer and select Add Folder, naming it NewAccount.

The Images Folder

One last setup detail is that we have an image we want to use for our header, and we need to add it to the project. Create a new folder in the project by right-clicking on the solution name in the Solution Explorer and selecting the Add Folder option. Name the folder *images*. Then add the image by right-clicking on the new folder name and selecting the Add Existing Item option from the menu. Browse to the file vc_prj08.jpg on the accompanying CD-ROM and add it in. It is now available for use by the application.

Configuring Security

Visual Studio created a Web.config file for us in the root directory of the project. You can open it like any other file, so let's do so and edit it a little. Notice that there are all sorts of things in this file, only some of which are related to security. The rest can be safely ignored for the time being (just don't do anything to it). Also notice that there is already an authentication section with some information in it and an authorization section with nothing in it. We're going to change that.

Edit the authentication section so that it does not use the Windows authentication method, but uses the Forms method instead. Also tell it to point to the login form that we're going to create for the security redirection. It should look like this:

```
<authentication mode="Forms">
    <forms loginUrl="prj08login.aspx" name=".ASPXFORMSAUTH"></forms>
</authentication>
```

The authorization portion is simple. We want to deny access to all anonymous users, which implies that we allow access to all authenticated users. This is exactly what we want in this case. Here's the authorization section for the root configuration file:

```
<authorization>
    <deny users="?" />
</authorization>
```

That takes care of that one. Now we need another one, which we'll have to create from scratch. This one is for the NewAccount directory, and we need it so that we can override the restrictive security we just set up at the root level. Lower-level (directory level) web.config files have priority over higher ones. So let's open it up with the following web.config file. You can create it in a text editor and then add it to the project.

```
<?xml version="1.0" encoding="utf-8" ?>
<configuration>
    <system.web>
            <authorization>
                    <allow users="*" />
            </authorization>
    </system.web>
</configuration>
```

The Forms

Now that we're all setup, we can actually create some content. The three forms we're making could be created using the Designer tools or the HTML window. Ours will be built by hand in the HTML window so that we can get the layout the way we wanted it.

The Login Form

Our primary form, which allows the user to login to the system, can be created by renaming the default form that Visual Studio created for us. Rename it *prj08login.aspx*. The form we're creating looks like Figure 8.4. It helps to have an image of what you're building before you build it.

Figure 8.4　The Login form.

The ASP/HTML code to create the form is listed below. Take a look at it and then I'll discuss what is relevant.

```
<%@ Page Language="vb" AutoEventWireup="false"
Codebehind="prj08login.aspx.vb" Inherits="prj08.WebForm1"%>
<!DOCTYPE HTML PUBLIC "-//W3C//DTD HTML 4.0 Transitional//EN">
<HTML>
    <HEAD>
        <title>Vulture Corp Login</title>
        <LINK rel="stylesheet" type="text/css" href="Styles.css">
        <meta name="GENERATOR" content="Microsoft Visual Studio.NET 7.0">
        <meta name="CODE_LANGUAGE" content="Visual Basic 7.0">
        <meta name="vs_defaultClientScript" content="JavaScript">
        <meta name="vs_targetSchema"
         content="http://schemas.microsoft.com/intellisense/ie5">
    </HEAD>
<body style="PADDING-RIGHT:0px; PADDING-LEFT:0px;
 PADDING-BOTTOM:0px; MARGIN:0px; PADDING-TOP:0px">
<form id="LoginFrm" method="post" runat="server">
    <table cellspacing="0" cellpadding="0" border="0" width="600">
        <tr valign="middle">
            <td background="images/vc_prj08.jpg" height="91"
             colspan="2">
            <span class="pageTitle">     
```

```
                             
                    Vulture Corp. Login</span>
                </td>
            </tr>
            <tr valign="top">
                <td colspan="2" class="infoText"
                style="PADDING-LEFT:35px">
                <br>Please login to the <span id="appname"></span>
                system. If you are new to this system, click the
                Create New Account link below.<br>
                </td>
            </tr>
            <tr valign="top">
                <!-- This column is for login information -->
                <td>
                    <table cellpadding="0" cellspacing="5" border="0">
                        <tr>
                            <td width="35"></td>
                            <td colspan="2"></td>
                        </tr>
                        <tr>
                            <td width="35"></td>
                            <td>
                                <span class="inputLabel">User ID:</span>
                            </td>
                            <td>
                                <asp:TextBox ID="tbID"
                                Runat="server"></asp:TextBox>
                            </td>
                        </tr>
                        <tr>
                            <td width="35"></td>
                            <td>
                                <spanclass="inputLabel">Password:</span>
                            </td>
                            <td>
                                <asp:TextBox ID="tbPwd" Runat="server"
                                TextMode="Password"></asp:TextBox>
                            </td>
                        </tr>
                        <tr>
                            <td width="35"></td>
                            <td></td>
                            <td>
                                <input type="submit" id="btnLogin"
                                name="btnLogin" value="Login"
                                runat="server">
                            </td>
                        </tr>
                        <tr>
                            <td width="35"></td>
```

```
                                    <td></td>
                                    <td class="errMsg">
                                        <asp:label id="errMsg"
                                         Runat="server"></asp:label>
                                    </td>
                                </tr>
                            </table>
                        </td>
                        <!-- This column is for the "Create New Account" link -->
                        <td valign="center" class="infoText">
                            Not a user yet? Create new new account here.<br>
                            <a href="NewAccount/prj08new.aspx"
                             class="LinkButton">Create new account</a>
                        </td>
                    </tr>
                </table>
            </form>
        </body>
</HTML>
```

We did a couple of interesting things here. We added a link to the default style sheet that VB created for us. We added a couple of styles here that make the site look better. Also, the image that we added to the project has been set up as a cell background in one of our tables. This will add some flair to the top of the page. Here are the styles we added to the style sheet:

```
A:hover
{
    color:#AAAAFF;
}


.pageTitle
{
    font-family: Haettenschweiler, Arial Black ;
    font-size: 36pt;
    color: Navy;
}

.inputLabel
{
    font-family: Verdana;
    font-size: 10pt;
    font-weight: bold;
}

.infoText
{
    font-family: Verdana;
    font-size: 10pt;
```

```
        font-weight: normal;
}


.errMsg
{
        font-family: Verdana;
        font-size: 10pt;
        font-weight: bold;
        color: Red;
}

.linkButton
{
        text-decoration: none;
        font-weight: bold;
        color: #ffffff;
        background-color: Navy;
}
```

In addition, there is a span in there with an ID of *appname*. In your code, you can change its innerHTML property to be the name of your application or Web site. There are two ASP TextBox controls, tbID and tbPwd, that we use to capture user input, a standard HTML anchor link to our forthcoming New Account page, and an ASP Label control with an ID of *errMsg* that we use to tell users about their typing mistakes.

 You can create a password field by adding a normal TextBox control to your form and then setting its TextMode property to the value TIP   Password, as we have done in this project. This hides the user's typing and echoes it with asterisks. However, it has an added benefit. Internet Explorer understands these fields, and once the user enters data, it will ask if the password should be saved in its password list. You've probably seen other sites do this, and it makes using your site very convenient.

At this point, we can add some code to the page. Everything can be handled in the compiled code-behind component that VB creates. Here's the listing:

```
Imports System.Data.SqlClient
Imports System.Web.Security


Public Class WebForm1
    Inherits System.Web.UI.Page
    Protected WithEvents tbID As System.Web.UI.WebControls.TextBox
    Protected WithEvents tbPwd As System.Web.UI.WebControls.TextBox
    Protected WithEvents btnLogin As
        System.Web.UI.HtmlControls.HtmlInputButton
    Protected WithEvents errMsg As System.Web.UI.WebControls.Label
```

```vb
#Region " Class Data and Types "

    ' Database connection string. We're using SQL Server. Change this if
    ' you want to use something else, like the Access db included with
    ' the book.
    Private Const CONNSTR As String = "PERSIST SECURITY INFO=False; " & _
        DATA SOURCE=tony; INITIAL CATALOG=prj08; UID=sa; PWD=;"

#End Region

#Region " User Code "

    Private Function GetPwd(ByVal sID As String) As String

        Dim conn As SqlConnection = New SqlConnection(CONNSTR)
        Dim sSQL As String

        ' SQL to retrieve alert rows that are current. By design,
        ' there is only ever intended to be one row in there, reflecting
        ' the current state of the company.
        sSQL = "SELECT pwd FROM VultureUser WHERE ID='" & sID & "'"

        ' Get our data objects ready for retrieval.
        Dim da As SqlDataAdapter = New SqlDataAdapter(sSQL, conn)
        Dim ds As DataSet = New DataSet()
        Dim theRow As DataRow

        ' Load the data.
        Try
            conn.Open()
            da.Fill(ds, "pwd")
            conn.Close()
            theRow = ds.Tables("pwd").Rows(0)
            GetPwd = theRow("pwd")
        Catch ex As SqlException
            GetPwd = ""
        End Try

    End Function

#End Region

#Region " Event Handlers "

    Private Sub btnLogin_ServerClick(ByVal sender As System.Object, _
        ByVal e As System.EventArgs) Handles btnLogin.ServerClick

        ' Get password from database. If it's not there, we're
        ' already done. If so, then validate it.
        Dim pwd As String = GetPwd(tbID.Text)
```

```
        ' Validate. Feel free to UCase() everything if you want
        ' case-insensitive passwords.
        If tbPwd.Text = Trim(pwd) Then
            ' Send them on their way; they are authenticated.
            FormsAuthentication.RedirectFromLoginPage(tbID.Text, False)
        Else
            ' Tell them something was not right.
            errMsg.Text = "The supplied user ID or password " & _
                "was not correct. If you do not " & _
                "have an account, use the link on this page to " & _
                "create one."
        End If

    End Sub

#End Region

#Region " Web Form Designer Generated Code "

    'This call is required by the Web Form Designer.
    <System.Diagnostics.DebuggerStepThrough()>
    Private Sub InitializeComponent()

    End Sub

    Private Sub Page_Init(ByVal sender As System.Object, _
        ByVal e As System.EventArgs) Handles MyBase.Init
        'CODEGEN: This method call is required by the Web Form Designer
        'Do not modify it using the code editor.
        InitializeComponent()
    End Sub

#End Region

End Class
```

The first step in the code is to import the namespaces that we need access to, specifically the SqlClient and Web.Security namespaces. This will make our job easier when coding. Second, we add a constant to hold the connection string that is used to access SQL Server.

Our code will need to compare the password that the user enters with the password stored in the database under the user's ID. I wrote a utility method that takes the user's ID and retrieves the password from the database that matches it. The method, GetPwd, retrieves the record if it exists, extracts the password from the DataSet, and returns it to the caller. If there is not a match, meaning the user is not in the database, it returns an empty string. Otherwise, the method uses standard ADO.NET techniques that you've seen in other projects.

Figure 8.5 The New Account form.

The event handler that traps the Login button click, btnLogin_ServerClick, retrieves the matching password and sees if the one the user entered matches the one in the database. If it does, it uses the FormsAuthentication object to redirect users to the page that they originally requested. If not, we display a nice error message for them and continue to wait.

The New Account Form

We would like to let users into our site, but we do need a user ID and password to work with. Therefore, we have a form that will allow them to create a new account, providing us with this information. It needs to take in a user ID and password and then add it to the database, but only if the ID does not already exist (we're requiring that it be unique). If users enter everything correctly and they are successfully entered into the database, we send them back to the login page so they can access the system.

The form, shown in Figure 8.5, is similar to the login screen, but simpler. The ASP/HTML code that is used to create the form follows. When you create the form, remember to create it in the NewAccount folder that we added to the project earlier.

```
<%@ Page Language="vb" AutoEventWireup="false"
Codebehind="prj08new.aspx.vb" Inherits="prj08.prj08new"%>
<!DOCTYPE HTML PUBLIC "-//W3C//DTD HTML 4.0 Transitional//EN">
<HTML>
    <HEAD>
        <title>New Vulture Account</title>
```

```
        <LINK rel="stylesheet" type="text/css" href="../Styles.css">
        <meta name="GENERATOR" content="Microsoft Visual Studio.NET 7.0">
        <meta name="CODE_LANGUAGE" content="Visual Basic 7.0">
        <meta name="vs_defaultClientScript" content="JavaScript">
        <meta name="vs_targetSchema"
         content="http://schemas.microsoft.com/intellisense/ie5">
</HEAD>

<body style="PADDING-RIGHT:0px; PADDING-LEFT:0px;
 PADDING-BOTTOM:0px; MARGIN:0px; PADDING-TOP:0px">
    <form id="frmNew" method="post" runat="server">
    <table cellspacing="0" cellpadding="0" border="0" width="600">
        <tr valign="middle">
            <td background="../images/vc_prj08.jpg" height="91">
                <span class="pageTitle">     
                         
                  Vulture Corp. New Account</span>
            </td>
        </tr>
        <tr valign="top">
            <td class="infoText" style="PADDING-LEFT:35px">
                <br>Enter the required fields below in order to
                create a new account. Click the Done button when
                you're finished.<br>
            </td>
        </tr>
        <tr>
            <td>
                <table cellpadding="0" cellspacing="5" border="0">
                    <tr>
                        <td width="35"></td>
                        <td colspan="2"></td>
                    </tr>
                    <tr>
                        <td width="35"></td>
                        <td>
                            <span class="inputLabel">User ID:</span>
                        </td>
                        <td>
                            <asp:TextBox ID="tbID"
                             Runat="server"></asp:TextBox>
                        </td>
                    </tr>
                    <tr>
                        <td width="35"></td>
                        <td>
                            <span
                             class="inputLabel">Password:</span>
                        </td>
                        <td>
                            <asp:TextBox ID="tbPwd"
```

```
                                        Runat="server"></asp:TextBox>
                                </td>
                            </tr>
                            <tr>
                                <td width="35"></td>
                                <td></td>
                                <td>
                                    <input type="submit" id="btnSave"
                                     name="btnSave" value="Done"
                                     runat="server">
                                </td>
                            </tr>
                            <tr>
                                <td width="35"></td>
                                <td></td>
                                <td class="errMsg">
                                    <asp:Label ID="lblInfo"
                                     Runat="server"></asp:Label>
                                </td>
                            </tr>
                        </table>
                    </td>
                </tr>
            </table>
            </form>
        </body>
</HTML>
```

There's not much that's different from the login page. There are two TextBox controls for the desired ID and password, as well as a button for users to tell the system that they're done. The code behind the page follows:

```
Imports System.Data.SqlClient
Imports System.Web.Security

Public Class prj08new
    Inherits System.Web.UI.Page
    Protected WithEvents tbID As System.Web.UI.WebControls.TextBox
    Protected WithEvents tbPwd As System.Web.UI.WebControls.TextBox
    Protected WithEvents lblInfo As System.Web.UI.WebControls.Label
    Protected WithEvents btnSave As
        System.Web.UI.HtmlControls.HtmlInputButton

#Region " Class Data and Types "

    ' Database connection string. We're using SQL Server. Change this if
    ' you want to use something else, like the Access db included with
    ' the book.
    Private Const CONNSTR As String = "PERSIST SECURITY INFO=False; " & _
        "DATA SOURCE=tony; INITIAL CATALOG=prj08; UID=sa; PWD=;"
```

```
#End Region

#Region " User Code "

    Private Sub SaveAccount(ByVal sID As String, ByVal sPWD As String)

        Dim conn As New SqlConnection(CONNSTR)
        Dim sSQL As String
        Dim cmd As New SqlCommand()

        ' First see if the user ID already exists in the DB.
        ' It must be unique.
        sSQL = "SELECT COUNT(*) FROM VultureUser WHERE ID='" & sID & "'"
        cmd.CommandText = sSQL
        cmd.Connection = conn
        Dim da As New SqlDataAdapter(cmd)
        Dim ds As New DataSet("idcount")
        Dim theRow As DataRow

        ' See if the requested new account already exists in the
        ' database.
        Try
            conn.Open()
            da.Fill(ds)
            conn.Close()
            theRow = ds.Tables(0).Rows(0)
            If CInt(theRow(0)) > 0 Then
                Throw (New System.Exception( _
                "That user ID already exists. Please select another."))
            End If
        Catch ex As SqlException
            Throw (New System.Exception( _
            "Could not create new user account. Try again later."))
        End Try

        ' Try to insert the new user account into the database.
        sSQL = "INSERT INTO VultureUser (ID, pwd) VALUES ('" & _
                sID & "', '" & sPWD & "')"
        cmd.CommandText = sSQL
        Try
            conn.Open()
            cmd.ExecuteNonQuery()
            conn.Close()
        Catch ex As SqlException
            Throw (New System.Exception( _
            "Could not create new user account. Try again later."))
        End Try
    End Sub

#End Region
```

```
#Region " Event Handlers "

    Private Sub Page_Load(ByVal sender As System.Object, _
        ByVal e As System.EventArgs) Handles MyBase.Load
        'Put user code to initialize the page here
    End Sub

    Private Sub btnSave_ServerClick(ByVal sender As System.Object, _
        ByVal e As System.EventArgs) Handles btnSave.ServerClick

        ' Take in the user's requested user ID and password, then add
        ' them to the database. If the user ID already exists, tell
        ' the user to try again.
        Try
            SaveAccount(tbID.Text, tbPwd.Text)
            lblInfo.Text = ""
            Response.Redirect("..\default.aspx")
        Catch ex As Exception
            lblInfo.Text = ex.Message()
        End Try

    End Sub

#End Region

#Region " Web Form Designer Generated Code "

    'This call is required by the Web Form Designer.
    <System.Diagnostics.DebuggerStepThrough()>
    Private Sub InitializeComponent()

    End Sub

    Private Sub Page_Init(ByVal sender As System.Object,
        ByVal e As System.EventArgs) Handles MyBase.Init
        'CODEGEN: This method call is required by the Web Form Designer
        'Do not modify it using the code editor.
        InitializeComponent()
    End Sub

#End Region

End Class
```

Like the other form, we import the SqlClient and Web.Security namespaces and create our database connection string. The real meat of the module is the SaveAccount method. It takes in the user-entered ID and password and uses standard ADO.NET techniques to do two things with them. First, it retrieves a COUNT(*) on the database for any matches on the user ID. If there are any results, the ID is a duplicate and the user has to try again. If it is not a duplicate, it then attempts to insert the new record in the database.

Notice that this time we are throwing our own custom exceptions if there are errors or conditions of our own that represent errors. Using this technique is not only solid error handling, but it also allows us to create accurate error messages for the user that are very easy to display later.

The event handler for the Done button, *btnSave_ServerClick*, is very simple. It calls the SaveAccount method inside a Try..Catch block. If any exceptions are thrown, we only have to display the message in the exception object for the user. If everything is okay, we redirect users to the login page to log in. Of course, we could just go ahead and log them in ourselves.

The Default Form

The Default form is merely a placeholder to represent your application's main page. It gives us something to secure. We create it as default.aspx so that we are, in effect, securing the entry into the Web site. The form looks like Figure 8.6, and the ASP/HTML code follows:

Figure 8.6   The Default form.

```
<%@ Page Language="vb" AutoEventWireup="false"
Codebehind="default.aspx.vb" Inherits="prj08.Cdefault"%>
<!DOCTYPE HTML PUBLIC "-//W3C//DTD HTML 4.0 Transitional//EN">
<HTML>
    <HEAD>
        <LINK rel="stylesheet" type="text/css" href="Styles.css">
        <title>Vulture Corp. Info</title>
        <meta name="GENERATOR" content="Microsoft Visual Studio.NET 7.0">
        <meta name="CODE_LANGUAGE" content="Visual Basic 7.0">
        <meta name="vs_defaultClientScript" content="JavaScript">
        <meta name="vs_targetSchema"
         content="http://schemas.microsoft.com/intellisense/ie5">
    </HEAD>
    <body style="margin:0px; padding:0px">
        <form id="Form1" method="post" runat="server">
        <table cellspacing="0" cellpadding="0" border="0" width="600">
            <tr valign="middle">
                <td background="images/vc_prj08.jpg" height="91"
                 colspan="2">
                    <span class="pageTitle">    
                              
                       Vulture Corp. Info</span>
                </td>
            </tr>
            <tr>
                <td>
                    <p class="infoText" style="padding-left:25px;
                     padding-top:15px">
                        This page represents your application's main
                        page.
                        If you got here, you must have been
                        authenticated!
                    </p>
                </td>
            </tr>
        </table>
        </form>
    </body>
</HTML>
```

Running the Project

At this point everything should be ready to roll. Build the project, and just to make sure everything is set up correctly, test the program externally from your browser. If you are working locally, you can use localhost to test it out, using the following URL: http://localhost/prj08.

Figure 8.7   The result of supplying invalid login information.

That should be all you need; it will try to load the default.aspx file in the root directory of the Web directory. Because of the way we configured the security using the web.config file, the request will be automatically redirected to our prj08login.aspx page. It should come up first. Enter valid login credentials, and you should be sent on to your requested page. If not, you'll get an error message, as shown in Figure 8.7.

Note that you could put any number of pages you like in the application root directory. If a user tries to access any of them (not just default.aspx) without being authenticated first, he or she will be sent to the login page. I'm no hacker, but I don't know of any way to get around this, and it seems pretty secure to me.

Enhancing the Project

This project gave you an overview of security and some details about Web security. It is certainly enough information to achieve a level of security that is acceptable for lower security needs on any sort of Web site. However, security is a vast and complex subject, one that you could spend a long time researching and playing with.

There are plenty of opportunities for adding functionality to this project. Many topics were only briefly discussed here, and some were not dealt with at all. Try some of these ideas for fun:

Secure your passwords. Using encryption and Authentication Ticket, you can make sure that passwords are encrypted on the client before they're sent over the HTTP wire and then decrypted on the server once they are received. This will complete the final step needed to solidly secure your site.

Improve the user data. We only stored primitive information about the user in the database. You could add a few more useful fields, including email address, home address, phone, and full name.

Validate fields. It would be a simple matter to add some of the ASP validator controls to the forms. The RequiredFieldValidator is a perfect example and can be used to make sure that the user has entered something in all the fields before trying to authenticate the user.

Email password feature. Users always forget passwords. Unless you don't mind personally calling them all to remind them of their passwords, you could send them out automatically. Ask the users for their ID; then look up their password and email address in the database and send it to them. If you want to get fancy, store a secret question and answer during the new account process. Then you could ask them the question and if they supply the correct answer, display the password for them.

WHAT'S COMING NEXT

Our next project is my favorite in the whole book. Web content and applications are fun to build. However, what would you say if I said you could easily build Web sites and applications for cell phones and other Web-enabled devices?

That's exactly what we'll be doing using the Microsoft Mobile Web SDK and Visual Studio .NET. We will create a Web site that uses ASP.NET, database access and even separate middle-tier business components to provide useful, current information to your company's employees through mobile devices. It will be exciting enough to make you go out and get a Web-enabled cell phone if you don't have one.

Employee Information System Using the Mobile Toolkit

If you watch television at all, you have surely seen one or more of the many advertisements for cell phone service providers. One in particular struck me, in which two people are sitting on a wooded cliff overlooking a dark city. They begin to access all sorts of features through their mobile phones, such as booking flights, reserving theater tickets, and accessing movie schedules. As they access each feature, parts of the city start to light up. I always thought that being able to access functionality like that from anywhere was a powerful capability, and I think that I'm right. The most amazing thing is that now the ability to provide this functionality can reside with any reasonably competent VB programmer.

An extension to ASP.NET and Visual Studio, the Mobile Internet Toolkit, adds functionality that allows you to build ASP.NET applications that are targeted toward Web-enabled personal devices, such as PDAs and cell phones. You can build applications very much like those in the television commercials. It's all very compelling.

All sorts of possibilities are opened up by the Mobile Internet Toolkit. Some are not so good; you may see a huge outpouring of really bad Web sites all over your cell phone. However, the positive possibilities are much more likely. Our project presents just one of those possibilities and will help you keep the employees of your company well informed.

THE PROBLEM:

As engineers, we are often asked to provide information to customers and other employees. Often, easy access to time-sensitive information is the problem. If information is not accessible, it usually gets ignored and is not seen. We also need to be able to provide information to remote employees and to employees during off hours.

THE SOLUTION:

A Web site is an obvious solution as a means to present data to remote and off-hours employees. However, not all of them will have access to a computer. With the incredible proliferation of Web-enabled devices like PDAs and cell phones, it would be beneficial to be able to provide the information to those platforms. Our project will do just that. We will build a Web application using the Microsoft Mobile Internet Toolkit and Visual Basic .NET that provides employees with access to important company information.

The Project

Our mobile employee information Web site consists of two primary parts: the business component and the Web front end. We'll cover each, including:

1. **Business component.**   Our site will need support on the back end, and we'll be creating a standalone class that will provide us with database support and anything else we might need.

2. **The Web application.**   We'll use the Mobile Internet Toolkit, Visual Basic .NET, and ASP.NET to create the main application. This is the fun part wherein we construct the mobile Web site that users will access through cell phones; it will include features like weather alerts, company announcements, company phone lookup, company events, and a next holiday function.

3. **Test it out.**   We'll test the program out once it's complete using the emulator, but you'll definitely want to give it a try with a Web-enabled cell phone.

You Will Need

✔ **Visual Studio .NET**

✔ **The Mobile Internet Toolkit SDK**

✔ **Microsoft Mobile Explorer 3.0 or later**

✔ **A basic knowledge of Visual Basic .NET**

✔ **Internet Information Server**

✔ **SQL Server (or other database)**

✔ **A basic knowledge of ASP.NET**

Technology Overview

The idea behind remote Web technology is not new. Back in 1996 when the first Windows CE devices came out, they came with Pocket Internet Explorer installed. You could use it to browse the Web, but it was designed to be small and simple and could only handle fairly simple Web sites. Even those had no color, and the device had limited screen space. The solution was a half-hearted recommendation from Microsoft that content providers make CE versions of their sites that were tuned to the limited capabilities of Pocket IE. This didn't go over well for many reasons, and you rarely saw Pocket IE versions of Web sites, unless the sites were about Windows CE.

Mobile devices today, particularly cell phones, have taken a different approach. They have their own browsers, often non-Microsoft browsers. The concept of the content they provide and form in which they provide it are completely different. Content is usually provided specifically for them, tuned to the device's capabilities. In addition, the availability of a large number of Web-enabled cell phones at reasonable prices has made them a success. It is into this world of customized Web content that we delve.

It would normally be quite a pain to create Web content that is customized for different mobile devices, especially given the wide variety of hardware and software running on them. You would either create your own generic isolation layer that would allow you to write generic code, which would get translated to something device specific, or go insane trying to write code for each device. The really, really good news, and the primary reason that mobile Web content will soon skyrocket, is that Microsoft has created the Mobile Internet Toolkit.

This Toolkit is essentially an add-in to Microsoft Visual Studio .NET that provides you with extensions, designers, and tools that allow you to easily create mobile Web content. Not only that, but it allows you to create code that will work on almost any portable Web-enabled device. If you need to go past the generic capabilities it provides, you can also write device-specific code. Microsoft even made it fairly easy to create your content, with excellent tools and controls, which I'll be covering in detail.

The Basic Idea

The first bonus that you run into with the Mobile Toolkit is that it's based on ASP.NET. If you know ASP.NET, you'll have a great start on mobile Web content. The process you use to create mobile Web sites is the same one you use to create regular ASP.NET Web sites or applications. You can write ASP code using any editor, or you can allow the tools to generate it for you. Other bonuses include a complete suite of controls that are made specifically for the mobile environment. Everything runs in regular old Internet Information Server, so you don't need anything special beyond the Mobile Toolkit SDK. Everything is rendered in device-independent HTML that is tuned for mobile devices. The Toolkit and your own code handle dealing with the fact that you're targeting mobile devices.

On the Device

Each device has its own particular implementation of a Web browser to interpret the content you create. PocketPCs have a version of Pocket IE. Cell phones have their own mini-browsers. We will be concentrating on cell phones for the following reasons:

- They're cheaper and more prolific.
- They are more or less the lowest common denominator, and code that we create for them will be upwardly compatible with devices like PocketPCs.

There are several mini-browsers from different manufacturers, each of which may have slightly different capabilities. Some support different flavors of HTML, such as cHTML or WML. However, the code that is emitted from the Mobile Toolkit should work on any of them.

Web Content for Cell Phones

If you haven't used the Web through a cell phone before, you might be a little under-whelmed. It's almost entirely black-and-white text right now (although there are browsers and phones in development that supply limited graphics and color). Not much will fit on one page, and you have limited navigation capabilities, usually only up and down arrows. Consequently, content for mobile devices must be handled differently. Some basic guidelines to follow when designing mobile content include:

Think small.   Web pages can scroll a little, vertically, but are severely limited in width. Your content must fit in this small space. For example, the display on my cell phone is four lines long and 96 pixels wide.

Focus your content.   This involves rethinking how a Web page is designed. You must limit the content of a Web page to a single, focused purpose. Concentrate on having less content per page and more pages.

Content, not appearance.   The display capabilities of the mini-browser are very limited, usually only black-and-white colors and very limited graphics. They tend to be mostly text, even the controls. Keep your content focused and don't worry too much about fancy visuals.

Reduce user input.   Remember that users are working with a cell phone, and input can be difficult. If you need input, try to use simple selections that users can make from lists or keep the input numeric. Alphabetic input is the most difficult for users to enter. You don't want people trying to enter the name of the movie they want to see while driving down the road.

You'll get a good idea of what's possible and practical by looking at the Web content that is available for mobile devices. Notice what sort of graphics limitations they have, how their content and user inputs are organized, and what kind of performance they have.

Tools Available

Visual Studio already provides you with excellent tools to design forms, build code, and debug and deploy your applications and components. You will continue to use these tools when building mobile Web content. However, you will also need the Mobile Internet Toolkit SDK.

The SDK, an add-on from Visual Studio, adapts the tools in Visual Studio to help you develop mobile content. The form designer will handle mobile forms and ASP pages. You also get a new category on the toolbar: Mobile Controls. The control list is quite extensive and can handle almost anything you might need to do. You will also be able to debug your mobile applications. The SDK is a free download from Microsoft.

In addition, available as a separate download, the Microsoft Mobile Explorer (MME) is an emulator, a version of Internet Explorer that emulates an actual cell phone mini-browser. The MME integrates tightly with Visual Studio and is the runtime environment for your mobile applications. When you run the application, it comes up in the MME (once you configure it to do so; more on this later). Figure 9.1 shows what the MME emulator looks like. Microsoft even went so far as to make it look like a cell phone.

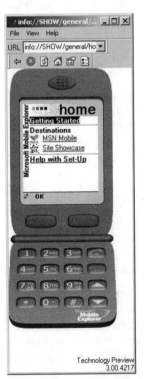

Figure 9.1   The Microsoft Mobile Explorer cell phone emulator.

Mobile Web Development

Mobile Web development is similar to ASP.NET development, but there are plenty of differences and unique aspects to this particular flavor. We'll be covering all the mobile Web development topics that you need to know to get rolling building your own applications.

How to Write a Mobile Web Application: An Overview

I always seem to understand new topics better when I have a quick overview and then fill in the details. Therefore, that's how we're going to start. An overview of the process can be a big help when it comes to understanding the individual topics we'll be covering. The steps listed below illustrate how to create your own mobile Web application, although there may be deviations given your own needs.

1. Create a new mobile Web application project in Visual Studio. This application type will be available to you once the Mobile Application Framework SDK is installed on your computer. Like other ASP applications, it creates the project in your InetPub directory under IIS.

2. Create any style sheets you might like to use. Style sheets are a powerful way to control the appearance of your application, and they are best created before you design your forms so that they can be used when the form is ready.

3. Layout your forms. The form designer has been updated and includes mobile controls in the toolbox. Create any forms you like, dropping controls on them as required. This works very much like designing Web forms.

4. Write code behind your controls and forms. This works just like VB, but you also have access to IIS objects. Your code will be a little different for mobile Web applications, but it is 98 percent like regular Visual Basic.

5. Run your application. It can be debugged much like regular applications. It will run in the MME.

6. Deploy your application. Place it on an IIS 5.0 server as you would any other Web site or application. Make sure the Mobile Internet Toolkit SDK is installed on the IIS server.

These steps should look very familiar. There are variations you can use as well. For example, when you use the form designer, it creates ASP code behind the scenes. If you prefer, you can, of course, create the ASP code yourself in text mode (you can toggle back and forth between Design and HTML view). Whatever your preferences, the tools make it easy for you to get your job done. However, some of the work is still up to you. One of the requirements you must meet is that every mobile ASP page must start with the same header, as follows:

```
<%@ Register TagPrefix="mobile" Namespace="System.Web.UI.MobileControls"
Assembly="System.Web.Mobile" %>
<%@ Page Language="vb" AutoEventWireup="false"
Codebehind="default.aspx.vb" Inherits="prj09.MobileWebForm1" %>
```

The first line you can include as is. The second one changes based on your specific application. If you use the form designer, these will be generated for you. If not, make sure you create them yourself.

Your code is actually built as a code-behind module. It is referenced as a code-behind module in the ASP code. You can see the reference to the module in the preceding ASP header.

Using Pages and Forms

VB programmers are used to the concept of forms. They are distinct units of UI that represent windows. Web programmers are used to the concept of pages. Each page is a distinct unit of UI directed to a specific purpose. Mobile applications have both concepts.

A form is actually a control, a container, that can hold other controls. A page can contain multiple forms. A form represents a distinct page on the mobile Web browser that can be seen and interacted with by the user. However, it is the page that is downloaded all at once to the client. You can place multiple forms on a single page and, through code, change which form is active. Only the active form, of which there is only one, can be visible on the browser at one time.

The mobile ASP page has a property called ActiveForm. It takes the name of one of the forms on the page and when set, makes that form the visible one. The first form defined on the page is the visible one by default. For example, you have two forms on a single page, Form1 and Form2. You could attach an event to any control on Form1, such as a command control, which calls the following line of code:

```
ActiveForm = Form2
```

This will change the form that is displayed on the UI. As mentioned, when designing Web UI for mobile devices, you need to think small and keep each form focused to a single function. This could mean that to build a particular function, you might need several forms. Suppose, for example, that you are presenting a Web page to list movie times. You would need to perform the following steps before actually presenting the movie times:

1. Get a ZIP code from the user.
2. Present a list of theaters to the user based on ZIP code and get the user's selection.
3. Present a list of films at the theater based on the user's theater selection.
4. Present a list of movie times based on the user's film selection.

A mobile form would represent each of these steps. All the forms for this related function could be placed on a single page. This is a standard and efficient design technique for mobile applications. It strikes a balance between forms and pages, preventing:

- Too many forms from collecting on a single page, which would make it inefficient to download from a single request and result in long waits for the user

- Too many small pages with a single form each, which would result in a much larger number of expensive round trips to and from the server

It is also much faster to switch between forms on a page than it is to download more pages. Keep this in mind when organizing your forms and pages.

Hello, World!

I know that when I'm learning a new technology, I want to dive in quickly and get the feel of what's going on. It gives me a nice, warm, fuzzy feeling that I have a clue about how it works. Assuming that most programmers are like this to one degree or another, I'll present a quick walkthrough by creating a mobile Hello World program. The following steps (and indeed, the rest of the content in this project) require that all the proper tools are ready to go, including Visual Studio .NET, the Mobile Internet Toolkit, and the Microsoft Mobile Explorer.

This is as simple as it gets: a form, a couple of label controls, and no user-entered code.

Create a new project of the mobile Web application variety. Name it HelloWorld and click the OK button to have Visual Studio create it for you. Figure 9.2 shows the New Project dialog.

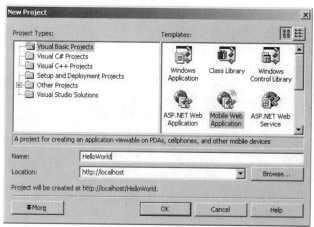

Figure 9.2   The New Project dialog for HelloWorld.

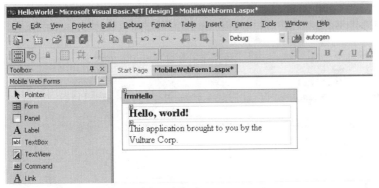

Figure 9.3   The HelloWorld mobile form.

Your project should start with one default form. Change the name of the form to frmHello in the properties window. Drag two label controls from the Mobile Controls and fill them in with the text illustrated in Figure 9.3.

Run the program by clicking the Play button or pressing F5. The application should show up in the Microsoft Mobile Explorer, as shown in Figure 9.4. You're done!

Figure 9.4   HelloWorld running in the emulator.

Lastly, let's take a quick peek at the ASP.NET code that was generated for us when we created the form (slightly reformatted to make it a little more legible):

```
<%@ Register TagPrefix="mobile" Namespace="System.Web.UI.MobileControls"
Assembly="System.Web.Mobile" %>
<%@ Page Language="vb" AutoEventWireup="false"
Codebehind="MobileWebForm1.aspx.vb" Inherits="HelloWorld.MobileWebForm1"
%>
<meta name="GENERATOR" content="Microsoft Visual Studio.NET 7.0">
<meta name="CODE_LANGUAGE" content="Visual Basic 7.0">
<meta name="vs_targetSchema" content="Mobile Web Page">

<body xmlns:mobile="Mobile Web Form Controls">

    <mobile:Form id="frmHello" runat="server">
    <mobile:Label id="Label1" runat="server" StyleReference="title">
     Hello, world!</mobile:Label>
    <mobile:Label id="Label2" runat="server">
     This application brought to you by the Vulture Corp.</mobile:Label>
    </mobile:Form>

</body>
```

There are a couple things to note here at this early stage. First, notice that the standard header for an ASP mobile application that we mentioned earlier has been included for us. Second, take a look at the tags that define the controls. Every one is preceded by the mobile attribute. This is required for mobile Web applications, and almost every tag will have the mobile attribute. Lastly, notice that all the controls have the following attribute:

```
Runat="server"
```

This is important, so let's talk about it.

Mobile Controls

The controls used on a mobile Web application are special creatures. With regular (non-mobile) applications and Web pages, you would include normal ActiveX controls, which would have to be downloaded to the client machine as binary images that can be executed by the browser. However, the browsers that run on mobile devices are not that sophisticated and cannot run ActiveX controls. Nor do they have anywhere to store items that large. And given the variety of browsers out there and the even larger variety of hardware on which they run, producing a binary that will run one each is impractical, to say the least.

The solution to the problem is a little gem called the Mobile Control. Each Mobile Control has the attribute mentioned earlier that tells the control to run at the server. These server-side Mobile Controls actually reside and execute on the server but not in the traditional sense. They execute on the server when the ASP code is requested and executed, and they emit generic HTML that looks and works like (to a greater or lesser degree depending on the browser) the actual control.

This type of control has plenty of advantages and is a clever idea. It allows you to work the controls in design mode, dropping them onto mobile forms and setting their properties. All these settings are translated to ASP code tags. The HTML for each control that is sent to the browser is generic and will work without worrying about binary compatibility. These controls are efficient because the HTML is much smaller than traditional binaries.

> **NOTE** Each Mobile Control has a fixed representation in design mode. When you drag a control onto a mobile form, it always looks the same to you. However, when you execute the program on a mobile device or in the emulator, the representation of the control might be quite different, though it will provide the functionality required in one way or another. The Calendar control is a perfect example. Try dropping a Calendar control onto a form and running the application. You'll see that it is not nearly the same as it was in design mode. Be prepared for this, and make sure you test all the controls on the emulator or a real mobile device before you settle on their use.

It is also worth noting that when you are designing forms, dragging and dropping controls onto forms, that controls can only be arranged vertically. They cannot be placed side by side (i.e., next to each other). Keep this in mind when you are planning your applications.

The Controls

Now that you know how they work, we're going to give you an overview and some examples of the more important controls that have been installed into your toolbox. The rest we'll leave to your own experimentation.

The Form Control

You've already had some basic exposure to the Form control. It's a control because it sits on an ASP page and needs to be rendered as HTML like any other control. You use the Form control to segregate mobile browser pages (not to be confused with ASP pages). They can be submitted to the server just like pages can. For example, they have a Method property that you can set to Get or Post, just like an ASP page for a form. There are also a few other properties you can use to control the appearance, such as Alignment and Font.

The Form is used to control what is on displayed in the browser window at any given time. The Form control was illustrated in Figure 9.3. When you need to change the currently visible form on the screen, you use the ActriveForm property of the page and assign it the name of the form you want to display, as in:

```
ActiveForm = frmResults
```

The Label Control

The Label control is very simple and works just like the label controls you are used to from normal Visual Basic forms. Simply set the Text property to change what it displays. The Label control was illustrated in Figure 9.3.

The Command Control

All users need a button that they can click on to make stuff happen. The Command control is the mobile version of the command button. It shows up in design mode as a button but may be rendered on the mobile device as a text link. It works just like a button, allowing you to change its caption and attach events to it.

The Text Control

The Text control is the mobile equivalent of the TextBox control. It allows you to accept alphanumeric user input. It does not have all the properties and capabilities of the regular TextBox, but it is sufficient for the mobile platform. Under certain circumstances and on varying platforms, the Text control will expand to become full-screen on the mobile device display so that more input can be entered.

You can change the style of the Text control to accept only numeric input (using the Numeric property) or to act like a password Text control, displaying only asterisks for the entered data (using the Password property). Make sure you test these features out on your target client device because some of them don't support these options.

It is a good idea to limit the use of the Text control. Directly entered values are the most cumbersome for users to supply. It is best to use controls that do not require data entry, such as List controls and Calendars, to collect input.

The TextView Control

The TextView control is similar to the RichText control in VB. It is intended to display larger volumes of text information with formatting. This control, unlike others of its ilk, can use HTML codes to format it. You can, for example, put your own line breaks in with the <BR> tag. If your display device supports it, you can also format text using bold attributes and other appearance attributes. The TextView control has a Text property that you can use to set its contents.

The Link Control

The Link control acts exactly like the Anchor tag, or link, on a Web page. Drop the control on a form and assign a Text value and URL to it, and you have a navigation link. Pretty simple.

The List Control

The List control is meant simply to display information in list form, much like the <UL> or <OL> lists in good old HTML. Use it to format text into bulleted or numbered lists. The items in the list are stored as a collection called Items. You add to the Items collection either at design time, through the UI, or at runtime, through code. Adding items through the UI is easy; just use the provided UI in the properties window. If you want to add them at runtime, it goes something like this:

```
Dim i As New MobileListItem()
i.Text = "My First Item"
i.Value = "1"
List1.Items.Add(i)
```

This will add one item to the list. Note, however, that you cannot reuse the declared object i for subsequent items. Each must be created separately. Otherwise, you will end up with a lot of list item references to the same MobileListItem object, and all the items that appear in the list will be the same.

You can also data bind the MobileListItem to a data source, including a DataSet. This will be covered in the Data Binding section.

The SelectionList Control

Although the List control is only used to display lists of items, the SelectionList control is used to allow the user to select from a list of items. It works very much like the List control in terms of adding items to the list. However, it also requires another control, such as a Command control, that will allow users to indicate that they are done making their selection. This control can also be used in multi-select mode, allowing users to make several selections before they are done.

The control allows the user to make selections but won't actually tell you when the user is done. That's up to you. Our little example here shows a form with a Selection list and a Command control that has an event attached to it, like an OK button. Figure 9.5 shows our forms in design mode.

Add some simple code to handle the click on the Command control, taking the selected value from the list and placing it in the Label control on the second form. Then make the second form active. The code is as follows:

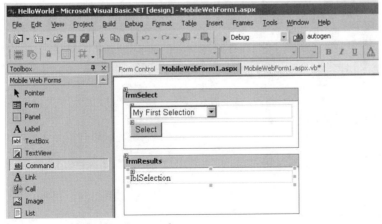

Figure 9.5 SelectionList on a form.

```
Private Sub Command1_Click(ByVal sender As System.Object, _
    ByVal e As System.EventArgs) Handles Command1.Click
    lblSelection.Text = SelectionList1.Selection.Text
    ActiveForm = frmResults
End Sub
```

The ObjectList Control

Another control in our list of lists, the ObjectList control, lets you create a list of objects. Often you will use this to store a list of instances of your own classes or rows of information in a DataSet. Add items to it just like the other list controls. You can add objects to the list either manually through code (a little tedious) or through data binding. There will be more on this later.

The Calendar Control

The Calendar control allows you to display a calendar of some sort on the client device. In design mode, it looks just like a month calendar, as in Figure 9.6. When it is rendered on a device, it could look quite different. However, it still allows a user to select a date. It will also allow a user to enter a date manually, rather than selecting it from a list.

The PhoneCall Control

The PhoneCall control is really cool. Drop it on a form and set its Text property, and it shows up on the display with the label you provide it. Set its PhoneNumber property, and when the user clicks on it (selects it), it will tell the cell phone to make the call.

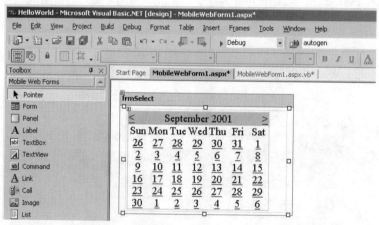

Figure 9.6   The Calendar control.

This is a very powerful capability. Any phone number that you present to the user can become a link that will allow the user to call that number immediately without dialing. We use this feature in this project.

And the Rest

There are a few additional Mobile Controls at your disposal. I won't be covering them in detail, but the summary of the rest of them in Table 9.1 will show you what's available.

Input Validation

The Mobile Internet Toolkit has some nice controls that make user input validations much easier. They help you reduce user input errors on the client before they get to the server. This makes server round trips more efficient because you're not sending erroneous input back and forth. That's why these controls were provided.

The controls each handle a specific type of validation, such as a comparison for a value or range of values. I'm going to pick one of them, the RequiredFieldValidator, and show you how it works. The other controls are similar, with a few differences based on the specific control involved. You can look them up to see how they work. For now, let's look at one example. Figure 9.7 shows a couple forms that you can create to test out our validator.

Table 9.1   Remaining Mobile Controls Summary

CONTROL	DESCRIPTION
Panel	A container control on which you can place other controls.
StyleSheet	Allows you to attach a style sheet to your application and control the appearance of the content.
Ad Rotator	Cycles images with links attached to them and presents advertisements to the user.
Validator Controls	An assortment of controls that help with user input validation.

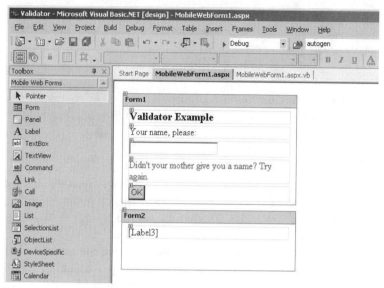

Figure 9.7 Validator control test forms.

The first form has a single TextBox that we can validate, a Command control to tell the page that we're done, and a RequiredFieldValidator control that we can use to validate the TextBox contents. Once you have the forms designed, set the properties of the RequiredFieldValidator as shown in Table 9.2.

Table 9.2 Validator Control Properties

PROPERTY	SETTING	DESCRIPTION
ID	rfv1	The ID is the control name referenced in code.
ControlToValidate	TextBox1	Set this to the specific control on the form that should be validated. The control to validate must be on the form before you set this property.
Text	\<see form\>	The text that is displayed when the control is visible in error.
Display	Dynamic	When set to dynamic, the control is visible when the control to validate is in error, and it is hidden when it is valid.
ErrorMessage	\<leave default\>	The ErrorMessage property is displayed when the control is in error. It is only displayed if the Text property is blank.

Now, add some code to the click event of the Command control, as follows:

```
Private Sub Command1_Click(ByVal sender As System.Object, _
    ByVal e As System.EventArgs) Handles Command1.Click

    If Page.IsValid Then
        Label3.Text = "Hi there, " & TextBox1.Text & _
            "! Thanks for telling us your name."
        ActiveForm = Form2
    End If

End Sub
```

The Page.IsValid property checks all the validation controls on the page and returns true if any are false. Our RequiredFieldValidator control automatically checks to make sure there is a value in the control to which it is assigned. If you leave our TextBox blank, the validator will return false, and the Page.IsValid property returns false. If it is false, the attached validator control automatically switches to error mode and displays itself and its error text. All the other validator controls work the same way; only their specific validations are different.

If Page.IsValid is true, meaning that the validator control is not in error, we can execute the success path, in this case, displaying the second form with the user's name. Figure 9.8 shows three images of the example during execution. The first is the basic UI, the second is the UI in its error state, and the last is its nonerror state.

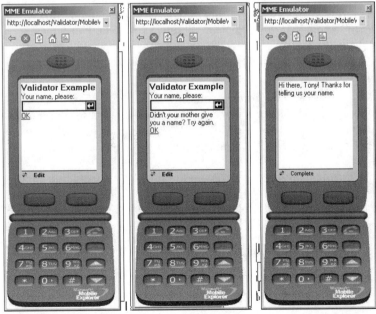

Figure 9.8 The Validator example during various stages of execution.

There are other validators and validation techniques at your disposal. Table 9.3 lists the rest of them and gives a brief description of each one.

You can also validate all the controls on the page at once using the Validation Summary control. It allows you to assign more than one validator control to a single control, performing several different kinds of checks on the control's value. The ValidationSummary control goes on a different form and is displayed if any of your validator controls are in error. The ValidationSummary control has a property called FormToValidate that you set to the form that contains the control to validate it and its validator controls. When the form containing the ValidationSummary control is displayed and the ValidationSummary control becomes active, it checks the state of all the validation controls on the page with which it is associated. It then displays all the errors from all the validator controls.

Displaying Images

You can display images in your mobile Web applications just like in other Web applications. However, there are limitations and design considerations that must be taken into account. For example, most Web-enabled cell phones cannot display color images; therefore, you must create your images accordingly.

Design Considerations

It is worth taking stock of the possible devices on which your mobile application will be used. Cell phones are the toughest because there are so many models. However, there are some basic assumptions you can stick to that will help you make sure that your mobile applications will work on most of the devices. Here are a few:

Use the lowest common denominator.   This applies to both size and color depth. Most devices are limited to about four lines of display room and a width of 96 pixels or less. If you keep your images to this size or smaller, you should be safe. Also, most phones can only display straight black-and-white images. A few support gray shades, but not enough to make it worthwhile yet. Stick to black and white for now.

Image formats.   There are several formats you can use, including BMP, JPG, and GIF. I have found, from a brief survey of cell phones and a few tests, that most of them handle GIF images the best. JPG images can have problems with the black-and-white color depth, and BMP images are significantly larger.

Displaying Images

It is pretty easy to display images using the Image control. Drag an Image control to your form and set its ImageURL property to point to the image. This works best if you add the image file to your project first using the Solution Explorer. Then the image will be easily available in the image browser for the ImageURL property.

You can also assign a URL link to an image using the NavigateURL property. This will make the image navigate to another URL when the image is selected and clicked.

Table 9.3   Summary of the Mobile Validation Controls

CONTROL	DESCRIPTION
RequiredFieldValidator	Makes sure there is a value of some sort in the associated control.
CustomValidator	Write your own validation code and use this control to attach it to another control.
Comparison Validator	Compare the value of two controls using the supplied comparison operators.
RangeValidator	Make sure that the value in the associated control is within a specified range.
RegularExpressionValidator	Check to make sure that the value in the associated control matches a supplied regular expression.

Pagination

Often you will have too much data to display on a single form. Pagination allows you to split the data into pages, either manually or automatically, to make display more convenient and efficient.

How It Works

Automatic pagination is the easiest to use form of pagination. You simply set the Paginate property of the form to true, and the server and the client will take care of automatically paginating your form content. For example, suppose you have a large list, such as a phone list, that is impractical to display on one page. The pagination feature will break the content into pages, inserting navigation controls for you to allow movement between the pages. It's pretty easy and suitable for most pagination needs.

This also works for forms that have lots of controls. If the form is too long, the system will insert page breaks between the controls on your form, splitting it into pages that the user can move between. If you do not like the way it breaks the pages for you, you can control it to some degree by placing your controls inside panels. The pagination system will not break within a panel, only between the panels themselves. However, paginated forms with controls are not so easy to use and should be restricted to those cases when they are absolutely needed.

You can also customize the pagination to some degree. The PagerStyle properties allow you to adjust the characteristics of the paging controls that are generated for you. They are shown in Figure 9.9. The most useful properties are the NextPageText and PreviousPageText properties. They allow you to change the text that is displayed for the next and previous page navigation controls. The rest are fairly obvious.

Figure 9.9   The PagerStyle properties.

If you have special cases where the automatic pagination does not operate the way you want it to, you can control it better by writing your own custom pagination code. Often referred to as *chunking*, this technique allows you to send partial data to the client pagination routine, holding the rest on the server until requested rather than sending all the data at once. If you have large amounts of data, this would be worth considering. However, it takes significantly more work than automatic pagination.

To Paginate or Not to Paginate

Usually you will want to stick with automatic pagination and use it when it is appropriate. For example, you could create a fairly long form with several controls that will not fit on the display. Automatic pagination would split it for you, but this is not terribly user friendly. You are better off not using pagination in this case and instead designing your form so that it fits on the screen better.

Data Binding

Controls in a mobile Web application can be bound to data sources very much like regular applications. On the server, you can load any data you like from a database and stuff it into a DataSet, which can be bound to controls. You can also create your own data and bind it to controls. For example, you could create your own class and create an ArrayList of instances of this class, binding the ArrayList to a control such as the ObjectList.

Controls that can be data bound have properties associated with them that handle the data binding. Each of them is important to grasp; they are explained in the following:

DataSource.   This property contains the name of the data container that holds all the data. This is usually a DataSet or an ArrayList, but it may also be a table or query.

DataMember.   A specific table, such as in a DataSet that can contain multiple tables.

DataItem.   A specific column from the DataSource or DataMember.

Often, setting the DataSource is sufficient to associate your data with your controls. Once you have these properties set, you call the DataBind() method to complete the connection. This is best illustrated by an example and comments about it along the way. We'll create a class called TVCharacters, make some instances of it, fill it with data, and then bind an array of the data to an ObjectList control. We'll see examples of data binding to actual DataSets in our project.

Start by creating a new mobile Web application. On the default form that shows up, drop an ObjectList control onto it. Now open the code window and we'll add some code to the PageLoad event. First is our TVCharacter class:

```
Public Class TVCharacter

    Private m_name As String
    Private m_show As String
    Private m_actor As String

    Public Sub New(ByVal sName As String, ByVal sShow As String, _
        ByVal sActor As String)
        m_name = sName
        m_show = sShow
        m_actor = sActor
    End Sub

    Public Property CharName() As String
        Get
            Return (m_name)
        End Get
        Set(ByVal Value As String)
            m_name = Value
        End Set
    End Property

    Public Property TVShow() As String
        Get
            Return (m_show)
        End Get
        Set(ByVal Value As String)
            m_show = Value
        End Set
    End Property

    Public Property Actor() As String
        Get
            Return (m_actor)
        End Get
        Set(ByVal Value As String)
```

```
                m_actor = Value
            End Set
    End Property

End Class
```

We have a basic class with three properties: CharName (the name of the TV character), TVShow (the name of the TV show where the character lives), and Actor (the actor who plays the character). There is also a simple constructor that allows you to create the objects by passing in data for all the properties.

Next we need some code to create a few of these objects and data bind them to the ObjectList. We put this code in the PageLoad event, which looks like this:

```
Private Sub Page_Load(ByVal sender As System.Object, _
    ByVal e As System.EventArgs) Handles MyBase.Load

    If (Not IsPostBack) Then

        Dim a As New ArrayList()
        Dim f(3) As ObjectListField
        Dim i As Int16

        For i = 0 To 2
            f(i) = New ObjectListField()
        Next

        a.Add(New TVCharacter("Homer Simpson", "The Simpsons", _
            "Dan Castellaneta"))
        a.Add(New TVCharacter("Sgt. Hans Shultz", "Hogans Heroes", _
            "John Banner"))
        a.Add(New TVCharacter("Basil Fawlty", "Fawlty Towers", _
            "John Cleese"))
        a.Add(New TVCharacter("Ginger Grant", "Gilligan's Island", _
            "Tina Louise"))

        f(0).DataField = "CharName"
        f(1).DataField = "TVShow"
        f(2).DataField = "Actor"

        For i = 0 To 2
            ObjectList1.Fields.Add(f(i))
        Next i

        ObjectList1.DataSource = a
        ObjectList1.DataBind()

    End If

End Sub
```

The code starts by surrounding everything with the following:

```
If (Not IsPostBack) Then
...
End If
```

This prevents the code from being run unintentionally, resulting in multiple erroneous copies of the objects being added to the list. Remove this check and then run the code to see what I mean. Next we create the ArrayList that will store our object instances and three ObjectListField objects that will represent our fields in the UI. Then we add four instances of our TVCharacter class, supplying each with data, and then stuff them into the ArrayList.

Now that our data is ready, we need to bind it. The first step is to create the fields in the ObjectList that will hold and display our data. The ObjectListFields we created earlier need to know which field of our data to display, and we do this through the DataField property of the ObjectFieldList. Assign the actual name of the property to the DataField. Once the ObjectListFields are set up, add them all to the Fields collection in the ObjectList control.

We're in the home stretch. Assign the ArrayList, a, to the DataSource property of the ObjectList, and then tell the ObjectList to complete the data binding with the DataBind method.

That takes care of everything. Note that a fair amount of this code is in support of the example classes that we need to illustrate the principles involved, and the process is easier than it looks. Run the program to see what we get. Figure 9.10 shows what the application looks like during execution.

Figure 9.10   The data binding example.

The left illustration in Figure 9.10 is how the application comes up, displaying the list with the first data field defined. Notice that each item looks like a link. You can click on each item in the list to see the rest of the fields, as shown in the right illustration of Figure 9.10. The complete record is shown on a second page to conserve screen space in the list.

So that's how it works. Later we'll see more data binding in our project.

Styles

Styles and style sheets in mobile Web applications work very much like styles in regular Web sites and Web applications. They are significantly more limited, however, and when used with a device with display capabilities as limited as those of a cell phone, are far less important. I will cover them briefly.

There are three ways of using styles in mobile Web applications: built-in styles, style properties, and style sheets (internal and linked). Built-in styles are predefined and can be used anywhere. At the time this was written, there were only two predefined styles: Title and Error. The Title style is usually represented as a larger and/or bold type. The Error style is usually rendered red (if the device can display colors). If you use these styles as intended, your text will be rendered properly on any mobile device. A simple example looks like this:

```
<mobile:label runat="server" stylereference="title">
    Hey, you!</mobile:label>
```

The second method involves using style attributes inline with your other controls or tags. For example, you could change the foreground color of a Command control using the following syntax:

```
<mobile:command runat="server" forecolor="#FF00FF" text="Purple"
    onclick="Purple_OnClick"/>
```

Lastly, you can create an actual style sheet that contains multiple styles. This can be implemented as an embedded or linked external style sheet. An embedded style sheet looks like this:

```
<mobile:stylesheet runat="server">
    <style name="purple" forecolor="#770077"/>
    <style name="purpleBigfont" stylereference="purple"
        font-size="large"/>
</mobile:stylesheet>
```

You get the idea. Use styles in mobile applications the way you do for other Web applications.

Mobile Capabilities

An object, called MobileCapabilities, is available for your use; it determines many capabilities of the browser in use on the client device. It is a lot like the Navigator object that you can use in regular Web sites to determine browser information. This object, however, has significantly more information for you. The basic usage is to create an instance of the object and then use its properties, like this:

```
Dim c As MobileCapabilities = CType(Request.Browser, MobileCapabilities)
If c.IsColor() Then
    ' Display using colors
Else
    ' Display using B&W
End If
```

You can use the information provided by the MobileCapabilities object to tune your display, formatting, and functionality to the capabilities of the device. There are lots of options, so this could take a while. It's easy to use, though, and even gives you a couple options for obtaining information. You can either use the properties, as shown in the preceding, or request the information by name, like this:

```
Dim c As MobileCapabilities = CType(Request.Browser, MobileCapabilities)
If Request.Browser("IsColor") Then
    ' Display using colors
Else
    ' Display using B&W
End If
```

Table 9.4 is a reference to all of the capabilities it provides.

Table 9.4   Mobile Capabilities Object Properties Reference

PROPERTY	RETURN TYPE	DESCRIPTION
ActiveXControls	Boolean	Determines whether or not the browser can handle ActiveX controls. This will always be false for the foreseeable future.
AOL	Boolean	Returns true if the client is running through America Online.
BackgroundSounds	Boolean	Returns true if the device supports the playing of background sounds.
Beta	Boolean	Returns true if the browser is a beta version.
Browser	String	Returns a string describing the browser in use. Two values I have seen are IE and Microsoft Mobile Explorer.

continues

Table 9.4 (Continued)

PROPERTY	RETURN TYPE	DESCRIPTION
CanInitiateVoiceCall	Boolean	Determines whether or not the device can make a phone call. For example, it would return false when executed on a PocketPC.
CanSendMail	Boolean	Tells you if the device can send email using the mailto: method.
GatewayMajorVersion	String	Gets the major version number of the wireless gateway in use.
GatewayMinorVersion	String	Gets the minor version number of the wireless gateway in use.
GatewayVersion	String	Gets the full version number of the wireless gateway in use.
HasBackButton	Boolean	Tells you if the browser supplies a Back button for navigation.
InputType	String	Lets you know what type of input mechanism is available on the device. Although there were no references about what the possible values are, I found the following possibilities: virtualKeyboard, telephoneKeyboard, telephoneKeypad, and keyboard.
IsColor	Boolean	If the display can show colors, this property returns true.
MaximumSoftkey LabelLength	Integer	Many cell phones have keys that can be defined and labeled by the software. This property tells you how much space is available for the screen labels for these buttons.
MobileDeviceManufacturer	String	Returns the name of the mobile device manufacturer.
MobileDeviceModel	String	Returns the particular model of the device being used.
NumberOfSoftKeys	Integer	Gives you the number of softkeys available for your use.
PreferredImageMIME	String	Delivers the name of the image type that is preferred by the device, such as image/gif.

PROPERTY	RETURN TYPE	DESCRIPTION
PreferredRenderingMIME	String	Returns the type of MIME content the device prefers, such as text/html.
PreferredRenderingType	String	Gives you the type of content that the device prefers. Some possible values are wml11, wml12, html32, and chtml10.
RendersBreaks AfterHtmlLists	Boolean	Tells if the device renders a break after HTML lists.
RendersBreaksAfter WmlAnchor	Boolean	Returns true if the device creates a break after a standalone anchor.
RendersWmlDo AcceptsInLine	Boolean	Tells you if the device creates a WML do accept for a button instead of a softkey.
RequiresHandheld FriendlyMetaTag	Boolean	Determines whether or not the device needs a metatag that tells the browser that it is handheld-compatible.
RequiresPhoneNumbers AsPlainText	Boolean	Some cell phones require plain text phone numbers rather than any special markup coding. This property returns true if this is the case.
RequiresUniqueHtml CheckboxNames	Boolean	Returns true if the device needs unique names for every <input> tag.
ScreenBitDepth	Integer	Returns the color depth of the display in bites per pixel.
ScreenCharactersHeight	Integer	Returns the height of the display in characters.
ScreenCharactersWidth	Integer	Returns the width of the screen in characters.
ScreenPixelsHeight	Integer	Returns the height of the screen in pixels.
ScreenPixelsWidth	Integer	Returns the width of the screen in pixels.
SupportCSS	Boolean	If the display supports CSS attributes for fonts, this property returns true.

Preparing Your Development Environment

We're getting close to the project, so we'd better make sure that your development environment is ready to go. There are a few things you'll need to get set up before any actual coding takes place. You'll also need to get the SDK installed and your emulator running. You might actually want to try things out on a real mobile device, too.

Install the SDK

This is pretty simple, but it has to happen before you can do any mobile Web development. Download the Mobile Internet Toolkit SDK from Microsoft. It's actually fairly compact, given what it does for you. You must have Visual Studio .NET installed prior to installing the SDK. When you have downloaded and installed the SDK, you will have access to the language extensions, the object libraries, the mobile Web controls, and the documentation.

Install the Emulator

Testing your application on a real mobile device is not only cumbersome and difficult to debug, but it can also be expensive, given the current mobile Internet access rates. Therefore, most of the mini-browser manufacturers, including Microsoft, have created emulators that run on your PC and act just like the device. The easiest and most generic one to use is the MME. You can download this from Microsoft at no cost. You have already seen it in the illustrations used for this project. Simply install it and Visual Studio will list it in the available browsers in the Browse With context menu in the Solution Explorer.

The emulator is easy to use, and it integrates very nicely with Visual Studio .NET. It works with the debugging system directly, and you can even dock it into your Visual Studio environment. The MME was used for all the testing and execution of all the code for this project.

If you are targeting a specific device, or would like to test your application on some specific devices, you might try looking at manufacturers' Web sites. Many manufacturers of cell phones or browsers provide emulators for their own hardware or software. You can usually download them at no cost. For example, Phone.com makes one of the more popular cell phone browsers and has an SDK and emulator of its own. You can even download skins for the emulator that look exactly like specific cell phone models.

Using a Real Mobile Device

Eventually you will want to make sure that your mobile Web application actually works on a real device. When you create a mobile Web application, Visual Studio creates the project directly in IIS. If the machine on which you develop the application can be connected to the Internet as a server, you can simply add a bookmark to it in your cell phone that points to your machine's IP address and the project directory. If not, you'll have to post your application to a server that has IIS 5.0 and the Mobile Internet Toolkit SDK installed and also has an Internet connection.

Let's Start the Project

Finally we arrive at the project that we'll be building using the Mobile Internet Toolkit SDK and Visual Basic. You will be making use of a fair amount of what you have learned so far when we created our Employee Information Application. It is targeted toward cell phones but should also work well with a PDA. Here are the features we will implement:

Weather alert.   If other companies are like mine, they are occasionally closed due to inclement weather. I normally have to call a phone number, a number that I can never remember, to check whether or not I should come in to work. Therefore I have provided a feature that anyone with a Web-enabled cell phone can access. It simply displays the company status for today, open or closed, with any message you would like to attach.

Announcements.   Companies make many announcements to employees, and it is important that the employees have access to them. This feature simply displays those announcements on their cell phone.

Company Events.   Companies have all kinds of events, from holiday parties to massive layoffs. Whatever the case, employees need to know about them. This feature allows users to select a date from a Calendar control, and all events for the month in which their selected dates falls are displayed.

Next holiday.   This feature is likely to be extremely popular. It looks at today's date and displays the next paid company holiday.

Phone lookup.   This feature is an online employee phone book. Users can enter an employee's last name, or the first part of a last name, and it will return any matches in a list. They can then see the entire record, including first and last name, phone number, and extension (if any). The best part, though, is that users can highlight the desired person and directly call the number without dialing it.

Design of the Application

It would be fairly easy to build this application in one big ASP.NET page with embedded code. That is not an ideal application design because it would be large, resulting in long download times. In addition, it would not be terribly reusable. So instead I have opted to break out the business functionality, largely database access routines, into a business component that we will compile as a DLL from a Class Library. UI code will go into the ASP page, which will contain all our forms on one page. The way I've split the business functionality out, you could easily use the same component for the back end of a normal Web site, such as your company's intranet site.

We need to create a database as well. It's a simple database with five tables and no relationships. The design of the tables is illustrated in Figure 9.11.

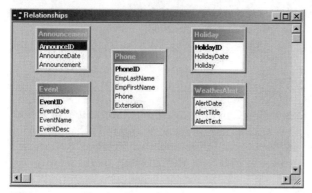

Figure 9.11 The database design.

Our application was written for Microsoft SQL Server. There is a Microsoft Access database on the accompanying CD-ROM that you can either import into SQL Server or change the code (particularly the connection string and the data access objects) so that you can read the Access database instead.

Part 1: The Business Component

The business component we're building has five methods in it, all of which perform essentially the same function: data retrieval. Some of the functions require special logic, most of which has been implemented in the SQL statements. I'll point it out when I use it. For now, let's just look at all the code at once, and then I'll discuss a few of the more interesting features.

Create a new project in Visual Studio, a standard Class Library. I called mine prj09logic. Rename the default class module MobileSvcs. Now we're ready to add code. The following listing is the complete content of the class:

```
Option Strict On
Option Explicit On

Imports System.Data.SqlClient

Public Class MobileSvcs

#Region " Class Data and Types "

    ' Database connection string. We're using SQL Server. Change this if
    ' you want to use something else, like the Access db included with
    ' the book.
    Private Const CONNSTR As String = "PERSIST SECURITY INFO=False; " & _
```

```
        "DATA SOURCE=tony; INITIAL CATALOG=prj09; UID=sa; PWD=;"

#End Region

#Region " User Code "

    ' This method retrieves the weather alert record from the database.
    Public Function GetWeatherAlert() As DataSet

        Dim conn As SqlConnection = New SqlConnection(CONNSTR)
        Dim sSQL As String

        ' SQL to retrieve alert rows that are current. By design,
        ' only one row is ever intended to be in there, reflecting
        ' the current state of the company.
        sSQL = "SELECT * FROM WeatherAlert WHERE AlertDate <= '" & _
            Now & "'"

        ' Get our data objects ready for retrieval.
        Dim da As SqlDataAdapter = New SqlDataAdapter(sSQL, conn)
        Dim ds As DataSet = New DataSet()

        ' Load the data.
        Try
            conn.Open()
            da.Fill(ds, "Alerts")
            conn.Close()
            GetWeatherAlert = ds
        Catch ex As SqlException
            GetWeatherAlert = Nothing
        End Try

    End Function

    ' This method loads announcement data from the database.
    Public Function GetAnnouncements() As DataSet

        Dim conn As SqlConnection = New SqlConnection(CONNSTR)
        Dim sSQL As String

        ' In this case, we simply retrieve all rows. It is assumed that
        ' the data will be properly maintained, with old records being
        ' removed on a regular basis.
        ' We added the DESC clause to bring the events back with the
        ' most recent events coming in first.
        sSQL = "SELECT * FROM Announcement ORDER BY AnnounceDate DESC"

        ' Get our data objects ready for retrieval.
        Dim da As SqlDataAdapter = New SqlDataAdapter(sSQL, conn)
```

```vbnet
        Dim ds As DataSet = New DataSet()

        ' Load the data.
        Try
            conn.Open()
            da.Fill(ds, "Announcements")
            conn.Close()
            GetAnnouncements = ds
        Catch ex As SqlException
            GetAnnouncements = Nothing
        End Try

End Function

' This method loads a list of matching employee phone
' records from the database. The sName parameter is the
' user-entered employee last name.
Public Function PhoneLookup(ByVal sName As String) As DataSet

        Dim conn As SqlConnection = New SqlConnection(CONNSTR)
        Dim sSQL As String

        ' The SQL loads data based on a complete or partial match of
        ' the first part of the last name. Ex: If the user enters a
        ' value of "POW", the SQL will return "Powers" and "Powell".
        sSQL = "SELECT EmpLastName, EmpFirstName, Phone, Extension " & _
                "FROM Phone " & _
                "WHERE EmpLastName LIKE '" & sName & "%' " & _
                "ORDER BY EmpLastName"

        ' Get our data objects ready for retrieval.
        Dim da As SqlDataAdapter = New SqlDataAdapter(sSQL, conn)
        Dim ds As DataSet = New DataSet()

        ' Load the data.
        Try
            conn.Open()
            da.Fill(ds, "PhoneNums")
            conn.Close()
            PhoneLookup = ds
        Catch ex As SqlException
            PhoneLookup = Nothing
        End Try

End Function

' This method loads the next available holiday from
' the database.
Public Function GetHoliday() As DataSet

        Dim conn As SqlConnection = New SqlConnection(CONNSTR)
```

```vb
    Dim sSQL As String

    ' This SQL will get the first record from a list of holidays
    ' that have a date following the current date.
    sSQL = "SELECT TOP 1 HolidayDate, Holiday " & _
           "FROM Holiday WHERE HolidayDate >= '" & _
           Now & "' ORDER BY HolidayDate"

    ' Get our data objects ready to load.
    Dim da As SqlDataAdapter = New SqlDataAdapter(sSQL, conn)
    Dim ds As DataSet = New DataSet()

    ' Load the data.
    Try
        conn.Open()
        da.Fill(ds, "Holiday")
        conn.Close()
        GetHoliday = ds
    Catch ex As SqlException
        GetHoliday = Nothing
    End Try

End Function

' This method loads event data from the database. The parameter
' is the user-selected date to match.
Public Function GetEvents(ByVal sDate As String) As DataSet

    Dim conn As SqlConnection = New SqlConnection(CONNSTR)
    Dim sSQL As String

    ' This SQL loads all event records whose month and year match
    ' the month and year of the date the user selected. The effect
    ' is that the users will get all the events for the month
    ' of the date that they entered.
    sSQL = "SELECT EventDate, EventName, EventDesc " & _
           "FROM Event " & _
           "WHERE (MONTH(EventDate)=MONTH('" & sDate & "')) " & _
           "AND (YEAR(EventDate)=YEAR('" & sDate & "')) " & _
           "ORDER BY EventDate"

    ' Get our data objects ready to load.
    Dim da As SqlDataAdapter = New SqlDataAdapter(sSQL, conn)
    Dim ds As DataSet = New DataSet()

    ' Load the data.
    Try
        conn.Open()
```

```
            da.Fill(ds, "Events")
            conn.Close()
            GetEvents = ds
        Catch ex As SqlException
            GetEvents = Nothing
        End Try

    End Function

  #End Region

  End Class
```

That's quite a listing. I promise we won't be going over every excruciating detail. We're only going to touch on a few of the more interesting parts. The basic idea of each of the five methods is to define a SQL statement to retrieve the data requested, fill a DataSet, and then return it to the caller.

The first method, GetWeatherAlert, is pretty simple. It assumes that there is only one record in the database table it reads, representing the current state of the company. You can change that single row as required to reflect the actual state of your company. The method GetAnnouncements is also fairly straightforward. The only interesting part is the DESC at the end of the SQL statement. It returns announcements so that the most recent come in first.

The PhoneLookup method is slightly more interesting. The functionality returns a list of rows whose associated last name matches a string that the user has entered. However, keeping with the practice of reducing the amount of data the user has to input, we look up matches based on the first part of the last name. For example, entering POW will return both Powell and Powers. We do this using the LIKE clause and the wildcard character, like this:

```
"WHERE EmpLastName LIKE '" & sName & "%'
```

All the results from the query are stuffed into a DataSet and returned to the caller.

The GetHoliday method is supposed to return the next paid holiday that the company has. It's easy to create a SQL statement to retrieve all the holidays after a certain date. We could write some code to then pull out the most recent one from the returned rows. However, we can do all the work in the SQL like this:

```
sSQL = "SELECT TOP 1 HolidayDate, Holiday " & _
       "FROM Holiday WHERE HolidayDate >= '" & _
       Now & "' ORDER BY HolidayDate"
```

The Top 1 clause returns the first row in the result set. As long as we have the ORDER BY clause at the end, which makes sure that the holidays come in the right order, everything works properly. We then return the top row in a DataSet.

Lastly, we have GetEvents. This method takes a date that the user has entered and retrieves all event rows from the database that fall in the same month as the passed-in date. The SQL looks a little more complex, but it really isn't:

```
sSQL = "SELECT EventDate, EventName, EventDesc " & _
       "FROM Event " & _
       "WHERE (MONTH(EventDate)=MONTH('" & sDate & "')) " & _
       "AND (YEAR(EventDate)=YEAR('" & sDate & "')) " & _
       "ORDER BY EventDate"
```

All we're doing here is extracting the MONTH part of the EventDate column and the passed-in date and making sure they're the same. We do the same thing with the YEAR, in case there are old or future rows in the database.

And that's about it for the business component. You can see how it would be very easy to use the exact same component to present the same information using a different venue, such as the company's intranet site. When you've got all this done (or loaded it from the CD-ROM), build the DLL and note where it is so that we can reference it shortly.

Part 2: The Mobile Web Application

Start this part of the project by creating a new mobile Web project. I called it prj09. Once the project is created, you'll be looking at a default form, ready for your ministrations. Rename the form default.aspx so that it will load automatically. You can create all the forms yourself or load the project from the accompanying CD-ROM. Figures 9.12 and 9.13 show what all the forms look like and the controls you'll want to drop on them. Table 9.5 also lists each control and any relevant properties that need to be set.

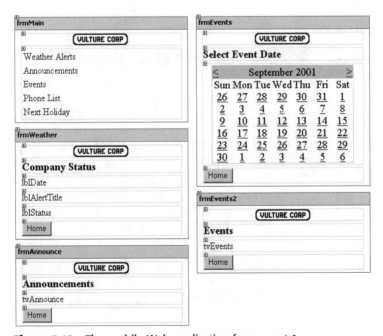

Figure 9.12   The mobile Web application forms, part 1.

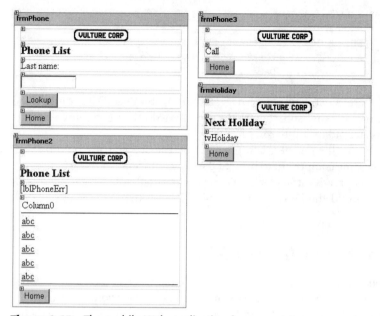

Figure 9.13 The mobile Web application forms, part 2.

Table 9.5 The Controls on the Forms

FORM	CONTROLS	PROPERTIES
frmMain	Image	ID=Image1, ImageURL=images/mobile_logo.gif, Alignment=Center
	List	ID=lstMenu
frmWeather	Image	ID=Image2, ImageURL=images/mobile_logo.gif, Alignment=Center
	Label	ID=Label1, Text="Company Status", StyleReference=Title
	Label	ID=lbllblDate
	Label	ID=lblAlertTitle
	Label	ID=lblStatus
	Command	ID=cmdHome, Text="Home"

FORM	CONTROLS	PROPERTIES
frmAnnounce	Form	Paginate=True
	Image	ID=Image3, ImageURL=images/mobile_logo.gif, Alignment=Center
	Label	ID=Label4, Text="Announcements", StyleReference=Title
	TextView	ID=tvAnnounce
	Command	ID=cmdHome2, Text="Home"
frmEvents	Image	ID=Image4, ImageURL=images/mobile_logo.gif, Alignment=Center
	Label	ID=Label8, Text="Select event date:"
	Calendar	ID=calEvents, Alignment=Center
	Command	ID=cmdHome3, Text="Home"
frmEvents2	Image	ID=Image5, ImageURL=images/mobile_logo.gif, Alignment=Center
	Label	ID=Label5, Text="Events", StyleReference=Title
	TextView	ID=tvEvents
	Command	ID=cmdHome4, Text="Home"
frmPhone	Image	ID=Image5, ImageURL=images/mobile_logo.gif, Alignment=Center
	Label	ID=Label6, Text="Phone List", StyleReference=Title
	TextBox	ID=txtName, Alignment=Left, Size=10, MaxLength=20
	Command	ID=cmdLookup, Text="Lookup"
	Command	ID=cmdHome5, Text="Home"
frmPhone2	Image	ID=Image7, ImageURL=images/mobile_logo.gif, Alignment=Center
	Label	ID=Label7, Text="Phone List", StyleReference=Title
	Label	ID=lblPhoneErr, StyleReference=Error, Visible=False
	ObjectList	ID=lstPhoneNums, Alignment=Left
	Command	ID=cmdHome6, Text="Home"

continues

Table 9.5 (Continued)

FORM	CONTROLS	PROPERTIES
frmPhone 3	Image	ID=Image8, ImageURL=images/mobile_logo.gif, Alignment=Center
	PhoneCall	ID=callSelected
	Command	ID=cmdHome7, Text="Home"
frmHoliday	Image	ID=Image9, ImageURL=images/mobile_logo.gif, Alignment=Center
	Label	ID=Label3, Text="Next Holiday", StyleReference=Title
	TextView	ID=tvHoliday
	Command	ID=cmdHome8, Text="Home"

Now that the forms are laid out, we need to make them do something. Let's take it one feature at a time, beginning with some of our generic code.

Supporting Code

We had to create some Command controls that go back to the main page. Each form has one at the bottom. Every control does the same thing. We created a method called *GoHome* that navigates back to the main menu. All the event handlers for those Command objects call GoHome. The GoHome method and one of the event handlers are as follows:

```
' A root method to go back to the main page.
Private Sub GoHome()
    ActiveForm = frmMain
End Sub


' The following event handlers all send the various pages
' back to the main form.
Private Sub cmdHome_Click(ByVal sender As System.Object, _
    ByVal e As System.EventArgs) Handles cmdHome.Click
    GoHome()
End Sub
```

The only other supporting code we need is a DataSet that sticks around beyond the scope of a method's boundaries. The code is outside a method, and the DataSet becomes part of the class data, like this:

```
Private dsPhone As DataSet
```

Main Menu Page

The main menu page is essentially a List control with five items in it. You can add the items as they are read on the form through the Items collection property for the List control. Add an event handler to the List's ItemCommand event. This will handle the feature selections for the application. The code looks like this:

```
' This method handles selections from our main page menu.
' It makes calls to the correct functionality based on the
' item selected from the list.
Private Sub lstMenu_ItemCommand(ByVal source As System.Object, _
    ByVal e As System.Web.UI.MobileControls.ListCommandEventArgs) _
    Handles lstMenu.ItemCommand

    ' The item 'e' represents the selected item from the list,
    ' and is passed to us through the event handler.
    Select Case CInt(e.ListItem.Value)
        Case 1    ' Weather Alert
            ShowWeatherAlert()
        Case 2    ' Announcements
            ShowAnnouncements()
        Case 3    ' Events
            ActiveForm = frmEvents
        Case 4    ' Phone list
            ActiveForm = frmPhone
        Case 5    ' Next Holiday
            NextHoliday()
        Case Else
    End Select

End Sub
```

Some of these items call methods, those that can execute right away. Others have secondary forms they need to move to first. Use the ActiveForm property of the page that makes the specified form the visible one. The other interesting item here is the passed-in parameter, *e*. In this case, because we're handling the ItemCommand event, e represents the selected list item. We are using its value property in the Select statement. Figure 9.14 shows what the main menu looks like running in the emulator.

Figure 9.14   The main menu seen in the emulator.

The Weather Alert

This feature is one of the simpler bits of functionality in this application, but it bears some scrutiny because we've patterned all our data retrieval methods after this one. We will use the business object we created earlier to access the data we need and then display it for the user. Our code is as follows:

```
' This method retrieves data about the weather status of the company
' and displays it for the user.
Private Sub ShowWeatherAlert()

    Dim o As New prj09logic.MobileSvcs()    ' Our business component
    Dim ds As DataSet                       ' Holds returned data
    Dim theRow As DataRow                   ' Holds a single row

    ' Get data about the weather alert status from our
    ' business component. There will be by design only be
    ' one row returned from this call.
    ds = o.GetWeatherAlert()

    ' If we got data back, then extract it from the
    ' DataSet and stuff it into our controls.
```

```
Try
    theRow = ds.Tables(0).Rows(0)
    lblDate.Text = CStr(theRow("AlertDate"))
    lblAlertTitle.Text = CStr(theRow("AlertTitle")) & " ---"
    lblStatus.Text = CStr(theRow("AlertText"))
Catch ex As Exception
    lblDate.Text = "No data available."
    lblAlertTitle.Text = "Try again later."
    lblStatus.Text = ""
End Try

' Finally make the weather alerts form the visible one.
ActiveForm = frmWeather

End Sub
```

Notice the creation of an instance of our business object, the MobileSvcs class. Once created, we only need to call its GetWeatherAlert method. The rest of the code copies data from its returned DataSet into the controls of the form. We place everything into a Try..Catch construct to make sure that we handle any errors that might crop up. Once the data is filled in, we make the form active and we're done. Figure 9.15 shows the Weather Alert screen.

Figure 9.15   The Weather Alert feature.

The Announcements

The Announcements feature retrieves a complete list of all rows in the Announcement table and displays them for the user. We are using a TextView control to present the data to the user because we can format the text a little more than a label allows. It's possible that this DataSet could be large, so we make sure that the automatic pagination is turned on, through the TextView properties, for the TextView control.

The code for the Announcement retrieval is similar to that of the weather alert feature. We load some data and present it to the user. The only real difference is the data processing. We could get multiple rows back from the database, so we need to deal with that. Take a look at the code:

```
' This method retrieves data about the currently available
' company announcements and displays them for the user.
Private Sub ShowAnnouncements()

    Dim o As New prj09logic.MobileSvcs()   ' Our business component
    Dim ds As DataSet                       ' Holds returned data
    Dim aRow As DataRow                     ' Holds a single row of
                                            '   data

    Dim s As String


    ' Get data about all current announcements from
    ' our business component.
    ds = o.GetAnnouncements()


    ' If we got data back, then extract it from the
    ' DataSet and stuff it into our controls.
    Try
        For Each aRow In ds.Tables(0).Rows
            s += CStr(aRow("AnnounceDate")) & "<BR>"
            s += CStr(aRow("Announcement")) & "<BR>"
        Next
    Catch ex As Exception
        tvAnnounce.Text = "No data available.<BR>Try again later."
    End Try
    tvAnnounce.Text = s


    ' Make the Announcements form visible.
    ActiveForm = frmAnnounce

End Sub
```

The business object gets our data for us with a single call. Once the DataSet is returned, we need to process each row in the DataSet and add it to the TextView control. For each announcement, we show the Date and Description. Note that we use the standard HTML <BR> tag to separate lines in the display. This is how the TextView allows you to format content, through the use of HTML tags.

Figure 9.16   The Announcements feature.

Once the string is assembled representing the announcement content, it is assigned to the TextView control, and the form is made active. As with the other forms, the user can click the Home Command to go back to our menu. The announcements feature is shown running in Figure 9.16.

The Phone Lookup

The Phone Lookup is our first feature that uses multiple forms; in this case there are three. The first form allows the user to enter all or part of an employee's last name. The second form displays the results of the query, where the user can select one of the returned names from a list. The third form displays the employee name and phone number as well as options, including the ability to actually call the phone number with a click.

Clicking the Lookup Command once you have entered an employee name activates the code behind the first form, as follows:

```
' Once a name or partial name has been entered on the phone list
' lookup, and the user clicks the lookup command, this method is
' called.
Private Sub cmdLookup_Click(ByVal sender As System.Object, _
```

```
        ByVal e As System.EventArgs) Handles cmdLookup.Click
        PhoneLookup()
        ActiveForm = frmPhone2
End Sub


' This method retrieves a list of matching names based on
' the user-entered name on the form, and binds it to a
' list.
Private Sub PhoneLookup()

    Dim o As New prj09logic.MobileSvcs()    ' Our business component

    ' Get a list of matching employee names from the database
    ' using our business component.
    dsPhone = o.PhoneLookup(Trim(txtName.Text))

    ' Stuff any returned data into our list the easy way
    ' (data binding)
    Try
        ' We want the user to be able to call the person
        ' automatically once the name is displayed for them, so add
        ' a command to the ObjectList that will show a "Place Call"
        ' option on the screen.
                    lstPhoneNums.Items.Clear()
                    lstPhoneNums.Commands.Clear()
        lstPhoneNums.Commands.Add(New ObjectListCommand("Call", _
            "Place Call"))

        ' Set up data binding from our DataSet to the ObjectList.
        lstPhoneNums.DataSource = dsPhone
        lstPhoneNums.DataMember = "PhoneNums"
        lstPhoneNums.DataBind()
                    lstPhoneNums.SelectedIndex=0

        ' Make sure the correct controls are visible.
        lstPhoneNums.Visible = True
        lblPhoneErr.Visible = False
    Catch ex As Exception
        ' Make sure the correct controls are visible.
        lstPhoneNums.Visible = False
        lblPhoneErr.Visible = True
        lblPhoneErr.Text = "No matches available."
    End Try

End Sub
```

The first method shown is called when the user clicks the Lookup Command on the first Phone form, assuming he or she has entered a value in the TextBox. The form is shown in Figure 9.17. It calls the next method, PhoneLookup, which takes care of retrieving the matching employee names and phone numbers and then adds them to our ObjectList. After PhoneLookup is done, the second phone form is ready for display, and we make it active.

Figure 9.17   The first Phone Lookup form.

PhoneLookup does all the work. We create an instance of our business object and use it to get matching data, passing the user-entered name to the method. Once it is returned, we use data binding to fill the data retrieved into the ObjectList. We use an object list because we want to attach complete data rows to the list. The DataSource is set to the DataSet that we got back from the business object, and the DataMember property is set to the particular table in the DataSet that we want to use (in this case it is the only table). Then we call DataBind and everything is set for a list full of data. The second phone form, filled with matching data records, is shown in Figure 9.18.

The last important point here is that, for something to happen when the user selects an item from the object list, we need to add a command to the ObjectList (not to be confused with a Command control). The ObjectList has a command collection, and we need to add one to activate our phone call once a name is selected. The ObjectList Control will give us a *Details* command automatically, which will allow the user to see all the fields associated with the selected object. The command we added to the collection will also be shown on the screen. The ObjectListCommand object is used to add the command to the command collection.

If the user clicks a name in our list, the UI displays a list of commands found in the command collection. This is shown on the left in Figure 9.19. We do not have to design this form; it is created for us. If the user selects Details, the details of the object clicked on are shown, in this case, the employee last name, first name, phone number, and extension as shown on the right in the figure.

Figure 9.18   The second Phone Lookup form.

Figure 9.19   The Commands and Details screens.

If the user selects the Place Call command, our own command, the code we have attached to the ItemCommand event of the ObjectList is executed. It looks like this:

```
' This method responds to a command from the ObjectList, in our
' case, the selected name that the user wants to see/call.
Private Sub lstPhoneNums_ItemCommand( _
    ByVal source As System.Object, ByVal e As _
    System.Web.UI.MobileControls.ObjectListCommandEventArgs) _
    Handles lstPhoneNums.ItemCommand

    ' Fill phone number into call control.
    callSelected.PhoneNumber = e.ListItem("Phone")

    ' Create the user name as we want to see it: Last, First, Phone.
    callSelected.Text = e.ListItem("EmpLastName") & ", " & _
        e.ListItem("EmpFirstName") & ": " & e.ListItem("Phone")

    ActiveForm = frmPhone3

End Sub
```

Because we have only one command available, this code is fairly simple. If we had multiple commands, we would have to know which one was selected by the user. The EventArgs parameter, e, gives us this information through the *CommandName* property. We could build a Select statement to decide what to do based on the chosen command. We can safely ignore that part of e for now. What we do instead is construct a complete name and phone number to display in the PhoneCall control on the third phone form. The e parameter also tells us which object was selected and gives us access to that object, via its *ListItem* property. As you can see in the code, we can get its properties, or in this case, the fields of data from the DataSet. Once we build the employee name and phone number string from the selected object, we add it to the PhoneCall control on the third phone form and make it active. It is shown running on the left in Figure 9.20. If you click on the name (the PhoneCall control), it will ask if you want to make a voice call, which it will do if you click OK. This is shown on the right in the figure.

That wraps up the Phone Lookup feature. If you fill the database with every employee in your company, this could be a very powerful feature. It was our most complicated feature in this project, but it was worth it.

Figure 9.20 The PhoneCall control and the result if you click on it.

The Next Holiday

Compared to the Phone Lookup, this feature is a walk in the park. We only have a single form, we only get a single row of data back from the database, and there's nothing complex in the UI. All the tricky bits of figuring out the next holiday are handled by the business logic. The user simply clicks on the menu item and the holiday is displayed. Let's take a look at the code:

```
' This method retrieves the next holiday for the company using
' our business component and displays it for the user.
Private Sub NextHoliday()

    Dim o As New prj09logic.MobileSvcs()  ' Our business component
    Dim ds As DataSet                     ' Holds returned data
    Dim theRow As DataRow                 ' Holds a single row of
                                          data
    Dim s As String                       ' Temp string space

    ' Get the next holiday from our business component.
```

```
ds = o.GetHoliday()

' If getting the holiday worked, then format it and
' display it for the user.
Try
    theRow = ds.Tables(0).Rows(0)
    s = CStr(theRow("HolidayDate")) & "<BR>"
    s += CStr(theRow("Holiday"))
    tvHoliday.Text = s
Catch ex As Exception
    tvHoliday.Text = "No data available.<BR>Try again later."
End Try

' Make the holiday form visible.
ActiveForm = frmHoliday

End Sub
```

We've seen all this before in the code for the other features. Get the data from the business object, format the data into a string with line breaks, and stuff it into a TextView control. Once that's complete, the target Holiday form is made active. The result is shown in Figure 9.21.

Figure 9.21 The Next Holiday feature.

The Company Events

The code for the event feature is not complex. The Calendar control makes the selection of a date fairly easy, although the date selector implementation on a cell phone client is a little cumbersome. It's much easier for users to simply type in a date, which the Date control allows them to do. We will use the business object to retrieve all the events that occur in the month of the date the user selects. For example, if 10/15/2001 is chosen, we pull all the events in the database for October 2001. Here's the code, which should look quite familiar by now:

```
' This method handles a date selection from the date control on
' our first events page.
Private Sub calEvents_SelectionChanged( _
    ByVal sender As System.Object, ByVal e As System.EventArgs) _
    Handles calEvents.SelectionChanged
    ShowEvents()
End Sub


' This method retrieves all company events for the month of
' the date selected and displays them for the user.
Private Sub ShowEvents()

    Dim o As New prj09logic.MobileSvcs()    ' Our business component
    Dim ds As DataSet                       ' Holds returned data
    Dim aRow As DataRow                     ' Holds a single row of
                                            '   data
    Dim s As String                         ' Temp string space

    ' Load event data using our business component.
    ds = o.GetEvents(calEvents.SelectedDate().ToString())

    ' If the event data load worked, then process each one in the
    ' DataSet, formatting it for display.
    Try
        For Each aRow In ds.Tables(0).Rows
            s += CStr(aRow("EventDate")) & "<BR>"
            s += CStr(aRow("EventName")) & "<BR>"
            s += CStr(aRow("EventDesc")) & "<BR><BR>"
        Next
    Catch ex As Exception
        s = "No data available.<BR>Try again later."
    End Try
    tvEvents.Text = s

    ' Make the event viewer form visible.
    ActiveForm = frmEvents2

End Sub
```

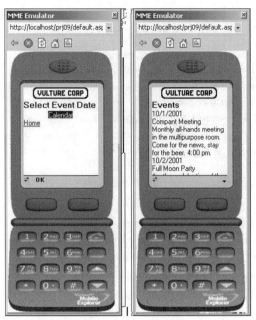

Figure 9.22   Using the Events feature.

The first method handles the event whereby the user makes a selection from the Calendar control. It simply calls the second method, although we could do some date validation here, which is why the method exists in the first place (otherwise, you could simply put the code in ShowEvents into this method). Beyond that, there's nothing peculiar here. Getting data back, formatting it into a string, and filling it into a TextView control should be old hat. The selection of a date and the resulting list of events is shown in Figure 9.22.

Running and Debugging the Project

Running your project is simple. You do it like you run any other project in Visual Basic. It executes in the MME. You can debug your application, setting breakpoints and examining values normally. The nifty part is that, when you create separate components to house your business logic, you can debug those, too.

Try this. Put a breakpoint on any call to our business object and run the application. Once the program stops there, you can step right into the business object (press F11). The code for that business object loads automatically and execution continues normally, seamlessly. If you've ever debugged DCOM components, for example, you know what a pain that was. This is like moving to another planet where debugging is pleasant and someone feeds you peeled grapes while you do it.

Enhancing the Project

You've now had a useful and exciting foray into the world of developing mobile Web applications. I personally think it's very exciting and opens up all kinds of possibilities for programmers interested in this area of development. It's easy, it's fun, and it's powerful. I'd say Microsoft has a big winner with this one.

There is more to this topic than could be covered in this project. Topics such as creating custom controls for Web applications, template forms, advanced pagination with headers and footers, and device-specific content give you plenty of areas to explore further.

There is a lot to cover in the topic of deployment and plenty of opportunities to use some of the capabilities we didn't get to, including:

Add it to your intranet.   The business component we created works for any application, and you could easily display the useful data it supplies on a corporate intranet. Add a status or information page that shows it to everyone all the time.

Create a content management Web site.   This mobile Web application depends on current data to be useful, but the people in a company are not going to maintain the data if it isn't easy. In particular, the weather alert data needs to be easily and quickly modified from a remote location. Create a basic Web site that allows authorized users to update the database content.

Create device-specific code.   There are more capable devices out there, and you could add some code to take advantage of some of those more interesting device-specific capabilities. Color, images, and fonts might be available.

Add more validation code.   We only did some basic error checking; you could use the Validator controls to add more robust error handling.

WHAT'S COMING NEXT

Our final project is up next, and it uses many of the techniques that you learned in all the previous projects to build an application for company use. It's similar to what we built here but can benefit those who don't have cell phones. It should help out all your employees.

NOTE   The last published version of the Microsoft Mobile Explorer as of this writing was a technology preview. While this worked fine with the beta versions of Visual Studio .NET, it has a few problems with the final released version. Some of the code in this chapter may not work properly with MME until a new version is released. However, the code here and any code you create yourself should work fine with Internet Explorer or your cell phone or other mobile devices.

Employee Intranet with .NET

So far in this book we have covered many of the new techniques in the Microsoft .NET Framework and Visual Basic .NET. Each project looked at a specific technique. This project will bring several of them together to create a solution that just about any company could use, given some adaptation. It will make it easier for individuals to deal with overhead tasks that almost every company has.

THE PROBLEM:

Most companies have overhead work that employees must do. It does not get their actual work done but needs to take place as part of almost any business. If we could make those tasks easier, or reduce the number of people involved to get them done, more time could actually be spent on building software, processing insurance claims, or whatever your company does.

THE SOLUTION:

I picked out three of these overhead tasks to automate or place in the hands of the employee, reducing the number of people involved. They are:

◆ Making vacation requests and managing your vacation time

◆ Adjusting or reviewing your personnel information

◆ Writing and submitting status reports

Tasks such as approving a vacation request or contacting your HR department for information or to make changes often require the interaction of more than one person at the same time. This system will help to put these tasks in the hands of one person (the employee) or at least make the interaction of people asynchronous so that they can each deal with it when they have time. The system is also available all the time, whether or not the multiple parties involved are at hand.

The Project

We will be building a company intranet site that allows employees to request vacation, manage vacation time, submit status reports, and review and edit their personnel information. We will also implement security so that only employees can get in. We will track which employees are logged in, restricting them to viewing and editing only their information. We'll even display a random joke, quote, or fortune for them on the main page. Along the way, we'll be using a lot of the technologies we've covered so far, including ASP.NET, ADO.NET, Web services, and .NET Forms Security. Here are the major parts of the project:

1. **The database.**   This is one of the more complex databases we've used so far, with six tables, all related in one fashion or another. I'll discuss the design of the database, as well as its contents.

2. **Web service.**   We'll build a Web service to handle the lookup of a random joke, quote, or fortune from the database. It could, of course, be used by any other application or by a Web site that has access to it. That's the fun of Web services.

3. **The main form.**   We'll build the main Web page and code that users will navigate to the rest of the application. It will also display the random fun item of the day.

4. **Security.**   Next we'll implement forms-based security for the Web site, just like we did in Project 8. We'll even take most of the code from that project, making some minor modifications to suit our specific needs.

5. **The vacation form.**   We will construct a form that allows users to see how much vacation time they have left this year and the past history of their vacation and to create new vacation requests.

6. **The employee information form.**   Users will be able to see the basic information that the company keeps on them, review it, and change some of it if they need to.

7. **The status reports form.**   Most companies require employees to create weekly (or otherwise) status reports. This provides a centralized location to enter status reports and to review past status reports.

You Will Need

✔ **Visual Studio .NET**

✔ **SQL Server (or other database)**

✔ **Internet Information Server**

Project Details and Design Notes

To build this project, you will need the technologies you have learned about already. We don't need to cover any new ones. However, you'll see how to integrate some of them to create a more complete solution.

Our project is mostly ASP.NET with VB code-behind modules. There is also a lot of ADO.NET. This application is fairly database-driven. The Web service that we will create helps add a light-hearted element to the system. The security that we implement makes use of the database without adding any new tables specifically for it.

UI Design

A few user interface design considerations were taken into account when I created the site. I decided to try to reduce the amount of navigation users have to perform to get tasks done. For example, the vacation form allows users to review their vacation information and make vacation requests on the same page. The sections of the page are separated, so they won't be confused. This way they don't have to look at their available vacation on one page and then go to another page to request time off.

The other advantage of keeping the navigation to a minimum is that we have fewer pages to create and maintain. This is a good principle to follow whenever designing applications. Especially with Web sites and Web applications, page proliferation tends to be like a runaway train. It's best to keep a tight rein on them.

Tracking Users

We need to be able to track users and who they are throughout the use of the application. We will be using the Session ASP.NET object to do this, much as we did in the Project 6, the ASP.NET project. Once users log in, we can stash their ID away in the Session object and refer to it on any page of the application, as long as we're in the same session.

We will also frequently need the Employee ID (EmpID) from the database. Typically, each page, in the page load event, will look up the EmpID from the database using the login ID that we save in the Session object. It will stay current as long as the page is active. The EmpID will be used in other database operations for the pages that need it.

Let's Start the Project

This is a fairly large project compared to most in this book, and it will be broken up into the following major parts:

Database.   We'll go over the design of the database and get it ready to use. We will need some sample data make the program function correctly.

Web service.   We will create a project just for the Web service that we will be using. Once this is in place and functional, we can close that project and start the new one.

The main form.   This will be built first as part of the main project. It will be easier to put this into place first and then implement security. The main form will give us something to access and help test security.

Security.   We'll put security in place next. For this project, we'll need security in place fairly early so that we have access to the user Login ID from the Session object.

And the rest.   Lastly, we'll build all three functional forms that make up the rest of the project: vacation, status reports, and employee information.

We have used our old pal, the Vulture Corporation, as an example company that might be building this intranet site. It should be fairly easy to change the title graphics and a few text items here and there to make this represent any company.

The Database

Our database, involving six tables, is more complicated than most in this book. There is a Microsoft Access version of the database on the accompanying CD-ROM that you can import into SQL Server. It also contains sample data that will be required before the program can run. Make sure you have data in place before you move on to the rest of the project.

Take a look at Figure 10.1, which shows all the database tables and fields. You can see how they are related and what exactly is in each one. Table 10.1 lists what each table is used for.

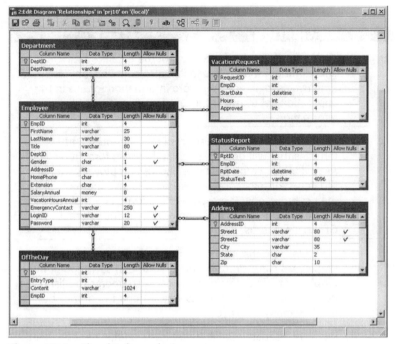

Figure 10.1   The database design.

The most complicated database query we perform during the course of the project is the retrieval of the complete employee record in the Employee Information page. This query needs to use a couple of JOINs to get meaningful information from the related tables. You'll see it once we get to that part of the application.

The Web Service

Now it's time for some real code. Ever since I discovered Web services and how much fun they are, I have been looking for excuses to make a few. This project provided an opportunity, so I took it. Our Web service gets a random record from the OfTheDay table in the database; it contains a joke, quote, or fortune. Our application simply needs one at random, regardless of which type is stored there. It will display a joke, quote, or fortune indiscriminately. However, we shouldn't punish the Web service just because we don't need to pick which type of entry we want.

I built the Web service and the database so that we can keep track of the different types of entries. We have three types, each of which is indicated by an integer value:

- Joke = 1
- Quote = 2
- Fortune = 3

Table 10.1 The Database Tables

TABLE	DESCRIPTION
Employee	The heart of the database. Most of the data is stored here, and all other tables relate to it. It also contains the employee's login and password information for use in this application, which makes it easy for use to access that information.
OfTheDay	This table stores our repository of jokes, quotes, and fortunes that will be displayed on the main form. It is related to the Employee table because employees submit the items for this table, and we want to give them credit for their submissions. Therefore, we associate an employee with each row in this table. An employee may submit many OfTheDay records.
Department	A simple table that lists departments in the company. Employees can belong to one department, so we point the Employee table to this one. We can also update the list of departments more easily this way. A department may be used by many employees.
Address	We have a separate table for addresses. I don't know about your company, but mine has a fair number of husband and wife teams that share the same address. This will help keep the database a little more efficient. An address may be used by more than one employee.
StatusReport	This table stores status reports submitted by employees. It is related to the Employee table so that we know which employee entered it. An employee may submit many status reports.
VacationRequest	Stores vacation time requests that users submit. An employee may submit many vacation requests.

The Web service lets you pass in one of these values to indicate which type you want. If you don't care, and will take anything, pass in a zero. The Web service itself has only one method, GetOne, that goes to the database, pulls a list of all available items back, and then picks one of the returned values at random.

This was a design decision I made. I could have also issued an initial SELECT COUNT statement to find out how many matching items there were in the database and then issued a second SELECT with a ROWNUM clause to pull back a randomly selected row. However, I opted for a larger DataSet return and a single trip to the database. You can take your pick, based on your needs.

Create a new Web service project and name it prj10OfTheDay. I renamed the class to OfTheDaySvc as well. The code for the Web service method follows. I have omitted the generated code. Take a glance at it; it is not very complex:

```
Imports System.Web.Services
Imports System.Data.SqlClient

Public Class OfTheDaySvc
    Inherits System.Web.Services.WebService

#Region " Class Data and Types "

    ' Database connection string used throughout the class.
    Private Const CONNSTR As String = "PERSIST SECURITY INFO=False; " & _
        "DATA SOURCE=tony; INITIAL CATALOG=prj10; UID=sa; PWD=;"

    ' These const values correspond to the types used in the database.
    Public Const ANYTYPE As Int32 = 0
    Public Const JOKETYPE As Int32 = 1
    Public Const FORTUNETYPE As Int32 = 2
    Public Const QUOTETYPE As Int32 = 3

#End Region

    <WebMethod()> Public Function GetOne(ByVal iType As Int32) As String

        Dim s As String     ' Return string
        Dim sSQL As String = "SELECT OfTheDay.EntryType, " & _
            "OfTheDay.Content, Employee.FirstName, Employee.LastName " & _
            "FROM OfTheDay, Employee " & _
            "WHERE OfTheDay.EmpID = Employee.EmpID"

        Dim conn As New SqlConnection(CONNSTR)
        Dim ds As New DataSet()

        ' Do we need a where clause? Only if a type was specified.
        If iType > 0 Then
            sSQL &= " AND OfTheDay.EntryType=" & iType
        End If
        Dim da As New SqlDataAdapter(sSQL, conn)

        Randomize()

        ' Load the data.
        Try
            conn.Open()
            da.Fill(ds, "oftheday")
            conn.Close()
        Catch ex As SqlException
            Throw ex
        End Try

        ' Select one at random.
        Dim aRow As DataRow
        Dim r As Int32 = Int(Rnd() * ds.Tables(0).Rows.Count)
```

```
          aRow = ds.Tables(0).Rows(r)
          s = aRow("Content") & "<BR><BR>Submitted by " & _
              aRow("FirstName") & " " & aRow("LastName")

          Return (s)

      End Function
```

We start with the usual database connection string, the Imports statements, and a few constants as needed. Then we move on to the GetOne method. Notice that we can accept a parameter to specify which type of item to retrieve.

The SELECT statement returns the data we need for the display of the item, as well as the name of the employee who submitted it. We have to get the name from the Employee table, so we do a match between the EmpID fields in the two tables. We'll format the returned string so that it contains the name of the person who submitted it to the system. If the caller requests a specific type of item, we add a WHERE clause to SELECT statement.

Lastly, we execute the query and return a formatted string. We use Web line breaks, <BR> tags, instead of vbCrLf because this is a Web service. If other types of applications want to use it, they'll have to parse it apart when they get the results.

Test It Out

You can try out the Web service once it is implemented just like we did with the Web service in Project 3. Run the application, and you get to see it in the browser. Figure 10.2 shows what it looks like, listing the single method available.

Click on the GetOne method. You'll see a new page that accepts parameters for the function. Enter a 0, 1, 2, or 3 and click the Invoke button. The Web service will run and return one of the items in the database. Figure 10.3 shows some sample results.

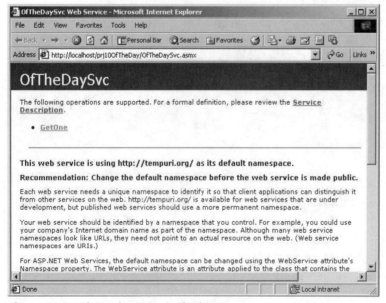

Figure 10.2   The Web service in the browser.

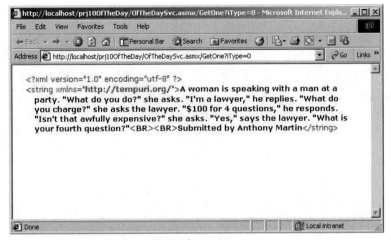

Figure 10.3   Results from the Web service.

The Main Form

We're going to launch into the main form now. We will need something in place to request and to subsequently show up once security is in place. So we'll do this now and then tackle security.

Start by creating our main project. Make a new ASP.NET Web application in Visual Studio .NET and name it *prj10*. Rename the standard Form1 default.aspx. This will allow it to come up automatically when the URL is requested.

This form makes use of some custom styles that we added to the default style sheet in the project. Open the style sheet, Styles.css, and add the following style to the end:

```
.MainTitle
{
    font-family: Haettenschweiler, Impact;
    font-size: 36pt;
}


.TitleContent
{
    font-family: Verdana, Arial;
    font-size: 10pt;
    padding-left: 10px;
}


.Content
{
```

```
    font-family: Verdana, Arial;
    font-size: 10pt;
}


.DescTitle
{
    font-family: Verdana, Arial;
    font-size: 14pt;
    font-weight: bold;
}


.Copyright
{
    font-family: Verdana, Arial;
    font-size: 8pt;
}
```

All the Web forms that we're building in this application were created the same way. We use FlowLayout mode, not GridLayout mode. Then we create the framework using a table manually, by entering HTML code. Once the cells are all in place, we switch to the Designer view and drag controls into the cells of the table. This works pretty well and gives us control over the layout. Figure 10.4 shows what the page looks like when we have completed entering the HTML and putting controls on it. Table 10.2 lists the controls and any important properties that need to be set.

Figure 10.4   The main form in the Designer.

Table 10.2 The Main Form Controls

CONTROL	NAME	PROPERTIES
Image	Image1	ImageURL="images/TitleHdr.jpg"
Label	lblUser	Text="", Font-Bold=True
Label	lblOfTheDay	CssClass="Content"

The Image control contains the title graphic. The other images on the page are simple IMG tags in the HTML; the listing for the page follows. You can enter it yourself or load it from the accompanying CD-ROM. There is nothing particularly complex; we use tables to control layout.

```
<%@ Page Language="vb" AutoEventWireup="false"
Codebehind="default.aspx.vb" Inherits="prj10.WebForm1"%>
<!DOCTYPE HTML PUBLIC "-//W3C//DTD HTML 4.0 Transitional//EN">
<HTML>
    <HEAD>
        <title></title>
        <meta content="Microsoft Visual Studio.NET 7.0"name="GENERATOR">
        <meta content="Visual Basic 7.0" name="CODE_LANGUAGE">
        <meta content="JavaScript" name="vs_defaultClientScript">
        <meta content="http://schemas.microsoft.com/intellisense/ie5"
         name="vs_targetSchema">
        <LINK href="http://localhost/prj10/Styles.css" type="text/css"
         rel="stylesheet">
    </HEAD>
    <body style="PADDING-RIGHT:0px; PADDING-LEFT:0px;
     PADDING-BOTTOM:0px; MARGIN:0px; PADDING-TOP:0px">
        <table cellSpacing="5" cellPadding="0" width="750" border="0">
            <tr>
                <td>
                    <asp:image id="Image1" runat="server"
                     ImageUrl="images/TitleHdr.jpg"></asp:image>
                </td>
            </tr>
            <tr>
                <td class="TitleContent" width="550">
                    Welcome to the Vulture Corp. Intranet site,
                    <asp:Label id="lblUser" runat="server"
                    Font-Bold="True"></asp:Label>
                    . You can come here any time and manage your
                    profile, request vacation, or
                    enter status reports.
                </td>
            </tr>
            <tr>
```

```
<td>
    <table cellpadding="10" cellspacing="0" border="0"
    width="750">
        <tr>
            <td align="middle" vAlign="middle"
             width="30%">
                <IMG SRC="images/Vacation.jpg"
                 border="0">
            </td>
            <td width="50%">
                <A class="DescTitle"
                 href="prj10vacation.aspx">Vacation
                 Planning</A>
                <br>
                <span class="Content">Use this feature
                 of the Web site to see how much
                 vacation you have left, or to request
                 time off.</span>
            </td>
            <td rowspan="3" valign="top">
                <span class="DescTitle">...Of the
                 Day</span>
                <br>
                <br>
                <asp:Label id="lblOfTheDay"
                 runat="server"
                 CssClass="Content">Of The Day content
                 goes here.</asp:Label>
            </td>
        </tr>
        <tr>
            <td align="middle" vAlign="middle"
             width="30%">
                <IMG SRC="images/StatusRpt.jpg"
                 border="0">
            </td>
            <td width="50%">
                <a class="DescTitle"
                 href="prj10status.aspx">Status
                 Reports</a>
                <br>
                <span class="Content">If your department
                 requires you to submit official status
                 reports, then you can enter them
                 here.</span>
            </td>
        </tr>
        <tr>
            <td align="middle" vAlign="middle"
             width="30%">
```

```
                                    <IMG SRC="images/EmployeeInfo.jpg"
                                     border="0">
                                </td>
                                <td width="50%">
                                    <A class="DescTitle"
                                     href="prj10empinfo.aspx">Employee
                                     Information</A>
                                    <br>
                                    <span class="Content">If you need to
                                     review or edit your personal
                                     information, stop by this part of our
                                     Intranet.</span>
                                </td>
                            </tr>
                            <tr>
                                <td colspan="3">
                                    <hr noshade size="1">
                                    <span class="Copyright">All content
                                     copyright (c) 2001 by Vulture Corp. All
                                     rights reserved.</span>
                                </td>
                            </tr>
                        </table>
                    </td>
                </tr>
            </table>
        <form id="Form1" method="post" runat="server">
        </form>
</body>
</HTML>
```

That's a hefty listing, but it turns into a nice page. We can now write code against the content of the page, wiring events up to the controls we placed there. We only need to worry about one event for this page, the load event. We need to pull some information from the database as well as call our Web service to retrieve a little humor for the day. The code for the Page Load event follows. I have omitted the generated code.

```
Option Explicit On

Imports System.Data.SqlClient

Public Class WebForm1
    Inherits System.Web.UI.Page

#Region " Class Data and Types "

    ' Database connection string. We're using SQL Server. Change this if
    ' you want to use something else, like the Access db included with
    ' the book.
```

```vb
        Private Const CONNSTR As String = "PERSIST SECURITY INFO=False; " & _
            DATA SOURCE=tony; INITIAL CATALOG=prj10; UID=sa; PWD=;"

#End Region

#Region " Event Handlers "

    Private Sub Page_Load(ByVal sender As System.Object, ByVal e As
System.EventArgs) Handles MyBase.Load

        ' Display a quote, joke, or fortune for the day.
        Dim wsvc As New prj10.localhost.OfTheDaySvc()
        Dim s As String
        s = wsvc.GetOne(0)

        lblOfTheDay.Text = s

        ' Get the user's name and use it.
        Dim conn As SqlConnection = New SqlConnection(CONNSTR)
        Dim sSQL As String
        Dim sUser As String = "Valued Vulture Corp. Employee"

        ' Load the employee names we'll need on this page.
        sSQL = "SELECT FirstName, LastName FROM Employee " & _
                "WHERE LoginID='" & Session("UserID") & "'"

        ' Get our data objects ready for retrieval.
        Dim da As SqlDataAdapter = New SqlDataAdapter(sSQL, conn)
        Dim ds As DataSet = New DataSet()
        Dim theRow As DataRow

        ' Load the data.
        Try
            conn.Open()
            da.Fill(ds, "employee")
            conn.Close()
            theRow = ds.Tables(0).Rows(0)
        Catch ex As SqlException
            conn.Close()
        End Try

        ' Display the user name.
        lblUser.Text = theRow("FirstName") & " " & theRow("LastName")

    End Sub

#End Region
```

Aside from the connection string, the first thing we do is to create an instance of the Web service. Before we can do this, however, we need to add a reference to it in the project so that the compiler knows what we are talking about. Right-click on the References section in the Solution Explorer, and from the context menu select Add Web Reference. You will see a dialog from Project 3, listing options for selecting Web references. On the left side, click the link that says "Web References on Local Web Server." This will provide you with a list of available Web services on your Web server. Figure 10.5 shows what this should look like. About half way down the list you can see the one we want. Click on it to add the reference to your project.

Now we can create the reference. It takes a grand total of two lines of code to get our item: one to create the object and another to make the call. We then assign the returned result to the text property of the lblOfTheDay control.

The rest of the code in the Page Load event is dedicated to the task of retrieving the full name of users from the database. We have their login ID through the Session object. We ship that off to the database and get the first and last name fields back. These are stuffed into a label control that is embedded in the text of the greeting on the page. This personalizes the site and assures users that they have been correctly recognized. Note that this will not show up correctly yet because we have not implemented security and thus do not have access to the user's login ID.

That's it for the main page. Figure 10.6 shows the page actually executing through the browser. Now it's time to secure the site so we have can get that user name, as well as proceed with the rest of the site implementation.

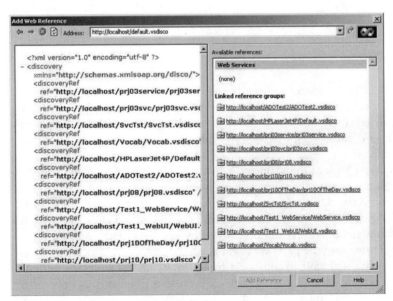

Figure 10.5 The Web references listing.

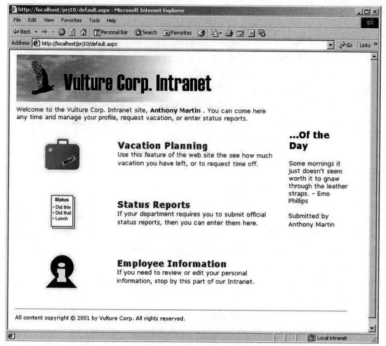

Figure 10.6 The main form running in the browser.

Security

You may recall our little chat about security from Project 8. We'll be using most of what we did in that project for security in this one. I chose to use forms-based security instead of Windows security to make it easier to run this project with multiple users. You could switch to Windows security, but you'd have to change a fair amount of the application.

For now, let's take a look at the main form. We simply copied the form from Project 8 and removed the section that allows users to create a new account. We want to restrict the access pretty tightly. Make a new Web form in the project and call it prj10login.aspx. Figure 10.7 shows what the form looks like in the Designer, with the appropriate portions removed. Create the content by copying the HTML/ASP code from Project 8 and removing the parts we don't need.

One other thing you will have to copy over from Project 8 is the styles we added to the style sheet. Make sure the following styles are present in your Styles.css, or the login form will look very strange:

```
.pageTitle
{
    font-family: Haettenschweiler, Arial Black ;
```

```
        font-size: 36pt;
        color: Navy;
}

.inputLabel
{
        font-family: Verdana;
        font-size: 10pt;
        font-weight: bold;
}

.infoText
{
        font-family: Verdana;
        font-size: 10pt;
        font-weight: normal;
}

.errMsg
{
        font-family: Verdana;
        font-size: 10pt;
        font-weight: bold;
        color: Red;
}

.linkButton
{
        text-decoration:        none;
        font-weight: bold;
        color:  #ffffff;
        background-color: Navy;
}
```

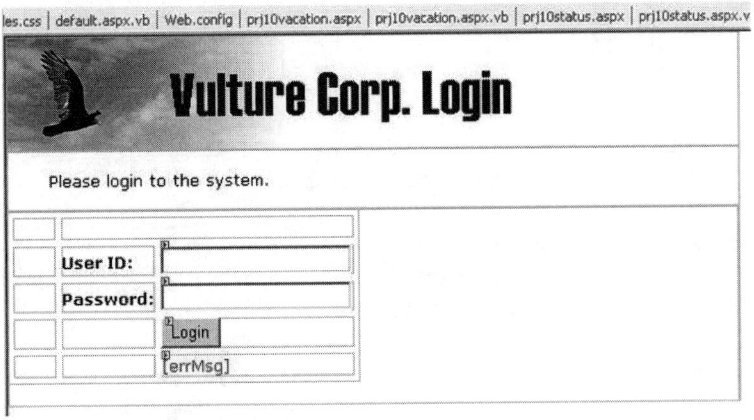

Figure 10.7 The login form in the Designer.

We are using essentially the same code as well, so you can copy that over to the new form, too. The code for the Button Click event and the Password lookup is a little different, so we list it here and point out the differences:

```
Private Function GetPwd(ByVal sID As String) As String

    Dim conn As SqlConnection = New SqlConnection(CONNSTR)
    Dim sSQL As String

    ' SQL to retrieve alert rows that are current. By design,
    ' only one row is ever intended to be in there, reflecting
    ' the current state of the company.
    sSQL = "SELECT Password FROM Employee WHERE LoginID='" & sID & "'"

    ' Get our data objects ready for retrieval.
    Dim da As SqlDataAdapter = New SqlDataAdapter(sSQL, conn)
    Dim ds As DataSet = New DataSet()
    Dim theRow As DataRow

    ' Load the data.
    Try
        conn.Open()
        da.Fill(ds, "pwd")
        conn.Close()
        If ds.Tables("pwd").Rows.Count > 0 Then
            theRow = ds.Tables("pwd").Rows(0)
            GetPwd = theRow("Password")
        Else
            GetPwd = ""
        End If
    Catch ex As SqlException
        GetPwd = ""
    End Try

End Function

Private Sub btnLogin_ServerClick(ByVal sender As System.Object, _
    ByVal e As System.EventArgs) Handles btnLogin.ServerClick

    ' Get password from database. If it's not there, we're
    ' already done. If so, then validate it.
    Dim pwd As String = GetPwd(tbID.Text)

    ' Validate. Feel free to UCase() everything if you want
```

```
' case-insensitive passwords.
If tbPwd.Text = Trim(pwd) Then
    ' Send them on their way - they are authenticated.
    Session("UserID") = tbID.Text
    FormsAuthentication.RedirectFromLoginPage(tbID.Text, False)
Else
    ' Tell them something was not right.
    errMsg.Text = "The supplied user ID or password was not " & _
        "correct."
End If

End Sub
```

The GetPwd function has been changed to work with our database. It uses our login ID to retrieve the matching password from the Employee table. The button click handler has been changed to work with the new controls on our form and to not refer to the "add a new account" functionality. Beyond that, the form should function like it did in Project 8.

Wiring It Up

The last step in security is to edit the Web.config file so that we restrict users properly and redirect them to the login page if they are not yet logged in. The authorization and authentication sections of this file should look like this:

```
<authentication mode="Forms">
    <forms loginUrl="prj10login.aspx" name=".ASPXFORMSAUTH"></forms>
</authentication>

<authorization>
    <deny users="?" />
</authorization>
```

Once you edit the Web.config file and make these changes, security will be active. Any time you run the program, the login screen will appear, and you will have to login to proceed.

> **TIP** Once you enable security in your application, you will be required to login whenever you run it. Every time you need to test anything or try out new functionality, you will have to login. If you do this as often as I do, it will become annoying very quickly. It is best to save security implementation until as late as possible during development to prevent this from happening, lest you become another victim of programmer rage.

Trying It Out

To test out security, simply run the program. You can also see it kick in by pointing to your local browser and requesting the default.aspx page, as in:

```
http://localhost/prj10
```

This will issue a request to the server for default.aspx. Because you are an unauthenticated user at this point, you will be redirected to the login form, shown running in Figure 10.8. Make sure you know a login ID and password from the sample database so you can test it out. Once you pass, the main page should be presented.

The Vacation Planning Form

We're finally getting to the core functionality of the application. The vacation planning page does three main things for users:

- It shows the current amount of vacation allotted to the user per year, the amount used so far this year, and the amount remaining for the year.

- The form shows a table of all vacation requests that the user has made so far and their approval state. This history allows users to balance their vacation checkbook, so to speak.

- Users can make new vacation requests from this form. It also does some basic validation to make sure they have enough vacation time left to make the request.

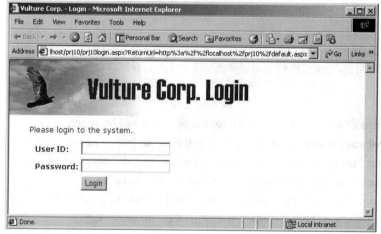

Figure 10.8 The login page running in the browser.

Begin by creating a new Web form and naming it prj10vacation.aspx. As with the other page, make sure you're working in FlowLayout mode instead of the default GridLayout mode. You can easily create everything you need by typing in the HTML here. It's easier than trying to figure out which parts to type in and which parts to create in the Designer. The HTML listing looks like this:

```
<%@ Page Language="vb" AutoEventWireup="false"
Codebehind="prj10vacation.aspx.vb" Inherits="prj10.prj10vacation"%>
<!DOCTYPE HTML PUBLIC "-//W3C//DTD HTML 4.0 Transitional//EN">
<HTML>
  <HEAD>
    <title></title>
    <meta name="GENERATOR" content="Microsoft Visual Studio.NET 7.0">
    <meta name="CODE_LANGUAGE" content="Visual Basic 7.0">
    <meta name="vs_defaultClientScript" content="JavaScript">
    <meta name="vs_targetSchema"
     content="http://schemas.microsoft.com/intellisense/ie5">
    <LINK href="http://localhost/prj10/Styles.css" type="text/css"
     rel="stylesheet">
  </HEAD>
  <body style="PADDING-RIGHT:0px; PADDING-LEFT:0px; PADDING-BOTTOM:0px;
   MARGIN:0px; PADDING-TOP:0px">
    <form id="frmVacation" method="post" runat="server">
      <table cellSpacing="5" cellPadding="0" width="750" border="0">
        <tr>
          <td>
            <asp:image id="Image1" runat="server"
             ImageUrl="images/VacationHdr.jpg"></asp:image>
          </td>
        </tr>
        <tr>
          <td class="TitleContent" width="550">
            Here you can review your current vacation time as well as
            request time off and view prior time off requests. Note that
            all information is for the current calendar year.
          </td>
        </tr>
        <tr>
          <td>
            <table cellpadding="10" cellspacing="0" border="0"
             width="750">
              <tr>
                <td class="DescTitle" width="150" align="left"
                 colspan="2">
                  Summary
                </td>
                <td rowspan="6" width="350" valign="top">
                  <!-- This cell handles the request part of the page -->
                  <span class="DescTitle">Request Vacation</span>
                  <table cellpadding="10" cellspacing="0" border="0">
```

```
          <tr>
            <td class="Content" align="right">
              Start Date:
            </td>
            <td class="Content">
              <asp:Calendar id="calStart" runat="server"
               Font-Size="X-Small" BackColor="LightBlue">
                <NextPrevStyle BorderStyle="None">
                </NextPrevStyle>
                <SelectedDayStyle BorderStyle="None"
                 BorderColor="Red" BackColor="RoyalBlue">
                </SelectedDayStyle>
                <TitleStyle Font-Bold="True" ForeColor="White"
                 BackColor="RoyalBlue"></TitleStyle>
              </asp:Calendar>
            </td>
          </tr>
          <tr>
            <td class="Content" align="right">
              Hours:
            </td>
            <td class="Content">
              <asp:TextBox id="tbHours" runat="server"
               Font-Bold="True" Height="26px" Width="139px">
              </asp:TextBox>
            </td>
          </tr>
          <tr>
            <td class="Content">
            </td>
            <td class="Content">
              <asp:Button id="btnRequest" runat="server"
               Text="Submit Request"></asp:Button>
            </td>
          </tr>
          <tr>
            <td class="Content">
            </td>
            <td class="Content">
              <asp:RangeValidator id="rvHours" runat="server"
               MinimumValue="1" MaximumValue="200"
               ControlToValidate="tbHours" Type="Integer">
              </asp:RangeValidator>
              <br>
              <asp:RequiredFieldValidator id="rqvHours"
               runat="server" ControlToValidate="tbHours">
              </asp:RequiredFieldValidator>
              <br>
              <asp:Label id="lblResult" runat="server"
               ForeColor="Red"></asp:Label>
            </td>
          </tr>
        </table>
      </td>
    </tr>
```

```
<tr>
  <td class="Content" width="150" align="right">
    Employee Name:
  </td>
  <td class="Content" style="FONT-WEIGHT: bold">
    <asp:Label id="lblEmpName" runat="server">
     Label</asp:Label>
  </td>
</tr>
<tr>
  <td class="Content" width="150" align="right">
    Total Vacation:
  </td>
  <td class="Content" style="FONT-WEIGHT: bold">
    <asp:Label id="lblTotal" runat="server">
     Label</asp:Label>
  </td>
</tr>
<tr>
  <td class="Content" width="150" align="right">
    Vacation Used:
  </td>
  <td class="Content" style="FONT-WEIGHT: bold">
    <asp:Label id="lblUsed"
     runat="server">Label</asp:Label>
  </td>
</tr>
<tr>
  <td class="Content" width="150" align="right">
    Vacation Remaining:
  </td>
  <td class="Content" style="FONT-WEIGHT: bold">
    <asp:Label id="lblRemaining" runat="server">
     Label</asp:Label>
  </td>
</tr>
<tr>
  <td colspan="2">
    <table cellpadding="10" cellspacing="0" border="0"
    width="400">
      <tr>
        <td class="Content">
          <b>Request History:</b>
          <br>
          <asp:DataGrid id="dgVacation" runat="server"
           PageSize="20" Font-Size="X-Small"
           BackColor="LightBlue" BorderWidth="1px"
           BorderStyle="Solid" BorderColor="White"
           CellPadding="3">
            <HeaderStyle Font-Size="X-Small"
             Font-Bold="True" Wrap="False"
             BorderWidth="2px"
             ForeColor="White" BorderStyle="Solid"
             BorderColor="White" BackColor="RoyalBlue">
            </HeaderStyle>
```

```
          </asp:DataGrid>
        </td>
      </tr>
      <tr>
        <td class="Content">
          <img src="images/bullet1.gif"><a
            href="default.aspx">Back to Main Page</a>
        </td>
      </tr>
    </table>
  </td>
 </tr>
</table>
</td>
</tr>
</table>
</form>
</body>
</HTML>
```

What a load! It's quite a big listing. It will be worth it though; this is the best page in the whole application. Once you get it entered, the result should resemble Figure 10.9, which shows the complete form in the Designer. Table 10.3 details all the controls on the form and any pertinent property settings.

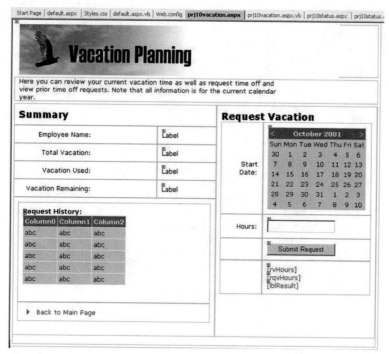

Figure 10.9 The vacation form in the Designer.

Table 10.3   The Controls on the Vacation Form

CONTROL	NAME	PROPERTIES
Button	btnRequest	Text="Submit Request"
Calendar	calStart	Font-Size=X-Small, BackColor= LightBlue, SelectedDayStyle BackColor=RoyalBlue, TitleStyle Font-Bold=True, TitleStyle ForeColor=White
DataGrid	dgVacation	PageSize=20, Font-Size=X-Small, BackColor=LightBlue, BorderWidth=1px, BorderStyle=Solid, BorderColor=White, CellPadding=3
Image	Image1	ImageURL="images/VacationHdr.jpg"
Label	lblEmpName	None
Label	lblTotal	None
Label	lblUsed	None
Label	lblRemaining	None
Label	lblResult	Text="", ForeColor=Red
RequiredFieldValidator	rqvHours	ControlToValidate="tbHours"
RangeValidator	rvHours	ControlToValidate="tbHours"
TextBox	tbHours	Text="", Font-Bold=True

The code for this form takes care of two primary tasks. First, it loads information from the database to display when the page loads. It also performs a few calculations so that we can display used and remaining vacation. Second, it handles a button click that submits a new vacation request and saves it in the database. Take a look at the code:

```
Option Explicit On

Imports System.Data.SqlClient

Public Class prj10vacation
    Inherits System.Web.UI.Page

#Region " Class Data and Types "

    ' Database connection string. We're using SQL Server. Change this if
    ' you want to use something else, like the Access db included with
    ' the book.
    Private Const CONNSTR As String = "PERSIST SECURITY INFO=False; " & _
```

```
                "DATA SOURCE=tony; INITIAL CATALOG=prj10; UID=sa; PWD=;"
        ' We will load the employee ID when the page loads and store it
        ' in here. That way we'll only have to load it once per page.
        ' Same with all the other stats.
        Private eID As Int32 = 0
        Private sName As String = ""
        Private iTotal As Int32 = 0
        Private iUsed As Int32 = 0
        Private iRemaining As Int32 = 0

#End Region

    Private Sub Page_Load(ByVal sender As System.Object, _
        ByVal e As System.EventArgs) Handles MyBase.Load

        Dim conn As SqlConnection = New SqlConnection(CONNSTR)
        Dim sSQL As String

        ' Load the initial employee information we'll need on this page.
        sSQL = "SELECT EmpID, FirstName, LastName, " & _
               "VacationHoursAnnual FROM Employee WHERE LoginID='" & _
               "Session("UserID") & "'"

        ' Get our data objects ready for retrieval.
        Dim da As SqlDataAdapter = New SqlDataAdapter(sSQL, conn)
        Dim ds As DataSet = New DataSet()
        Dim ds2 As New DataSet()
        Dim theRow As DataRow

        ' Load the data.
        Try
            conn.Open()
            da.Fill(ds, "employee")
            theRow = ds.Tables(0).Rows(0)
            eID = theRow("EmpID")
            sName = theRow("FirstName") & " " & theRow("LastName")
            iTotal = theRow("VacationHoursAnnual")
        Catch ex As SqlException
            conn.Close()
            Throw (ex)
        End Try

        ' Fill in what we can so far on the form.
        lblEmpName.Text = sName
        lblTotal.Text = iTotal

        ' Now that we have the Employee ID, we can load, calculate
        ' and display vacation data.
```

```
sSQL = "SELECT StartDate, Hours, Approved " & _
        "FROM VacationRequest WHERE EmpID = " & eID
da.SelectCommand.CommandText = sSQL
Try
    da.Fill(ds2, "vacation")
    conn.Close()
Catch ex As SqlException
    Throw ex
End Try


' Calculate everything. Only count hours as used if
' they are approved hours.
Dim aRow As DataRow
For Each aRow In ds2.Tables("vacation").Rows
    If aRow("Approved") = 1 Then
        iUsed += aRow("Hours")
    End If
Next
iRemaining = iTotal - iUsed


' Fill in the rest of the labels.
lblUsed.Text = CStr(iUsed)
lblRemaining.Text = CStr(iRemaining)


' Populate the datagrid.
dgVacation.DataSource = ds2
dgVacation.DataBind()


' Configure the validator controls on the page.
rvHours.MinimumValue = 1
rvHours.MaximumValue = iRemaining
rvHours.ErrorMessage = "The hours you request must be " & _
        "between 1 and " & CStr(iRemaining) & "."

rqvHours.ErrorMessage = "You must enter a value for the " & _
        "hours requested, from 1 to " & CStr(iRemaining) & "."

End Sub

' If the user clicks the Submit Request button, this code
' handles actually saving it to the database.
Private Sub btnRequest_Click(ByVal sender As System.Object, _
    ByVal e As System.EventArgs) Handles btnRequest.Click


    ' Save the request to the database. It could be
    ' reviewed later by a manager.
```

```vb
        Dim conn As New SqlConnection(CONNSTR)
        Dim sSQL As String

        ' Make sure we are using a valid date.
        If calStart.SelectedDate() < Now Then
            lblResult.ForeColor = System.Drawing.Color.Red
            lblResult.Text = "You must select a date equal to or " & _
                "later than today."
            Exit Sub
        End If

        ' Prepare our INSERT statement that will save the request.
        sSQL = "INSERT INTO VacationRequest (EmpID, StartDate, " & _
            "Hours, Approved) " & _
            "VALUES (" & eID & ", '" & _
            calStart.SelectedDate.ToString() & "', " & _
            CInt(tbHours.Text) & ", 0)"

        ' Attemp the INSERT.
        Dim cmd As New SqlCommand(sSQL, conn)
        Try
            conn.Open()
            cmd.ExecuteNonQuery()
            conn.Close()
            lblResult.ForeColor = System.Drawing.Color.RoyalBlue
            lblResult.Text = "Vacation request was successfully " & _
                "submitted (" & calStart.SelectedDate() & ", " & _
                "tbHours.Text & " hours)."
        Catch ex As SqlException
            conn.Close()
            lblResult.ForeColor = System.Drawing.Color.Red
            lblResult.Text = "There was a database error: " & ex.Message()
        End Try

    End Sub

    ' If the user changes the selection on the calendar, we want
    ' to make sure it is today or later. If not, tell the user.
    Private Sub calStart_SelectionChanged(ByVal sender As System.Object, _
        ByVal e As System.EventArgs) Handles calStart.SelectionChanged

        ' Make sure we are using a valid date.
        If calStart.SelectedDate() < Now.Date Then
            lblResult.ForeColor = System.Drawing.Color.Red
            lblResult.Text = "You must select a date equal to or " & _
                "later than today."
```

```
            Else
                lblResult.Text = ""
            End If

        End Sub

    End Class
```

We define our connection string, as usual, but this time we actually have some class data to store. All the class variables are related to saving the various vacation statistics, as well as the employee ID once we load it from the database.

Then we handle the page load event. We start it out by retrieving some employee information from the database, including the employee ID, the first and last names, and the amount of vacation the employee is allotted for the year. We'll use these shortly because we need them before we can get any work done. We use standard SQL and ADO.NET to get the information back. Once we get the data back, we fill in the user name and total vacation hours on the form.

Next we must load all the vacation request records for the user for several reasons. First, we need to iterate through them all, totaling the amount of vacation used this year. Second, we will hook the list of records up to the DataGrid so that users can see the history of all their requests. We retrieve the vacation date, hours used, and approval state for all the records that match the employee ID.

Once all the records are loaded, we iterate through them using a For..Each loop totaling the amount of vacation used. This is stored in the iUsed class variable. After the loop completes, we calculate the amount of vacation remaining and store that. Those values are then filled into the form.

> **NOTE** The amount of vacation used is calculated in this application based only on approved hours. Any stored requests that are not approved yet do not count toward the used total. This may not suit your needs, and it is very easy to change. Simply remove the condition in the For..Each loop that checks the approval status.
>
> If the total amount of vacation used or remaining looks wrong, it's probably because the unapproved requests were not counted.

The last thing we do in the page load handler is to configure the validator controls. We wait until now because we don't know the maximum value that should be allowed until we calculate the amount of vacation remaining for the employee. Once we do, we can set the MaximumValue property and the error messages, all of which reference the total remaining vacation hours.

Our next function handles the Submit Request button that indicates that the user is saving a new vacation request. We first check to make sure that the date the user has selected in the calendar is equal to or later than today's date. It does not make sense to retroactively request vacation. If the date is invalid, we tell the user and exit the Procedure.

We handle errors in this application in one of two ways. You've already seen the validator controls that check input as the user enters it. However, what do you do if you have an error in the code? You can't display a message box because you are running on the server. I decided to create a label control called lblResult that initially has no text value and is thus invisible. If we encounter an error in the code during a Try..Catch construct, we set the text of the label to describe the error and change its color to red.

We also use the same label to report that a requested operation succeeded. If everything goes well, we set the text to indicate this and change the color to a friendlier blue. You can use the same technique anywhere, and we do for each form in the application.

As long as the start date is okay and we have a valid number of hours requested, we go ahead and attempt to INSERT the request data into the database. If all goes well, we tell the user. If something goes wrong, we also tell the user. And that's it for saving the request.

Try It Out

You should be able to run the application now and access the vacation planning page. Figure 10.10 shows the page running in the browser.

Run around the form and try a few things. First, you can verify that the calculations are being done correctly. Then you can attempt to submit a vacation request. Select an old date and see that you get an error reported properly, as shown in Figure 10.11. Save the request and make sure it gets put into the database.

Figure 10.10   The vacation planning page in the browser.

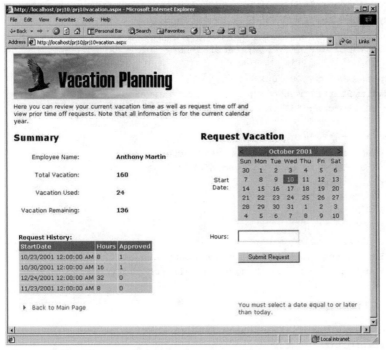

Figure 10.11 The vacation planning page, with error.

The Employee Information Form

Most of your employees will typically want to make sure you have the right information or occasionally to edit the information. It can save time when employees need to verify their salary or emergency contact if they can do it themselves without having to bother your other staff to get the information. So we created this page to allow the user to do just that.

Start by creating a new Web form and naming it prj10empinfo.aspx. Enter the following HTML to create the form:

```
<%@ Page Language="vb" AutoEventWireup="false"
Codebehind="prj10empinfo.aspx.vb" Inherits="prj10.prj10empinfo"%>
<!DOCTYPE HTML PUBLIC "-//W3C//DTD HTML 4.0 Transitional//EN">
<HTML>
  <HEAD>
    <title></title>
    <meta content="Microsoft Visual Studio.NET 7.0" name="GENERATOR">
    <meta content="Visual Basic 7.0" name="CODE_LANGUAGE">
    <meta content="JavaScript" name="vs_defaultClientScript">
    <meta content="http://schemas.microsoft.com/intellisense/ie5"
     name="vs_targetSchema">
```

```
      <LINK href="http://localhost/prj10/Styles.css" type="text/css"
        rel="stylesheet">
    </HEAD>
    <body style="PADDING-RIGHT: 0px; PADDING-LEFT: 0px; PADDING-BOTTOM:
0px;
    MARGIN: 0px; PADDING-TOP: 0px">
      <form id="frmStatus" method="post" runat="server">
        <table cellSpacing="5" cellPadding="0" width="700" border="0">
          <tr>
            <td align="left" colSpan="4">
              <asp:image id="Image1" runat="server"
               ImageUrl="images/EmployeeInfoHdr.jpg">
              </asp:image>
            </td>
          </tr>
          <tr>
            <td class="TitleContent">
              Review the information that company has on file about you.
              You can make a few changes as well, should you need to.
            </td>
          </tr>
          <tr>
            <td class="DescTitle" style="PADDING-LEFT: 10px">
              Information Summary
            </td>
          </tr>
          <tr>
            <td>
              <table style="PADDING-LEFT: 10px" cellSpacing="0"
              cellPadding="10" width="700" border="0">
                <tr height="40">
                  <td class="Content" vAlign="middle" align="right"
                   width="25%">
                    First Name:
                  </td>
                  <td class="Content" vAlign="middle" align="left"
                   width="25%">
                    <asp:label id="lblFirstName" runat="server"
                     Font-Bold="True"></asp:label>
                  </td>
                  <td class="Content" vAlign="middle" align="right"
                   width="25%">
                    Annual Salary:
                  </td>
                  <td class="Content" vAlign="middle" align="left"
                   width="25%">
                    <asp:label id="lblSalary" runat="server"
                     Font-Bold="True"></asp:label>
                  </td>
                </tr>
                <tr height="40">
```

```
  <td class="Content" vAlign="middle" align="right"
   width="25%">
    Last Name:
  </td>
  <td class="Content" vAlign="middle" align="left"
   width="25%">
    <asp:label id="lblLastName" runat="server"
     Font-Bold="True"></asp:label>
  </td>
  <td class="Content" vAlign="middle" align="right"
   width="25%">
    Vacation Hours:
  </td>
  <td class="Content" vAlign="middle" align="left"
   width="25%">
    <asp:label id="lblHours" runat="server"
     Font-Bold="True"></asp:label>
  </td>
</tr>
<tr height="40">
  <td class="Content" vAlign="middle" align="right"
   width="25%">
    Title:
  </td>
  <td class="Content" vAlign="middle" align="left"
   width="25%">
    <asp:label id="lblTitle" runat="server"
     Font-Bold="True"></asp:label>
  </td>
  <td class="Content" vAlign="middle" align="right"
   width="25%">
    Emergency Contact:
  </td>
  <td class="Content" vAlign="middle" align="left"
   width="25%">
    <asp:TextBox id="tbContact" runat="server"
     Font-Bold="True"></asp:TextBox>
  </td>
</tr>
<tr height="40">
  <td class="Content" vAlign="middle" align="right"
   width="25%">
    Department:
  </td>
  <td class="Content" vAlign="middle" align="left"
   width="25%">
    <asp:label id="lblDept" runat="server"
     Font-Bold="True"></asp:label>
  </td>
  <td class="Content" vAlign="middle" align="right"
   width="25%">
```

```
      Login ID:
    </td>
    <td class="Content" vAlign="middle" align="left"
     width="25%">
      <asp:label id="lblLogin" runat="server"
      Font-Bold="True"></asp:label>
    </td>
  </tr>
  <tr height="40">
    <td class="Content" vAlign="middle" align="right"
     width="25%">
      Gender:
    </td>
    <td class="Content" vAlign="middle" align="left"
     width="25%">
      <asp:label id="lblGender" runat="server"
      Font-Bold="True"></asp:label>
    </td>
    <td class="Content" vAlign="middle" align="right"
     width="25%">
      Street 1:
    </td>
    <td class="Content" vAlign="middle" align="left"
     width="25%">
      <asp:label id="lblStreet1" runat="server"
      Font-Bold="True"></asp:label>
    </td>
  </tr>
  <tr height="40">
    <td class="Content" vAlign="middle" align="right"
     width="25%">
      Home Phone:
    </td>
    <td class="Content" vAlign="middle" align="left"
     width="25%">
      <asp:TextBox id="tbHomePhone" runat="server"
      Font-Bold="True"></asp:TextBox>
    </td>
    <td class="Content" vAlign="middle" align="right"
     width="25%">
      Street 2:
    </td>
    <td class="Content" vAlign="middle" align="left"
     width="25%">
      <asp:Label id="lblStreet2" runat="server"
      Font-Bold="True"></asp:Label>
    </td>
  </tr>
  <tr height="40">
    <td class="Content" vAlign="middle" align="right"
     width="25%">
```

```
      Extension:
    </td>
    <td class="Content" vAlign="middle" align="left"
     width="25%">
      <asp:label id="lblExt" runat="server" Font-
       Bold="True"></asp:label>
    </td>
    <td class="Content" vAlign="middle" align="right"
     width="25%">
      City, State, ZIP:
    </td>
    <td class="Content" vAlign="middle" align="left"
     width="25%">
      <asp:label id="lblCityStateZip" runat="server"
       Font-Bold="True"></asp:label>
    </td>
  </tr>
  <tr height="40">
    <td class="Content" vAlign="middle" align="right"
     width="25%">
    </td>
    <td class="Content" vAlign="middle" align="left"
     width="25%">
    </td>
    <td class="Content" vAlign="middle" align="right"
     width="25%">
      Password:
    </td>
    <td class="Content" vAlign="middle" align="left"
     width="25%">
      <asp:textbox id="tbPwd" runat="server"
       TextMode="Password" Font-Bold="True"></asp:textbox>
    </td>
  </tr>
  <tr height="40">
    <td class="Content" vAlign="middle" align="left"
     width="25%">
      <IMG src="images/bullet1.gif"><A href="default.aspx">
       Back to Main Page</A>
    </td>
    <td class="Content" vAlign="middle" align="left"
     width="25%">
    </td>
    <td class="Content" vAlign="middle" align="left"
     width="25%">
      <asp:label id="lblResult" runat="server"
       ForeColor="Red"></asp:label>
    </td>
    <td class="Content" vAlign="middle" align="left"
     width="25%">
      <asp:Button id="btnSubmit" runat="server"
```

```
                   Text="Save Changes"></asp:Button>
               </td>
           </tr>
         </table>
       </td>
     </tr>
   </table>
 </form>
 </body>
 </HTML>
```

That was our biggest listing yet, primarily due to the number of controls on the page. They are detailed in Table 10.4, and Figure 10.12 shows what the form should look like in the Designer. Most of these are label controls used to display data and field names. There are three edit fields and a button to break up the monotony a little.

Table 10.4   The Employee Information Controls

CONTROL	NAME	PROPERTIES
Button	btnSubmit	Text="Save Changes"
Image	Image1	ImageURL="images/EmployeeInfoHdr.jpg"
Label	lblFirstName	Text="", Font-Bold=True
Label	lblLastName	Text="", Font-Bold=True
Label	lblSalary	Text="", Font-Bold=True
Label	lblTitle	Text="", Font-Bold=True
Label	lblDept	Text="", Font-Bold=True
Label	lblLogin	Text="", Font-Bold=True
Label	lblGender	Text="", Font-Bold=True
Label	lblStreet1	Text="", Font-Bold=True
Label	lblStreet2	Text="", Font-Bold=True
Label	lblExt	Text="", Font-Bold=True
Label	lblCityStateZip	Text="", Font-Bold=True
Label	lblResult	Text="", Font-Bold=True
Label	lblHours	Text="", Font-Bold=True
TextBox	tbPwd	Text="", Font-Bold=True, TextMode=Password
TextBox	tbContact	Text="", Font-Bold=True
TextBox	tbHomePhone	Text="", Font-Bold=True

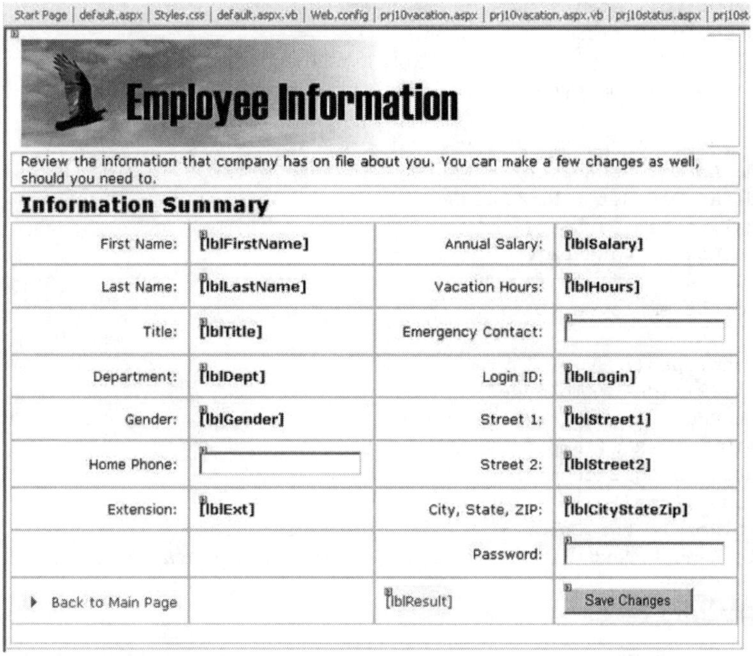

Start Page | default.aspx | Styles.css | default.aspx.vb | Web.config | prj10vacation.aspx | prj10vacation.aspx.vb | prj10status.aspx | prj10st

Figure 10.12 The employee information form in the Designer.

We begin the code in our usual fashion, with a database connection string and any class data we might need. In this case, we need something to keep track of the employee ID and the password, once we pull them out of the database:

```
#Region "Class Data and Types "

    Private Const CONNSTR As String = "PERSIST SECURITY INFO=False; " & _
        "DATA SOURCE=tony; INITIAL CATALOG=prj10; UID=sa; PWD=;"

    Private eID As Int32 = 0
    Private sPwd As String = ""

#End Region
```

The Page Load event takes care of loading the employee information and filling it into the labels on the form. Here's the code:

```
    Private Sub Page_Load(ByVal sender As System.Object, _
        ByVal e As System.EventArgs) Handles MyBase.Load

        Dim conn As SqlConnection = New SqlConnection(CONNSTR)
        Dim sSQL As String
        Dim s As String
```

```
' The SQL for retrieving the Employee ID based on
' the login ID from the Session.
sSQL = "SELECT Employee.EmpID FROM Employee " & _
       "WHERE Employee.LoginID = '" & Session("UserID") & "'"

' Get our data objects ready for retrieval.
Dim da As SqlDataAdapter = New SqlDataAdapter(sSQL, conn)
Dim ds As DataSet = New DataSet()
Dim ds2 As New DataSet()
Dim theRow As DataRow

' Load the employee ID.
Try
    conn.Open()
    da.Fill(ds, "employee")
    theRow = ds.Tables(0).Rows(0)
    eID = theRow("EmpID")
Catch ex As SqlException
    conn.Close()
    lblResult.ForeColor = System.Drawing.Color.Red
    lblResult.Text = "There was a database error: " & ex.message()
    Exit Sub
End Try

' Load the initial employee information we'll need on this page.
' A little complex, but it works.
sSQL = "SELECT Employee.EmpID, Employee.FirstName, " & _
       "Employee.LastName, Employee.Title, " & _
       "Department.DeptName, Employee.Gender, " & _
       "Address.Street1, Address.Street2, Address.City, " & _
       "Address.State, Address.Zip, Employee.HomePhone, " & _
       "Employee.Extension, Employee.SalaryAnnual, " & _
       "Employee.VacationHoursAnnual, " & _
       "Employee.EmergencyContact, Employee.Password " & _
       "FROM Employee INNER JOIN " & _
       "Department ON Employee.DeptID = Department.DeptID " & _
       "INNER JOIN " & _
       "Address ON Employee.AddressID = Address.AddressID " & _
       "WHERE (Employee.LoginID = '" & Session("UserID") & "')"

da.SelectCommand.CommandText = sSQL

' Load the employee data.
If Not (Page.IsPostBack) Then

    Try
        da.Fill(ds2, "employeeinfo")
        conn.Close()
    Catch ex As SqlException
        conn.Close()
        lblResult.ForeColor = System.Drawing.Color.Red
        lblResult.Text = "There was a database error: " & _
            ex.message()
        Exit Sub
    End Try
```

```
        ' Fill in the fields on the form.
        Dim aRow As DataRow
        If ds2.Tables(0).Rows.Count > 0 Then
            ' First column
            aRow = ds2.Tables(0).Rows(0)
            lblFirstName.Text = aRow("FirstName")
            lblLastName.Text = aRow("LastName")
            lblTitle.Text = aRow("Title")
            lblDept.Text = aRow("DeptName")
            lblGender.Text = aRow("Gender")
            lblHomePhone.Text = aRow("HomePhone")
            lblExt.Text = aRow("Extension")
            ' Second column
            lblSalary.Text = CStr(aRow("SalaryAnnual"))
            lblHours.Text = CStr(aRow("VacationHoursAnnual"))
            lblContact.Text = aRow("EmergencyContact")
            lblLogin.Text = Session("UserID")
            lblStreet1.Text = aRow("Street1")
            If Not (aRow("Street2") Is System.DBNull.Value) Then
                lblStreet2.Text = aRow("Street2")
            End If
            lblCityStateZip.Text = aRow("City") & ", " & _
                aRow("State") & " " & aRow("Zip")
            sPwd = aRow("Password")
        Else
            lblResult.ForeColor = System.Drawing.Color.Red
            lblResult.Text = "No information was found for " & _
            "login ID" & Session("UserID") & "."
        End If
    Else
        conn.Close()
    End If

End Sub
```

We go through the usual routine of loading the employee ID from the database to begin with. We'll need it for other database operations later. So we get it and save it in a class variable, eID.

Next we load the employee data. This pulls back a large number of columns from three different tables and results in a large and complex-looking SQL SELECT statement. The only complex parts are the two INNER JOINs we use to pull out actual values from the Department and Address tables. Without the JOINs, we would have only meaningless IDs to display for the employee. Beyond that, the loading of the data is perfectly normal.

> **TIP** We're all used to checking for null values returned from the database. We do it the way VB taught us to. However, this is a little different in Visual Basic .NET. We need to make use of a class in the .NET framework called DBNull and one of its properties, Value. To check a value for null, do it like this:

```
If Row("Street2") Is System.DBNull.Value Then
```

Once we have the data, we need to stuff it into the form. Each column of data in the returned row is used to populate a label control on the form. That's all there is to the Page Load event. However, we also allow users to make changes to three of the fields on the form. We need to make sure that there are valid values there and to actually save the changes to the database using a SQL UPDATE statement. Here is the code we'll be referring to:

```
' Handle a click on the Save Changes button.
Private Sub btnSubmit_Click(ByVal sender As System.Object, _
    ByVal e As System.EventArgs) Handles btnSubmit.Click

    Dim conn As New SqlConnection(CONNSTR)
    Dim sSQL As String
    Dim s As String

    ' Make sure that something actually exists in the
    ' the three edit fields.
    If Len(tbHomePhone.Text) = 0 Then
        lblResult.ForeColor = System.Drawing.Color.Red
        lblResult.Text = "You must enter a value for Home Phone."
        Exit Sub
    End If
    If Len(tbPwd.Text) = 0 Then
        lblResult.ForeColor = System.Drawing.Color.Red
        lblResult.Text = "You must enter a value for Password."
        Exit Sub
    End If
    If Len(tbContact.Text) = 0 Then
        lblResult.ForeColor = System.Drawing.Color.Red
        lblResult.Text = "You must enter a value for " & _
            "Emergency Contact."
        Exit Sub
    End If

    ' Take care of any single quotes in the contact text field.
    s = tbContact.Text.Replace("'", "''")

    ' Prepare our UPDATE statement to save the data.
    sSQL = "UPDATE Employee SET HomePhone='" & _
        tbHomePhone.Text & "', " & _
        "EmergencyContact = '" & tbContact.Text & "', " & _
        "Password = '" & tbPwd.Text & "' " & _
        "WHERE EmpID = " & CStr(eID)

    ' Attempt the update.
    Dim cmd As New SqlCommand(sSQL, conn)
    Try
        conn.Open()
        cmd.ExecuteNonQuery()
        conn.Close()
```

```
            lblResult.ForeColor = System.Drawing.Color.RoyalBlue
            lblResult.Text = "Employee information was " & _
                "successfully updated."
        Catch ex As SqlException
            conn.Close()
            lblResult.ForeColor = System.Drawing.Color.Red
            lblResult.Text = "There was a database error: " & ex.Message()
        End Try

    End Sub
```

The first part of the button click handler makes sure that we have values of some sort in each of the text boxes. If those all pass, we attempt to save the changes using an UPDATE. Whatever the results, success or failure, we tell the user how it went. This form was not complicated; it just looks that way due to the amount of data on the page.

Try It Out

Run the application and access the employee information page. Once the page is displayed, verify that the correct data is being loaded for the particular user you are impersonating. Try out the update for a field or two to make sure it works. The form is shown executing in the browser in Figure 10.13.

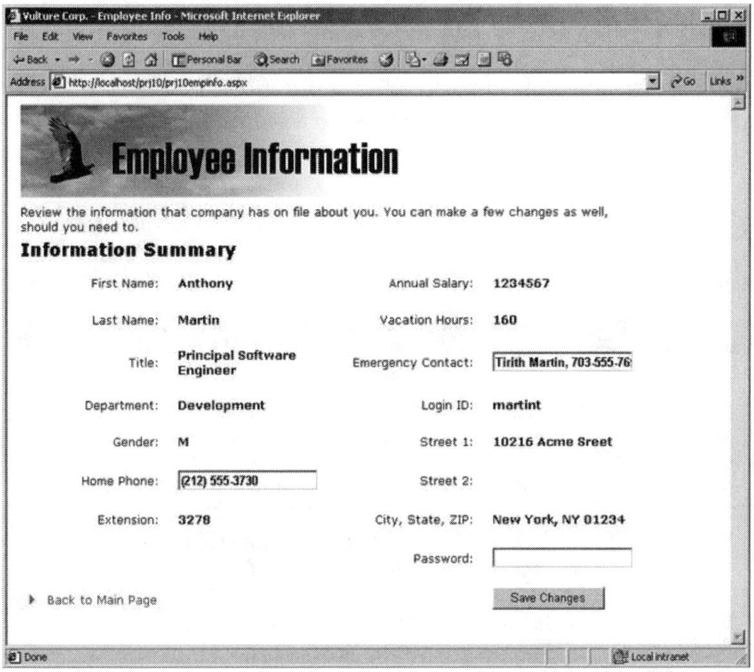

Figure 10.13   The employee information form in the browser.

Figure 10.14 The status report form in the Designer.

The Status Report Form

The status report form is probably the simplest in the application. It has a couple text fields to accept and display status report information, and a button to save it. That's it! Take a look at Figure 10.14 to see what it looks like sitting in the Designer. The controls are listed in Table 10.5.

Table 10.5 The Status Report Controls

CONTROL	NAME	PROPERTIES
Button	btnSubmit	Text="Submit Report"
Image	Image1	ImageURL="images/StatusRptHdr.jpg"
Label	lblResult	Text="", ForeColor=RoyalBlue
TextBox	tbNew	Text="", Width=340px, Height=250px, MaxLength=4096, Rows=1, TextMode=MultiLine
TextBox	tbOld	Text="", Width=340px, Height=250px, MaxLength=4096, Rows=1, TextMode=MultiLine

Even the HTML is much shorter than the other pages we've dealt with in this application. Again, this is due to the smaller number of controls and a layout that is not as complex. Take a look at it and you'll see what I mean:

```
<%@ Page Language="vb" AutoEventWireup="false"
Codebehind="prj10status.aspx.vb" Inherits="prj10.prj10status"%>
<!DOCTYPE HTML PUBLIC "-//W3C//DTD HTML 4.0 Transitional//EN">
<HTML>
  <HEAD>
    <title>Vulture Corp. - Status Reports</title>
    <meta name="GENERATOR" content="Microsoft Visual Studio.NET 7.0">
    <meta name="CODE_LANGUAGE" content="Visual Basic 7.0">
    <meta name="vs_defaultClientScript" content="JavaScript">
    <meta name="vs_targetSchema"
     content="http://schemas.microsoft.com/intellisense/ie5">
    <LINK href="http://localhost/prj10/Styles.css" type="text/css"
    rel="stylesheet">
  </HEAD>
<body style="PADDING-RIGHT:0px; PADDING-LEFT:0px; PADDING-BOTTOM:0px;
 MARGIN:0px; PADDING-TOP:0px">
    <form id="frmStatus" method="post" runat="server">
      <table cellSpacing="5" cellPadding="0" width="700" border="0"
       style="PADDING-LEFT:10px">
        <tr>
          <td colspan="2">
            <asp:image id="Image1" runat="server"
             ImageUrl="images/StatusRptHdr.jpg"></asp:image>
          </td>
        </tr>
        <tr>
          <td class="TitleContent" colspan="2">
            Enter a new status report here if your department requires
            it. You can also review previous status reports.
          </td>
        </tr>
        <tr>
          <td class="Content" valign="top" width="50%">
            <br>
            <span class="DescTitle">Enter New Report</span>
            <br>
            <br>
            <asp:TextBox id="tbNew" runat="server" Width="337px"
             Height="250px" MaxLength="4096" Rows="1"
             TextMode="MultiLine"></asp:TextBox>
            <br>
            <br>
            <asp:Button id="btnSubmit" runat="server"
             Text="Submit Report"></asp:Button>
             
            <br>
```

```
          <br>
          <img src="images/bullet1.gif"><a href="default.aspx">
          Back to Main Page</a>
      </td>
      <td class="Content" valign="top" width="50%">
          <br>
          <span class="DescTitle">Review Prior Reports</span>
          <br>
          <br>
          <asp:TextBox id="tbOld" runat="server" Width="340px"
          Height="250px" Rows="1" TextMode="MultiLine"></asp:TextBox>
          <br>
          <br>
          <asp:Label id="lblResult" runat="server"
          ForeColor="RoyalBlue"></asp:Label>
      </td>
    </tr>
  </table>
</form>
</body>
</HTML>
```

That's an awfully short page, but it does what it needs to. The code is not especially complex either, given what we've seen already. We start off predictably by setting up the database connection string and class data:

```
#Region "Class Data and Types "

    Private Const CONNSTR As String = "PERSIST SECURITY INFO=False; " & _
        "DATA SOURCE=tony; INITIAL CATALOG=prj10; UID=sa; PWD=;"

    Private eID As Int32 = 0

#End Region
```

Our Page Load event does its usual job: load the employee ID and the data to initially display on the page. We have to actually build the contents of the existing status reports. Take a look at the code:

```
    Private Sub Page_Load(ByVal sender As System.Object, _
        ByVal e As System.EventArgs) Handles MyBase.Load

        Dim conn As SqlConnection = New SqlConnection(CONNSTR)
        Dim sSQL As String
        Dim s As String

        ' Load the initial employee information we'll need on this page.
        sSQL = "SELECT EmpID FROM Employee WHERE LoginID='" & _
                "Session("UserID") & "'"
```

```
    ' Get our data objects ready for retrieval.
    Dim da As SqlDataAdapter = New SqlDataAdapter(sSQL, conn)
    Dim ds As DataSet = New DataSet()
    Dim ds2 As New DataSet()
    Dim theRow As DataRow

    ' Load the employee ID.
    Try
        conn.Open()
        da.Fill(ds, "employee")
        theRow = ds.Tables(0).Rows(0)
        eID = theRow("EmpID")
    Catch ex As SqlException
        conn.Close()
        Throw (ex)
    End Try

    If Not (Page.IsPostBack) Then

        ' Now load the matching status report records.
        sSQL = "SELECT RptDate, StatusText FROM StatusReport " & _
            "WHERE EmpID=" & CStr(eID) & " ORDER BY RptDate DESC"
        da.SelectCommand.CommandText = sSQL
        Try
            da.Fill(ds2, "statusreport")
            conn.Close()
        Catch ex As SqlException
            conn.Close()
            Throw ex
        End Try

        ' Loop through each record and build the string
        ' for display in the textbox.
        Dim aRow As DataRow
        If ds2.Tables(0).Rows.Count > 0 Then
            For Each aRow In ds2.Tables(0).Rows
                s &= "Date: " & aRow("RptDate") & vbCrLf & _
                    "--------" & vbCrLf
                s &= aRow("StatusText") & vbCrLf & vbCrLf
            Next
        Else
            s = "No reports available."
        End If

        ' Stuff it in the control.
        tbOld.Text = s
    Else
        conn.Close()
    End If

End Sub
```

Once all of the status reports have been loaded into a DataSet, we iterate through them and build a single string that can be displayed in the large text box. We do a little formatting along the way to make the whole thing more readable. Once this is done the form is displayed.

The only other thing our page (and at this point, our application) needs to do is save a new status report. Users can enter any text they like in the left text box and click the Submit Report button to save it. The code that handles this follows:

```
' This button click handler will save any new status report
' text in the database.
Private Sub btnSubmit_Click(ByVal sender As System.Object, _
    ByVal e As System.EventArgs) Handles btnSubmit.Click

    Dim conn As New SqlConnection(CONNSTR)
    Dim sSQL As String
    Dim s As String

    ' Make sure there's something in the text box to save.
    If Len(tbNew.Text) = 0 Then
        lblResult.ForeColor = System.Drawing.Color.Red
        lblResult.Text = "You must enter something before your " & _
            "report can be submitted."
        Exit Sub
    End If

    ' Make sure any single quotes are properly handled.
    s = tbNew.Text.Replace("'", "''")

    ' Prepare our INSERT statement using data from the UI.
    sSQL = "INSERT INTO StatusReport (EmpID, RptDate, StatusText)" & _
        " VALUES (" & eID & ", '" & Now.ToString() & "', '" & _
        s & "')"

    ' Attempt to save the data.
    Dim cmd As New SqlCommand(sSQL, conn)
    Try
        conn.Open()
        cmd.ExecuteNonQuery()
        conn.Close()
        lblResult.ForeColor = System.Drawing.Color.RoyalBlue
        lblResult.Text = "Status report was successfully " & _
            "submitted (" & Now & ")."
    Catch ex As SqlException
        conn.Close()
```

```
                lblResult.ForeColor = System.Drawing.Color.Red
                lblResult.Text = "There was a database error: " & ex.Message()
            End Try

        End Sub
```

We check to make sure that there is actually something in the text box control, and if there is, we try to insert it into the database. We let the user know how it went by updating the results label on the form.

Try It Out

Take this form for a test drive. Log in as someone who has a few reports and see that they are returned properly, newest to oldest, as dictated by the ORDER BY clause we used. Enter a new status report and save it. The next time you come back to the form, the new one will be reported on the right. Figure 10.15 shows the form running in the browser.

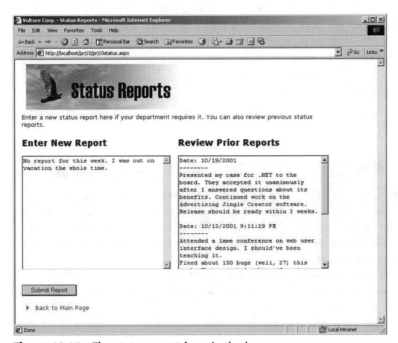

Figure 10.15   The status report form in the browser.

Enhancing the Project

This project illustrated how to pull several .NET technologies together to create a real-world application. You could use similar techniques to build any application that strikes you as interesting.

Although this is a sizeable project, there are plenty of things you could do beyond just adding new features for your employees to use:

Site and data management.   Add a page or two to help you manage the site contents. For example, you will want to be able to manage the information in the database that employees have no access to, such as adding new employees and departments.

Approval of vacation.   Vacation requests can be submitted, but how do they get approved? You could start by adding manager information to the database and associating employees with that manager. Then create a page that would allow managers to approve vacation requests for the employees associated with them. You could do this with a fairly simple Web form.

Review status reports.   Like vacation requests, status reports must be reviewed by managers. Create a page that would allow managers to look at the status reports for all the employees associated with them. You could optionally create a special page that managers use to create their status reports. It would show all the reports of the employees associated with them so that they could review their department status as they write their own reports. Or is this making life too easy for managers?

Edit addresses.   Change the employee information page to allow editing of users' addresses. This would be handy for employees but was left out of the project due to space considerations. The update SQL would have to be changed quite a bit, though, to handle the related table.

THAT'S IT

I hope that you see incredible success and fun in the world of .NET and Visual Basic .NET! I know I had a blast writing all these programs and learning about all the new goodies along the way. .NET is very powerful, and my number one priority is to get my company to move to it. This initiative has purely selfish motivations, however. I will find it very difficult to go back to VB6 after all this.

Thanks for coming, and have a wonderful time with .NET!

What's on the CD-ROM?

The CD-ROM that accompanies this book contains all the source code for all the projects. It also contains any supporting files you might need, including images, solution files, image files, and sample databases. Whenever possible, the structure of the directories and files for the project have been maintained as needed so that they may be loaded directly into Visual Studio.

The disc is organized by project. The main directory is called Projects, and each project is contained underneath the main directory. For example, the code for project 5 is stored in a directory structure like this:

```
Projects\Project 5
```

Using the CD-ROM

The CD-ROM has a Web browser interface that allows you to view information about the projects, access the code, and see what else is on there. It should start automatically when you insert the CD-ROM into the drive. If it does not, simply open the file *index.htm* in the root directory.

A Free Utility?

There is a small utility on the CD-ROM in the root called *autorunit.exe*. It allows you to pass a command line document to it which it will then launch. We use it to implement the autorun feature of the CD-ROM. If you examine the file *autorun.inf*, you will see how it is used. A typical example looks like this:

```
Autorunit index.htm
```

This sort of utility can be very useful if you plan on creating any sort of autorun interface that must launch a document. You could launch a Web page as we've seen, or a Microsoft Word document, or an image file; anything that is associated with a program. We created this utility using C++, and are providing it for you use, royalty and guilt free. Use it in your own programs or installations if you like.

By the way, if you run the utility without a command line argument, it will launch a Windows shell displaying the content of the current directory.

Bonus Content

Project 6 is a Web portal built using ASP.NET. It's a big project, but not as big as we wanted to make it. We have created an extended version of the portal that adds an entire section to the site. The new section displays news headlines from Moreover.com, and shows how to extract content from the Web, distill it for your user's needs, and funnel it to your Web site.

The complete project, as well as additional explanatory text, is included on the CD-ROM in a subdirectory called Project 6b. You can find all the source code and other information you need to run the enhanced project there.

Experiments

During the course of writing this book, experimental code was written for various reasons: exploring new technology, testing out a theory or technique, or perhaps just learning a new feature of the Visual Studio environment. Some of the experiments became smaller examples in the explanatory sections of the projects.

We have selected a few of the experiments and put the code for them on the CD-ROM. We chose some of the more interesting or more complete experiments that we thought you might find interesting. Feel free to prowl through the code to see if you can glean any useful bits of information. Who knows, one of them might be useful.

The code for the experiments is stored in a directory off the root called Experiments.

TcpTrace

This utility was written by a very sharp programmer named Simon Fell. It appears to be a simple program at first, but reveals its utility as soon as you run into your first problem trying to debug Web services.

One of the most difficult aspects of tracking down Web service problems is knowing what is traveling back and forth between the client and the service. You will need to see what SOAP messages are being passed, and whether or not they are getting to the intended recipient. TcpTrace allows you to watch all the SOAP messages traveling across your wires between your code.

The utility is free for use, but make sure that you read through the usage license. If you have any questions about its use or the license, visit the Web site at http://www.pocketsoap.com. Thanks to Simon not only for allowing us to include the utility on the CD-ROM, but also for creating the utility in the first place. It helped me out when I was working with Web services, and cut down development time quite a bit.

Hardware Requirements

The hardware requirements for the CD-ROM are fairly small. You only need a CD-ROM drive. Other requirements for the code on the CD-ROM are covered by the individual project chapters.

User Assistance and Information

The software accompanying this book is being provided as is without warranty or support of any kind. Should you require basic installation assistance, or if your media is defective, please call our product support number at (212) 850-6194 weekdays between 9AM and 4PM Eastern Standard Time. Or, we can be reached via e-mail at: **techhelp@wiley.com**.

To place additional orders or to request information about other Wiley products, please call (800) 879-4539.

Index

CUSTOMER NOTE: IF THIS BOOK IS ACCOMPANIED BY SOFTWARE, PLEASE READ THE FOLLOWING BEFORE OPENING THE PACKAGE.

This software contains files to help you utilize the models described in the accompanying book. By opening the package, you are agreeing to be bound by the following agreement:

This software product is protected by copyright and all rights are reserved by the author, John Wiley & Sons, Inc., or their licensors. You are licensed to use this software as described in the software and the accompanying book. Copying the software for any other purpose may be a violation of the U.S. Copyright Law.

This software product is sold as is without warranty of any kind, either express or implied, including but not limited to the implied warranty of merchantability and fitness for a particular purpose. Neither Wiley nor its dealers or distributors assumes any liability for any alleged or actual damages arising from the use of or the inability to use this software. (Some states do not allow the exclusion of implied warranties, so the exclusion may not apply to you.)